Foundations of Object-Oriented Programming Using .NET 2.0 Patterns

Christian Gross

Apress®

Foundations of Object-Oriented Programming Using .NET 2.0 Patterns

Copyright © 2006 by Christian Gross

Lead Editor: Jonathan Hassell
Technical Reviewer: Brian Myers
Editorial Board: Steve Anglin, Dan Appleman, Ewan Buckingham, Gary Cornell, Tony Davis, Jason Gilmore, Jonathan Hassell, Chris Mills, Dominic Shakeshaft, Jim Sumser
Project Manager: Sofia Marchant
Copy Edit Manager: Nicole LeClerc
Copy Editor: Ami Knox
Assistant Production Director: Kari Brooks-Copony
Production Editor: Linda Marousek
Compositor: Susan Glinert Stevens
Proofreader: Elizabeth Berry
Indexer: Valerie Perry
Interior Designer: Van Winkle Design Group
Cover Designer: Kurt Krames
Manufacturing Director: Tom Debolski

Library of Congress Cataloging-in-Publication Data

Gross, Christian.

  Foundations of object-oriented programming using .NET 2.0 patterns / Christian Gross.

    p. cm.

  ISBN 1-59059-540-8

  1. Object-oriented programming (Computer science) 2. Microsoft .NET. 3. Software patterns. I. Title.

QA76.64.G8 2005

005.1'17--dc22

2005025961

Printed and bound in the United States of America (POD)

Trademarked names may appear in this book. Rather than use a trademark symbol with every occurrence of a trademarked name, we use the names only in an editorial fashion and to the benefit of the trademark owner, with no intention of infringement of the trademark.

Distributed to the book trade worldwide by Springer-Verlag New York, Inc., 233 Spring Street, 6th Floor, New York, NY 10013. Phone 1-800-SPRINGER, fax 201-348-4505, e-mail orders-ny@springer-sbm.com, or visit http://www.springeronline.com.

For information on translations, please contact Apress directly at 2560 Ninth Street, Suite 219, Berkeley, CA 94710. Phone 510-549-5930, fax 510-549-5939, e-mail info@apress.com, or visit http://www.apress.com.

The information in this book is distributed on an "as is" basis, without warranty. Although every precaution has been taken in the preparation of this work, neither the author(s) nor Apress shall have any liability to any person or entity with respect to any loss or damage caused or alleged to be caused directly or indirectly by the information contained in this work.

The source code for this book is available to readers at http://www.apress.com in the Source Code section. You will need to answer questions pertaining to this book in order to successfully download the code.

Contents at a Glance

Contents

About the Author

This guy has three requirements: a computer, high-speed Internet connection, and a pay TV subscription.

—Said by a woman when asked what her husband needs when choosing a place to live

 **CHRISTIAN GROSS** says of himself: "Computers have always fascinated me. When I started high school, my homeroom was the computer room. I remember arriving earlier so that I could write little programs to chase pixels across the screen. From there on everything else is history.

"Many people like to write programs; personally I like to figure out how best to write programs. Often I will look at a piece of source code and think of all the permutations and combinations for how that source code can be written. And while going through those permutations and combinations, what interests me is why it works or does not work."

About the Technical Reviewer

BRIAN MYERS is the author of the book *Beginning Object-Oriented ASP.NET 2.0 with VB .NET: From Novice to Professional*, available from Apress. He is a software engineer and database administrator for a large manufacturing company. He is a Microsoft Certified Solution Developer for .NET, a Microsoft Certified Application Developer for .NET, and a Microsoft Certified Professional.

Brian has worked with VB since VB 5 and has written OOP applications for over seven years. He has over seven years of experience as a software developer, mostly with Microsoft technologies.

Brian has also written articles for *ASP Today* (http://www.asptoday.com) as well as taught courses in .NET development and SQL Server.

Introduction

Patterns are an interesting topic that has already been thoroughly discussed. The book that originally started the pattern phenomenon was *Design Patterns: Elements of Reusable Object-Oriented Software* by Erich Gamma et al. (Boston: Addison-Wesley, 1995). At the time the book was published, it presented new ideas and concepts. Now it has become the reference book of design patterns, and the described design patterns have become the basis of all sorts of applications.

This book is an explanation of design patterns as applied to the .NET 2.0 Framework. Some of the patterns are from *Design Patterns: Elements of Reusable Object-Oriented Software*, and others are from other sources. The focus of this book is not to explicitly define the patterns, but to illustrate the patterns in the context of using them with a programming language like C#, because the original design patterns were illustrated using C++, and there are major differences between that language and .NET and C#.

Why Patterns?

You might be wondering, "Why this book, and why patterns?" Oddly enough, the idea occurred to me while training some students on how to use design patterns. The students were doing their exercises, and I saw one student in particular write code in which the base type was a class and not an interface. I asked him why he was writing code like that, and his response was, "Because that is what I have been doing all this time." The student's method was wrong, but his response revealed an interesting perspective: why use an interface when a base class is good enough? Right then, it hit me like a ton of bricks: object-oriented programming, or OOP, can be easier understood when one is first taught patterns.

When learning traditional OOP techniques, you are taught about shapes, squares, and other abstract topics. You learn about how a class is responsible for its own data, and how classes implement responsibilities. The problem with this form of learning is that it explains object-oriented programming, but it does not explain how to solve a problem with concrete solutions. For example, how do you instantiate a type, pass its references to another class, and persist that information to a medium? The problem with traditional object-oriented programming is that it gives vague guidance in implementing a solution.

Patterns are different in that they give you a predefined form of what to do and when. Consider it as follows: you want to learn how to bake a cake. You know a cake is made of flour, eggs, milk, baking powder, and perhaps a few additional ingredients, yet not all cakes are equal. Add too much baking powder, and your cake will rise too much. Add too many eggs, and your cake will taste like an omelet. Object-oriented programming is like baking a cake: you know the ingredients, and know what the ingredients do, but have no idea of the proportion of the ingredients or steps to make a cake. Just as a good recipe will help you turn your ingredients into a delicious cake, patterns will help you convert your code into efficient programs.

It is possible to cook and bake using only recipes, without knowing what the ingredients do or how they interact. The problem with such an approach is that it does not work. For example, imagine making a meal where your starter is pea soup, main entree is salmon with peppermint sauce and a side of pumpkin and soya noodles, and finally a dessert of maple ice cream. The menu does not sound appetizing, even though the individual courses may taste great. The problem is that patterns, like recipes, interact with each other, and hence need to be coordinated. The only way to coordinate patterns is to have some basic understanding of the object-oriented programming techniques.

What Are Patterns?

A pattern is like a recipe, except that the ingredients used to create a pattern are object-oriented principles. For example, consider the following source code:

```
interface IBaseInterface { }

class Derived : IBaseInterface { }
```

A class, Derived, implements the interface IBaseInterface. This is the classical implementation of the Bridge pattern. Yet the question must be asked, Why an interface, and why not a class? From an object-oriented perspective, the results are similar enough. This begs the question, Why are there interfaces in a programming language? The answer: because a pattern defines a best practice based on an implementation that has proven itself to be useful when developing applications. The results from extensive coding experience is that interfaces are more useful than classes when using base types and implementing the Bridge pattern.

Patterns differ from best practices in the same way that theories differ from hypotheses. A theory is based on ideas that have proven themselves repeatedly using the scientific method, which is a way of performing an experiment so that someone else can reproduce the results. A pattern is like a recipe book that defines a series of steps, and ingredients that, when used according to the defined steps, will result in identical cakes. A hypothesis is an idea that is most likely correct, but has not yet proven itself using the necessary repeated experiments by different individuals. Hypotheses are precursors to theories, meaning that best practices are precursors to patterns.

The patterns defined in the book *Design Patterns: Elements of Reusable Object-Oriented Software* have been proven to work and apply to multiple contexts. For example, using the structure defined in the Factory pattern, the same results can be expected in different programming languages and different programming contexts.

What to Expect from This Book

In addition to patterns and object-oriented principles, this book is about learning to read code like a musician reads sheet music. If you think about it, musicians express their thoughts using a notation that only musicians can understand. A score, which represents the music to be played, looks like a bunch of scratch marks to the untrained eye. Yet to musicians, it is Bach, Mozart, AC/DC, or Eminem, and makes perfect sense. Musicians, when reading a score, will know when to play their musical instruments, and what emotions are being generated at that moment.

There is no simplification or abstraction of the score. Musicians just know what a piece of music does by reading its score.

The purpose of this book is to make it possible for you to read a piece of code and decipher its intent. This already is the case in many Open Source projects where individuals constantly read code created by others. With other types of projects, this is not the case, as each coder writes code using their preferred tricks and techniques. For example, something as trivial as where to put curly brackets unleashes a torrent of debates. The reason this happens is each coder will have learned some trick or technique based on an experience, or some slides at a conference, or an individual comment made by somebody. Reading a piece of code is not just about recognizing some keywords; it is about seeing a block of keywords used in a context that solves a specific problem. In short, reading a piece of code is about interpreting OOP in the context of patterns.

Consider why a programming language exists at the philosophical level and ask yourself, Why does a programming language contain a particular keyword, concept, or strategy? The answer is because that keyword, concept, or strategy solves a particular problem when used in a given context. What is not explained is when it is best to use the feature. For example, in C#, it is possible to use the keywords `struct`, `class`, `interface`, `abstract`, and `sealed` to define a type that is used in a program. Usually the coder will know the technical cause and effect of the mentioned keywords. However, that coder generally does not know the context for when each keyword should or should not be used. This goes back to the original point that coders will rely on their own tips and tricks, regardless of where they picked them up. This is not the right way to code, as it essentially relies on trial and error.

What This Book Covers

Each of the chapters in this book is incremental in knowledge and serves a specific purpose:

- *Chapter 1, "Essentials of Object-Oriented Programming"*: In this chapter, I present the essentials of object-oriented programming. Defined and illustrated in C# are concepts like modularization and exceptions. Reading this chapter makes it simpler for you to understand various OOP buzzwords.

- *Chapter 2, "Logging, Errors, and Test-Driven Development"*: The main aim of Chapter 2 is to define and illustrate test-driven development, which is a method of developing software by creating tests and source code in unison. The advantage of this approach is source code that is stable and consistent.

- *Chapter 3, "Defining the Foundation"*: In this chapter, you encounter the essential design patterns that serve as the basis of all other design patterns: Factory and Bridge.

- *Chapter 4, "Application Architecture"*: The design patterns in Chapter 3 are universal and do not enforce an overall architecture. In Chapter 4, I demonstrate applying the basic patterns to the creation of architecture strategies. The architecture strategies, which you can easily extend and maintain, illustrate how to solve application problems. Using the defined patterns, I demonstrate how you begin creating an application with the correct foot forward.

- *Chapter 5, "Implementing Component Groupings"*: When implementing applications, often the main problem is making the application work properly using well-developed code. Often what happens is that a developer will create a set of well-defined and implemented classes. Then subsequent requests and requirements cause additional classes to be added or the existing ones to be modified. Those additions and changes cause problems, and Chapter 5 addresses this issue by proposing a set of patterns that can be used to make it easier to implement applications.

- *Chapter 6, "Writing Algorithms"*: Often when writing code, you will be tempted to introduce a shortcut when trying to solve a problem. The shortcut may be a little one, but it could have large ramifications. In Chapter 6, I present patterns that define how to deal with situations where you might have been tempted to use shortcuts. The illustrated patterns are more verbose, which might seem like overkill. However, the main aim of the patterns is to simplify extending and maintaining the written code.

- *Chapter 7, "Efficient Code"*: When writing code, your aim is to make the code as efficient as possible. Chapter 7 teaches you how to write efficient code that can be extended and maintained without making the code hard to comprehend.

- *Chapter 8, "Data Persistence"*: Serialization and persistence are topics that many pattern books avoid. Yet they are extremely important, and Chapter 8 addresses them. The patterns and strategies illustrated in this chapter dramatically simplify writing data to another medium.

- *Chapter 9, "Refactoring to Patterns"*: The last chapter wraps everything up by introducing refactoring. The focus of the chapter is not to introduce all aspects of refactoring, rather to define and illustrate how you can use the patterns defined in the book to refactor written code.

■ ■ ■

CHAPTER 1

Essentials of Object-Oriented Programming

Before you can understand patterns, you need to be familiar with some common nomenclature used in object-oriented programming (OOP). In this chapter, and throughout this book, I'll use C# to demonstrate some key OOP ideas. When writing OOP code using the C# language, you need to know about four main concepts: type, scope, inheritance, and generics. The combination of the four considerations makes an OO application work—or not work. The four main concepts are implemented as language keywords, such as `class` or `interface`, and I discuss what you need to know about these concepts in this chapter.

C# is an object-oriented programming language you can use to create applications on the .NET platform using the .NET runtime. When talking about C#, it's hard not to talk about the .NET platform, as C# requires the .NET runtime. Some consider C# the best language you can use to interact with the .NET runtime. This book discusses specific details about .NET and its API only in passing, and these details are secondary to the OOP information here.

Understanding Types

A type is a block of code that encapsulates data and methods. The simplest of all types is a class, which could be defined as follows:

```
class SimpleClass { }
```

In C#, you define types using keywords, identifiers, and curly brackets. The identifier `class` is a keyword that defines a class with the identifier `SimpleClass`. The curly brackets define a code block where everything between the curly brackets belongs to the `SimpleClass` type. Attributes can be associated with the `class` keyword; however, in the preceding example there are no additional attributes. Other types you can use are `struct`, `interface`, and generics. (Generics are discussed later in this chapter, in the "Writing Generic Code" section.)

Let's take a moment to look at `struct`s. The following example shows how to define a `struct` type:

```
struct SimpleStructure { }
```

The difference between a `struct` and a `class` is that the former is a value type and the latter is a reference type. The difference between a reference and a value type is an example of an implementation detail. There are some conceptual differences, but they are a direct result of the implementation. From an object-oriented conceptual perspective, both define types.

A type is necessary because it defines a piece of code that another piece of code can reference. The following code example illustrates how to reference types:

```
struct SimpleStruct {
}
class SimpleClass {
    SimpleStruct _myStruct;
    public SimpleStruct getData() {
        return _myStruct;
    }
}

class MainApp
{
    static void testMethod() {
        SimpleClass cls = new SimpleClass();
        SimpleStruct structure = cls.getData();
    }
}
```

The class MainApp has a method testMethod, which references types SimpleClass and SimpleStruct. The class SimpleClass references the type SimpleStruct. The sample code looks simple, and is an example of what a coder would typically write. What makes the code complex is that the references create dependencies. These dependencies can force major changes, even though the change in the dependency was simple.

In the sample code, the type SimpleStruct doesn't reference—and doesn't need to know— the details of SimpleClass. But SimpleClass has to know about SimpleStruct. The types SimpleClass and SimpleStruct are considered to be one module. Source code that uses the functionality exposed by the module is called a *consumer*. The method testMethod, which represents a consumer, has to know about the types SimpleClass and SimpleStruct. If a change in SimpleStruct were to occur, then two code sections, the consumer and the SimpleClass implementation, would have to be checked and potentially changed. Checking for implementation changes in a module is straightforward, because a module is self contained. The headaches begin in the consumer code, because a change in SimpleStruct requires a change in the consumer code, which could be more complicated than the module.

This is the irony of reusable object-oriented code. As more consumers reference and use a module's code, the more potential problems arise. This is because the module cannot dictate how the consumer uses itself. The consumer can do things that might work, but when the module is updated, such changes will cause logical errors in the application. The next section discusses the kinds of errors you might encounter.

There are two types of errors: syntactical and logical. In syntactical (or syntax) errors, the type details change, and the compiler catches the changes due to extra or missing information. Most often, parameters cause these problems. Syntax errors aren't wholly problematic, as a programmer can quickly fix the errors, but many errors are tedious to fix.

Logical errors are more problematic. A logical error is when the type changes its details without causing a syntax error. These types of errors are especially challenging because the compiler won't report the error. Defensive code (code that has built-in error mechanisms) can catch the error when the program is running. Logical errors are more commonly called *bugs*, or in slang terms, "features." Logical errors are often due to bad code design, poor implementation, or lack of testing. Logical errors arise because of a misunderstanding between the consumer and the module. It could be argued that a logical error isn't an error, but the result of a necessary change. However, this brings back what my Engineering Statics professor said: "Either the bridge stands or it falls; there is no middle ground." It doesn't matter what a logical error is called; the code still doesn't work, and it needs to be fixed. Regardless of why the logical error occurred, the costs of a logical error can be disproportionately high in financial or political impression terms.

A logical error can occur because the code contains uncontrolled or unmanageable referencing of other types. In the simple consumer code example you saw previously, only two types were referenced. Imagine four simple consumer code examples that only reference two or three types. If any of the consumer code implementations made a method call at the wrong moment, or made certain assumptions, the number of logical errors—once you factor in combinations and permutations—can be staggering. The logical-error scenario gets worse when a fix causes other logical errors to occur, a symptom known as *feature interaction* that's a particularly deadly form of logical error.

Feature-interaction errors are difficult and tedious to battle, and more often than not result in code that needs to be rewritten. Feature-interaction errors should be avoided; patterns help with this problem. Test-driven development keeps feature-interaction errors in check because any changes that cause other problems to occur are immediately recognized. An immediate recognition causes an immediate fix, ensuring that a feature-interaction error is squashed while it's still small and tamable.

Consider the following: imagine a room of people. Each person is a type, and like a party where each person can communicate with each other person, types can reference one another without regard. If the communication is organized, then there will be only a slight murmur of voices when several people are communicating at one time. If things were to get out of control, the noise would reach extremely loud levels, spiraling into cacophony. This is because for somebody to communicate with another person, he has to speak louder than the noise level of the room. The next person does the same thing, and shortly, you'll find everybody shouting. If the sound can be kept to a lower level, then everything is still controllable. Relating this back to types and referencing, if types reference one another without any order, the code will quickly become hard to understand because too many types reference other types.

Modular vs. Reusable Code

Modular code is code that has been split into blocks of functionality. Reusable code is code that's usable in different situations. It's important to understand that modular code isn't necessarily reusable code, and reusable code isn't necessarily modular code. Reusable code that has been reused often tends not to be modular code. These two statements might confuse, because we tend to think of reusability and modularity as the same thing.

One of the best explanations of modularity is given in the book *Software Engineering: A Practitioner's Approach.*[1] In the book, modularity is explained as a four-decade-old concept that can be best summarized as "software that has been split into distinct separately named and addressed blocks of source code, which are integrated into a program to solve a problem."

A modular program contains unique pieces of code that interface with each other to solve a problem. Modularity makes it possible to use a divide-and-conquer strategy when implementing the solution. A module is defined by its *contract*, which specifies the module's functionality. When developers know the contract, they only have to write source code to meet the requirements of the contract. At a later point in time, the individual modules are combined, and if the contracts are correctly defined and implemented, the resulting program works. Metaphorically speaking, this process is comparable to building a bridge by starting on both sides. If the contracts are properly defined and implemented, then the two bridge segments will meet at the right place in the middle.

The following source code is an example of a modular application:

```
class User1 {
}
class User2 {
}
class User3 {
}
class MainApp
{
    static void testMethod() {
        User1 cls1 = new User1();
        // Do something with cls1
        User2 cls2 = new User2();
        // Do something with cls2
        User3 cls3 = new User3();
        // Do something with cls3
    }
}
```

User1, User2, and User3 are three unique and distinct types that have no interaction with one another. The method testMethod instantiates the three types and uses them to execute some logic. The consumer of the three types uses the types independently of one another. In a real-world scenario there might be some interaction, but the objective of modularizing an application is to separate the code pieces so that they don't interact.

▓Note Reusability has a different aim than modularizing source code, and is best defined as behavior that would "be more useful in more than one context."[2]

---

1. Roger S. Pressman, *Software Engineering: A Practitioner's Approach, European Adaptation*, 3rd ed. (London: McGraw-Hill, 1994), p. 325.
2. Grady Booch, *Object-Oriented Analysis and Design with Applications*, 2nd ed. (Boston: Addison-Wesley, 1993), p. 138.

The idea behind reusability is to define a piece of code that multiple consumers use. A reusable piece of code would be used often, and in theory reduces the developer's need to write code. There's a problem with this scenario, in that writing code that's reusable creates code that's difficult to change (a symptom known as brittle code), because there are too many changes to make when a small modification in the reused code takes place. Consider the following code segment, which illustrates the point:

```
class BaseClass {
}
class User1 {
    BaseClass _inst1;
}
class User2 {
    BaseClass _inst2;
}
class User3 {
    BaseClass _inst3;
}
class MainApp
{
    static void testMethod() {
        User1 cls1 = new User1();
        // Do something with cls1
        User2 cls2 = new User2();
        // Do something with cls2
        User3 cls3 = new User3();
        // Do something with cls3
    }
}
```

The type BaseClass is used in three different classes (User1, User2, and User3), which makes the type BaseClass reusable. The downside is that if the type BaseClass is altered, then the usage of BaseClass has to be inspected in each of the three different classes. This is the basis of the brittle-code problem. A change in BaseClass requires inspection in how BaseClass is used. The compiler finds syntax errors relating to how the type BaseClass is used. Logical errors in how BaseClass is used are more complicated to find and require well-defined testing procedures.

The type BaseClass isn't modular because usage of the type spans different modules. An argument could be made that the type BaseClass is a module in its own right. The problem with that argument is that the reusable type is used too often to be considered a module. Some books define a reusable type or collection of reusable types as being smaller in size.[3]

Remember that modularity and reusability should be considered orthogonal to each other. Neither modularity nor reusability should be a means to an end, and you should use each in doses. As a general rule, modules implement a divide-and-conquer strategy, and reusable types implement functionality in different contexts. There's a need for each, which this book will explain in more detail throughout.

3. Steve McConnell, *Rapid Development* (Redmond, WA: Microsoft Press, 1996), p. 533.

Using Scope to Control Access

Going back to the people-in-the-room analogy illustrated in the section "Understanding Types," every person can approach another person and speak to that person. Were the room a party, then having different people talk to each other is a good thing and a way to network. If instead the room were a court scenario, then chaos would ensue as everybody attempts to talk to somebody else. A courtroom requires order and that only certain individuals speak at certain times. The C# programming language can be either a party or a courtroom, and that environment is determined by which accessibility modifiers are used.

Accessibility modifiers can apply both to type declarations and their associated methods and data. Imagine the party scenario in which you approach to speak to another person. Just because you can speak to the other person doesn't give you the right to reach into his or her pockets and see how much money that person is carrying. C# has the same concept, in that you can use the same type, but maybe not the same methods or data members. Accessibility modifiers make it possible to manage the referencing of a type's methods and data.

Before explaining the nature of the scope modifiers, an additional piece of information needs to be explained. Usually when you create a .NET application, the C# compiler takes a set of source-code files that are compiled into a binary .NET module.[4] The .NET module can be considered a raw form of .NET executable code. The problem is that the .NET runtime has no idea how to run the module. Therefore, the module has to be wrapped as something, which could be a program that can execute on its own, or an assembly. Scope identifiers not only affect the code that's compiled as one assembly, but they affect how types can see other types in other assemblies.

The .NET environment includes the following scope modifiers: `public`, `internal`, `protected`, `internal protected`, and `private`. Not all scope modifiers can be used at all times. When declaring types, only the modifiers `public` and `internal` can be used. All scope modifiers can be used when declaring methods or data members belonging to a type.

Following are the different types of scope modifiers:

- `internal`: Defines a type, method, or data member that has a public scope in the context of an assembly. The type, method, or data member cannot be accessed from outside the assembly.

- `internal protected`: This protection can only be applied to methods or data members, and is a combination of the `internal` and `protected` scope modifiers. This means a method or data member has public scope in the subclassed type.

- `private`: Defines a method or data member that's private and only accessible to the type defining the method or data member.

- `protected`: Protected methods and data members are scoped as private by any code that attempts to use the method or data type directly. If the method or data member is called from a subclassed type, then the scope is more akin to public. For quick reference, `protected` means public or private scope depending on the context. The next section outlines the specifics of inheritance.

---

4. Don Box with Chris Sells, *Essential .NET Volume 1: The Common Language Runtime* (Boston: Addison-Wesley, 2003), pp. 13–23.

- public: Defines a type, method, or data member to be considered visible regardless of assembly or program scope. The public scope modifier is considered the loosest of scope modifiers, and therefore the most dangerous with respect to managing unwanted references.

Throughout the book, the illustrated patterns will use scope modifiers to define how a consumer can reference and use the type. Scope modifiers are important and must be carefully considered. Too often, when confronted with a complicated situation, developers automatically use the public scope modifier. This is a bad practice, and causes problems with respect to uncontrolled referencing of types. Remember the party where the noise level went out of control; using the wrong scope modifier results in the same sorts of problems.

Understanding Inheritance

Inheritance is an extremely powerful concept that allows one type to subclass another type. Using inheritance, it's possible to define some functionality in the base class, which is then modified or defined in a derived class. Inheritance is much like building a house, where you start with the foundation and then build on the foundation.

A simple example of a class subclassing another class is as follows:

```
class BaseClass {
}
class Derived : BaseClass {
}
```

The class BaseClass is a type definition that's considered the foundation. The class Derived inherits the functionality from the base type BaseClass. In C#, inheritance is defined by the class or interfaces after the colon character, and three main types support inheritance.

The three types that support inheritance are defined as follows:

- class: A generic type that supports most inheritance operations. A class can define methods, data members, and most things that .NET classes need to implement.

- interface: A special class type that doesn't support an implementation. Interfaces are used to define a contract in the form of a type.

- struct: A special type of class that's a value type and considered to be a sealed class. (A sealed class is a class that can be used, but not subclassed from. In a value type, contents of the type are stored on the stack.)

▓**Note** enum has a restricted inheritance notation, so it isn't considered a main type that supports inheritance.

In general notation terms, you code the three main types that support inheritance as follows:

```
class TYPE : [class type] [, interface type, ...] { }
interface TYPE : [interface type,...] { }
struct TYPE : [interface type,...] { }
```

The type class can inherit from another class, but only one class and not multiple classes. This is called a single-inheritance object model. (There are arguments for other inheritance models, and the reason for each is beyond the scope of this book.) With a single-inheritance object model, any other identifier after the subclassed class must be an interface. Also, a class doesn't have to subclass another class if the class wants to subclass an interface. Both the type interface and the type struct can subclass only other interfaces.

Inheritance is a controversial topic for some people because of the problems that it causes. Many of those individuals promote using only interfaces. An example of a problem with inheritance is the fragile base-class problem, which is illustrated in Chapter 5. .NET is different from other frameworks, in that to a large degree, .NET has solved many of the inheritance problems that occur using other programming languages, and allows the developer to control how inheritance is used. However, keep in mind that inheritance, like interfaces, is a tool to be used in the right situation. For example, implementations are used to define a class with multiple personalities, where a personality is an implementation of an interface, and inheritance is used to specialize a behavior.

Differences Between Inheritance and Structs

A struct is a value type, and a class is a reference type. They can have radically different behavior when used in conjunction with inheritance. This behavior can lead to undesired side effects.

Consider the following example, in which two types are defined with the same data member:

```
struct ExStruct {
    public int value;
}
class ExClass {
    public int value;
}
```

The types ExStruct and ExClass define a public data member value. When the type ExStruct is manipulated and passed as a parameter to a method, the stack is used. In contrast, the type ExClass is a reference to some data in the heap. The easiest way to illustrate the difference is to pass an instance of each as a parameter to a method, as shown by the following code example:

```
class ExMethodCall {
    public static void SecondMethod( ExStruct param1, ExClass param2) {
        DebugMgr.start( 10, "ExMethodCall.SecondMethod");
        param1.value ++;
        param2.value ++;
        DebugMgr.output( 10, "During ExStruct.value = " + param1.value);
```

```
            DebugMgr.output( 10, "During ExClass.value = " + param2.value);
            DebugMgr.end( 10);
        }
        public static void FirstMethod() {
            DebugMgr.start( 10, "ExMethodCall.FirstMethod");
            ExStruct cls1 = new ExStruct();
            ExClass cls2 = new ExClass();
            DebugMgr.output( 10, "Before ExStruct.value = " + cls1.value);
            DebugMgr.output( 10, "Before ExClass.value = " + cls2.value);
            SecondMethod( cls1, cls2);
            DebugMgr.output( 10, "After ExStruct.value = " + cls1.value);
            DebugMgr.output( 10, "After ExClass.value = " + cls2.value);
            DebugMgr.end( 10);
        }
    }
```

The type ExMethodCall has two methods: FirstMethod and SecondMethod. The method FirstMethod instantiates the types ExStruct and ExClass, which are then passed as parameters to the method SecondMethod. The data member values are incremented within the method SecondMethod. The idea behind the SecondMethod method is to illustrate how methods can modify the values of a type. When the code is executed, the following output is generated:

```
start (TestInheritance.IllustrateStructAndClass)
    start (ExMethodCall.FirstMethod)
        Before ExStruct.value = 0
        Before ExClass.value = 0
        start (ExMethodCall.SecondMethod)
            During ExStruct.value = 1
            During ExClass.value = 1
        end (ExMethodCall.SecondMethod)
        After ExStruct.value = 0
        After ExClass.value = 1
    end (ExMethodCall.FirstMethod)
end (TestInheritance.IllustrateStructAndClass)
```

In the output, the value of the data member value for each type is zero before the SecondMethod method call. The values are incremented within the SecondMethod method. However, things change after the call to SecondMethod. The instance of type ExStruct has a data member value of zero, which wasn't the value within the context of the SecondMethod method call. This is because the type ExStruct is a value type, and the entire contents of the structure are stored on the stack. When a value type is passed to a method, the value of the type is copied to the stack. Then, whenever the value on the stack is modified, a copy is modified, not the original instance.

The behavior of a value type when compared to a reference type is a purposeful behavior. In fact, all languages make a difference between value and reference types. I'll illustrate where value types can become tricky by rewriting the example of value versus reference type, as follows:

```
interface RunningTotal {
      int GetValue();
      void IncrementValue();
   }

   struct ExStruct2 : RunningTotal {
      private int _value;

      public int GetValue() {
         return _value;
      }
      public void IncrementValue() {
         _value ++;
      }
   }

   class ExClass2 : RunningTotal {
      private int _value;

      public int GetValue() {
         return _value;
      }
      public void IncrementValue() {
         _value ++;
      }
   }
```

This time the types ExClass2 and ExStruct2 subclass the interface RunningTotal. The idea behind the RunningTotal interface is to define the increment operations as part of a generic type. Further developing the rewritten example, the SecondMethod method references the interface RunningTotal, as shown in the following example:

```
class ExMethodCall2 {
      public static void SecondMethod( RunningTotal param) {
         DebugMgr.start( 10, "ExMethodCall.SecondMethod");
         param.IncrementValue();
         DebugMgr.output( 10, "During RunningTotal.value = " + param.GetValue());
         DebugMgr.end( 10);
      }
      public static void FirstMethod() {
         DebugMgr.start( 10, "ExMethodCall.FirstMethod");
         ExStruct2 cls1 = new ExStruct2();
         ExClass2 cls2 = new ExClass2();
         DebugMgr.output( 10, "Before ExStruct2.value = " + cls1.GetValue());
         DebugMgr.output( 10, "Before ExClass2.value = " + cls2.GetValue());
         SecondMethod( cls1);
         SecondMethod( cls2);
```

```
            DebugMgr.output( 10, "After ExStruct2.value = " + cls1.GetValue());
            DebugMgr.output( 10, "After ExClass2.value = " + cls2.GetValue());
            DebugMgr.end( 10);
        }
    }
```

Notice how the types are instantiated and then passed to the method SecondMethod. The method SecondMethod expects the type RunningTotal, so a cast automatically happens. When running the example code, the following output is generated:

```
start (TestInheritance.IllustrateStructAndClass)
    start (ExMethodCall.FirstMethod)
        Before ExStruct2.value = 0
        Before ExClass2.value = 0
        start (ExMethodCall.SecondMethod)
            During RunningTotal.value = 1
        end (ExMethodCall.SecondMethod)
        start (ExMethodCall.SecondMethod)
            During RunningTotal.value = 1
        end (ExMethodCall.SecondMethod)
        After ExStruct2.value = 0
        After ExClass2.value = 1
    end (ExMethodCall.FirstMethod)
end (TestInheritance.IllustrateStructAndClass)
```

Notice again, after the SecondMethod method has been called, the original value for the type ExStruct2 hasn't been altered. This shows that the value behavior applies if a value type implements the interface.

What's stressful about this entire situation is that SecondMethod doesn't know whether the RunningTotal type instance is a value type or a reference type. The method SecondMethod is making changes via method calls on the RunningTotal interface, assuming that the changes are kept. Yet those changes aren't kept when the SecondMethod returns control, resulting in code that could potentially create buggy results.

The observant reader will say that my example is biased because the behavior for a value type passed as a parameter for a method has already been illustrated. The same behavior could have been illustrated without a method call. The same happens when a value type is downcast to an interface, as illustrated by the following example:

```
((RunningTotal)cls1).IncrementValue();
```

The class instance cls1 is downcast to RunningTotal, then the method IncrementValue is executed. When the method cls1.GetValue is called, the results of the method IncrementValue will have disappeared. A simple rule of thumb is not to subclass interfaces in a struct type unless you have a good reason.

Simple Inheritance

Now that you've learned about the differences between inheritance and structs, it's time to move on to simple inheritance. The simplest kind of inheritance is when one type defines a method and a subclass redefines that method. Here's an example:

```
class BaseClass {
    public void SimpleMethod() {
            DebugMgr.start( 10, "BaseClass.SimpleMethod");
            DebugMgr.end( 10);
    }
}


class Subclassed : BaseClass {
    public new void SimpleMethod() {
        DebugMgr.start( 10, "Subclassed.SimpleMethod");
        DebugMgr.end( 10);
    }
}
```

The class BaseClass defines the method SimpleMethod. The class Subclassed subclasses the BaseClass and redefines the method SimpleMethod. Notice the use of the new keyword. The new keyword is what makes .NET and C# a software-engineering language with useful and consistent inheritance management.

When a class subclasses another class and defines a method identical to a method in the subclass, that class is *overriding* a method. Overriding means that old functionality is replaced with new functionality. Having new functionality potentially results in code that might introduce new problems. To subvert such problems, C# and .NET require the developer to indicate explicitly when a method is overridden. This makes the developer aware that functionality will be altered in some base class.

The following code illustrates how to use the defined types:

```
Subclassed subcls = new Subclassed();
subcls.SimpleMethod();
DebugMgr.output( 10, "Now assigning to type BaseClass");
BaseClass basecls = subcls;
basecls.SimpleMethod();
```

The type Subclassed is instantiated and assigned to the variable subcls, which is of the same type. Next, the method SimpleMethod is called, and then a downcast to the subclassed type BaseClass is made and assigned to the variable basecls. The method SimpleMethod is called again. The following output is generated when the sample code is executed:

```
 start (Subclassed.SimpleMethod)
 end (Subclassed.SimpleMethod)
Now assigning to type BaseClass
 start (BaseClass.SimpleMethod)
 end (BaseClass.SimpleMethod)
```

When using the new keyword, the functionality used by the consumer is based on the type and the casting. Let's say BaseClass is instantiated. If the instance is downcast to Subclassed, then Subclassed is called because it has an implementation of SimpleMethod. If the instance is cast back to BaseClass, which has its own SimpleMethod implementation, then BaseClass will be called. This is a clean inheritance model because the implementation you execute is based on the cast type.

Inheritance Using Virtual Functions

In the simple inheritance example you saw in the previous section, the method of the type is the method that's called. That kind of inheritance is limiting because it requires that the type's user know about the type. When writing components, which Chapter 3 will discuss in more detail, having to know the type in order to call the appropriate method defeats the purpose of having and creating components.

More conveniently, inheritance can make use of virtual functions. A virtual function is designed to redirect the method call to a derived class, even when the method being called belongs to a base class. Going back to the simple inheritance example, the code results in the method Subclassed.SimpleMethod being called, regardless if the method call is called from the type Subclassed or BaseClass. Virtual functions implement an object-oriented technique called polymorphism. Polymorphism is defined as follows:

> *The idea behind polymorphism is that a group of heterogeneous objects (for example, apples, oranges, bananas) can be made to look homogenous (for example, a bunch of fruit), but can then be distinguished based on their own specific type at run time.* [5]

An example of polymorphic types is as follows:

```
class Animal {
    public virtual void WhatAmI() {
        DebugMgr.output( 10, "I don't know what you are");
    }
}

class Human : Animal {
    public override void WhatAmI() {
        DebugMgr.output( 10, "I am a human");
    }
}

class Dog : Animal {
    public override void WhatAmI() {
        DebugMgr.output( 10, "I am a dog");
    }
}
```

---

5. Arthur J. Reil, *Object-Oriented Design Heuristics* (Boston: Addison-Wesley, 1996), p. 95.

The type Animal defines a single method WhatAmI, which is defined as virtual using the virtual keyword. Using the virtual keyword means that the method has declared itself as a candidate for being overridden. The types Human and Dog subclass the type Animal, and redefine the method WhatAmI. The keyword override is used to indicate that the virtual method will be overridden, and any reference to the WhatAmI method will be redirected to the appropriate method.

An example of calling polymorphic types is as follows:

```
DebugMgr.output( 10, "Created Human and assigned to Animal");
Animal animal1 = new Human();
animal1.WhatAmI();
DebugMgr.output( 10, "Created Dog and assigned to Animal");
Animal animal2 = new Dog();
animal2.WhatAmI();
```

The types Human and Dog are instantiated and assigned to the variables animal1 and animal2, which are the type Animal. Essentially, the calling code instantiates a type and downcasts the instantiated type to the subclass type. Then the subclass type method WhatAmI is called. Running the calling code generates the following output:

```
Created Human and assigned to Animal
I am a human
Created Dog and assigned to Animal
I am a dog
```

In the generated output, unlike the simple inheritance example where a downcast calls the base type method, the subclassed method is called.

Polymorphic code allows the developer to create general code that manipulates specific types. From the previous example, this means that general code would manipulate the Animal type, but call the specific types Dog or Human.

Inheritance in a Software-Engineering Context

C# and the .NET runtime go beyond regular polymorphic code. They make it possible to develop polymorphic code that's time proof—or at least mostly time proof. The difficulty is that if a later version implements newer functionality, then older consumers will receive the newer functionality.

Consider the case of extending the Animal class with a more specific Dog type, as shown by the following example:

```
class EnglishBulldog : Dog {
    public override void WhatAmI() {
        DebugMgr.output( 10, "I am an English Bulldog");
    }
}
```

The type EnglishBulldog extends the type Dog, and overrides the method WhatAmI. If the old code were modified to use the new type, the following code would result:

```
private static Animal CreateCurrentDogInstance() {
      DebugMgr.start( 10, "TestInheritance.CreateCurrentDogInstance");
      DebugMgr.end( 10);
      return new EnglishBulldog();
      // return new Dog(); Original version
}
private static void TimeProofPolymorphicInheritance() {
      DebugMgr.start( 10, "TestInheritance.TimeProofPolymorphicInheritance");
      Animal animal = CreateCurrentDogInstance();
      animal.WhatAmI();
      DebugMgr.end( 10);
}
```

This time, when the method CreateCurrentDogInstance is called, the method implementation from EnglishBulldog is called, not Dog as in previous examples. This is a desired behavior, but consider the ramifications of this context. You're writing some code, and your code intends to describe all animals on the planet. But then time passes, and it's realized that the application is used mostly with dogs. At this point, the developers of the application have decided to add more functionality for dog breeds. New functionality is added, and old functionality needs to keep working as is. The implementation needs to support two functionalities, the old and the new, which share the same interface.

The newly defined Dog type is called EnglishBulldog, and the new users of the application like the update. Now comes the question: do the old users who generally aren't interested in dogs get the update as well? In the previous code example, the method CreateCurrentDogInstance would force all old users to get the new update, and that isn't necessarily the best result. In a software-engineering context, old features and bugs that are suddenly fixed could cause more difficulties and anomalies than the fix itself.

C# solves this problem by using the new keyword. In the example in the "Simple Inheritance" section, the new keyword was used to indicate that a method is overriding another method. But you can also use the new keyword if you're defining new functionalities while using old methods. Using the new keyword, you could redefine the Bulldog type as follows:

```
class EnglishBulldog : Dog {
      public new virtual void WhatAmI() {
          DebugMgr.output( 10, "I am an English Bulldog");
      }
}
```

By adding the new virtual keywords, users of the Animal type get the old functionality of the Dog type. If the method CreateCurrentDogInstance is called and the Animal type is executed, the following output is generated:

```
start (TestInheritance.TimeProofPolymorphicInheritance)
   start (TestInheritance.CreateCurrentDogInstance)
   end (TestInheritance.CreateCurrentDogInstance)
   I am a dog
end (TestInheritance.TimeProofPolymorphicInheritance)
```

This is interesting, in that even though the EnglishBulldog type is instantiated, the method WhatAmI of EnglishBulldog isn't called. This means users of the old type get the old functionality, and users of the new type get the new functionality. You can use the new keyword to define new functionality. You can convert a virtual method into a nonvirtual method, and vice versa.

Writing Generic Code

Writing generic code means writing libraries in a general reusable sense. The word *Generics* with a capital G means something entirely different. In a nutshell, Generics is the writing of libraries that can be generally reused using a specific notation. The new definition and the old definition sound similar, but the notation makes a world of difference.

The Case for Generics

Let's imagine writing a reusable class that manages a reference to another type, which is illustrated as follows:

```
class OldContainer {
    private Object _contained;

    public Object MyProperty {
        get {
            return _contained;
        }
        set {
            _contained = value;
        }
    }
}
```

The type OldContainer has a private data member _contained, which is of the type Object. In .NET speak, referencing the Object type means referencing the instance of any type (object). All objects in .NET eventually subclass the Object type, even if it isn't written as it's implied.

Following is an example code piece that uses the type OldContainer:

```
OldContainer container = new OldContainer();
container.MyProperty = 2;
int value = (int)container.MyProperty;
```

The property MyProperty is assigned the value of 2, even though MyProperty expects an assignment of type Object. Some readers might expect a type conflict, but the number 2 is being boxed by .NET and downcast to the type Object.

The code becomes problematic when the value is retrieved from the property MyProperty. Because MyProperty is of type Object, and the variable value is of type int, a typecast has to be performed. The typecast is tedious and introduces a potential runtime error. The problem with using the Object type as a basis reference type is that any type can be referenced. For example, the type OldContainer could reference the type Foo, and when a cast to int is performed a runtime type exception is generated.

The following is a rewritten version of the type OldContainer to use Generics:

```
class NewContainer< item> {
    private item _contained;

    public item MyProperty {
        get {
            return _contained;
        }
        set {
            _contained = value;
        }
    }
}
```

After the identifier NewContainer are a set of angle brackets. Within the angle brackets is an identifier item. You define Generics with the identifier item and the angle brackets. The identifier item isn't a type, but a named placeholder for a type. The best way to understand Generics is to say that the identifier item is a placeholder for a type replaced in the context of a method or type declaration.

An example of using the type NewContainer is as follows:

```
NewContainer< int> container = new NewContainer< int>();
container.MyProperty = 2;
int value = container.MyProperty;
```

The type NewContainer is defined with the type int within the angle brackets. The type int replaces the placeholder item in the NewContainer definition. The data member _contained is defined to be the type int. When MyProperty is assigned the value of 2, the value isn't boxed and then downcast. Instead, the value is assigned directly, and when the value is retrieved from MyProperty, a typecast isn't necessary, because the type of the container is an int.

Constraints

The type NewContainer defines a placeholder, but the placeholder type is used as a black-box reference. A black box is so defined because the holder of the box has no idea what the box contains, nor does the holder care. With respect to the type NewContainer, the placeholder is a black box because NewContainer doesn't call any methods or use any data members of the placeholder. Had the type NewContainer attempted to call a method or data member, a compilation fault would occur. This is because the type NewContainer doesn't know what methods or data members are supported.

Following is an example of how to constrain the NewContainer type:

```
class BaseType< mytype> {
    public virtual void DoSomething( mytype value){
    }
}
```

```
class NewContainerConstrained< item> : NewContainer< item>
    where item : BaseType< item> {
    public void ActionMethod( item param) {
        param.DoSomething( MyProperty);
    }
}
```

The sample code can be a bit confusing because multiple actions are going on with the same type. The class NewContainerConstrained subclasses the NewContainer type. Because the NewContainer type is a Generic class, something has to be defined for the placeholder, which happens to be the placeholder identifier for the type NewContainerConstrained. As a side note, it's possible to specify a type for the subclassed type NewContainer, as shown by the following example:

```
class NewContainerConstrained< item> : NewContainer< int>
```

Going back to the constrained-example code, the identifiers after the where item specify the constraint. The first identifier after the where keyword must be a placeholder identifier. The colon after the placeholder identifier specifies the types that the placeholder identifier has subclassed. The additional type identifier new() indicates that the placeholder type must support a no-parameter constructor.

Once the placeholder has been constrained, then the supported methods can be called. In the case of this example, that means that the item placeholder has to subclass the type BaseType, which is also a Generic type. The type BaseType has a single method DoSomething that can be called within the context of the type NewContainerConstrained. Because all Generic types use the same placeholder identifiers, there are no cast problems when the Generic types are specialized.

Now let's go back to the problem of specializing the Generic type too early. The problem with early specialization is that it prematurely constrains the Generic code. If the NewContainer subclass had been specialized to be the int type, then the method call param.DoSomething would have to be specialized as well. The reason is because the constraint of the BaseType method DoSomething is defined as a placeholder. An example of rewriting the Generic code using a specialized form is as follows:

```
class BaseType {
    public virtual void DoSomething( int value){
    }
}

class NewContainerConstrained< item> : NewContainer< int>
    where item : BaseType {
    public void Method( item param) {
        param.DoSomething( MyProperty);
    }
}
```

The rewritten NewContainerConstrained type specializes the type NewContainer, and the type BaseType isn't a Generic type. The result is that you can't use the BaseType type generically to process other types. In many cases that's entirely acceptable, but it does illustrate an important Generic code fact. When writing code, your use of Generics is either entirely generic, or specialized. This means your classes should either all contain placeholders for the generic parts, or the generic parts all have defined specializations. Trying to be partially specialized is asking for problems, because errors result when constraints aren't fulfilled.

Writing code generically means writing your types as reusable code pieces. Writing your code in a specialized context means writing modules. It will be difficult, and will require many hacks, if you attempt to write some code generically and other code in a specialized fashion. This book makes extensive use of .NET Generics because they solve many problems elegantly.

Some Considerations

Whenever you use a Generic type, a specific version of the Generic type is dynamically created. If the Generic type were used with three different types, then three different versions would be dynamically created. This results in a larger application requirement when the .NET application is executed. The size change can either be negligible or significant. It only depends on the number of different types, and how often a Generic type is embedded within another Generic type.

For example, in the mid-1990s when templates were introduced in C++ (a feature similar in theory to C# Generics), I had to compile a set of Generic types that expanded 65 levels. The resulting code size meant every time the type was instantiated, two megabytes of memory space was required. It's doubtful that C# will suffer from the same problems as C++ templates. It does mean that some developers will overuse Generics.

When illustrating Generics, many developers will show how much better it is to write a list or stack class. They demonstrate how type-safe the list or stack is, thus making the classes stable and robust. These demonstrations aren't without merit, even though they offer a false sense of security. As explained earlier, there are two types of errors: logical and syntax. Syntax errors aren't a problem, and generally speaking, doing an improper cast is also not a major problem. It's easy to find and fix this type of problem. More problematic are logical errors, a kind of error that Generics don't address. In fact, in some cases, Generics amplify the problem, because the source code that uses Generics extensively is abstract and requires some thinking to figure out what's being defined. Putting it simply, imagine developing an architecture that can be abstracted. When implementing the abstraction, another abstraction is created, and when creating that abstraction, yet another abstraction is created. To make all these abstractions work together, the developer has to assign the correct classes with one another. The problem is that what seems obvious to one person isn't obvious to another person. Hence, the advantage of the abstraction is lost. In contrast, when writing a class that implements an interface and references another class, you know what the intention is.

For example, what happens when a generic type uses a generic type, which in turn uses a generic type? Unless the developer has an intimate understanding of Generics, conceptual problems will arise. My point is neither to scare nor to be a naysayer of Generics. Rather, I say to use Generics, as they solve many problems elegantly, but realize that Generics are a powerful mechanism that should be treated with respect and used in proper doses.

Composition

When writing code, inheritance allows one type to subclass another type. Often inheritance is abused, and used in contexts that aren't applicable. In those contexts, the best approach is to use composition.

Composition occurs when work that's associated with a type is delegated to another type. For example, classical OOP would use inheritance to expose all functionality associated with a type. A smarter approach would be to use composition to implement functionality that's only partially related to the type. When used in conjunction with Generics, composition provides a powerful and flexible solution.

The following quotes best describe when to use each:

> *Use composition to extend responsibilities by delegating work to other more appropriate objects.*
>
> *Use inheritance to extend attributes and methods.*[6]

A simple example of composition follows:

```
class BaseClass {
    public void Method() {
    }
}

class User1 {
    BaseClass _inst1;

    public DoSomething() {
        _inst1.Method();
    }
}
```

The type User1 has a data member of the type BaseClass. Calling the method DoSomething calls the method Method of the data member _inst. The method DoSomething is delegating the bulk of the work to the type BaseClass.

Asynchronous Code

When instantiating types, making method calls, and modifying data, all the operations occur synchronously. That's a logical approach, as you'd expect an answer when a method is called.

Writing asynchronous code is another programming methodology that isn't covered extensively in this book, outside of delegates. The reason is because asynchronous programming introduces concepts that are entirely alien and complicated. When I say "asynchronous," I mean true asynchronous code, such as Microsoft Message Queue. The reason why asynchronous code is less commonly used than synchronous code is because it isn't convenient for the programmer. Using a mail metaphor, synchronous programming is like sending a package via a courier. The courier picks up the package, and you know that, barring catastrophic circumstances, the package will arrive. Asynchronous programming is like sending a letter in the mail. The letter will arrive, but there's no tracking of the letter, no verification that the letter has arrived. Using the mail, you assume that sometime in the future, the letter will arrive.

---

6. Peter Coad et al, *Java Design: Building Better Apps and Applets*, 2nd ed. (Upper Saddle River, NJ: Prentice Hall, 1998), p. 49.

Asynchronous programming is reactionary programming, in that code reacts to triggers sent to it. In the simplest case, you implement asynchronous code using C# delegates, as shown by the following example:

```
delegate void DoItNow( string param);

class ReceiveMessage {
    public void MethodToDoItNow( string param) {
        DebugMgr.start( 10, "ReceiveMessage.MethodToDoItNow");
        DebugMgr.output( 10, "Received message " + param);
        DebugMgr.end( 10);
    }
}

public class RunExamples {
    public static void DoIt() {
        DebugMgr.start( 10, "RunExamples.DoIt");
        ReceiveMessage receiver = new ReceiveMessage();
        DoItNow myDelegate = new DoItNow( receiver.MethodToDoItNow);

        myDelegate( "do something");
        DebugMgr.end( 10);
    }
}
```

In C#, the keyword delegate is used to define a method signature that a sender and receiver use to exchange data. A delegate is intended to be neutral and matched on the basis of a method signature. In the example code, the type ReceiveMessage has a method MethodToDoItNow that has the same method signature as the delegate DoItNow.

The type RunExamples has a method DoIt, which instantiates the delegate and assigns the instance to the variable myDelegate. The instantiated delegate has a single constructor parameter that's a method reference to a method with the same signature as the defined delegate. In the case of the example, the method reference is from an instantiated type. It's possible to assign a delegate with a static method.

When calling the delegate instance, the call is delegated to the registered methods. Running the example, the following output is generated:

```
start (RunExamples.DoIt)
    start (ReceiveMessage.MethodToDoItNow)
        Received message do something
    end (ReceiveMessage.MethodToDoItNow)
end (RunExamples.DoIt)
```

The output verifies that the type ReceiveMessage receives a message, even though the type RunExamples hasn't explicitly called the method.

A delegate is an example of writing asynchronous code, and .NET also supports a system called *events*. Events are an extension of the asynchronous programming methodology. Regardless, though, of the mechanism used, the receiver of the message never knows when a message will arrive with asynchronous programming. When a message is sent, the receiver has to establish a context and process the data.

The other part of asynchronous programming is the trigger that sends the message. There are three types of triggers, which are defined as follows:

- *Passive*: A trigger that consistently polls for a change in some state. When the state changes, the trigger propagates the change.

- *Timer-based*: A trigger that propagates a message using a countdown mechanism that could be a single shot or periodic propagation.

- *Active*: A trigger that's part of another type that calls the delegate. The trigger code is distributed throughout different code pieces.

Some Final Thoughts

Knowing OOP and its associated terms means that you know the ingredients of the various patterns. You won't know how to apply the ingredients properly, as the patterns will cover that aspect. But when the term *virtual* or *inheritance* is used, you'll know what that encompasses with respect to the .NET platform. When a pattern is explained and implemented, you can pick apart the different OOP techniques used and learn the abstract idea behind the pattern. This makes it possible to see beyond the individual keywords and start thinking in strategies.

CHAPTER 2

Logging, Errors, and Test-Driven Development

The purpose of this chapter is to show you how to log, generate exceptions, and do test-driven development (TDD). These three topics aren't generally covered in books on patterns or object-oriented design, but are extremely important for understanding OOP. It's important to cover these topics early in this book, because these concepts make an application stable, robust, and—if an error does occur—reproducible. The worst thing that can happen to an application is finding a bug that cannot be tracked or reproduced. If you implement the three topics from this chapter in your application, those problems cannot happen.

Implementing Logging Management

You use logging to allow an application to indicate what it's doing, and to specify where any problems are. The simplest way for an application to indicate what it's doing is to use the method `Console.WriteLine`. However, the simplest way is also the worst way, because it assumes that there's a console to write to. If the application were a component executing in the context of an application server, a console wouldn't be available.

The best way to implement logging is to use log4net. The log4net library is a port from the Java log4j library, and is available at `http://logging.apache.org/log4net`.

A Simple Log4net Example

You need to know about two implementation details when using log4net: changing the source code and changing the application configuration file. The changes in the source code require writing method calls that check if logging is enabled, and subsequently making the logging calls. The application's configuration file modifications enable or disable the logging.

Following is an example implementation of how you might use log4net to perform a simple debug logging operation:

```
using System;
using log4net;

[assembly: Config.DOMConfigurator(Watch=true)]

public class MainApp
{
    public static void Main(string[] args)
        ILog log = LogManager.GetLogger( "Chapter2.Logging");

        if (log.IsDebugEnabled)
            log.Debug("Hello world");
    }
}
```

Let's walk through this. You reference the namespace log4net so you can use the log4net assembly. You must add the attribute [assembly: . . .] to enable the log4net listener. You use the listener to capture log4net messages that are then output to the logging outputs defined in the application configuration. If you don't activate the listener, logging isn't activated, and any logging messages made are lost. You can add the attribute to the main application, or to an assembly that's loaded by the main application. The location doesn't matter; it only matters that the attribute is executed.

You make logging calls by calling methods on the ILog interface. You call the method LogManager.GetLogger to get an interface instance of ILog. The parameter "Chapter2.Logging" represents a logging configuration that's loaded from the application configuration file. Loading a logging configuration loads and defines logging levels. In the source code, the property IsDebugEnabled only returns true if the loaded configuration file has enabled the debug logging level. Otherwise, false is returned. If true is returned, then you can call the method log.Debug to indicate a logging message at the debug level.

You can make logging method calls anywhere in the source code. However, only the configuration file determines whether or not logging output is generated. The configuration file determines which data is logged, and where that logged data is generated. In big-picture terms, the developer adds all the logging hooks, but the administrator determines what's logged and where. Following is an example modified application-configuration file that contains a minimal number of configuration entries that you can use to generate logging output:

```
<?xml version="1.0" encoding="utf-8" ?>
<configuration>
    <configSections>
        <section name="log4net"
            type="System.Configuration.IgnoreSectionHandler" />
    </configSections>
    <appSettings>
    </appSettings>
```

```
<log4net>
    <appender name="ConsoleAppender"
        type="log4net.Appender.ConsoleAppender">
        <layout type="log4net.Layout.PatternLayout">
            <param name="ConversionPattern" value="Tracer %m%n" />
        </layout>
    </appender>
    <root>
        <level value="ERROR" />
        <appender-ref ref="ConsoleAppender" />
    </root>
    <logger name="Chapter2.Logging">
        <level value="ALL" />
    </logger>
</log4net>
</configuration>
```

When adding log4net configuration information to a standard application configuration file, you must define a log4net configuration section. In the preceding example, you define the log4net configuration block using a log4net XML tag. The log4net configuration block typically contains three types of blocks: the appender XML tag, which defines a logging destination; the root XML tag, which defines a default logging functionality; and the logger XML tag, which defines a specific logging configuration. When you call the method GetLogger, the parameter for the method references a configuration defined by the logger XML tag. Going back to the .NET code example, the method parameter references the logging configuration "Chapter2.Logging".

Looking closer at the appender XML tag, you see an attribute type, which defines the destination of the logged messages. Log4net has various destinations that include e-mails and the Microsoft Windows event log. (I'll define all the destination possibilities shortly.) The appender XML tag can contain the layout XML tag, which you use to control the layout of the logged message. There are various types of layout possibilities, but the simplest is to use the type log4net.Layout.PatternLayout, which uses an escaped string approach.

The configuration information doesn't activate logging, and is only responsible for defining what information is logged and how it's logged. Two pieces make logging work: a program that activates log4net by calling the appropriate logging methods, and a configuration file that specifies how the data is logged.

Let's go back to the original logging source code. If the "Chapter2.Logging" configuration were not specified in the configuration information, then a default configuration would be used. The root XML tag defines the default logging configuration information.

If the source code was compiled and the defined configuration file was used, the application would generate the following output when executed:

```
Tracer Hello world
```

Generating Messages Using the ILog Interface

When using log4net, it's only necessary to understand the configuration file entries and the `ILog` interface. All the other interfaces and classes are implementation details useful for those individuals who want to extend the default log4net functionality. You define the `ILog` interface as follows:

```
public interface ILog : ILoggerWrapper {
    void Debug(object message);
    void Debug(object message, Exception t);
    void Info(object message);
    void Info(object message, Exception t);
    void Warn(object message);
    void Warn(object message, Exception t);
    void Error(object message);
    void Error(object message, Exception t);
    void Fatal(object message);
    void Fatal(object message, Exception t);

    bool IsDebugEnabled { get; }
    bool IsInfoEnabled { get; }
    bool IsWarnEnabled { get; }
    bool IsErrorEnabled { get; }
    bool IsFatalEnabled { get; }
}
```

In the `ILog` interface, a number of methods and properties have the same method or property signatures, but different identifiers. This is done on purpose, and illustrates how logging output can be generated on different degrees of importance. Log4net assumes that not all logged messages are as important as other logged messages. In log4net terms, the different degrees of importance are defined as priorities. There are five priority levels, defined in increasing priority, as follows:

- *Debug*: The lowest priority, used to generate debugging or contextual information while an application is executing. For this priority, the generated output should only be useful for the developer.

- *Info*: A priority used to generate application information that's useful for users of the application. You could use the generated information to define a context to isolate a bug or programmatic problem.

- *Warn*: A priority used to generate messages to indicate that executing conditions aren't valid. However, the messages aren't enough to cause problems. These messages are generated before the problems start.

- *Error*: A priority used to indicate that an error has occurred. The error isn't a fatal error, meaning that the program or user can recover from this level of error. For example, for this priority an error could occur when the user asks a program to open a nonexistent file.

- *Fatal*: The highest priority, indicating that the program cannot continue. After generating a fatal error message, the program should exit.

In the generated logging output, the medium in which the message is transmitted reflects the priority of the message. The high-level idea is to define which priorities are logged, and the destinations of those priorities. For example, let's say that when an application sends a fatal log message, you want to receive that message using a pager or telephone. However, an info message could be stored in a database for later perusal. It's important to understand that using log4net doesn't invoke some other mechanism. This means that a fatal error message won't exit your application or generate an exception. Your application needs to do those things manually. Log4net is intended to be used in conjunction with other error-handling mechanisms.

In the example source code, the property IsDebugEnabled was tested before calling the method Log. This is necessary for performance reasons. Otherwise, there are performance ramifications, and an application is slowed down unnecessarily. The log4net framework doesn't verify that the proper enabled property is called before calling a logging method. For example, if you can call the property IsErrorEnabled to test for an Error priority, you can also call the Debug method. You must remember that log4net expects you to execute the correct method call. From a performance perspective, calling the enabled methods doesn't incur a large overhead.

Managing a Configuration File

When an application uses the ILog interface, this doesn't mean that logging messages are generated. Whether a message is generated depends on the configuration information. You can define log4net configuration information in three ways: within an application configuration file, within a custom configuration file, or using source-code commands. The simplest and probably the most common way is to use the application configuration file.

The application configuration file defines the configuration identifier, priority, destination, and format of the message. Retrieving an ILog interface instance using the method call GetLogger also retrieves a configuration identifier. A configuration identifier defines different logging configurations within an application. For example, often in my own applications I have a tracing mode and an application-logging mode. In tracing mode, the generated output is nested and extensive. In application-logging mode, a specific logging format is generated, so that it's easy to inspect what the application is doing.

When defining a configuration identifier, there's a default definition and a specific definition. The default definition provides default functionality that the custom configuration definition does or doesn't inherit. An example of defining a configuration identifier follows:

```
<root>
    <level value="ERROR" />
    <appender-ref ref="ConsoleAppender" />
</root>
<logger name="logger.tracer" additivity="false">
    <level value="ALL" />
    <appender-ref ref="TracerAppender" />
</logger>
```

The root XML tag defines the default configuration. Contained within the root XML tag are the XML tags level and appender-ref. The XML tag level defines which priority is logged, and the XML tag appender-ref references a message destination. The logger XML tag is a custom configuration definition, where the identifier is defined by the attribute name. When the attribute additivity is false, it means that the custom configuration doesn't inherit the default configuration details. The default is for the custom configuration to inherit from the root configuration.

Log4net supports inheritance using the additivity attribute, allowing an administrator to log messages to multiple destinations simultaneously. Let's reconsider the previously defined custom configuration logger.tracer without the additivity attribute. When a message is generated, that message is generated in both the TracerAppender destination and the ConsoleAppender destination. For every message logged, two messages are generated. In contrast, when the additivity attribute is assigned a value of false, a single message is generated for the TracerAppender destination.

For this example, the default configuration has a defined priority of ERROR, meaning that only messages having a priority of ERROR and higher are generated. Whenever an inherited custom configuration is defined, then the default priority of the custom configuration would be ERROR. In the preceding example, the custom definition logger.tracer has assigned the attribute additivity a false value, meaning that the default message priority level isn't inherited, and the custom configuration must define its own priority. For the example, the priority is ALL, indicating that all logging messages are to be generated.

Configuration definitions reference a message destination, which is called a log4net appender. An *appender* defines the layout and filter for a message. Following is an example definition of the configuration reference appender-ref TracerAppender:

```
<appender name="TracerAppender" type="log4net.Appender.ConsoleAppender">
        <layout type="log4net.Layout.PatternLayout">
                <param name="ConversionPattern" value="Tracer %m%n" />
        </layout>
</appender>
```

The XML element appender requires two attributes: name and type. The name attribute is a user-friendly name of the message destination that's referenced in the logger or root XML tags. The type attribute is a class name that's loaded when a message is generated. For most cases, you'll use a log4net-defined implementation, but you could reference a custom class by implementing the proper interfaces. In the example, the class name log4net.Appender.ConsoleAppender references an appender that generates a message on the console.

The following appenders are defined within the log4net package (note that all class names are prefixed with the namespace log4net.Appender):

- ADONetAppender: Appends the data to a SQL database using the ADO.NET API. You append the data using a prepared SQL statement or stored procedure.

- ASPNetTraceAppender: Appends messages to an ASP.NET trace context.

- BufferingForwardingAppender: A special type of forwarder that propagates the messages as events. The events are sent when you define a condition.

- ColoredConsoleAppender: The messages are appended to the standard output, or standard error output, but you can color or highlight specific message priorities. Remember that not all consoles support all color codes.

- ConsoleAppender: The messages are appended to the standard output, or standard error output.

- EventLogAppender: The messages are appended to the Application log of the Windows event log.

- FileAppender: The messages are sent to a file.

- ForwardingAppender: This Appender is similar to the BufferingForwardingAppender, except that messages aren't filtered and are sent immediately.

- MemoryAppender: The messages are appended to an in-memory Appender.

- NetSendAppender: The messages are sent using the Windows Messenger Service.

- OutputDebugStringAppender: The messages are sent to a Windows debug facility.

- RemotingAppender: The messages are sent to a remote sink.

- RollingFileAppender: This Appender is similar to a FileAppender, except that a new file is used when certain conditions arise. For example, if the output file exceeds a certain size or date, a new file is generated. For production scenarios, use RollingFileAppender.

- SmtpAppender: Sends a message using the SMTP e-mail protocol.

- SmtpPickupDirAppender: Writes an SMTP-formatted message to a directory. An SMTP engine can then pick up the message for forwarding to an e-mail address.

- TextWriterAppender: This Appender writes to the standard .NET TextWriter class.

- TraceAppender: Appends all messages to a Trace system.

- UdpAppender: Sends a message to a specific client or broadcast group, using the connectionless User Datagram Protocol (UDP).

The details of each appender are beyond the scope of this book, and I recommend that you read the log4net documentation for further details.

Within each appender is the layout XML element, which specifies the format of the message that is output. There are two main layouts: log4net.Layout.PatternLayout and log4net.Layout.XMLLayout. The layout PatternLayout generates a single line, formatted using a set of escape sequences. You can find the individual escape sequences and their purposes in the log4net PatternLayout class documentation. The XMLLayout engine generates an XML-compliant log-output file suitable for later processing. Within the layout XML element are other XML parameter elements that define how the layout appears.

Setting Up a Real-Life Configuration

The purpose of logging is to understand what an application is doing, and when it's doing it. A simple way to generate logging messages would be to use the priority levels to generate the errors and everything else. Generating errors isn't the problem, because errors are easy to locate. The rest of the priorities are more difficult. For example, when generating debug messages, you might wonder what constitutes a debug message. If the debug message is overused, then the generated messages are too numerous, and they make it hard to know what the application is doing. In a nutshell, you must define a strategy when generating logging messages.

Defining the Configuration File

Let's define a scenario of logging messages in an application. When an application is running in production, you should log fatal and error priorities. Logging these messages in production or during development would be a good default behavior. Therefore, to assign a default behavior, you would define the priorities in the root XML element. Following is an example configuration:

```
<root>
        <level value="ERROR" />
        <appender-ref ref="ErrorAppender" />
        <appender-ref ref="PanicAppender" />
</root>
```

In the example configuration, the priority logged is ERROR, meaning that all ERROR and FATAL messages will be processed. There are also two message destinations. The ErrorAppender message destination is a generic error-handler message destination. The PanicAppender message destination is a special destination used to broadcast high-priority messages. For example, if an application has crashed, the administrator will want to know as quickly as possible that the application doesn't work anymore. The PanicAppender broadcasts a high-priority message via the Windows event log or via e-mail, allowing for immediate attention.

Using two logging destinations seems illogical and wasteful of resources, as two logging messages are generated. However, you define two destinations so that two messages can be sent to two *different* destinations. If an application in production generates a FATAL priority message, then the you-know-what has hit the fan, and somebody has to react quickly before managerial problems arise. When an application generates an ERROR priority message, that message is important, but probably not as important as a FATAL priority message. Having both messages sent to the same destination is generally a bad idea, because the receiver has to decipher whether the message is bad, or really bad. Therefore, it's necessary to distinguish between fatal and error exceptions.

Another way to separate the two error levels is to define a default and custom configuration for each error level. The default configuration would log all FATAL priorities, and a custom configuration would assign a priority to log all ERROR priorities. There's nothing wrong with this approach, except that the default wouldn't be to log both priorities, and the administrator would need to inform the developer of his or her deployment solution.

What hasn't yet been covered, and would clarify the reasoning of the decision, is the ability of a destination to filter messages, making it possible to define a priority filter in two places. Following is an example of an appender that can filter messages:

```
<appender name="PanicAppender" type="log4net.Appender.SmtpAppender">
        <filter type="log4net.Filter.LevelRangeFilter">
            <levelMin value="FATAL" />
            <levelMax value="FATAL" />
        </filter>
        <layout type="log4net.Layout. SimpleLayout " />
</appender>
```

```
<appender name="ErrorAppender" type="log4net.Appender.ConsoleAppender">
        <layout type="log4net.Layout.SimpleLayout" />
</appender>
```

The destination PanicAppender has a built-in filter that's defined by the XML child element filter. The purpose of the filter element is to process only those priorities that apply to the context. In the overall scheme of things, the PanicAppender is meant for big problems, so when a FATAL priority message is generated, it's sent via an e-mail. The ErrorAppender has no filter defined, so it processes all messages sent to it. Using this approach, you can define multiple destinations in a configuration that processes different priorities.

Having said all that, some people would consider ERROR and FATAL priorities to have equal importance for paying-attention purposes. To generate a strong, but not high-importance message, use the WARN priority. You define a modified root configuration as follows:

```
<root>
        <level value="WARN" />
        <appender-ref ref="ProblemAppender" />
        <appender-ref ref="PanicAppender" />
</root>
```

The difference in the redefined root configuration definition is that the WARN, ERROR, and FATAL message priorities are processed. However, don't confuse ERROR and FATAL priorities as being identical priorities. A FATAL priority is when the application is exiting or is about to crash. An ERROR priority is when the application is still functioning, but doesn't have a correct state. When an ERROR priority message has been sent, the application executes and functions with a fallback configuration. When an application is executing after an ERROR priority message, immediate attention is needed, but at least the application might still be running. With the modified priority, the PanicAppender destination is modified to filter a priority with a levelMin of ERROR, and a levelMax of FATAL.

An example of how you could use this new priority is the monitoring of hard disk space. A message of priority WARN would be sent if a hard disk has less than 100MB. The priority WARN is used because the application can execute without any difficulties. When the hard disk has less than 10MB left, a message of priority ERROR is sent. The application can still execute, but conditions are becoming complicated, and the application could potentially crash or be forcibly exited. Finally, a message of priority FATAL is sent when less than 1MB is left on the hard disk. When less than 1MB of space is on the hard disk, the application cannot continue to function and must exit before other problems occur.

The modified configuration that started with WARN is a usual ideal root configuration because all important information is logged, but not so much that the information becomes too large. All priorities below WARN are additional troubleshooting priorities, and should be designated as a custom configuration, as illustrated by the following example definitions:

```
<logger name="logger.tracer " additivity="false">
        <level value="DEBUG" />
        <appender-ref ref="TracerAppender" />
</logger>
```

The logger definition logger.production has no child elements and inherits all the definitions from the root. The logger.tracer definition has an additivity of false to indicate that none of the root information should be used. Within the `logger.tracer` logger element are the definitions of the priority and the message destination.

In a big-picture sense, the purpose of this example configuration illustrates how an administrator and developer define the default streams used in an application. You use the identifier `logger.tracer` to log debug messages, as reflected by the DEBUG priority. In coding terms, the developer would load multiple ILog instances, reflected by the priority and purpose of the log message to send. The log messages could be further refined to specific assemblies or application functionalities. By subdividing the logging, it's possible to keep an eye on specific pieces of the application while ignoring the other parts. Subdivision makes it possible for an administrator to react quickly to potential problems. A bad idea is to generate only one stream that contains all logging output. That's a recipe for confusion.

Generating Application Errors That Log

The configuration file is used by an application that has logging enabled. Logging doesn't happen magically, and does require programmatic intervention. The configuration file has two major logging streams: `root` and `logger.tracer`. Let's start with the simple `root` destination, which is illustrated as follows:

```
public class MyObject {
    private static readonly ILog log = LogManager.GetLogger( "root");

    public void DoSomething( int val) {
        if( val < 0 && log.IsErrorEnabled) {
            log.Error( "oops wrong value");
            return;
        }
    }
}
```

In the preceding example, the class MyObject has a private static data member that references the ILog instance `logger.production`. The data member is declared as static because then only one instance needs to be instantiated. If you're wondering, log4net is thread safe and capable of dealing with concurrent access to the ILog instance. In the method DoSomething, the property IsErrorEnabled is tested along with two tests of the parameter. If both tests are true, then a log entry is written.

The code, as presented here, has two problems: what happens if the logging configuration file is incorrect, or if the message priority isn't enabled? The answer is that if the parameter val is less than zero and logging isn't enabled, a message won't be logged, and the application thinks everything is executing correctly. This is an example of where writing clever or compact code introduces an error. The better way to implement the DoSomething method is as follows:

```
    public void DoSomething( int val) {
        if( val < 0) {
            if( log.IsErrorEnabled) {
                log.Error( "oops wrong value");
            }
            return;
        }
    }
```

In the rewritten example, the test val is separated from the test of the property IsErrorEnabled. The code as it's written is correct, because even if logging isn't enabled, the method will function correctly. But now another inconvenience is created. Let's say there's an error, and logging isn't activated. The program exits as required, but there's no reason why the program exited. If nobody is aware that logging isn't working, everybody will be scratching their heads as to the nature of the problem. Sure, the fact that logging might not be activated is one of those problems that can be classified as "duh" solutions, but it still doesn't mean that it won't happen.

What's unattractive about the programmatically correct solution is that it's ugly. The code is ugly because there are two tests on separate lines. This increases the space required by the code and adds overhead in mentally figuring out what the code does. Additionally, the code contains a hard-coded string "oops wrong value" that makes some coders want to scream and run to the hills. The solution is to test using an assertion, as shown in the following example:

```
public void DoSomething ( int val) {
    Verification.IsFalse( val < 0);
    return;
}
```

The method Verification.IsFalse is a compact method that tests a condition. If the condition fails, an error is logged, and an exception is thrown. The class identifier Verification was used instead of Assert, because the term Assert conflicts with the identifier Assert in other packages. It's possible to use absolute namespace identifiers, but that only increases the amount of coding. Getting back to the solution, the advantage is that it's easy to read and understand. A later section of this chapter ("Using Assertions") discusses more details about the Verification type.

Generating Tracing Output

For the priority levels below WARN, when a message is logged it's typically logged for tracing purposes. Tracing output is generally only useful for the developer, and generates information that's used in post-mortem debugging. In the early days of writing code, there were no such things as debuggers. All code was debugged by generating a bunch of text that told the programmer what the program was doing. The problem was that the programs that generated the text tended to be assembly or C programming-language oriented. When things went wrong, debugging output tended to become corrupted. The solution was debuggers, which allow a programmer to step through actively and analyze what the program is doing.

The debugger has become a problem, and can lead to unstable code that's only tested in targeted sections. Debuggers have become crutches for developers to find problems quickly and eradicate them. People freely step through lines and lines of code, wasting hours on a single problem. Yet tell some developers to spend a fraction of the time to add test scripts with tracing, and they'll say it's a waste of time adding "printfs." Tracing is a pulse of your application that provides a logical trail of execution when used properly. If you have a logical trail, it's possible to figure out what went wrong. This section illustrates how to generate a trace log.

Following is an example of some source code that calls methods on a trace framework:

```
public static void TestExamples() {
    CallTracer.Start( System.Reflection.MethodBase.GetCurrentMethod());
    CallTracer.Output("Some message in this context");
    BetterExamples();
    BadExamples();
    CallTracer.End();
}
```

When the code is executed, output similar to the following is generated:

```
start (Chap02SectImplError.ProcessErrorHandlingExamples.TestExamples)
    Some message in this context
    start (Chap02SectImplError.ProcessErrorHandlingExamples.BetterExamples)
    end (Chap02SectImplError.ProcessErrorHandlingExamples.BetterExamples)
    start (Chap02SectImplError.ProcessErrorHandlingExamples.BadExamples)
    end (Chap02SectImplError.ProcessErrorHandlingExamples.BadExamples)
end (Chap02SectImplError.ProcessErrorHandlingExamples.TestExamples)
```

Looking at the output, there are a number of start and end identifiers. Each of the identifiers represents a block of functionality. The source code that generates the block is associated with the methods TestExamples, BetterExamples, and BadExamples. Based on the nesting, the method TestExamples calls the methods BetterExamples and BadExamples. Notice also that when standard text is generated using the method CallTracer.Output, it follows the nested offset of the parent block.

The first impression is that you use the class CallTracer to trace each method call. This is an incorrect impression, because the purpose of CallTracer is to track blocks of functionality. In many cases, a block of functionality starts and ends with a single method call. The idea is to use the CallTracer class to track the flow of the program, adding messages at critical points.

You shouldn't implement tracing under all circumstances, because doing so complicates many pieces of code. Following is a list of scenarios in which tracing sequences are implemented:

- *Interface and component implementations*: An important functionality is implied whenever an interface is implemented. Therefore, you should trace all methods of an interface.

- *Major change of functionality*: A major change of functionality happens when a method calls another method that's the start of another task. For example, when an application initializes itself, the initialization functionality is self-contained in another module. When writing tracing code, you would log the start and end of the initialization.

- *Complex functionality*: Sometimes complex algorithms are hard to debug because they're too tedious to single-step. Using tracing, you can incrementally watch the values of the algorithm to find any potential bug.

- *Important events*: There are many situations in which an important value, event, or action needs to be logged. You log these situations because they can clarify something that's about to happen. For example, you can log an important test for success or failure.

Using tracing for other situations than those mentioned is also acceptable, if the tracing helps the developer understand the application's execution path. Any further tracing will confuse the reader of the generated log output.

Developers also require the ability to add tracing method calls on a temporary basis. Consider the context of a developer running an extensive test framework. While running the tests, a problem occurs and debugging isn't possible. The already defined tracing calls aren't sufficient to pinpoint the exact problem. The developer needs to add a number of additional tracing calls to follow the logic of an application.

The problem of adding additional tracing calls is that for the specific problem, the logic is explained in detail. However, in a higher-level sense, adding the additional tracing calls confuses because there could be multiple subsystems that have implemented a more detailed logic.

A solution is to use two different priorities for generating tracing information. Using log4net, the default tracing would generate messages at the priority INFO, and for specific messages to understand a block of functionality, the default tracing would use the priority DEBUG. Separating the two types of tracing makes it possible to get a high-level understanding using the INFO priority first; then you can drill down into the specific problem using the DEBUG priority. When writing tracing code, you can add INFO priority messages to the source code ahead of time. You shouldn't add the DEBUG priority messages ahead of time, because you use DEBUG priority messages to illuminate problems. It isn't easily possible to know ahead of time what the problems will be.

Following is an example of source code that illustrates the additional methods used to send DEBUG priority messages:

```
public static void TestExamples() {
    CallTracer.Start( System.Reflection.MethodBase.GetCurrentMethod());
    CallTracer.DebugOutput( "Output only visible when debugging");
    BetterExamples();
    BadExamples();
    CallTracer.End();
}
```

The CallTracer class would have additional methods with the Debug identifier that create log messages sent at the DEBUG priority. The other methods Start, End, and Output would create log messages at the INFO priority.

Now I've explained all the log4net priorities, and I've defined a purpose for each. Initially, the different priorities were too numerous and not necessary, but with the explanations of errors and debugging code, the purposes are associated with a specific action. Even though the examples in this book illustrate specific CallTracer or Verification types with associated methods, there's no reason why you couldn't create your own tracing and error-handling types.

Using Configuration Inheritance

Log4net can do additional things, and many are beyond the scope of this book. One item that isn't beyond the scope of this book, and needs to be discussed, is log4net namespaces.

When log4net loads a configuration file, a resolution happens. The resolution allows a configuration to be loaded according to a namespace, if the specified configuration doesn't exist. Consider the following example configuration:

```
<logger name="a">
    <level value="WARN" />
    <appender-ref ref="ConsoleAppender" />
</logger>
```

In the example, the logging destination a is defined. It's both an identifier and a base namespace identifier. Following is some example source code that attempts to load another logging destination:

```
ILog log = LogManager.GetLogger( "a.b.c");
```

The GetLogger method asks for the logger identifier a.b.c, which doesn't exist. Thus far, you've seen that if the logging destination doesn't exist, then the default logging destination is used. But a namespace resolution also happens. A number of namespace identifiers are in the example logging destination. The first resolution attempts to load the logging destination a.b.c. If that destination doesn't exist, the logging destination a.b is loaded. If that destination doesn't exist, then the logging destination a is loaded. In the example, a exists and is loaded. However, if the logging destination a didn't exist, then the default logging configuration would be loaded.

The main use of namespaces is to define and load configurations associated with types. For example, if a type devspace.subsystem.type was defined, then a logging destination devspace could be defined. The following source code illustrates the way to implement this:

```
ILog log = LogManager.GetLogger(
System.Reflection.MethodBase.GetCurrentMethod().DeclaringType);
```

Calling the property DeclaringType returns the type of the current executing method, including the namespace of the type. The idea would be to associate the namespace of the type with the namespace of the defined logging destination.

Implementing ToString

I happen to write code for both Java and .NET. A discussion of both platforms is beyond the scope of this book, but I mention Java because the Java platform implements the ToString method, whereas on .NET ToString exists, but is rarely implemented.

The collection classes are the simplest illustration of where ToString should have been implemented in .NET. Calling a collection's ToString implementation in Java iterates and outputs the various elements. However, that doesn't happen in .NET, and when writing code using test-driven development (TDD), ToString makes it possible to figure out what the state of the type instance is.

Consider the following simple example of implementing the ToString type:

```
class MyClass {
    private string _buffer;

    public override string ToString() {
        return "Buffer (" + _buffer + ")";
    }
}
```

The class MyClass has a data member _buffer, which should be represented when the ToString method is called. In the implementation of ToString, return is a descriptive buffer. The format of the return buffer is dependent on the need. The format could be an XML buffer, or something else. Regardless of the format, a type should always implement the ToString method.

For illustration purposes, the classes and tests defined in this book use a set of classes that are used as in the following example:

```
class MyClass {
    private string _buffer;

    public override string ToString() {
        MemoryTracer.Start( this);
        MemoryTracer.Variable( "buffer", _buffer);
        return MemoryTracer.End();
    }
}
```

In the example, a class called MemoryTracer is used to generate a formatted output of the type. The methods Start and End create an indented block, and the method Variable outputs the contents of the variable _buffer.

Implementing Exception Handling

In the logging examples, the Verification type was illustrated and defined to throw an exception when a test returns a value of false. The Verification type is an example of an exception-handling strategy. Exceptions indicate an error, and handling errors appropriately is a programming strategy with the same level of complexity as designing classes. When an error occurs, the objective is not simply to report the error, but to do something meaningful. Many programs display the error and exit the program upon encountering an error. This hit-error-and-exit strategy is tedious if an application has multiple problems. A user will be constantly starting and exiting an application. A good error-handling strategy can generate an error, then do something to continue operating. For example, an acceptable solution would be to use a default state or configuration. If an error does happen, then the application should roll back any changes made before the error, before the application exits.

Consider this: you're writing a program to copy files. During the copying process, you encounter a file that cannot be copied. What do you do? Do you stop copying, or continue? If the application stops copying, then the already copied files need to be deleted because the file state is inconsistent. Think of it as follows: one file causes an error, the error is fixed, and the files are copied again. The problem is, which files need to be copied? Unless you keep a log, it's hard to know what to copy and not to copy. If you do a rollback and delete the copied files, the state will be consistent, but potentially gigabytes of data need to be recopied. The point is that there's no ideal solution; there are advantages and disadvantages to each.

When writing an application that generates errors, you need to think about state and the types of errors. A well-written application behaves well both when the conditions and state are correct, and when conditions and state are incorrect.

Classifying an Error and an Exception

When implementing an error- and exception-handling infrastructure, you need to define the difference between an error and exception. An error occurs when something happens that shouldn't have happened, but is predictable. An exception occurs when something happens that shouldn't have happened, and isn't predictable. An exception should never happen, whereas an error could happen.

The best way to illustrate the difference is the following bad example of using exceptions, in which an error handler would be the correct solution. (Note that the example could have been written more succinctly using other keywords, but that's not the point.)

```
int[] args = new int[ 4];

try {
    for( int c1 = 0; ; c1 ++) {
        args[ c1] = 1;
        Tracer.output( 10, "Counter " + c1);
    }
}
catch( IndexOutOfRangeException excep) {
    Tracer.output( 10, "You've hit the end of the array");
}
```

In the example, a for loop is created that incrementally counts and assigns the array args with a value of 1. In the definition of the for statement, there's no upper limit. The for loop will continue indefinitely, at least in theory. What happens in reality is once the boundary of the array has been exceeded, an exception is generated. An exception is always generated, so you need an exception handler that encapsulates the for loop.

Looking at the solution, everyone will say that the problem is that there's no test for the upper limit in the for loop. Of course that's the problem, but I illustrated how it's possible to use exceptions when an upper limit test isn't used. This structure of putting together an application does happen—albeit not with loops, but with other algorithms. This structure is wrong because an error handler, which is the upper limit, should have been used.

Running the example code without the exception block generates the following exception:

```
Unhandled Exception: System.IndexOutOfRangeException: Array index is out of range.
in <0x00098> Chap02SectImplError.BadExceptionUsage:ExampleMethod ()
in <0x0001c> MainApp:DifferenceErrorAndException ()
in <0x00018> MainApp:Main (string[])
```

The exception that's generated is the IndexOutOfRangeException. Using the try and catch block catches the exception and ends the loop. Following is the generated output when the exception is caught:

```
Counter 0
Counter 1
Counter 2
Counter 3
You've hit the end of the array
```

Not all of the example is bad, because it illustrates how to deal with an exception when it does happen. The try and catch block is strategically added to encapsulate the potentially problematic code, and not all the code in general. A good exception-handling strategy does that because it allows you to focus on specific exceptions. Focusing on the exception makes it possible to develop an exit strategy that may involve keeping the application running, and not arbitrarily exiting the application.

When an exception is generated, many applications will exit, which isn't the best strategy as a general approach. Often the reason why applications exit is that it's the simplest method to implement.

The clever reader will say that using an exception to indicate an end-of-array condition isn't a bad idea, and can even be efficient. Think of it as follows. To implement an error handler or upper limit test requires one clock cycle. To catch an exception requires 20 clock cycles. Therefore, if the array is 21 elements long, throwing an exception is more efficient than testing for an end of the array. However, even with a performance improvement, using exceptions in lieu of good error-handler functionality is wrong from a software engineering perspective.

One of the main reasons not to use exceptions instead of error handlers is that code can become unpredictable, because there may be too many exception handlers. Consider the following modified source code based on the original example, which could be potentially unpredictable:

```
int[] args = new int[ 10];

try {
    for( int c1 = 0; ; c1 ++) {
        int calculation = 1;
        try {
            Tracer.Output( "Counter " + c1);
            calculation = 23;
        }
        catch( Exception ex) {
            ;
        }
        args[ c1] = calculation;
    }
}
catch( IndexOutOfRangeException excep) {
    Tracer.output( 10, "You've hit the end of the array");
}
```

In the modified source code, two pieces of functionality have been added. The first addition is a nested exception handler that catches the exception Exception. The second source code addition is the variable calculation. Going through the logic of the code, the variable calculation is defined and assigned a value of 1. Then, within the nested exception handler, the variable calculation is assigned a value of 23. Now imagine if the method Tracer.Output were to generate an error. The assignment of the calculation variable to 23 would be ignored, and the loop would continue processing the data without further consideration.

What has happened is that the nested exception handler irons out any problems that result in allowing the application to continue. Yet the result is an invalid state as the assigning of calculation = 23 has been skipped. The assignment is an invalid assignment, and the result is an inconsistent application that appears to function properly.

Focusing on the consistency problem, what's happening is the hiding of problems. Because there are a larger number of exception blocks, real exceptions are masked and captured by exception blocks intended for another purpose. In a big-picture perspective, the error isn't reported, and errors will propagate themselves to other parts of the application. When the exception does appear due to an inconsistent state created elsewhere, the original source of the problem has been lost, making finding bugs that much more difficult. Implementing an exception-handling scheme requires careful forethought and implementation.

An exception is an occurrence that can happen, but shouldn't be happening. An exception cannot be predicted at a specific location in your code, but can be predicted in a general area of your code. For example, an exception is a type-casting problem, or inconsistent file state. An exception that can be pinpointed to a specific area of code isn't an exception, but an error. An example of an error would be a file that isn't found, or an end-of-an-array condition. Errors and exceptions are different, and each requires its own strategy.

Implementing an Error Strategy

Handling errors is not about checking for an error and then returning an error code. In program-ming languages such as C++ or Component Object Model (COM), there were exceptions and error codes. Error codes existed because exceptions couldn't easily cross process or Dynamic Link Library (DLL) boundaries. .NET uses exceptions, so it isn't necessary to return error codes. As seen previously, implementing exceptions isn't just about throwing errors and catching them. Exceptions need to be intelligently managed, so that when an exception happens there are reasons to be concerned.

How Not to Manage Objects

When implementing an error strategy, you aren't creating an error-return–code strategy like COM used to do. Implementing an error strategy means writing code that deals with problems as they arise. To understand the problem fully, consider the following source code, which implements two functions that return a value:

```
class BadExampleErrorHandling {
    public static int[] GetArrayValues() {
        return null;
    }
    public static string GetStringValue() {
        return null;
    }
}

class ProcessErrorHandlingExamples {
    public static void BadExamples() {
        Tracer.start( 10, "ProcessErrorHandlingExamples.BadExamples");
        int[] arr = BadExampleErrorHandling.GetArrayValues();
        if( arr != null) {
            for( int c1 = 0; c1 < arr.Length; c1 ++) {
                Tracer.output( 10, "Value is " + arr[ c1]);
            }
        }
```

```
        string value = BadExampleErrorHandling.GetStringValue();
        if( value != null) {
            if( value.Length > 0) {
                Tracer.output( 10, "Not an empty String");
            }
        }
        Tracer.end( 10);
    }
}
```

In the preceding example, the class BadExampleErrorHandling has two methods: GetArrayValues and GetStringValue. The return value signature for each of the methods is an object. In the first case the object is an array of values, and in the second case the object is a string. The return values from the individual methods are null to indicate that an instance value cannot be returned. In a programming context, null would be correct, because it means that something went wrong in the method and that the caller should take some other action.

The problem of returning a null object is that an unknown state is created. A null object doesn't indicate to the caller of the method what went wrong. A null object only indicates something isn't right and the caller needs to figure out the problem. Also problematic is that the caller of the method must add additional error handling to compensate for the problem.

The question is, what is the correct value to return? When the caller calls a method, it expects an appropriate answer. An appropriate answer is an object instance, and if that isn't possible, then an exception must be raised. Let's say that a caller calls a method and expects an object that contains the configuration of the application as a return answer. If the configuration file or repository cannot be found, would an exception be an appropriate course of action? Could another appropriate course of action be defined as a default configuration? These questions are examples of error conditions and not exception conditions.

How to Manage Objects

The reason why this extra thought has to go into exceptions and error handling is because code can become complicated. Consider the following source code, which makes poor use of error handling and results in a more complicated implementation:

```
NameValueCollection pluginConfig = (NameValueCollection)
    ConfigurationSettings.GetConfig("settings/tracer");

if( pluginConfig != null) {
    if( pluginConfig["isactive"] != null && pluginConfig[ "isactive"] == "true") {
        Console.WriteLine( "Woohoo is active");
    }
}
```

You use the preceding example source code to retrieve a value from an application configuration file. Notice how many tests there are before a valid value can be tested. First, you test to check if the variable pluginConfig is not null to indicate that a configuration file has been loaded. Second, you test to check if the isactive variable exists. The problem with the two tests is that they're of no interest to the coder who wants to retrieve the value of a variable, and two tests aren't necessary.

From a coding perspective, either an exception is generated, or the error is dealt with appropriately. The caller of the method shouldn't have to figure out if something strange happened. In the case of the preceding example, that means either pluginConfig references a valid object instance, or an exception is generated. Having pluginConfig reference a null object means something went wrong, but it's unknown what went wrong. For example, maybe the application execution directory is incorrect, or the application configuration file has XML problems, or doesn't exist.

A better strategy is never to return a null object, and either return an empty object, return an object with some default data, or generate an exception that says something meaningful. The following rewritten example returns an empty object:

```
class BetterExampleErrorHandling {
    private static readonly string EmptyValue = "";

    public static int[] GetArrayValues() {
        return new int[ 0];
    }
    public static string GetStringValue() {
        return EmptyValue;
    }
}


class ProcessErrorHandlingExamples {
    public static void BetterExamples() {
        Tracer.start( 10, "ProcessErrorHandlingExamples.BetterExamples");
        int[] arr = BetterExampleErrorHandling.GetArrayValues();
        for( int c1 = 0; c1 < arr.Length; c1 ++) {
            Tracer.output( 10, "Value is " + arr[ c1]);
        }
        if( BetterExampleErrorHandling.GetStringValue().Length > 0) {
            Tracer.output( 10, "Not an empty String");
        }
        Tracer.end( 10);
    }
}
```

In the rewritten example, the methods GetArrayValues and GetStringValue return not a null value, but default object instances. In the examples, the valid object instances are null-length arrays and empty string buffers. Looking at the implementation of the BetterExamples, the code has been immensely simplified because there's no need to test the validity of the objects. It's assumed that the individual methods always return a valid object. In the case of the for loop, the empty value is an array of length zero, which means no iterations are performed. In the end, simpler methods make it simpler to find errors and then fix them. If an empty object or an object with a set of data cannot be returned, then the application should throw an exception.

If it's necessary to indicate an inconsistent state and you don't wish to throw an exception, then you can define a property. You'd use the property to test the validity of the state, and the program uses it for further actions. The following example modifies the BetterExampleError➥ Handling class to include a test property:

```
class BetterExampleErrorHandling {
    private static readonly string EmptyValue = "";

    public static bool IsArrayValid {
        get {
            return false;
        }
    }
    public static int[] GetArrayValues() {
        return new int[ 0];
    }
    public static string GetStringValue() {
        return EmptyValue;
    }
}
```

The method `IsArrayValid` as it's implemented always returns false. Calling the property and returning false means that the method `GetArrayValues` will always return an object of inconsistent state.

Defining Default Values

Some methods return empty values when called. Consider the example of loading a configuration file, but the file doesn't exist. The loading routines could generate an exception, or generate an empty configuration structure. In either case, the caller of the configuration loader will receive a condition in which no configuration is available. At that point, the loading routines could return an exception that then leads to a program exiting. Or the loading routines could define a default configuration that allows a program to continue executing.

It's important not to confuse *empty* with *default*, and *default* with an unstable condition of the application. The objective of returning an empty or a default structure is to ensure that a program is operating with the correct state at all times. When a program doesn't have the correct state, that means bugs can arise, and the program becomes unstable.

The following example type declaration includes a default state declaration:

```
class ExampleDefault {
    private int _value;

    ExampleDefault() {
        AssignDefault();
    }
    ExampleDefault( int param) {
        _value = param;
    }
    public void AssignDefault() {
        _value = 12;
    }
}
```

The class ExampleDefault has two constructors, one without any parameters and another with a single parameter. Having a constructor without parameters means that when the object is instantiated without constructor parameters, that object is initialized with a default state. You use the constructor with a single parameter to initialize the object with a caller-defined state. The purpose of both constructors is to define a valid state regardless of how the object is instantiated.

When the constructor without any parameters is executed, the constructor implementation calls the method AssignDefault, which creates the default state. You shouldn't code the default state in the constructor because that makes it more complicated to use the type. Consider a scenario in which a type is instantiated. Because the instantiation is complicated and lengthy, pooling the instance would increase performance. The problem with pooling is that the state needs to be reset to the default value before the object can be used again. If the default state was coded in the constructor, then it won't be possible to recycle an object instance. Having a method to initialize an object makes it simpler to reset the state without having to allocate a new instance.

Single Entry and Single Exit

In the early days of programming, there was a technique called single entry, single exit. The idea is that when the method is called, the method can only return in a single location. Consider the following sources, which illustrate a normal method and another method that's written using a single entry, single exit strategy:

```
class ExampleSingleEntrySingleExit {
    private int _defaultValue = 12;

    public int MethodNormal( int param1) {
        if( param1 < 10) {
            return param1 / 2;
        }
        else if( param1 > 100) {
            throw new Exception();
        }
        return _defaultValue;
    }
    public int MethodSeSx( int param1) {
        int retval = _defaultValue;
        if( param1 < 10) {
            retval = param1 / 2;
            goto exit_method;
        }
        else if( param1 > 100) {
            throw new Exception();
        }
    exit_method:
        return retval;
    }
}
```

The method MethodNormal is an example method coded with a single entry point, but multiple exit points. There's the return when param1 is less than ten, and there's a default return at the end of the function. Another return occurs when an exception is executed, but for now the code ignores that. The original problem in C and C++ with this way of writing a method was that if any resources were allocated, then they might not be freed because the method returns in multiple places.

Now consider the single entry, single exit strategy by implementing the method MethodSeSx. In the test of param1, which is less than ten, instead of using a return statement, use a goto. The goto jumps to the label exit_method that's at the end of the method. You use the end of the statement to terminate the method functionality and ensure the returned state is valid. In the implementation, the only return logic added is to return the variable retval. When implementing single entry, single exit methods, use the goto statement. Many programmers don't appreciate gotos because they can lead to messy code. However, some programmers have realized gotos are acceptable, so long as they don't backtrack a method execution.

The advantage of the single entry, single exit method is to free resources consistently that were allocated within the method. That's not an issue anymore because .NET is a garbage-collected environment, and it would seem that there's no need for a single entry, single exit strategy. The single entry, single exit strategy does help in the implementation of state-safe methods. Using single entry, single exit makes it possible to determine the state of the system before and after the method call. In most .NET applications, it isn't necessary to use single entry, single exit, and this method is almost exclusively needed when methods have complex state relationships.

Dealing with Errors and State

When an application encounters a problem, the application attempts to fix the problem dynamically, but the application has to generate an exception if the problem cannot be fixed. What is often forgotten when throwing exceptions is the need to repair the state to its condition before the problem started. Consider the following source code, which has a problematic state:

```
class ProgramState {
    private int _variable1;
    private int _variable2;

    public void AssignState( int param2) {
        if( param2 < 1) {
            throw new Exception();
        }
        _variable2 = param1;
    }
    public void DoSomething( int param1, int param2) {
        _variable1 = param1;
        AssignState( param2);
    }
}
```

In the example, imagine calling the method DoSomething, where the parameter param2 has a value of 0. Calling DoSomething assigns the variable _variable1. Then you call the method AssignState, and because param2 has a value of zero, an exception is generated. Neither AssignState nor DoSomething have a try . . . catch block, meaning that the exception thrown in AssignState is passed to the caller of DoSomething. The lack of a try . . . catch or try . . . finally block is problematic, because when the exception in AssignState is thrown, _variable1 has already been assigned, but _variable2 hasn't been assigned. The inconsistent state results in the ProgramState class instance being corrupted.

A corrupted state results in programs that execute inconsistently, and makes it hard to isolate bugs. Imagine the bigger picture. A type calls the method DoSomething with a bad param2. An exception is thrown to the caller of DoSomething. The caller catches the exception and fixes up the problem, but doesn't call the method DoSomething again. The program continues, and another routine uses the ProgramState class instance that previously threw an exception. The other routine considers everything to be in a consistent state and extracts the values of _variable1 and _variable2. Then the other routine realizes that things don't compute and generates an exception that cannot be fixed. The application exits and a log file is generated.

The administrator or developer will read the log file and attempt to fix the other routine. However, the problem is that the other routine is working perfectly, which dumbfounds the developer. The developer puts in a patch that fixes the program, but doesn't fix the logic. The result is that a bug still exists, a buggy patch has been added, and most likely nobody in the future will be able to decipher exactly what is going on. All these problems could have been avoided if the developer was careful with his or her state.

In the .NET environment, there's no solution to this type of bug, other than making sure data consistency is always maintained. The Java runtime implements something called *checked exceptions*. This means that when a method is called that throws an exception, the caller must either catch the exception or delegate it to the caller of the caller. Checked exceptions force the programmer to realize that an exception may be thrown, and that the method needs to deal with the exception.

The only option in .NET is to set up a try and catch block that catches all exceptions, resets the state, and throws the caught exception. Following is an example implementation of method DoSomething that manages state properly:

```
public void DoSomething( int param1, int param2) {
    int temp = _variable1;
    try {
        _variable1 = param1;
        AssignState( param2);
    }
    catch( Exception ex) {
        _variable1 = temp;
        throw ex;
    }
}
```

In the rewritten DoSomething method, the state is written, but a temporary variable temp is defined. The variable temp contains the data stored by _variable1, which is reassigned to _variable1 if an exception occurs. DoSomething doesn't want to process the exception, and simply throws the caught exception for further processing.

Another solution to the consistent state problem is to modify the state after the methods have executed. The solution would involve changing the method DoSomething to use temporary variables that are assigned at the end of the method. The following rewritten DoSomething method can cope with exceptions:

```
public void DoSomething( int param1, int param2) {
    int temp = param1;
    AssignState( param2);
    _variable = temp;
}
```

In the rewritten example of DoSomething, the parameter param1 is written to a temporary variable that's stored locally within the function. The variable _variable is only assigned once all the child methods have been called. The solution is correct, but a new coding style is defined, and the rules of thumb are defined as follows:

- *Assign state as late as possible*: Assigning state as late as possible dramatically reduces the chances that an exception will arise that violates state.

- *If state must be assigned use a* try . . . finally *block*: Using a try . . . finally block, it's possible to catch any thrown exception and fix up the modified state to the original state before the method is called.

- *In general, write code that modifies as little global state as possible*: Often it isn't possible to write code that doesn't modify state, but making an effort to work with local objects reduces the chances that a state error will occur.

Implementing an Exception Strategy

When something goes wrong in an application, the best way to indicate that a failure has occurred is to use an exception. Exceptions are generally expensive in computational terms, but remember exceptions only occur when something goes wrong. Ideally, nothing goes wrong in an application and only a few exceptions are generated. If too many exceptions are generated, then there are problems in the design of the application.

Exceptions 101

In the .NET environment, all exception classes are subclasses of the type Exception. Trying to throw an exception using a type that doesn't directly or indirectly inherit from the Exception type generates an error when the code is compiled. The following example generates an exception:

```
public void ThrowException() {
    throw new Exception( "My error");
}
```

You use the keyword throw to generate an exception, and an instantiated class is thrown. In the preceding example, the constructor parameter is a message that indicates why the exception was thrown. The Exception type can still be thrown if you don't supply any type of message. However, if you don't provide a message, then when the exception is thrown, the exception catcher has no idea what the problem was.

To catch an exception, you need to define a try and catch block; an example follows:

```
public void CatchException() {
       try {
           ThrowException ()
       }
       catch( Exception ex) {
           // Do something with exception
       }
}
```

The method CatchException has an embedded try and catch block that's used to trap an exception that's thrown. All methods called within the try block are tracked for possible exceptions to trap. The exceptions that are caught depend on the contents of the catch "method" call. I put the quotes around the word method in the context of catch because the catch statement defines a sub-block. The sub-block is executed if the types of the catch "method" match, or are a subclass of, the exception being thrown. In the example, the type is Exception, which means the sub-block will catch all exceptions that can be thrown.

The Exception type has the following properties, which you can query or assign:

- InnerException: References the embedded exception, which the following section will explain in greater detail.

- Message: A string property that's a textual representation of the exception's cause.

- Source: A string property that represents the name of the application that causes the exception.

- StackTrace: A string property that contains the function stack state at the time the exception was thrown. This property is useful when performing a postmortem analysis of what went wrong.

- TargetSite: References an object instance of type MethodBase that references the method that threw the exception.

An exception can embed other exceptions. For example, imagine writing an assembly that uses an externally developed assembly. If an exception arises within the external assembly, the assembly will catch it. The problem is: what does the assembly do with the exception? The simplest solution is to catch the exception, analyze it, and throw the exception again. It's possible to process the exception, but if the error is fatal then the calling application needs to know about the problem. The following example analyzes a caught exception and then throws it again:

```
public void MyAssembly() {
    try {
        externalAssembly.externalMethod()
    }
    catch( Exception ex) {
        // Do something
        throw ex;
    }
}
```

The method MyAssembly encapsulates the external-assembly method call externalMethod within an exception block. When the external assembly throws an exception, it's caught, analyzed, and thrown again.

The problem with throwing an exception from the external assembly is that the application will catch something that's unknown. Consider it as follows: you're driving the car, and the carburetor complains that the air mixture contains too little fuel. As a driver, you have no idea what's going on, as you might not even know what a carburetor is. The driver wants a message that processes the problem of the carburetor into something that the driver can understand. You can nest exceptions in .NET to address this problem, as illustrated by the following example:

```
public void MyAssembly() {
    try {
        externalAssembly.externalMethod()
    }
    catch( Exception ex) {
        // test the type of exception and generate a new one
        throw new Exception( "MyAssembly Exception", ex);
    }
}
```

In the rewritten MyAssembly method, a new exception is instantiated within the catch block. When instantiating the Exception type, the constructor has two parameters: "My Assembly Exception" and ex. The first parameter is a buffer that indicates an error message that the application can understand. The second parameter is the external assembly exception. When the new exception is thrown, the old exception is embedded within the new exception.

The receiver of the new exception reacts to the exception, and processes the embedded exception if necessary. However, processing the embedded exception is optional, and provides details about the problem. It's a good idea to nest exceptions so that the application can react in a meaningful manner when an exception is generated. Referencing the carburetor example, that would mean generating a low-fuel message.

You can define multiple catch statements to indicate multiple exceptions that can be caught. The following example illustrates how to catch multiple exceptions:

```
public void MyAssembly() {
    try {
        externalAssembly.externalMethod()
    }
    catch( IOException ex) {
        // Catch an Input Output Exception
        throw new Exception( "MyAssembly Exception", ex);
    }
    catch( Exception ex) {
        // Catch all of the other exceptions
        throw new Exception( "MyAssembly Exception", ex);
    }
}
```

In the preceding example, there are two catch blocks, and each block catches a different set of exceptions. The exceptions caught by each catch block depend on the type of the exception being thrown. In the first catch block, all exceptions that have IOException as a direct or indirect subclass are caught. In the second catch block, all exceptions that have Exception as a direct or indirect subclass are caught.

It would seem that because all exceptions subclass the type Exception, the second catch block would process all exceptions. However, that's not how the catch mechanism works. When an exception is thrown, the individual catch blocks are sequentially iterated. For each block, .NET tests if the thrown exception has the exception type of the block as a direct or indirect subclass. Once the catch block makes a match, the catch block processes the exception and ignores all the other blocks.

When writing your own catch blocks, the order is important. You order the blocks from specialized to generic. Going back to the preceding example, the exception IOException is specialized because IOException subclasses Exception. The simplest way to understand the catch blocks is to think of them as a huge switch statement, where Exception is the default.

Implementing Your Own Exceptions

When writing applications that generate exceptions, you can use both custom Exception types and the default .NET runtime exceptions. The default .NET runtime exceptions follow a common naming convention, in which the identifier Exception is appended to the purpose of the exception (for example, ArgumentOutOfRangeException).

When defining your own exceptions, in all likelihood you'll derive from the ApplicationException type. At the time of this writing, there was a problem in the MSDN documentation. In the description of the type, the first paragraph said that nonfatal application exceptions derive from the type ApplicationException. However, the next paragraph mentions that an application defining its own exceptions should derive from ApplicationException. The problem is, what does the developer do for fatal application exceptions?

The MSDN documentation attempted to add the ability to filter exceptions according to their severity. In the logging section, there were multiple levels of logging (fatal, nonfatal, warning, and so on). You need to represent only the fatal and nonfatal errors as exceptions. Therefore, you derive the custom exception from Exception for fatal errors. For nonfatal application errors, you derive from ApplicationException. Implementing exceptions using that strategy makes it possible to write catch filters; an example follows:

```
public void Method() {
    try {
    }
    catch( ApplicationException ex) {
        // Catch all nonfatal application errors
    }
    catch( Exception ex) {
        // Catch all fatal application errors
    }
}
```

To dovetail the functionality of the exceptions into the logging levels, you could define the following base exception types:

```
public class ApplicationFatalException : Exception {
    public ApplicationFatalException( string message) : base( message) {
        Logging.Fatal( message);
    }
}

public class ApplicationNonFatalException : ApplicationException {
    public ApplicationNonFatalException( string message) : base( message) {
        Logging.Error( message);
    }
}
```

The type ApplicationFatalException derives from the type Exception. Then, in the constructor, the method Logging.Fatal calls the logging routines outlined in the log4net section. The type ApplicationNonFatalException derives from the type ApplicationException, and likewise logs its message in the constructor. The developer would then derive his or her own exceptions from either ApplicationFatalException or ApplicationNonFatalException, and logging would happen automatically. These classes are convenient because the developer can use exceptions that make implicit use of the logging libraries.

Using Assertions

When writing applications that verify the values of parameters, the resulting code can become large and hard to maintain. To compact the verification code, a potential solution is to use the Assert class.

The Assert class doesn't exist in the .NET class library in the sense of performing a verification of a test and then generating an exception. You'll need to write your own, use the Assert class from the NUnit library, or use the Verification class that's available at the web site http://www.devspace.com/Wikka/wikka.php?wakka=BookReLearningOOPUsingNetPatterns. For illustration purposes, I'll demonstrate the Verification class, but the Assert class in NUnit functions in a similar manner. Regardless of which assertion library you use, assertions all function similarly.

The idea behind an assertion library is to provide a framework in which you can use a method to test a value's validity or invalidity. If the test fails, then the assertion framework will execute some routines to deal with the inconsistency. Assertions are most often used to validate parameters before they're processed. The following simple assertion tests for a positive integer:

```
Verification.IsTrue( param1 > 0,
                new InstantiateException( AssertionFailure.Instantiate));
```

The class Verification has a method IsTrue, which has two parameters. The first parameter is the test that must be true. The test param1 must be greater than zero and must return a true value. The second parameter is a delegate that's used to instantiate an exception when necessary. Had a delegate not been used, then whenever the IsTrue method is called, the exception would be instantiated, but not thrown. The downside to the instantiation is that an automatic log file entry would be created, and that isn't desired.

You define the class AssertionFailure as follows:

```
class AssertionFailure : ApplicationFatalException {
    public AssertionFailure( string message) : base( message) {
    }
    public static Exception Instantiate() {
        return new AssertionFailure( "Could not assert");
    }
}
```

The class AssertionFailure subclasses the class ApplicationFatalException. You use the static method Instantiate to create a new instance of the class AssertionFailure.

Many assertion libraries, including the referenced Assert class, have additional methods such as IsNull, AreSame, Fail, and so on, which you can use to test and generate exceptions in different contexts.

Using NUnit for Test-Driven Development

Software engineering books always stress the need to test an application. The purpose of testing is to ensure that no bugs—or at least a minimal amount of bugs—exist in the application. Traditionally, testing in a software engineering context is considered a step of the development process. When creating software applications, the usual sequence of steps are requirements, analysis, design, implementation, testing, and deployment. The traditional sequence is a serial operation and considers testing as something that starts after the initial development has started. Over time, there have been some modifications to the steps (for example, iterative development), but in general, the steps still exist and are followed in a serial fashion.

Understanding Test-Driven Development

Object-oriented programming doesn't directly relate to TDD, because object-oriented development is possible with a single class. What's different is that instead of designing an overall object-oriented architecture ahead of time, the types evolve with the application's implementation. The ramification of this is that you don't know what all the types are ahead of time. This ramification doesn't fall within the parameters of traditional object-oriented development.

A new development strategy has been created called test-driven development (TDD). It says for each piece of functionality introduced, a test is written before the code is written. Many developers consider test scripts as being created and executed by another department or individual. The result is an inconvenient timeline. Consider it as follows: you have five months to complete an application. In the original timeline, three months are planned for development, and two months for testing. However, the real time for development is four months, and as a result testing has to be accomplished in one month. Testing suffers because it's forced to make up for the lost time that development or the earlier steps exceeded. Sadly, too often people use a result that's only tested somewhat, and offer a service pack or hot fix if there are any serious problems. This isn't what the customer wants or needs. Imagine creating a car, and saying, "Yeah, sometimes the wheels fall off, but let's get the car out, and if that problem happens, we'll fix it." The problem is that people use cars to do critical tasks, such as dropping off children, driving people to the doctor, and picking up groceries. If a wheel were to drop off, a chain of disasters would ensue. My point is that these types of application problems aren't necessary. Applications will suffer, and have suffered, because of this lack of attention to testing. I'm pointing fingers, but stating the fact that all people who are part of a development cycle are forced to produce under tight timelines. The results aren't hard to guess.

TDD improves the development process, because the application is done when the last line of code is written. The difference is that the last line of code means that the last test script has been written and executed. If the last test script has been executed, then the application has been tested properly. As a result, an application doesn't need to compress the test times. Using the previous example timeline, development can take all five months.

There are several good side effects of TDD. Code and tests that are written simultaneously expose integration and grey zones early. It's possible to find bugs in tested code that in other situations would be considered hard to track. All in all, there are no bad side effects of TDD. Having to write the scripts and probably modify them multiple times could be considered a bad side effect by some people. However, rewriting a test script isn't done lightly, and is done for a reason. This means that in any case, the test script would have to be rewritten even without TDD. The difference is that the rewrite wouldn't have been done because it would have involved too much work. With TDD, the problem would have been caught earlier and the changes wouldn't have been quite as dramatic.

Another reason for using TDD is that it improves the coding experience and doesn't require as much use of the debugger. You use a debugger to find a problem when it occurs. A developer would start the application, define some breakpoints, and watch some variables. Starting the application and stepping through the code highlighted is the problem. What happens is that the application is usually too large, and too much time is spent trying to figure out where the problem is. Then, when the problem is pinpointed, several executions are necessary to define the exact problem. In contrast, combining TDD with logging and a good exception-and error-handling implementation, the bug can be found in one execution. This is because the tests should work without problems, and if there are problems the log file will highlight the area of the problem in the code. Using these technologies in unison makes a debugger irrelevant, to a large degree.

Enabling NUnit in Your Application

You use the NUnit framework to run tests in an organized manner. NUnit is so simple and straightforward that it's tempting to believe that NUnit is missing something. However, NUnit is complete, and when used in conjunction with logging and proper exceptions, tells you what's working and not working.

Remember, when using NUnit and TDD you don't need to test each method individually. TDD is about testing scenarios and defining what all the possible scenarios are. For reference purposes, scenarios that fail are just as important as scenarios that succeed. As much as we'd like to have shortcuts to develop test scripts using auto-generated code, this neither works nor helps the test. Auto-generated code is good if you're testing mathematical algorithms or programming languages. Auto-generated code generates a large list of numbers that you can use as a check mark to indicate success or failure. These numbers make it sound good that an application passes x thousand tests. I'd rather have three well-defined scenario tests than a hundred auto-generated tests.

There's no best way to write tests. Essentially, tests need to provide coverage and be realistic. The best way to start writing tests is to choose a problem that the assembly or application attempts to solve. From there, determine the overall operation, define the correct parameters, and then test the generated outputs when the operation has been called.

To illustrate the test-script design process, consider the following class:

```
class Mathematics {
    public int Add( int param1, int param2) {
        return param1 + param2;
    }
}
```

The class Mathematics has one method, Add, which has two parameters: param1 and param2. The method Add adds two numbers together and returns the sum. The following code illustrates how to test the Add operation:

```
[TestFixture]
public class TestMath {
    [Test] public void Add() {
        Mathematics obj = new Mathematics();
        Assert.AreEqual( 6, obj.Add( 2, 4), "Addition of simple numbers");
    }
}
```

The class TestMath has the attribute TestFixture associated with it. You use the attribute TestFixture to define a class that contains tests. There can be multiple classes with the TestFixture attribute. A test is defined when you assign the attribute Test to a particular method, which in the example is the method Add. The class doesn't need to inherit from a particular type, and the test methods have no parameters.

In the test methods, you use the Assert class to test whether something works as expected. In the example, the Assert.AreEqual method was used to test the addition of 2 and 4 to get the expected result of 6. If another result were generated, then an exception would be generated, and the text would be "Addition of simple numbers".

Running NUnit Tests

Once you've defined the individual tests, they need to be executed. NUnit tests aren't executed directly, but rather the NUnit application bootstraps the application or assembly. There are two ways to run NUnit tests: from the console or the GUI. For this book's purposes, I use the console application.

Assuming that the name of the application to execute is called chap02NUnit.exe, then the command line to run the tests is as follows:

```
nunit-console.exe chap02NUnit.exe
```

The application nunit-console.exe loads the application chap02NUnit.exe, and searches for the attribute TestFixture. Upon finding those attributes, the classes are iterated for tests that are then executed. Running NUnit then generates the following output. (Note that NUnit works, and has been personally tested, on multiple platforms and using multiple toolkits. The illustrated examples were executed on a Mac OS X computer running Mono.)

```
centaur:~/bin cgross$ mono ../../nunit/bin/nunit-console.exe chap02NUnit.exe
NUnit version 2.2.0
Copyright (C) 2002-2003 James W. Newkirk, Michael C. Two,
Alexei A. Vorontsov, Charlie Poole.
Copyright (C) 2000-2003 Philip Craig.
All Rights Reserved.

OS Version: Unix 7.7.0.0    Mono Version: 1.1.4322.573

.
Tests run: 1, Failures: 0, Not run: 0, Time: 0.400054 seconds


centaur:~/Desktop/active/oop-using-net-patterns/src/bin cgross$
```

In the example, ignore that Mono bootstraps the nunit-console.exe application, which then bootstraps the applications containing the tests. What's important is the generated output. In the output, the operating system and .NET runtime are generated, which happens to be Mono running on a Mac OS X computer. The runtime illustrates that Mono 1.1 was used, but NUnit is compatible with Mono and .NET 2.0. Below that line is a single dot that represents a test method being executed. After all the tests have been executed, a report is generated, indicating which tests failed and succeeded. In the case of the example, there were no failures and only successes.

More Detailed NUnit Tests

The example test was successful, and proved that the method Add worked. But when developing using TDD, that single test isn't enough. Included in the test scenarios are tests that need to fail. A good testing strategy includes tests that succeed and tests that fail. Tests that fail are necessary because they indicate whether the operations can cope with failure.

In the implemented Add method, it would seem that there's no way a failure can occur, but there is. The type int is a 32-bit integer, which means the maximum value is 2×31, because one bit is used to sign the value. A test would then be to check if adding two large numbers results in an overflow. You'd write an example overflow test as follows:

```
[Test]
public void OverflowAdd()
{
    Mathematics obj = new Mathematics();
    Assert.IsTrue( 4000000000 != obj.Add( 2000000000, 2000000000),
        "Overflow condition");
}
```

The test adds two billion to two billion, which results in an overflow, not four billion, as we would expect. Using the method Assert.IsTrue, you can test the return value from the Add method; it shouldn't equal four billion. Running the test yields the following generated output:

```
centaur:~/bin cgross$ mono ../../ nunit/bin/nunit-console.exe chap02NUnit.exe
NUnit version 2.2.0
Copyright (C) 2002-2003 James W. Newkirk, Michael C. Two,
Alexei A. Vorontsov, Charlie Poole.
Copyright (C) 2000-2003 Philip Craig.
All Rights Reserved.

OS Version: Unix 7.7.0.0    Mono Version: 1.1.4322.573


..
Tests run: 2, Failures: 0, Not run: 0, Time: 0.658305 seconds
```

The NUnit test run reported that two tests were run, and no failures, which is what we expected. We expected the OverflowAdd method to fail, and not to give the result of four billion to indicate that overflow has happened. The problem is the test worked, and it only worked because of a fluke. To understand the fluke, consider the following Intermediate Language (IL) of the test:

```
method public hidebysig instance void  OverflowAdd() cil managed
{
  .custom instance void [nunit.framework]
      NUnit.Framework.TestAttribute::.ctor() = ( 01 00 00 00 )
  // Code size       45 (0x2d)
  .maxstack  5
  .locals init (class Mathematics V_0)
  IL_0000:  newobj      instance void Mathematics::.ctor()
  IL_0005:  stloc.0
  IL_0006:  ldc.i4     0xee6b2800
  IL_000b:  conv.u8
  IL_000c:  ldloc.0
  IL_000d:  ldc.i4     0x77359400
  IL_0012:  ldc.i4     0x77359400
  IL_0017:  callvirt    instance int32 Mathematics::Add(int32,
                                                           int32)
  IL_001c:  conv.i8
  IL_001d:  ceq
  IL_001f:  ldc.i4.0
  IL_0020:  ceq
  IL_0022:  ldstr       "Overflow condition"
  IL_0027:  call        void [nunit.framework]NUnit.Framework.Assert::IsTrue(bool,
                                                                           string)
  IL_002c:  ret
} // end of method TestMath::OverflowAdd
```

In the IL, the numbers are converted into 64-bit integers that are compared. The IL command conv.i8 converts the stack value into a 64-bit integer. This means that the comparison of values is between two 64-bit integers. The problem in the comparison is that you can avoid an over-flow using a simple typecast. Consider the following changed comparison:

```
Assert.IsTrue( 4000000000 != (uint)obj.Add( 2000000000, 2000000000),
    "Overflow condition");
```

In this rewritten comparison, in which the data type is converted into an unsigned integer, the test will fail. This means the addition of two billion to two billion results in a total of four billion. By adding a typecast, a test that worked doesn't work anymore, even though the implementation of the Add method stayed the same. This indicates that the tests are poorly written.

When writing tests, you need to test conditions and their expected results or failures succinctly. The best way to test for an overflow condition is to test if a method throws the OverflowException exception. Following is the ideal test script:

```
[Test]
[ExpectedException(typeof(OverflowException))]
public void OverflowAdd()
{
    Mathematics obj = new Mathematics();
    obj.Add( 2000000000, 2000000000);
}
```

In the rewritten test method OverflowAdd, the attribute ExpectedException is used to test if an exception of type OverflowException is thrown. If the exception isn't thrown, then the test fails. If the exception is thrown, then the test is considered a success. The Add method doesn't throw an exception, so the test fails, meaning that the Add method needs to be reengineered.

To fix the Add method to generate the exception, you should rewrite the method to the following:

```
class Mathematics {
    public int Add( int param1, int param2) {
        checked {
            return param1 + param2;
        }
    }
}
```

In the rewritten Add method, you use the checked keyword to see if any overflow condition exists. If so, an OverflowException is generated. Another solution is to compile the assembly with the "Check for Arithmetic Overflow" flag. However, my opinion is not to rely on this, because it's an extra step that must be remembered. Anything extra to remember will go wrong somewhere, sometime.

In writing the two separate tests, the TestMath object was instantiated in each method call. Instantiating the object twice could be considered wasting resources, or not similar to actual operating conditions. Allocating the object once and reusing that instance could fix that. Following is a rewritten test class that instantiates the TestMath type once, and is used in two different methods:

```
[TestFixture]
public class TestMath {
    private Mathematics _obj;

    [TestFixtureSetUp] public void Init(){
        _obj = new Mathematics();
    }
    [TestFixtureTearDown] public void Dispose() {
    }
    [Test] public void Add() {
        Assert.AreEqual( 6, obj.Add( 2, 4), 6, "Addition of simple numbers");
    }
    [Test]
    [ExpectedException(typeof(OverflowException))]
    public void OverflowAdd()
    {
        obj.Add( 2000000000, 2000000000);
    }
}
```

In the rewritten TestMath class, two additional methods and attributes have been added. The attribute TestFixtureSetUp is a constructor method for the test class that NUnit calls before executing the test methods. The name of the method isn't important, and in the example it's used to instantiate the type Mathematics. The attribute TestFixtureTearDown is a destructor used to clean up resources that have been allocated and initialized within the test class.

When writing test scripts that use constructors and destructors, it's important to realize that state will be created. Maybe the state is desired, but bugs can arise due to state. Maybe a test is to run tests with and without state. In any case, writing tests does require some thinking about what the component does.

The main reason for using a set of classes is when objects reference other objects. For example, MyClass could be part of a list. When generating a list, you'd want a formatted output to make it simpler to see if the state of the objects is correct.

Some Final Thoughts

This is the second chapter that doesn't explicitly reference any patterns. I've done this on purpose, because the material presented in this chapter represents the new generation of object-oriented development processes. These processes are pioneered in a large part by the Open Source community. Even though some editions of the 2005 version of Visual Studio include testing and logging utilities, the toolkits presented have been around for years and have proven their worth. The best part is that they're free, and the source code is available.

Regardless of which toolkits you use, TDD, logging, and proper exception and error handling are key parts of developing an application. Combining the three pieces, a developer has the pulse of an application, and knows when the application is "healthy" or "sick." If an application is "sick," then the developer will have early warning signals, and will be able to find out what's causing the sickness.

Writing code using TDD takes some getting used to, but there are huge advantages, and it works. However, this chapter only touches the surface of TDD. For further reading, I recommend the book *Test-Driven Development By Example* by Kent Beck (Addison-Wesley, 2003).

CHAPTER 3

■■■

Defining the Foundation

In this chapter, I introduce two main patterns: the Bridge pattern and the Factory pattern. These two patterns provide the basis of all applications. Think of a program as a house: metaphorically speaking, the two patterns provide the foundations and the walls of that house. Without these patterns, no assembly or application would ever be maintainable. The Bridge pattern separates interface from implementation, which is useful from a maintenance and extension perspective. And the Factory pattern instantiates the types that implement the Bridge pattern.

Defining a Base for the Application

When writing code for an application, the basis of the application will be the infrastructure, namely types without an implementation. These types define an overall application and its execution without getting bogged down in the details of implementation. What you are doing when creating the types this way is called *defining an intention*. Typically, intentions are defined using interfaces, and classes that implement interfaces are generally called *components*.

In this section of the chapter, you'll learn how to define intentions and implement test-driven development as a means of creating the base for your applications.

Defining Intentions

An intention is something an application should do, without knowing the details of how to do it. An intention could be the definition of a mechanism to load a configuration. Excluded would be the details of whether that configuration could have been loaded from a database, or an XML file, or some other binary file. When defining an intention, the idea isn't to be vague, but to be as specific as possible without having to define minute details. It's possible to specifically indicate how the configuration is manipulated, and it's even possible to define the information that a configuration references. What is left as a detail for the interface implementation is the creation and wiring of configuration information to the interface instance.

The Bridge pattern[1] provides a way to express an intention and its associated implementation in technical terms. And the Factory pattern illustrates how an implementation is instantiated, but the Factory pattern returns to the caller an instance of the intention, and not

---

1. Erich Gamma et al., *Design Patterns: Elements of Reusable Object-Oriented Software* (Boston: Addison-Wesley, 1995), p. 151.

the implementation. When implementing the Bridge and Factory patterns, the overall architecture is made up of what are known as *development components. Component* is a general term that describes the development of interfaces and assemblies that are distributed as pieces used to build an application. Components have the advantage that multiple parties can work together towards a common goal without having to interact with each other, except for implementing the required interfaces.

Components are useful because a boundary is defined on what can and can't be referenced. Remember from Chapter 1 how uncontrolled references represent a development problem. Components use scope declarations like `internal` and `public` constructively, which requires developers to follow a coding convention.

The general idea of the Bridge pattern is to separate intention from implementation. When a consumer uses the intention, it doesn't know about the implementation. This is done on purpose so that the implementation can be altered or updated without having to update the consumer. Consider the following source code, which is a realization of the Bridge pattern:

```
public interface Intention {
    void Echo( string message);
}

internal class Implementation : Intention {
    public void Echo(string message) {
        Console.WriteLine( "From the console " + message);
    }
}
```

The interface `Intention` defines a method `Echo` that generates an output. The interface doesn't define where the output will be generated because it's an intention of generating output. The class `Implementation` implements the interface `Intention` and provides a meaning to the intention. From the perspective of the class `Implementation`, the intention of generating output means to generate output on the console. Another implementation could define the intention to mean generating output to an e-mail.

For either implementation, the consumer only knows about the intention and that the output is being generated somewhere. The consumer of the interface `Intention` doesn't need to know how the intention is implemented—it simply uses the interface. An example of consuming the interface is as follows:

```
Intention obj = new Implementation();
obj.Echo( "hello anybody there");
```

In this example, the variable `obj` is of type `Intention`, and instantiated is the type `Implementation`. Then when calling the method `obj.Echo`, the actual method called is `Implementation.Echo`.

So far so good, but then a problem arises, and it's the reason why the Factory pattern exists. The objective of the Bridge pattern is to separate the intention from the implementation so that the consumer of the intention has no idea of the implementation type. Yet in the consumer example, the implementation type is instantiated using the new statement. Therefore, the consumer does know the type of the implementation, so the example includes an interface just for the sake of using patterns in the source code, which of course is silly.

The solution to the type problem is solved using the Factory pattern. Included as part of the Factory pattern is a change in scope conventions for the intention and implementation types. Look back at the definition of the interface Intention and class Implementation. The interface scope is public, and the class scope is internal. When these declarations are used in an assembly, it means that all consumers of the assembly can see the interface, but the implementation is only visible within the assembly. To get an instance of the class Implementation, a helper type is needed. This type is an implementation of the Factory pattern.

Following is an example Factory implementation:

```
public class Factory {
    public static Intention Instantiate() {
        return new Implementation();
    }
}
```

The class Factory scope is public, and it contains a single static method, Instantiate. The method Instantiate, when called, creates a new instance of the class Implementation, but returned is an Intention interface instance. When a consumer calls the method Instantiate, an interface instance is returned, without the consumer knowing the type of the interface instance. The consumer code is rewritten as follows:

```
Intention obj = Factory.Instantiate();
obj.Echo( "hello anybody there");
```

The consumer code calls the method Factory.Instantiate, which returns an interface instance of Intention. The consumer code uses patterns and is a good example of writing the correct code. Yet, you may have the gnawing feeling that this example passes the buck. To instantiate the type Implementation, the method Factory.Instantiate will always have to be called. So instead of using the new keyword, a method is used; this is trading one type for another type, which is known as *using a helper type*.

The reason why it's better to use a helper type is because it makes it simpler to update the implementation of the interface. If the consumer knows about the implementation types, then when the implementation types are updated, the consumer might need to be updated. If the consumer only knows about the interfaces and uses a helper type to instantiate the implementations, then an update in the implementations will never need an update in the consumer. The helper type reference remains identical.

Implementing Test-Driven Development

As demonstrated in Chapter 2, writing tests is as important as writing components. To test the interface Intention, you could write a test like this one:

```
[TestFixture]
public class IntroTests {
    [Test]public void SimpleBridge() {
        Intention obj = Factory.Instantiate();
        obj.Echo( "hello anybody there");
    }
}
```

Running the test class results in the following output:

```
centaur:~/src/bin cgross$ mono ../../apps/nunit/bin/nunit-console.exe chap03.exe
NUnit version 2.2.0
Copyright (C) 2002-2003 James W. Newkirk, Michael C. Two, Alexei A. Vorontsov,
Charlie Poole.
Copyright (C) 2000-2003 Philip Craig.
All Rights Reserved.

OS Version: Unix 7.7.0.0    Mono Version: 1.1.4322.573

.From the console hello anybody there

Tests run: 1, Failures: 0, Not run: 0, Time: 0.312191 seconds
```

NUnit reports that a single test was run, and there were no failures. The output of the Implementation class is dumped to the same output stream as the one where the NUnit output is generated. What is interesting about this test is that it's extremely useless. Sure, you can cross off the writing and execution of a test from your to-do list, but the interface and implementation haven't been tested.

Implementing a proper test isn't that simple for the Implementation type because the type generates an output that isn't captured by the test. Essentially, the problem is how to generate feedback to the testing application that indicates that the Implementation type did everything correctly. In test-driven development terminology, the solution is to create a mock object.

A *mock object* behaves like the object it's mimicking, but it doesn't actually perform the actions. For example, in a database scenario, such an object would verify a particular SQL statement and not execute the SQL statement. The mock object for the Implementation class is the type Console. The Console type was chosen as a mock object because it's a lower-level class than Implementation. In general, mock objects are created for the lower-level called classes. Mock objects enable a subsystem to be tested in isolation.

Creating a mock object for the System.Console class is a bit tricky because it means replacing a method call from the standard .NET libraries. The solution is to use namespaces and aliases. The mock object needs to reside in its own namespace as shown in this example:

```
namespace Chap03MockObjects {
    public class Console {
        public Console() { }
        public static void WriteLine( string message) {
            System.Console.WriteLine( "-" + message + "-");
        }
    }
}
```

The class Console lies within the namespace Chap03MockObjects, which ensures no conflict will happen with Console in the namespace System. For the time being, the output of the mock object will be generated on the console. This means the System.Console class is called again.

■**Caution** Use the full namespace identifier `System.Console`, otherwise the `Console.WriteLine` will be redirected to `Chap03MockObjects.Console`.

The output is generated on the console to illustrate how it's possible to make a mock object appear like the real object, which then redirects to the real object.

To use the mock class instead of the class `System.Console` within the class `Implementation` requires an alias. The alias will cause the type `Console` to be identified as another type, which may or may not be related to the original type. Following is an alias declaration for this type:

```
using System;
using Console = Chap03MockObjects.Console;
```

The `System` namespace is still included, but the `Console` type is redirected to be the type `Chap03MockObjects.Console`. This means whenever the `Console` type is called, the mock object is called. It's advisable to encapsulate `Console` in an if statement that is only included in a debug build or a test build. To accomplish this, the example can be modified like so:

```
using System;
#if TEST_BUILD
using Console = Chap03MockObjects.Console;
#endif
```

Mock objects are an important part of writing applications, as they make it possible to test individual types or subsystems in isolation. Mock objects don't need to be written for every type, just for those at the lowest level. For example, let's say that type A references type B, which references type C. Whatever type C references will need a mock object. When testing type B, there doesn't need to be a mock object for type C. It's assumed that type C will be tested before type B, and therefore type C is considered programmatically correct.

A scenario does exist in which there would be a mock object for type C. If two different teams are developing types B and C, then potentially the team that implements type B might need a mock object of type C. The reason is the team of type B will only get paid if their implementation works. The team won't want to rely on type C as that means testing a type they didn't implement. The team that implements type C could be lazy and say privately that they will let the team implementing type B test their work, saving them from testing type C. Hence, if the team working on type B implements their own mock objects, they aren't dependent on the code of the team working on type C and can get paid once their work is complete.

Mock objects are created for the following scenarios:

- *You need references to types that aren't under your control*: This is part of the internal quality assurance process ensuring that an application isn't working because it isn't working correctly, not because the dependencies are working incorrectly.

- *You need isolation of types to test a set of functionality to simplify testing of the types*: Some subsystems are so complex that the only way to write tests that can verify the correctness of such subsystems is to write mock objects.

- *You would like to simplify the test environment*: For example, testing the type `Implementation` without a mock object is very difficult as there is no direct feedback. The only way to get feedback is to implement more complicated scripts.

- *You want to use recursive type references*: Consider the scenario where a subsystem requires a delegate callback. The testing environment would have to provide mock objects to successfully test the subsystem. Another scenario is when `Assembly1.A` calls `Assembly2.B`, which calls `Assembly1.C`. It isn't possible to test `Assembly1.A` without testing at the same time `Assembly2.B` and vice versa. The only solution is to test `Assembly2.B` and create a mock object for `Assembly1.C`.

Going back to the `System.Console` example, the mock object `Chap03MockObjects.Console` doesn't need to contain all of the functionality of `System.Console` to provide a meaningful test environment. The purpose of the `Chap03MockObjects.Console` is to implement only as much functionality as necessary to make the tests do something meaningful. The class `Chap03MockObjects.Console` is incomplete in that the output is still output to the console, and not verified. To perform a verification, a callback needs to be added. Consider the following source code as a rewritten mock object that has built-in callback facilities:

```
namespace Chap03MockObjects {
    public delegate void FeedbackString( string message);

    class NoCallbackDefinedException : ApplicationFatalException {
        public NoCallbackDefinedException() : base( "No callback is defined") { }
    }

    public class Callback {
        private static FeedbackString _feedback;

        public static FeedbackString CBFeedbackString {
            get {
                if( _feedback == null) {
                    throw new NoCallbackDefinedException();
                }
                return _feedback;
            }
            set {
                _feedback = value;
            }
        }
    }

    public class Console {
        public Console() { }
        public static void WriteLine( string message) {
            Callback.CBFeedbackString( message);
        }
    }
}
```

The general idea in the rewritten classes is to define a delegate that will be implemented by the test infrastructure, which the mock object can call into. The delegate FeedbackString pipes the content written to the method Console.WriteLine back to whomever implements the delegate. The delegate is stored and referenced in the class property Callback.CBFeedbackString. If the property CBFeedbackString is referenced without having a valid delegate assigned to the variable _feedback, the exception NoCallbackException is thrown. This is done on purpose because the property should never be referenced if there is no valid delegate value.

The test needs to be rewritten and a callback needs to be provided so that a complete feedback loop is created, as shown here:

```
[TestFixture]
public class IntroTests {
    private string _strHelloAnybodyThere = "hello anybody there";

    [Test]public void SimpleBridge() {
        Intention obj = Factory.Instantiate();
        Chap03MockObjects.Callback.CBFeedbackString =
            new Chap03MockObjects.FeedbackString( this.CallbackSimpleBridge);
        obj.Echo( _strHelloAnybodyThere);
    }
    void CallbackSimpleBridge( string message) {
        string test = "From the console " + _strHelloAnybodyThere;
        if( message != test) {
            throw new Exception();
        }
    }
}
```

The class IntroTests has an additional method, CallbackSimpleBridge, that is the delegate the FeedbackString method used to provide the feedback. In the method SimpleBridge, the interface instance Intention is created using the factory method Factory.Instantiate. Then the delegate is assigned to the property CBFeedbackString to complete the structural parts of the feedback loop. Finally, the method obj.Echo can be called.

When the method obj.Echo is called, the method CallbackSimpleBridge is called in turn; this results in the parameter message being tested against the variable test, which is the combination of some text in the string buffer _strHelloAnybodyThere. If the buffers are identical, then the test is successful, but if the data isn't identical, an exception is generated. A special exception type doesn't need to be used because the NUnit framework will catch any generated exception. When NUnit catches the exception, the appropriate error messages are generated.

The feedback loop is completed, and it's possible to effectively test a method that seemed untestable. Overall, the callback mechanism is very easy to understand and implement. The callback mechanism provides a method whereby the higher-level testing infrastructure can interact with the lower-level types. Without the feedback loop, it isn't easy to discover whether or not a test has succeeded.

The callback mechanism also needs to be considered very carefully. In the example, a delegate was used, but that isn't the only possible technique. The class Chap03MockObjects. Console could have contained some properties that represented the data that was generated. The calling test would reference the properties and verify that everything is OK. If there are data consistency problems, then an exception is generated. There is no advantage or disadvantage to using either a callback or populated properties. To a large degree, it's the choice of the test writer.

Now that you have an understanding of how to define the base of your application and a general idea of how the Bridge and Factory patterns are involved, let's take a closer look at these patterns, starting with the Bridge pattern.

Implementing the Bridge Pattern

The big picture concept of the Bridge pattern is to separate implementation from intention. But the philosophical question is, Why do you want that? One of the big problems in the software industry is change. It isn't that change is bad, just that change is a fact of life. What is bad is change that is disruptive.

Many architects and developers try to minimize change or make it less disruptive by future-proofing an application or a design. To *future-proof* is to add features to an application that will protect it from early obsolescence. Often in discussions about future-proofing, you'll hear buzzwords like platform neutral, interoperability, language neutral, location transparent, and flexible application environment.

The problem with future-proofing software is that you can only ever achieve limited success. Let me give an example from my personal life. In the late 1990s, I was consulting for a customer and providing them with Visual Basic architectural guidance. The customer's language of choice was Smalltalk, and often I had meetings with higher-level managers who attempted to convince me of the virtues of Smalltalk. I'm not picking on Smalltalk, as Smalltalk is fine language. It was just the way that Smalltalk was sold was wrong. The customer built a huge framework in an attempt to future-proof their applications. The framework was started in the early 1990s, almost done in late in that decade, and cost seven digits. What happened? Java came along and caused the client to throw all of the work out the window and restart with Java.

Future-proofing in literal terms means being certain of the future, which is impossible. We should change the term *future-proofing* to fit an alternative outlook: closing the absolute minimum number of doors for the future. It's simply impossible to future-proof software, as decisions will have to be made and those decisions will eventually need to be locked in.

For example, writing an application in .NET means using .NET. Whatever code you write won't work in Java because Java uses its own runtime. It could be debated that, using J#, it's possible to write code that works in both .NET and Java. However, the obstacles are very high, and the code uses the lowest common denominator libraries and coding techniques. Instead, the objective should be to code using .NET, and write code that is CLS compliant and executes on multiple platforms. Using such a strategy, it's at least possible to be flexible and potentially shift operating systems when necessary. But in the end, the application is and always will be .NET, and if .NET were to be terminated, there might be a problem. Where the future-proofing comes into play is the fact that there is Mono and it's open source.

The main objective with future-proofing is to make decisions that will keep as many doors open as possible using reasonable means. With this in mind, let's look at how you should approach defining interfaces.

Keeping Options Open Using Interfaces

When defining interfaces, the objective should be to solve the task at hand, no more, no less. Many developers attempt to future-proof interfaces by adding features that could potentially be used in the future. The problem with adding such features is that they need to be tested and documented. The reality is features will be added, not properly tested, not properly used, and become dead code that has to be maintained in the future. By keeping interfaces to the minimal requirements, it's possible to solve the problem without getting bogged down in extra work.

For example, from Chapter 2, recall that the type Mathematics was defined as well as a single method, Add, that calculated everything using the type int. A good way to future-proof the type would be to not use the type int, but use some general type. An example of using a general type is to employ Generics, as illustrated here:

```
public interface IMathematics< numbertype> {
    numbertype Add( numbertype param1, numbertype param2);
}
```

The interface IMathematics is defined using a Generic data type, which allows you to define the specific data type at a later point in time. An implementation of the IMathematics interface is as follows:

```
internal class IntMathematicsImpl : IMathematics< int> {
    public int Add(int param1, int param2) {
        checked {
            return param1 + param2;
        }
    }
}
```

The class IntMathematicsImpl implements the interface IMathematics and defines the data type to be an int. Then, like the original implementation of Mathematics, the two integers are added in the context of checked block.

A factory that instantiates the class IntMathematicsImpl is defined as follows:

```
public class FactoryIMathematics {
    public static IMathematics< int> Instantiate() {
        return new IntMathematicsImpl();
    }
}
```

The method Instantiate returns a specialized form of the IMathematics interface that uses the int data type. The code within the method Instantiate instantiates a new instance of the class IntMathematicsImpl.

Too Much of a Good Thing

The interface that used Generics to keep options open allows different types to be manipulated. A developer might come up with the idea to convert the implementation and factory to use Generics, thus making it possible to manipulate all types without having to explicitly provide an implementation for the type. The following example illustrates how the factory could be converted into a Generic type:

```
public class FactoryIMathematics< basetype> {
    public static IMathematics< basetype> Instantiate() {
        return new IntMathematicsImpl< basetype>();
    }
}
```

The class FactoryIMathematics is converted into a Generic type, and the method Instantiate uses the Generic type, as does the class IntMathematicsImpl. Following is the Generic type IntMathematicsImpl:

```
internal class IntMathematicsImpl< basetype> : IMathematics< basetype> {
    public basetype Add( basetype param1, basetype param2) {
        checked {
            return param1 + param2;
        }
    }
}
```

The converted IntMathematicsImpl class is based entirely on using a Generic type. In theory, it's possible to use any data type, and through the "magic" of Generics, it's possible to perform add operations on any type. The problem is that it isn't possible to magically add any data type. This is an example of abusing Generic types. The class IntMathematicsImpl won't compile because C# has no idea how to translate the expression param1 + param2, as the compiler doesn't understand how to add two unknown types together. This means it isn't possible to use Generics to add two unknown types. A developer might then come up with the idea of abstracting the Add method to use another interface that a type must implement à la .NET constraints.

Using constraints, the Generic implementation knows how to add two unknown data types. This solution would work, but it's a delegation, which adds complexity. Remember, the original interface generically defined how to perform mathematics in a general fashion. The added complexity in the example might be obvious, but it happens because one idea leads to another idea, which leads to yet another idea.

It's very easy to overuse Generics, as it's so tempting to define everything in abstract terms. You might want to think that, once those abstract terms have been defined, magically plugging in a data type will result in a working system. The problem is that it's impossible to do that. Adding methods or properties to make the Generic types work is adding complexity. Remember the focus of the Bridge pattern: to separate intention from implementation. An intention can and needs to be described in abstract terms, but an implementation should be specific.

Another danger of attempting to define in abstract terms an addition is that adding integers isn't like adding complex numbers, floating-point numbers, or even different bases. The result is that the different types share the same intention of adding, but their implementations will be entirely different.

What About .NET 1.x?

Without the ability to use Generics, it isn't easily possible to define generic interfaces that can be applied with multiple data types. In essence, it's easy to say that is why Generics were added to .NET 2.0 in the first place. However, it still doesn't help those developers who are using .NET 1.x.

The simplest solution to the Generics problem is to use the `object` type as follows:

```
public interface IMathematics {
    object Add( object param1, object param2);
}
```

In the declaration of the IMathematics interface, the method Add uses the type object for all of the types. As the type object is the basis for all other types, it's possible to define multiple implementations that use different data types. Following is an example implementation that adds two integers:

```
public class IntMathematicsImpl : IMathematics {
    public object Add(object param1, object param2) {
        checked {
            return (int)param1 + (int)param2;
        }
    }
}
```

In the implementation of the Add method for the class IntMathematicsImpl, the types are converted from object to int. If the type can't be converted from object to int, then a typecast exception will be generated. This means another test case must be added to determine whether an exception is thrown. After the typecast, the numbers are added together and returned to the caller as an object type. The answer will be correct, as the code is programmatically correct.

Looking at the solution, it's probably easier to stick with the int data type. The reason is because the boxing conversion from int to object and then back to int is too expensive. The working code is fairly expensive in computational terms when executed many times. This would mean that individual interfaces for each type (int, long, float, etc.) would have to be defined and implemented. However, often native data types aren't used, and in that case it's absolutely acceptable to use the object type. In fact, the list classes in .NET 1.x use that strategy.

This wraps up our look at the details of Bridge pattern implementation. Next up, you get a chance to see variations of this pattern.

Bridge Pattern Implementation Variations

The Bridge pattern has many facets, all of which relate to each other. For example, when defining reusable classes, often the better approach is to use not interfaces, but classes. What will be defined in this section are the different variations and the contexts that they apply to. Note that some of the examples may bear resemblance to patterns defined later. Not all examples are similar to patterns, and it's important to get a feeling for how the Bridge pattern can be used.

Implementing Application Logic

One purpose of the Bridge pattern is to simplify application logic. The interfaces are combined with another type to perform a particular operation. The type that does the combining is called a *controller*. The controller represents the abstract application logic. It's important to realize that the controller only performs actions, as illustrated by the following example of adding a list of numbers:

```
public class Operations {
    private IMathematics _math;

    public IMathematics Math {
        get {
            if( _math == null) {
                throw new PropertyNotDefined( "Operations.Math");
            }
            return _math;
        }
        set {
            _math = value;
        }
    }
    public int AddArray( int[] numbers) {
        int total = 0;

        foreach( int number in numbers) {
            total = this.Math.Add( total, number);
        }
        return total;
    }
}
```

The class Operations is used to perform a higher-level operation that utilizes the lower-level interface IMathematics. The Operations class is considered a controller because it does something with the lower-level interface. Note that the example uses a single interface instance, but there could be multiple interface instances involved.

The Operations class doesn't instantiate the interface instance, but exposes a property Math that some other type must assign. The reason why the Operations class doesn't instantiate an interface instance is for maximum flexibility. The focus of the controller class is to perform some operations using the interfaces provided. It's also expected that the controller doesn't consider specifics, as it's like the interface intention in that the controller implements an abstract application process logic.

The method AddArray then implements the process by using the interface instance. The purpose of the AddArray method is to add integer values to generate a grand total that is then returned to the caller. The array parameter numbers is iterated using a foreach loop that sequentially calls the method obj.Add, where the first parameter is a running total and the second parameter is a value from the array of numbers.

To use the Operations class, I've written the following test:

```
[Test]public void AddListDotNet1() {
    Operations ops = new Operations();
    ops.Math = Factory.Instantiate();

    int[] values = new int[] {1,2,3,4,5};

    Assert.AreEqual( 15, ops.AddArray( values), "List did not add");
}
```

The class Operations is instantiated using the new statement and assigned to the variable ops. Then the Operations.Math property is assigned using the Factory.Instantiate method. After that, an array of integer values is created and passed to the Operations.Add method. The Assert.AreEqual method tests to make sure that the list is properly added.

What is confusing in the test code is that the Operations class wasn't instantiated using a factory. A factory is generally not necessary because the Operations class is a controller, and there will only ever be one definition and one implementation. Consider it as follows: the controller only uses interfaces and represents an abstracted logic. Typically, there is only one type of application logic, and hence using an interface and factory complicates a scenario that doesn't need complications. In some instances, the controller will be defined using an interface, and these instances will be discussed later. What I want to point out here is that you shouldn't feel guilty using a class declaration for a controller. It's acceptable so long as the controller uses general types.

Having read all that regarding the direct instantiation of a class, note that the class Operations is specific in that the int type is used to add numbers. Ideally, the controller class shouldn't be type specific. A solution would be to use the redefined IMathematics interface that uses the type object. Using that interface definition then, the Operations.AddArray method would be rewritten as follows:

```
public object AddArray( object[] numbers) {
    object total = this.Math.Reset();
    foreach( object number in numbers) {
        total = this.Math.Add( total, number);
    }
}
```

In the rewritten AddArray method, there is no type defined, and every value referenced is of type object. The rewritten method is truly abstract and can add any type of objects. But to make the addition work properly, an additional method needs to be included in the IMathematics interface. This method, Reset, is used to return a default empty value. An empty object is necessary because AddArray is adding an unknown type to another unknown type. The variable total can't be assigned a value of zero, because total is an object, and .NET requires assigning total something. Using the value null is not appropriate because, as specified in Chapter 2, a null object isn't an empty object, and all methods should return an empty object.

The rewritten AddArray method works, but as mentioned previously, based on the type object, there is a performance cost. The performance cost is due to boxing and unboxing of the types from a native type to an object instance. Using .NET Generics, it's possible to solve this problem, but then it's necessary to use .NET 2.0. Of course, not all operations are math operations, and using the object type is most likely acceptable.

Using .NET Generics, the Operations class is implemented as follows:

```
public class Operations< type> {
    private IMathematics< type> _math;

    public IMathematics<type> Math {
        get {
            if( _math == null) {
                throw new PropertyNotDefined( "Operations.Math");
            }
            return _math;
        }
        set {
            _math = value;
        }
    }
    public type AddArray( type[] numbers) {
        type total = this.Math.Reset();

        foreach( type number in numbers) {
            total = this.Math.Add( total, number);
        }
        return total;
    }
}
```

In the .NET Generics version of the Operations class, the type has become a parameter that is the base type for the interface IMathematics. The method AddArray has no types and only uses the type employed to define the Operations class. Notice with .NET Generics the Operations class is a pure abstract application logic class, and is type safe.

The following test uses the .NET Generics version of the Operations class:

```
[Test]public void AddListDotNet2() {
    MathBridgeDotNet2.Operations< int> ➥
ops = new MathBridgeDotNet2.Operations< int>();
    ops.Math = MathBridgeDotNet2.Factory.Instantiate();

    int[] values = new int[] {1,2,3,4,5};

    Assert.AreEqual( 15, ops.AddArray( values), "List did not add");
}
```

In this test version, the same methods and instantiations are used. The only difference is that the type int is used to convert a Generic type to a specific type.

Inspecting the code closer, a potential additional optimization would be to instantiate the types using a factory that is parameterized using a type. An example of such an optimization would be as follows:

```
ops.Math = MathBridgeDoNet2.Factory.Instantiate<int>();
```

In this example, the Factory.Instantiate method has an additional type identifier that would be used to instantiate the correct implementation type. The solution is elegant and rather clever. Consider the following implementation:

```
public class Factory {
    public static IMathematics Instantiate<type>() {
        if( typeof( type) is int) {
            return new ImplIMathematics();
        }
    }
}
```

In the implementation of Instantiate, an if block tests which type the Generic .NET parameter is. Then, depending on the type, the appropriate implementation is instantiated. The advantage of this approach is that the Factory class can be extended to support new types without needing the client to be recompiled or changed.

Controller Interfaces

In general, the controller class is defined as a class, but sometimes the controller class needs to be defined as an interface. There are several reasons for doing this, and the most important relate to flexibility and convenience.

Let's start out by focusing on the flexibility issue. Imagine the controller is implementing a taxation system. The general intention of taxation is similar regardless of the country. What's different are the details of calculating the deductions, amortizations, etc. Some developers might be tempted to abstract the details as parameters that can be activated to determine which calculations are performed by the controller. The controller class would then need to be constantly extended to support yet another taxation system. Such an approach is futile and leads to complicated and messy code that should be avoided.

When a controller class needs to switch personality, an interface should be defined for a taxation system such as the following:

```
namespace ITaxation {
    public interface IIncomes {
    }
    public interface IDeductions {
    }
    public interface ITaxation {
        IIncomes [] Incomes { get; set; }
        IDeductions [] Deductions { get; set; }

        Decimal CalculateTax();
    }
}
```

The interface ITaxation has two properties, Incomes and Deductions, and a single method, CalculateTax. The properties are assigned the incomes and deductions of the individual. Instead of properties, you might think another solution would be to convert the properties into parameters for the method CalculateTax; but that would be incorrect, because the taxation system might want to perform multiple taxation calculations. Hence, the data is best defined as properties, since the properties are central to the calculation of taxes for the ITaxation interface. As a rule of thumb, if the data is needed in more than two methods, then you should create a property.

Let's ignore the implementations of the IIncomes and IDeductions for the time being and consider them as general implementations that will be instantiated and assigned somewhere. Instead, let's focus on the ITaxation interface. Unlike the previous controller definition, there are multiple controller implementations. Each controller implementation would be specific to a country and its tax structure. Following is an example implementation:

```
internal class SwissTaxes : ITaxation {
    public IIncomes[] Incomes {
        get { return null; }
        set { ; }
    }
    public IDeductions[] Deductions {
        get { return null; }
        set { ; }
    }
    public Decimal CalculateTax() {
        return new Decimal();
    }
}
```

The class SwissTaxes implements all of the methods. Again, ignore the properties, but consider the method CalculateTax. The method CalculateTax would be a custom implementation of the Swiss tax code. If the class were AmericanTaxes, the method CalculateTax would be an implementation of the American tax code.

Implementing a Default Base Class

From the class SwissTaxes just presented, let's consider the properties Incomes and Deductions. In the example class, the properties weren't properly implemented, but this wouldn't be the case in an actual working example. Implementing SwissTaxes means implementing the properties using some type of assignment and retrieval. When coding AmericanTaxes, the same properties have to be implemented, and the exact same source code, or at least very similar, will be used to code American taxes. The problem with an interface is that there is no implementation. When an interface is implemented multiple times, it could occur that multiple implementations are similar if not identical.

The solution to the redundancy problem is to include a default base class that implements a base logic. The default base class would then be subclassed by the different controller implementations. An example default base class is as follows:

```
public abstract class BaseTaxation : ITaxation {
    private IIncomes[] _incomes;
    private IDeductions[] _deductions;
```

```
    public IIncomes[] Incomes {
        get {
            if( _incomes == null) {
                throw new PropertyNotDefined( "BaseTaxation.Incomes");
            }
            return _incomes;
        }
        set { _incomes = value; }
    }
    public IDeductions[] Deductions {
        get {
            if( _deductions == null) {
                throw new PropertyNotDefined( "BaseTaxation.Deductions");
            }
            return _deductions;
        }
        set { _deductions = value; }
    }
    public abstract Decimal CalculateTax();
}
```

The class BaseTaxation has the scope public abstract and implements the interface
ITaxation. The properties Incomes and Deductions are implemented in the class and provide
the base logic for all taxation implementations. The C# compiler will require the method
CalculateTax to be implemented and is therefore declared as abstract.

The use of the keyword abstract is targeted and makes it simpler to implement a base
logic. When using the abstract keyword in the context of a class, it means that the class can be
subclassed, but can't be instantiated. This is appropriate because the defined base class is a
helper class and not a full implementation. It's absolutely vital to remember this; otherwise the
class might be inappropriately instantiated. Consider any implemented method in the base
class as a method that all derived implementations will use without change. And consider any
implemented method as an implementation that is structural and has less to do with application process logic.

When implementing an interface in a default base class, all methods have to be implemented,
even though the methods might not be relevant for the default base class. For example, the
class BaseTaxation requires the implementation of the method CalculateTax. As the default
base class doesn't actually provide a default implementation for the methods, the appropriate
choice for each method is to use the keyword abstract. By using this keyword on a method, the
method doesn't have to be implemented, but requires any subclass to implement the method.

Default base classes are a very powerful mechanism used by controller classes. But they
aren't limited to controller classes and can be used in different contexts where a basic functionality
is required. Default base classes will often be exposed using the internal keyword, even though
the class BaseTaxation is public in scope. The scope identifier depends on how many implementations will use the default base class. All implementations of ITaxation will subclass
BaseTaxation, as the properties are useful for all implementations and the public scope is
appropriate.

If you are using .NET Generics, default base classes are an excellent opportunity to include .NET Generics. For example, the class BaseTaxation could be defined in terms of Generic types. When implementing taxation for a particular country, the type BaseTaxation would be subclassed using specific types.

Multiple default base classes could be defined. For example, a BaseEUTaxation abstract class would subclass the BaseTaxation class. This is because the tax systems within the EU use similar rules even though the rates and calculations are different. Then the German and French tax implementations would derive from the BaseEUTaxation abstract class. When defining multiple default base classes, it's important to use the abstract keyword to ensure no factory attempts to instantiate an incomplete class.

Abstract classes are useful, but they also create problems when testing the individual classes. The abstract class can't be instantiated, and therefore it's necessary that mock objects derive from the default base classes. Following is an example of a test for the BaseTaxation class:

```
internal class MockBaseTaxation : BaseTaxation {
    public override Decimal CalculateTax() {
        throw new MockNotImplemented();
    }
}

internal class MockIncome : IIncomes {
    public void SampleMethod() {
        throw new MockNotImplemented();
    }
}

[TestFixture]public class TaxTests {
    [Test]public void TestAssignIncomeProperty() {
        IIncomes[] inc = new IIncomes[ 1];
        inc[ 0] = new MockIncome();
        ITaxation taxation = new MockBaseTaxation();
        taxation.Incomes = inc;
        Assert.AreEqual( inc, taxation.Incomes, "Not same object");
    }
    [Test]
    [ExpectedException(typeof(PropertyNotDefined))]
    public void TestRetrieveIncomeProperty() {
        ITaxation taxation = new MockBaseTaxation();
        IIncomes[] inc = taxation.Incomes;
    }
}
```

Mock objects were created for the IIncomes and BaseTaxation types. In real life, the IDeductions interface would have had an associated mock object, but it wasn't implemented for the purpose of clarity. A mock object was created for the IIncomes interface because the focus of the test is to determine the BaseTaxation type. The required methods to be implemented by the types IIncomes and BaseTaxation will generate an exception. This is done on purpose and reflects the nature of the BaseTaxation type in that none of those methods should be used or called. The test methods that are part of the TaxTests class are generic test methods that have been described previously in Chapter 2 and in this chapter, and won't be discussed further.

There is a problem when implementing mock objects for default base classes in that the mock objects need to implement some methods or properties. Going back to the BaseTaxation base class, this means the method CalculateTax needs to be implemented. The problem is what the mock object implements. The simplest and logical answer is to throw an exception. An exception is the appropriate action because the purpose of the mock object is to provide a placeholder to test other functionality. The only scenario where an exception isn't appropriate is when the mock object method implementation is expected to do something. Then the mock object needs to implement some default behavior.

For example, let's say a test required that the CalculateTax method be called. In implementation terms, the BaseTaxation mock object would be written as follows:

```
internal class MockBaseTaxationRequiresCall : BaseTaxation {
    private bool _didCall;
    public MockBaseTaxationRequiresCall() {
        _didCall = false;
    }
    public bool DidCall {
        get { return _didCall; }
    }
    public override Decimal CalculateTax() {
        _didCall = true;
        return new Decimal();
    }
}
```

The class MockBaseTaxationRequiresCall has a property, DidCall, that indicates whether or not the method CalculateTax was called. The state of the property is set to false when the class is instantiated.

Note In Chapter 2, I mentioned that initialization code shouldn't be located in the constructor, but in a reset method. For a test, it's acceptable to use the constructor because of the narrow focus of the test.

The method CalculateTax implements an expected action, which in the example is nothing, and assigns the DidCall property to true. The test that uses the class MockBaseTaxationRequiresCall is written as follows:

```
[Test]public void TestDidCallMethod() {
    MockBaseTaxationRequiresCall taxation = new MockBaseTaxationRequiresCall();
    // Call some methods
    Assert.IsTrue( taxation.DidCall);
}
```

It's important to write tests for default base classes, because otherwise it's unknown whether the default functionality works. The tests for default base classes will involve writing mock objects, and it's highly recommended that the code be kept in a separate namespace, because there might be multiple different implementations of the same mock object type to test different aspects of the base class.

Interface and Class Design Decisions

Interfaces aren't always the best ways to define types. The reason why interfaces are constantly referenced is because in past technologies that was the only way to separate intention from implementation. Interfaces were used for technological reasons and not just design reasons. With .NET, you don't need to use interfaces other than for design reasons. In fact, it isn't even necessary to use interfaces at all, since abstract classes and abstract methods can be used as substitutes. This then raises the question, Is the need for interfaces passé? Interfaces are necessary, but there are specific contexts. The Bridge pattern is designed to separate implementation from intention, and thus interfaces are an ideal context and the most appropriate.

In .NET, it isn't possible to create a class that subclasses multiple classes, as .NET doesn't support multiple inheritance. .NET only supports the implementation of multiple interfaces. This means when a class wants to offer multiple pieces of differing functionality, interfaces must be used. When a class wants to offer a major piece of functionality, then abstract classes can be used. Abstract classes can even be used to control what classes offer as functionality.

The argument is as follows: defining an interface means defining a piece of functionality. When a class implements multiple interfaces, multiple functionalities are combined. In some situations, combining multiple functionalities is entirely inappropriate. But at other times, it's entirely appropriate. For example, the interfaces IIncomes and IDeductions could be implemented as a single class that implements two interfaces, or as two classes that implement a single interface.

To see how you can implement interfaces, let's extend the taxation example. The Swiss tax system calculates taxes to the nearest Swiss Franc. When filling out a tax form, the amounts are always rounded to the nearest Swiss Franc, and that makes it simpler to add the various amounts. Other tax systems require rounding to the nearest hundredth of a currency unit. An argument could be made that there is a requirement for defining specific methods to perform tax calculations. The question, though, is where this method goes. The simplest solution is to make the method part of the ITaxation interface as shown by the following example:

```
public interface ITaxation {
    IIncomes [] Incomes { get; set; }
    IDeductions [] Deductions { get; set; }

    Decimal IncomeTax( Decimal rate, Decimal value);
    Decimal CalculateTax();
}
```

The method IncomeTax calculates the income tax for a given rate and value. The calculation method used depends on the implementation. The design at this moment would include two calculation implementations, round off to the nearest currency unit, and round off to the nearest 100th of a currency unit.

Let's consider the ramifications of adding the method IncomeTax to the ITaxation interface. The main problem is that the method IncomeTax has nothing to do with the functionality offered by the ITaxation interface, because the calculation of a taxation is separate from determining the numbers used to calculate the taxation. Simply put, calculating the tax at a mathematical level doesn't depend on the deductions or incomes. Calculating the tax depends on tax rate and taxable income.

If default base classes were defined, then the method IncomeTax would have to be referenced. The question is whether a base class defines a base calculation, because after all, the math of calculating taxes is identical across implementations. It could be argued that the math of calculating taxes is a structural issue, and hence needs to be in the default base class. The issue, though, is that not everybody calculates the tax the same way. As odd as it may sound, the mathematics of tax calculation is different in that Americans uses dollars and decimals of dollars, the Swiss use only Francs, and the Japanese have no part values in that there is only the yen and no decimals. Yet Americans and Canadians calculate their taxes using the same mathematical rules. The dilemma is that the functionalities are similar, yet dissimilar. The object-oriented character of a software engineer is screaming to create a default base class and use inheritance.

The solution is to not consider everything as one interface, but as two interfaces:

```
public interface ITaxMath {
    Decimal IncomeTax( Decimal rate, Decimal value);
}
public interface ITaxation {
    IIncomes [] Incomes { get; set; }
    IDeductions [] Deductions { get; set; }
    ITaxMath [] TaxMath { get; set; }

    Decimal CalculateTax();
}
```

With two interfaces, ITaxMath and ITaxation, the logic is clearer to understand. One interface figures out what the numbers are for calculating the tax, and the other does the actual calculation. Since there are two interfaces, the logical solution is to use two implementations. Yet the better solution is to use a single class as illustrated by the following example:

```
interface class SwissTax : ITaxMath, ITaxation { }
```

The class SwissTax implements both interfaces ITaxMath and ITaxation, and it would seem doing so is counterproductive. In fact, it would probably drive a classical object-oriented designer batty (especially after my long discussion about separating functionality into two interfaces). Then along comes the Swiss taxation example that binds everything into a single class. The difference with the SwissTax class is that the implementation of the interfaces ITaxMath and ITaxation are related. Swiss taxes must be calculated using a Swiss calculator. Therefore, a single class can easily implement both interfaces. Only Swiss taxes will use the Swiss calculator. An argument could be made that the Japanese use the same calculation and hence could use the Swiss calculator, but in fact that is incorrect. The Japanese have no hundredths of a currency unit, but the Swiss do. What this means is that to calculate Japanese taxes, a third tax calculator needs to be implemented. And since the Japanese tax calculator is specific to Japan, a single class as in the SwissTax example would be appropriate. Yet when calculating American and Canadian taxes, there will be three classes: AmericanTaxation, CanadianTaxation, and the taxation calculator CalculateTaxDecimal. The main point to remember is that you have the choice and should use what is most appropriate.

There is nothing wrong with implementing multiple interfaces using a single class. It's a technique that is used very often and has proven to be a useful solution. However, some important ramifications exist, as implementing multiple interfaces means combining multiple implementations. Following are two of the most important:

- *Resource changes*: Implementing two interfaces using a single class should only be done when both interfaces are going to be used. In the taxation system, a controller requires a calculator, hence both interfaces will be instantiated.

- *Consistency changes*: When both interfaces are instantiated, it's important to consider data consistency. For example, calling some methods on one interface could impact the outcome of methods from another interface. If the original design of the interfaces didn't take this into account, then when testing the interfaces, there could be data consistency issues.

Often when designing applications, in some scenarios it isn't necessary to use interfaces. Sometimes interfaces are overused, and that leads to problems. An example is the XML document object model (DOM). The XML DOM is entirely interface based, and in many respects it leads to slower applications that don't work as well. As a result, many XML libraries are rewritten to not use interfaces. The problem isn't the use of interfaces, but the overuse of interfaces. For example, the interface ITaxMath could have been easily implemented as a class as illustrated by the following example:

```
public class TaxMath {
    public virtual Decimal IncomeTax( Decimal rate, Decimal value) {
        return new Decimal();
    }
}
public class TaxMathFactory {
    public static TaxMath Instantiate() {
        return new TaxMath();
    }
}
```

The class TaxMath has replaced the ITaxMath interface, and the method IncomeTax has been declared as virtual so that any other classes derive their own functionality. In the case of calculating Swiss taxes, this means rounding off the values created by the base class TaxMath.

Even though a class has replaced the interface, a factory must exist. The factory class TaxMathFactory treats the class TaxMath as a base class. This is done on purpose because every class that uses the TaxMath functionality only needs to consider the type TaxMath, and not the types of the derived classes. When implementing the Swiss tax calculation, the code would appear similar to the following:

```
public class SwissTaxMath : TaxMath {
    public override Decimal IncomeTax( Decimal rate, Decimal value) {
        return new Decimal();
    }
}
```

```
public class SwissTaxMathFactory {
    public static TaxMath Instantiate() {
        return new SwissTaxMath();
    }
}
```

The class `SwissTaxMath` derives from `TaxMath`. The factory `SwissTaxMathFactory` instantiates the type `SwissTaxMath` and returns the type `TaxMath`.

When using classes as "interfaces," don't ignore the use of the keyword `abstract`. In the previous examples, it wasn't necessary, but it avoids the problem of having a user instantiate the type directly. For example, to avoid instantiating the `TaxMath` class directly, the following code can be used:

```
public abstract class TaxMath {
    public virtual Decimal IncomeTax( Decimal rate, Decimal value) {
        return new Decimal();
    }
}
internal class StubTaxMath : TaxMath {
}
public class TaxMathFactory {
    public static TaxMath Instantiate() {
        return new StubTaxMath();
    }
}
```

In the example, the class `StubTaxMath` derives from the abstract-scoped class `TaxMath`. The scope of the class `StubTaxMath` is internal, so it can't be inappropriately instantiated. The factory `TaxMathFactory` instantiates the type `StubTaxMath`, but returns the abstract class `TaxMath` type.

Using classes and abstract classes instead of interfaces is useful when the implementations are narrowly scoped and tend to be reusable. For example, nobody would ever think of defining strings as an interface. The `string` type solves a narrowly scoped problem and is often used.

Interfaces define reusable contracts that are implemented in different contexts, and they solve a narrowly defined problem. If an interface tries to solve too many problems, the resulting implementations become unwieldy and problematic. An implementation of an interface is considered a modular solution and not reusable because it solves a single problem. For example, the Swiss or American taxation implementations aren't reusable because they solve a narrowly scoped problem. The Swiss and American taxation implementations are modular because they are used in the overall application to calculate taxations for various countries.

When using classes as interfaces, the classes are considered reusable and not modular. For example, a tax calculator is used in multiple contexts such as for the American, Canadian, German, and British taxation systems. But when defining a reusable class, often it's necessary to specialize the functionality, and as such keywords like `virtual` or `abstract` need to be used.

Now that you've become familiar with the Bridge pattern and it's variations, I want to turn your attention next to instantiating types with the Factory pattern.

Instantiating Types with the Factory Pattern

The Factory pattern[2] is used to instantiate a type. The simplest of factories is one that has a single method and instantiates a single type. Such a factory doesn't solve all problems in all contexts, and therefore different instantiating strategies have to be employed. All of these strategies are creational patterns that operate similarly to the factory. Specifically, in this section we'll explore why you want to use helper types, as well as how to create plug-ins, how to implement objects according to a plan, and when to clone objects.

The Need for a Helper Type

The helper type used to instantiate another type has been illustrated in multiple places thus far in the chapter. Also outlined were some reasons why using helper objects is a good idea. What wasn't covered are the detailed reasons why it's a good idea.

Helper objects make it simpler to keep the details of instantiating a type hidden from the consumer. Let's say that a type needs to be instantiated. The consumer uses the new keyword to instantiate a type that implements an interface. Remember that the implementation of an interface is modular. It could be that one implementation operates under one set of conditions, and another uses a different set of operating conditions. The simplest example is that one implementation needs to be used as a singleton, and another can be instantiated for each method call. (A singleton is a single instance of a type.) Consider the following code that illustrates different operating conditions:

```
public interface SimpleInterface {
}
internal class MultipleInstances : SimpleInterface {
}
internal class SingleInstance : SimpleInterface {
}
public class SimpleInterfaceFactory {
    public static SimpleInterface FirstType() {
        return new MultipleInstances();
    }
    private static SingleInstance _instance;
    public static SimpleInterface SecondType() {
        if( _instance == null) {
            _instance = new SingleInstance();
        }
        return _instance;
    }
}
```

The interface SimpleInterface is considered a reusable type that is implemented by the classes MultipleInstances and SingleInstance. The difference with the class SingleInstance is that there can only ever exist a single instance. The factory class SimpleInterfaceFactory has

---

2. *Design Patterns: Elements of Reusable Object-Oriented Software*, pp. 87, 107.

two methods that will instantiate both types. The method FirstType is a standard factory. What is different is the method SecondType, as it only ever instantiates one instance of the class SingleInstance. In the method SecondType, a test is made against the global variable _instance. If the variable _instance is null, then a new instance of SingleInstance is assigned. After the test, the reference of the variable _instance is returned to the caller. Then no matter how often the method SecondType is called, the same instance will be returned.

The caller of the method SecondType doesn't realize that the interface instance returned is the same instance. This is the main objective behind using a helper type to instantiate a type. The helper type can set the operating conditions of the type being instantiated. It doesn't matter whether the type to be instantiated returns an interface or a default base class, or class. The consumer of a helper type can be assured that whatever object instance is returned is consistent and has the right operating environment.

The factory SimpleInterfaceFactory contained two methods, FirstType and SecondType. Most factories will be structured with multiple instantiation methods. Typically, such a factory will have instantiation methods suitable for a grouping of implementations. If the interface related to transportation methods, then for all cars there would be a factory, and for all ships there would be another factory. The idea behind such multimethod factories is to be able to create all types of implementations that belong to a group based on a single factory.

Implementing a Plug-In Architecture

A more sophisticated factory is the plug-in factory. The plug-in factory instantiates types based on textual definitions extracted from a configuration file. A plug-in factory is flexible and is an effective way to separate intention from implementation. The general idea behind a plug-in factory is to be able to instantiate an interface instance based on some textual representation of an implementation that is part of an assembly. A full plug-in implementation is available in the downloadable source code for this book, which you can get from the Apress website (http://www.apress.com). Only covered here are the essential details of a fully functional plug-in factory.

From the consumer perspective, the way to instantiate an interface instance using a plug-in factory is as follows:

```
ITaxation obj = (ITaxation)(Factory.GetObject( "Taxation.SwissTaxationImpl"));
```

The consumer would instantiate the interface ITaxation using the type identifier of an ITaxation implementation. Because the code is written using .NET 1.x, a typecast is required as the GetObject method is implemented using the type object.

Using Generics, the method GetObject would be rewritten as follows:

```
ITaxation obj = Factory.GetObject<ITaxation>( "Taxation.SwissTaxationImpl");
```

As this demonstrates, the advantage of a plug-in factory is that it's an elegant solution that can be used generically.

The implementation of the plug-in factory is a bit more complicated because multiple actions have to be fulfilled:

- Identify the Generic types that are shared by the consumer and implementations. What binds the consumer and the implementation together is the interface, default base class, or some Generic class. The Generic types should be stored in a separate assembly referenced by both.

- Identify the assembly(ies). The interface implementations are located in separate assemblies, which need to be loaded when an interface instance is instantiated.

- When requested, load an assembly, instantiate the object, and typecast to the Generic type.

- Return the instantiated and typecast object to the consumer.

Following is an example that loads an assembly:

```
Assembly assembly = Assembly.LoadFrom( path);
```

The method LoadFrom is a static method that loads an assembly based on the path stored in the path variable. When an assembly is loaded, the types implemented within the assembly can be instantiated using the following method call:

```
object obj = assembly.CreateInstance( typeidentifier);
```

The type that is instantiated is the text-based identifier in the variable typeidentifier. An example might be Taxation.SwissTaxationImpl. If the type could be instantiated, then the object instance will be stored in the variable obj. If the object couldn't be instantiated, then the variable obj will be null.

Another solution to dynamically loading and instantiating an object instance is to use the Activator class type as shown here:

```
object obj = Activator.CreateInstance( Type.GetType( typedidentifier));
```

When called from the Activator class, the method CreateInstance requires a .NET type class instance. The type class instance is identified by the variable typeidentifier, which is a string. The string has a special notation: "{type name},{Assembly path}". Returned will be an object instance.

When loading assemblies dynamically, it isn't easy to debug the assembly. This is because the debugger doesn't know about the assembly, and hence trying to set breakpoints is difficult. However, since we are using test-driven development, this isn't an issue, as the assemblies are tested in isolation.

The illustrated plug-in architecture works for scenarios where the type is specified via a configuration defined elsewhere (for example, in a file) that won't change throughout the execution of an application. The plug-in architecture can't be used to reload or update an assembly while the application is executing. To do that, you will need to use the Client-Dispatcher-Server pattern, which is discussed in Chapter 4.

Creating Objects According to a Plan

In previous examples, the interfaces ITaxation and ITaxMath were defined. Within the interfaces defined was the property TaxMath. The idea is to associate a generic tax calculator with a taxation system. Each interface would have its own factory, but some code would have to associate the ITaxMath instance with the ITaxation instance. To solve this problem, you use a pattern called the Builder pattern.

The general idea of the Builder pattern is to be able to create a set of object instances. Remember, previously I mentioned that the helper types used to instantiate the objects are intended to define an operating context. The Builder pattern extends this by instantiating multiple objects in the context of one method. Following is an example of the Builder pattern that creates a complete Swiss taxation system:

```
public class Builder {
    public ITaxation InstantiateSwiss() {
        ITaxation taxation = new SwissTaxationImpl();
        taxation.TaxMath = new SwissTaxMathImpl();
        return taxation;
    }
}
```

The method `InstantiateSwiss` instantiates two types, `SwissTaxationImpl` and `SwissTaxMathImpl`, and wires them together. It's important to have the type `SwissTaxationImpl` not implicitly create the type `SwissTaxMathImpl` because that would corrupt the functionality of the controller. A controller is a generic operations type that only manipulates Generic types. The controller expects the right types to be associated with each other and the controller.

Between the Builder and Factory patterns, there isn't that much difference. The only real difference is that the Builder pattern will instantiate multiple types and wire them together. This raises the question whether the Builder pattern should only use Factory classes. The answer is no for most cases. A builder class needs to have intimate knowledge about the types that it's instantiating. Adding another abstraction layer will, for most cases, complicate the application architecture.

Where factory classes must be used is if a plug-in architecture exists. Plug-ins are referenced using general identifiers and not specific type identifiers. Therefore, when wiring together plug-ins, the plug-in factory is used, and the instances are wired together using the provided interfaces.

Cloning Objects

The last major way to instantiate a type is to instantiate the type based on an object instance. This is called *cloning an object*, or *implementing the Prototype pattern*. The big picture idea of this pattern is to be able to create a copy of an object that already exists.

In .NET, the way to clone an object is to implement the `ICloneable` interface as shown by the following example (ignore the lack of implementation details for the property TaxMath, which was done for clarity):

```
class SwissTaxationImpl : ITaxation, System.ICloneable {
    ITaxMath _taxMath;
    public ITaxMath TaxMath { get {;} set {;} }
    public Object Clone() {
        SwissTaxationImpl obj = (SwissTaxationImpl)this.MemberwiseClone();
        obj._taxMath = (ITaxMath)((System.ICloneable)_taxMath).Clone();
        return obj;
    }
}
```

The method Clone implements both a shallow clone and deep clone. A shallow clone is when only the type's local data members are copied. The shallow clone is realized using the method call MemberwiseClone. It isn't necessary to call the method MemberwiseClone and a type instantiation using the new keyword. The method MemberwiseClone was used for safety purposes. To implement a deep clone, the clone method of the classes' data members is called.

One of the debates of cloning is whether or not to implement a deep clone. For example, if type A references type B, then a deep clone will copy both type instances. But imagine if type A references type B, and type B references another instance of type B, which references the original type B instance. A cyclic reference scenario has been established, which when cloned using a deep clone could lead to a never-ending cloning scenario. To avoid those tricky situations, adding a didClone flag could be useful. However, even with a didClone flag, problems will arise. The better solution is to rethink the cloning scenario and to manually clone each data member and rebuild the structure using manual object assignment. There is no silver bullet solution to implementing a deep clone.

Some Final Thoughts

This chapter provided a look into how to develop code that defines an intention and implementation that is instantiated using a factory type. The key aspect to remember is that intentions can be defined using interfaces or classes. Intentions are a mechanism used to describe generic actions using a general type that makes it simpler for a consumer to interact with other types. Implementations are shielded from each other and are specific solutions to an intention.

Intentions are generally reusable, and implementations are generally modular, but usually not vice versa. Keeping this philosophy in mind makes it simpler to define and implement applications.

For a consumer to interact with an implementation based on an intention, you have to create a helper object called a factory. The factory object is the "middleman" that knows how to instantiate a type and create the proper operating environment. The factory object may be realized as a single method, a group of methods, or methods that wire multiple objects together. The essential point is that there is a helper class that is responsible for instantiating the right types, and it establishes a state and context so that consumers can execute their logic.

The information in this chapter serves as a foundation for the rest of the chapters. In a way, it's interesting that the Bridge and Factory patterns, including their variations, are the basis of all modern object-oriented applications. It also means that if you don't properly understand the Bridge and Factory patterns, you won't properly understand the other patterns described in this book.

CHAPTER 4

■■■

Application Architecture

The purpose of this chapter is to introduce three patterns that solve application structural problems. For instance, it would be useful to be able to dynamically load an assembly, use the contained types, and then unload the assembly. This is called a *structural pattern* because it doesn't directly solve any business problem. A structural pattern helps you to write an application more efficiently. Taking another example, a classical approach to processing data would be to use objects, but the Pipes and Filters pattern might be more efficient, because it enables you to dynamically alter the data processing without having to rewrite the objects. In this chapter, I'll cover this pattern, as well two other structural patterns, Client-Dispatcher-Server and Micro-Kernel. But first, let's look at how design patterns help you ensure your application works properly.

Making an Application Work Properly

Many design patterns are focused on programming constructs that are micro in nature. This doesn't mean design patterns can't address programming constructs at a macro level. Often patterns defined at the macro level are called *analysis* or *UML patterns.* There does exist a set of patterns that are higher level and implemented by code, albeit by multiple code blocks. Often these code blocks contain other patterns.

When working with patterns at the macro level, the focus isn't on the individual mechanics of the constructs, but on how the pieces are assembled. The assembled pieces are important because they determine whether or not a macro-level pattern is extendable and maintainable. Very often patterns at the macro level try to ignore the assembling of the pieces, specifically threading and synchronization, and consider those details as implementation issues. For example, if I knew a program would never use threads, then most likely I would write my code without worrying about synchronization and data corruption problems. Now imagine having to implement threading when the macro-level pattern doesn't consider it. The result is that code will have to be rewritten. Maybe using macro-level patterns would make the code thread safe, but the question is whether it is possible to apply the macro-level pattern. When using macro-level patterns from the get-go, you are assured that code that was not thread safe can be made thread safe.

In this chapter, I discuss three patterns, but highlight throughout the chapter two attributes that uniquely describe each of these patterns: extensibility/maintainability and black boxes. Understanding these attributes makes it simpler to write code that is reusable when it needs to be reusable, and modular when it needs to be modular.

Extensibility and Maintainability

The idea behind macro-level patterns is to define an architecture that solves a specific problem, but in solving the problem doesn't preclude the solving of other problems in the future. What this means is that you don't attempt to create an architecture that solves all problems, but create an architecture that is as open ended as possible while solving the problem at hand.

Looking back at Chapter 3, let's consider the Factory pattern. The idea behind the Factory pattern is to separate intention from implementation. At a macro level, the Factory pattern locks you into using a specific factory implementation, but left open is the implementation of an intention. Also left open is how the implementation is instantiated and the surrounding context. This is the sort of implementation that a macro-level pattern attempts to present, except patterns are assembled to create a higher-level pattern. To illustrate how a Factory pattern leaves the instantiation open ended, consider the following source code:

```
namespace MoreEfficientArchitecture {
    class ToCreate {
    }

    public static class Factory {
        private static ToCreate _singleton = new ToCreate();

        public static ToCreate FactoryVer1() {
            return new ToCreate();
        }
        public static ToCreate FactoryVer2() {
            return _singleton;
        }
    }
}
```

The type ToCreate is instantiated using two methods, ToCreateFactoryVer1 and ToCreateFactoryVer2. The result of calling either of these methods is an instance that implements ToCreate. A caller that manipulates the instance doesn't know where the instance is from, how it was instantiated, and what context was used. The caller only cares that the instance implements ToCreate. Yet the difference between the implementation of ToCreateFactoryVer1 and ToCreateFactoryVer2 is immense. The method ToCreateFactoryVer1 creates a new instance of the type ToCreate each time it's called, and the method ToCreateFactoryVer2 returns the same instance each time it's called.

These example factory methods aren't representative of the Factory pattern because of the missing Bridge pattern functionality. What the preceding code shows is that a factory doesn't need to use types that implement a Bridge pattern. The Factory pattern illustrates a simple macro-level pattern that can be used in multiple contexts and doesn't cause problems with respect to maintenance and extensibility.

Using Black Boxes

A *black box*, in literal terms, is a box that you have in your hand. You know it's in your hand because you can feel it, but you have no idea what is inside it. Frankly, often you don't care.

Postal workers carry black boxes around every day in the form of the letters or packages they deliver, which contain things that they never open or read. In coding terms, black boxes are extremely useful because they delegate functionality to another area of your code.

Consider the factory methods shown earlier that created the type ToCreate. Those methods are similar to black boxes, but not entirely because the methods FactoryToCreateVer1 and FactoryToCreateVer2 are committed to creating objects of the type ToCreate. It's never possible for those methods to create anything else, except something that subclasses the type ToCreate. A black box is something that you don't know anything about and don't want to know about, whereas the factory methods create types that are expected. You can't say to a factory method, "Please create for me an object instance, where you decide what the object instance is and which methods are implemented." Factory methods that did that would be potluck-like and a surprise for the caller, and applications tend to not like surprises. A real black box uses types transparently or as placeholders.

In .NET 1.1, black boxes can be defined using the Object type, as every other type is derived from the Object type. One place where black boxes are essential is in the collection classes. The collection classes could manage cow types, truck types, and any other type a developer could think of. In a nutshell, collection classes don't care what the types are because all a collection does is group the instances for use by some other functionality. In .NET 1.1, classes like ArrayList have to manipulate Object instances; otherwise, for each type there would have to be an implementation that subclasses ArrayList.

With the release of .NET 2.0, true black boxes have been implemented in the form of Generics. Most people consider Generics useful for containers like collection classes. A *container* is a type that contains black boxes, much like a truck can carry boxes. But there are other uses for black boxes, such as functionality delegation. Consider the following source code:

```
namespace Blackboxes {
    interface Math<type> {
        type Add( type param1, type param2 );
    }

    class Manipulations {
        public type SeriesAdd<type>( Math<type> adder, type[] values ) {
            type runningtotal = default( type );
            foreach( type value in values ) {
                runningtotal = adder.Add( runningtotal, value );
            }
            return runningtotal;
        }
    }
}
```

The type Math is an interface defined using Generics. There is a method, Add, that is defined using the Generic parameter type. The Generic parameter type is a delegation of functionality because it says whatever type implements the interface Math will define what is going to be added. The Generic parameter type could be a double, float, integer, or some object. From the perspective of the Math interface, what the type is and how it's added isn't its responsibility. The Math interface is defining an intention of what it wants to do.

Defining an interface based on Generics makes it possible to build subsystems that implement functionality that uses black boxes. The advantage is that algorithms can be specialized to use a specific type at the last moment. The type `Manipulations` is a subsystem that exposes a method, `SeriesAdd`, used to add together a series of elements based on the Generic parameter `type`. Notice that within the implementation of the method `SeriesAdd` the Generic parameter `type` is never used, but passed from one method to another. Only the implementation of the interface `Math` has to be concerned with what the Generic types are. When used in this fashion, the Generic parameter `type` is a true black box that is defined in another block of code.

Black boxes and Generics are useful because they make it possible to delegate the implementation of functionality. .NET Generics are type safe in contrast to using the `Object` type, and they make it possible to build code blocks that can be tested independently.

▓**Note** Often developers think that writing Generic code is similar to writing classical object-oriented code. Black boxes are useful because they define a self-contained architecture. When writing Generic code in the .NET Framework, the code includes black boxes that can have associated constraints.

Now that you've learned about the two attributes common to the patterns in this chapter, extensibility/maintainability and black boxes, let's turn our attention to the patterns themselves, starting with the Pipes and Filters pattern.

Pipes and Filters Pattern

It's possible to process a data set in two different ways, and the only real difference between the two ways depends on the nature of the data set. If the data set is structural, for example, files based, network based, etc., then the solution is stream based. Typically, the data is read using an input stream and written to an output stream. If the data set is application based (bank accounts, mortgages, and so on are examples of such data sets), that generally involves reading some data, iterating the data, and reading more data based on the iterated data. These two different ways of defining data would require two different methodologies to process the data.

Two different solution methodologies aren't necessary if the problem is to find, filter, and process data using tasks and subtasks that operate relatively independently. The Pipes and Filters pattern[1] provides solutions where there are tasks and subtasks. For example, when iterating a database, a main task would be to find all of the employees who have worked at an employer longer than a certain time. A subtask would be to perform an operation on the found employees.

Considering the last paragraph, you might be thinking that the employee example constitutes a non-stream-based solution. What I've done is converted a traditional object-oriented application into a stream-based application. We consider stream applications to be the processing of a single stream. Yet there is nothing wrong with combining multiple sources to generate an output stream.

To help you understand how the Pipes and Filters pattern works, the next section walks you through an example of using this pattern.

---

1. John M. Vlissides et al., *Languages of Program Design 2* (Boston: Addison-Wesley, 1996), p. 430.

An Example: Buying a Television from Amazon.com

The classical examples of illustrating the Pipes and Filters pattern are to show how a data stream could be encrypted and decrypted or how a token can be replaced in a stream. While such examples are illustrative of the Pipes and Filters pattern, they aren't useful in the context of application development. An improved example would be an application that allows you to buy a TV from Amazon.com.

Let's say that you are creating an ASP.NET application, and the application will search and find the best television for the client's requirements. The traditional approach is to search a site like Amazon.com, and then from the result set pick out the elements that are of interest.

Figure 4-1 illustrates the use case for the example ASP.NET application.

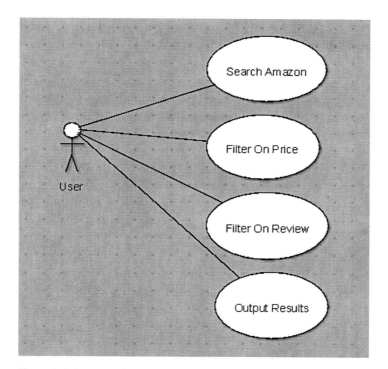

Figure 4-1. *Use case for example ASP.NET application*

In Figure 4-1, the actor is a user who has to perform four steps: search Amazon.com, filter the results on a price band, filter the resulting results based on user reviews, and then output the final results. Notice in the use case diagram how the individual use cases are sequential and operate on the results of the previous use case. This is a very common and essential attribute of the Pipes and Filters pattern. Even though the example doesn't illustrate the addition of other streams, it's also part of the pattern. If the data isn't processed using those attributes, then the Pipes and Filters pattern might not be suitable.

The advantage of the Pipes and Filters pattern is its ability to substitute and modify the sequence of events used to process a data set. For example, to search eBay for a television isn't difficult—it only requires adding an additional use case before the filtering is started. The strength of the Pipes and Filters pattern is its ability to add, remove, or shift the sequence of processing in a process. For example, imagine after having applied all of the filters an additional search is made to find an accompanying DVD player for each found television. Adding that use case wouldn't disrupt the overall processing, because the other use cases aren't modified.

Now that you have an overview of the television selection application, we'll look first at the architecture of the application, and then how to put it together.

Architecting the Television Selection System

Employing the use case diagram in Figure 4-1 as a basis for an architecture, note there are three distinguishing features in the architecture defined as follows:

1. Individual uses cases must be interchangeable.

2. Uses case can be chained together.

3. The generated output of one use case is the input for another use case.

The three distinguishing features are converted into an architecture by considering the uses cases as components derived from a common interface that are assembled into a linked list. In class diagram terms, the resulting architecture would resemble Figure 4-2.

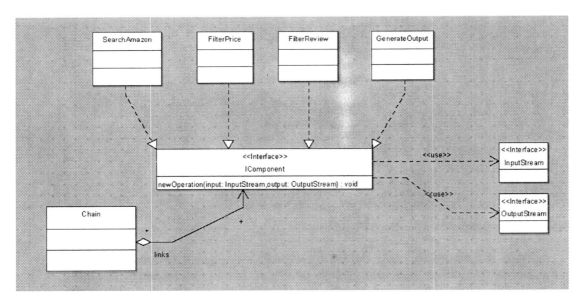

Figure 4-2. *Architecture of the Pipes and Filters pattern*

In Figure 4-2, the type Chain is a class that a client will use to employ the Pipes and Filters pattern. The type Chain contains a collection of IComponent interface types. The IComponent interface is implemented by the individual use cases (for example, SearchAmazon, FilterPrice, and so forth). The interface IComponent exposes a method, Process, that uses the types InputStream and OutputStream.

The types `InputStream` and `OutputStream` represent the input and output results of an individual `IComponent` implementation. When implementing the `IComponent` interface, you have three different implementation styles available, defined as follows:

- *Input sink*: An input sink adds data to the data stream by generating data locally or from an external stream such as a web service. The input sink is responsible for adding content to the stream. An input sink won't remove content.

- *Filter*: A filter will read the input stream, process the data, and generate an output stream. Some filters may add data like an input sink, but more importantly filters are responsible for transferring the data from the input stream to the output stream.

- *Output sink*: An output sink doesn't add data to the output stream and only reads the data to transfer the information to another streaming mechanism. Other stream mechanisms could include web services or a database.

When populating the `Chain` type with `IComponent` implementations, the collection would contain one or more input sinks, followed by none or multiple filters, and terminated by an output sink. Each `IComponent` implementation has the responsibility to transfer data from the `InputStream` interface stream to the `OutputStream` interface stream.

Implementing the Television Selection System

The formal specification of the Pipes and Filters pattern frequently mentions that a filter can process and write data while previous filters are still generating data. Adding this functionality isn't difficult and can be done by using the Producer-Consumer pattern illustrated in Chapter 7. For now, I'll restrict this discussion to a simpler capability of the Pipes and Filters pattern—sending and receiving data as a lump—so as to familiarize you with its basic functionality before tackling a complicated example.

What isn't referenced in the formal specification in great detail is how individual `IComponent` implementations discover each other. In the formal specification, one solution is the use of a parent type that manages all of the `IComponent` implementations. For this book, this is the solution employed, and it's referenced as the type `Chain`.

Implementing the television selection system involves defining the base types and streaming base types, creating some helper streaming classes, and finally adding the business logic, all of which I discuss in the following sections.

Defining the Base Types

The implementation of the Pipes and Filters pattern requires four types: `IComponent`, `InputStream`, `OutputStream`, and `Chain`. In the definition of the formal pattern, the input and output streams can be in one of three forms: method call with parameter, control component that is passed from `IComponent` implementation to the next `IComponent` implementation, and separate streaming objects.

The Amazon.com example illustrates the need for a streaming approach, but there is also a need for the control component approach. Consider, for example, the validation of a mortgage application that is based on the elements within a GUI. Converting a GUI to a streaming context, control elements are created dynamically, added to a list, read, destroyed, and then created again. Passing the individual GUI elements as streamed elements would be incorrect and resource intensive. So it would seem that applying the Pipes and Filters pattern would be inappropriate because it would involve either streaming GUI controls or passing a modifiable control structure from one chain element to another. The solution is to bring the two approaches together and use black boxes to encapsulate blocks of functionality.

This solution is based on a two-tier approach, with the first tier being illustrated in Figure 4-3.

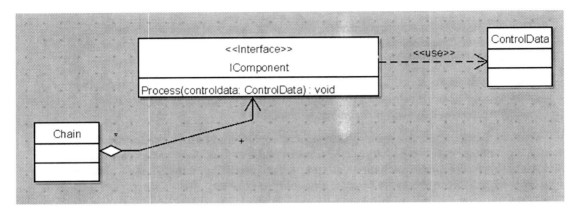

Figure 4-3. *First tier of a two-tiered Pipes and Filters pattern architecture*

The UML diagram in Figure 4-3 is a simplified version of the Pipes and Filters pattern in that there are only three types, Chain, IComponent, and ControlData. In implementation terms, the type Chain would contain a linked list of IComponent implementations. The ControlData type is passed from one IComponent implementation to another and references the control data. The ControlData type is a black box that can be anything. Using .NET 1.x, the ControlData type would have to be defined as Object. Using .NET 2.0, the ControlData type is a Generic parameter. Following is an example implementation of the IComponent interface that uses Generics:

```
public interface IComponent<ControlData> {
    void Process( ControlData controldata );
}
```

The interface IComponent has a single method, Process, that has a method signature based on the Generic type ControlData.

For the purposes of illustration only, the following source code example shows the IComponent interface using .NET 1.x code:

```
public interface IComponent {
    void Process( Object controldata );
}
```

I show you the .NET 1.x interface to demonstrate how to write Generic-based code using .NET 1.x. I don't recommend this, and will only do the conversion this one time. I do recommend that you start coding using the .NET 2.x platform, since it gives you more expressive capabilities for writing code.

The Chain type implementation is defined as follows:

```
public class Chain<ControlData> where ControlData : new() {
    LinkedList<IComponent<ControlData>> _links =
        new LinkedList<IComponent<ControlData>>();

    public void AddLink( IComponent<ControlData> link ) {
        _links.AddLast( link );
    }

    public void Process( ControlData controldata ) {
        foreach( IComponent<ControlData> element in _links ) {
            element.Process( controldata );
        }
    }
}
```

The Chain type is a Generic class parameterized by the ControlData type. The only constraint applied to ControlData is the new operator, allowing Chain instantiation rights. The method AddLink adds an IComponent implementation to the linked list variable _links. The linked list _links contains all of the IComponent implementations used to implement the Pipes and Filters pattern. The method Process iterates the IComponent implementations. For each iteration, the same ControlData instance is passed to the IComponent implementation.

Defining the Streaming Base Types

The implementation of the base types Chain and IComponent is uncomplicated, yet these types don't even come close to solving the problem at hand. This is because the ControlData type is a Generic type and isn't streaming based.

To solve the problem, you need streaming capabilities, and this requires a second-tier solution that implements the Generic parameter ControlData type as streaming compatible. The advantage of this approach is that the original architecture solves the single control data problem useful in a GUI context; and defining the black box to be streaming compatible solves the problem of searching for a television at Amazon.com. The challenge now is to define a ControlData type that doesn't disrupt the first tier solution and solves the problem without large complications.

Figure 4-4 shows a Generic-based solution that defines a ControlData type and associates it with an input stream and output stream.

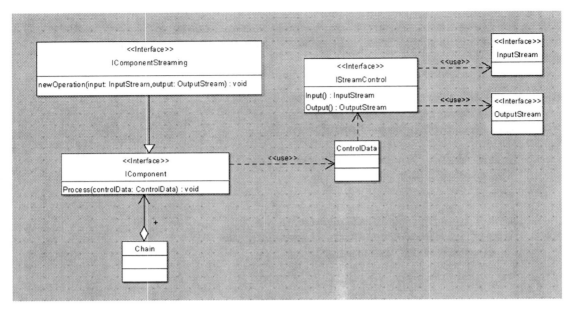

Figure 4-4. *Second tier of a two-tier Pipes and Filters pattern architecture*

In Figure 4-4, the original architecture from Figure 4-3 has been extended to include two additional interfaces, IComponentStreaming and IStreamControl. The InputStream and OutputStream interfaces are new in this UML diagram, but their purpose has already been illustrated in Figure 4-2.

The IComponentStreaming interface derives from the IComponent interface, which means any implementation of the IComponentStreaming interface requires implementing two Process methods. This can be tedious, but as previously discussed, abstract helper classes make implementations simpler. The interface IComponentStreaming isn't necessary, as the abstract helper class could handle all of the messy work itself. The reason why it's there is to make the processing of the data set friendlier and more obvious.

For reference purposes, the IComponentStream interface is implemented as follows:

```
public interface IComponentStreaming< type> :
    IComponent< IStreamingControl< type> > {
    void Process( InputStream<type> input, OutputStream<type> output );
}
```

To understand why IComponentStreaming is friendlier, consider a scenario where the IComponentStreaming interface isn't defined. Each IComponent implementation would have to manipulate the IStreamingControl interface that is defined as follows:

```
public interface IStreamingControl< type> {
    InputStream< type> Input {
        get; set;
    }
```

```
        OutputStream< type> Output {
            get; set;
        }
        InputStream< type> FactoryInputStream();
        OutputStream< type> FactoryOutputStream();
    }
```

The IStreamingControl interface is a Generic type, where the Generic parameter type references a type declaration for a buffer. There are two properties, Input and Output, and two factory methods, FactoryInputStream and FactoryOutputStream. The interface seems simple, but the IStreamingControl interface isn't just a ControlData type. The additional requirement relates back to the original problem of manipulating a single object or a set of streams. Look again at Figure 4-2 where the types SearchAmazon, FilterPrice, FilterReview, and GenerateOutput are chained together. When the type SearchAmazon generates output, the generated output is input for the FilterPrice type. The generated output for the FilterPrice type is input for the FilterReview type. It isn't possible to generically say all implementations manipulate the same input and output. Yet in the first tier implementation, there is a single instance of the DataControl Generic type.

Defining an additional interface, IComponentStreaming, makes it simpler to implement the conversion from a single instance to multiple stream instances. The conversion implementation is defined in an abstract helper class like this one:

```
public abstract class StreamingComponentBase<type> :
    MarshalByRefObject, IComponentStreaming<type> where type : new() {
    public virtual void Process( InputStream<type> input,
        OutputStream<type> output ) {
        foreach( type element in input ) {
            output.Write( element );
        }
    }
    public void Process( IStreamingControl<type> controlData ) {
        if( controlData.Input == null ) {
            controlData.Input = controlData.FactoryInputStream();
        }
        if( controlData.Output == null ) {
            controlData.Output = controlData.FactoryOutputStream();
        }
        Process( controlData.Input, controlData.Output );
        if( controlData.Output is StreamingControlImpl<type>.BridgedStreams ) {
            controlData.Input = (InputStream<type>)controlData.Output;
            controlData.Input.Reset();
        }
        else {
            controlData.Input = null;
        }
        controlData.Output = null;
    }
}
```

StreamingComponentBase is an abstract helper class that implements the default functionality of the IComponent interface, but the Process method of IComponentStreaming is defined as an abstract method. It's important to realize that the abstract base class is both Generic and specialized. The abstract base class has a Generic parameterized parameter type, but it refers to a Generic type that is stored in a buffer. It defines a buffer much like a set of characters in a string. Where the abstract base class is specialized is in the definition of the method Process, which has as its parameter a control data type.

The definition of the control data type has to match the definition specified in the interface IComponentStreaming. In both cases, the specialization is IStreamingControl< type>. In the implementation of the IComponent.Process method, the input and output streams are created if they don't already exist using the factory methods FactoryInputStream and FactoryOutputStream. Then the IComponentStreaming.Process method is called using the interface-defined input and output streams. After the method call, the output stream has to be converted into an input stream for the next IComponent implementation.

The stream conversion can only happen if the InputStream and OutputStream implementations allow it. As the interfaces are currently defined, no method call exists to extract the data that is implemented. To solve this problem, a special type is created that implements both InputStream and OutputStream. This special type, called BridgedStreams, makes it possible to convert an output stream into an input stream. I won't go into any more detail about this type, as it combines the functionality of two already existing types, and is thus relatively simple.

If the Input property isn't a type that can be bridged, then it's assigned a null value. The Output property is assigned a null value regardless. Then when the next component is iterated, the factory methods are executed to reassign the properties.

It would seem wasteful of resources to constantly instantiate and assign the Input and Output properties. The reason why it isn't wasteful is that an input stream or output stream might contain a state that, when reused, would corrupt the data stream. It would be possible to add a Reset method to the InputStream or OutputStream interfaces, but that is adding complexity and an added responsibility for StreamingComponentBase.

Not having a Reset method doesn't mean a reset can't occur. An implementation of IStreamingControl has to implement the factory methods. Since an implementation is aware of the types used, it wouldn't be difficult for it to call an internally defined Reset method. The client of IStreamingControl wouldn't realize that a recycled instance is being used. This is the same strategy that appears at the beginning of the chapter. By not adding the Reset method, the client is saying to the factory, "You figure it out." A delegation of functionality has occurred.

To finish the definition of the base streaming types, the types InputStream and Output stream are defined as follows:

```
public interface InputStream< type> {
    bool Available();
    type Read();
    ulong Read( out type[] data );
    ulong Read( out type[] data, ulong offset, ulong length );
    void Reset();
    void Skip( ulong offset );
    System.Collections.IEnumerator GetEnumerator();
}
```

```
public interface OutputStream<type> {
    void Flush();
    void Write( type data );
    void Write( type[] data );
    void Write( type[] data, ulong offset, ulong length );
}
```

Both InputStream and OutputStream are interfaces defined using .NET Generics that have a single Generic parameter type. A Generic parameter type could be an int, double, or some other object. The base assumption used by both interfaces is that the input and output stream are stored as an array of typed elements.

The input stream data can be read multiple times using the method Reset, which resets the internal reference pointer. The method Available tests whether data is available. The method GetEnumerator makes it possible to iterate the data using the foreach loop. The output stream has multiple Write methods used to write the data. The Flush method resets the internal buffers to remove any existing data.

■**Note** Within the System.IO namespace are a number of definitions for input, output, and streams. All of these definitions relate to streaming text or binary and aren't applicable to the Pipes and Filters pattern.

Figure 4-5 illustrates the final implementation architecture.

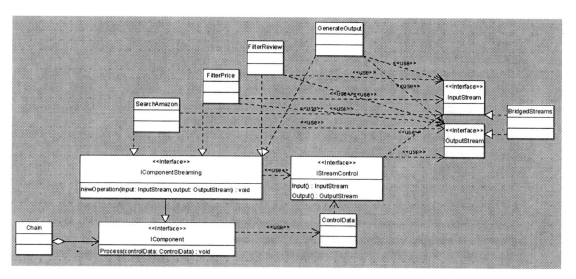

Figure 4-5. *Full architecture of the Pipes and Filters pattern for the Amazon application*

Notice in Figure 4-5 the additional complexity that results by adding the types InputStream and OutputStream. This is because a full architecture has been defined that has quite a number of types.

Implementing Some Helper Streaming Classes

The method IComponentStreaming.Process has two parameters, input and output, that represent the InputStream and OutputStream types, respectively. The abstract base class StreamingComponentBase implements the IComponentStreaming interface. Any implementation of IComponentStreaming only needs to subclass the StreamingComponentBase class. Defined earlier in the section "Architecting the Television Selection System" were three different IComponent implementation types: input sink, output sink, and filter. A further optimization is to define input sink and output sink abstract base classes that subclass StreamingComponentBase as follows:

```
public abstract class InputSink<type> :
    StreamingComponentBase< type> where type : new() {
    public abstract void Process( OutputStream<type> output );

    public virtual void Process( InputStream<type> input,
        OutputStream<type> output ) {
        foreach( type item in input ) {
            output.Write( item );
        }
        Process( output );
    }
}

public abstract class OutputSink<type> :
    StreamingComponentBase<type> where type: new() {
    public abstract void Process( InputStream<type> input );

    public virtual void Process( InputStream<type> input,
        OutputStream<type> output ) {
        Process( input );
    }
}
```

InputSink and OutputSink are defined as Generic types and as abstract classes that derive from the StreamingComponentBase type. Abstract classes are used because both InputSink and OutputSink are helper classes that shouldn't be instantiated on their own. Each class implements the Process method with the input, output parameter signature. In the case of InputSink, the Process implementation copies the input stream to the output stream. Having copied all elements, a modified Process method is called that only passes in the OutputStream parameter. OutputSink doesn't copy any data and exposes a Process method with only the InputStream parameter.

Adding the Business Logic

The last step is to implement the IComponent interfaces, which are defined as follows. (The details of the implementation classes have been omitted for clarity. The associated source code that can be downloaded does work and performs a search on Amazon.com.)

```
internal class SearchTV : InputSink<Item> {
    // Omitted for clarity
}

internal class FilterPrice : ComponentInputIterator<Item> {
    // Omitted for clarity
}

internal class ReviewRating : ComponentInputIterator<Item> {
    // Omitted for clarity
}

internal class Output : OutputSink<Item> {
    // Omitted for clarity
}

public static class Factory {
    public static IComponent<StreamingControlImpl< Item>> CreateSearchTV(
        string keywords) {
        return (IComponent<StreamingControlImpl< Item>>)new SearchTV( keywords);
    }
    public static IComponent<StreamingControlImpl<Item>> CreateFilterPrice(
        double maximum, double minimum) {
        return (IComponent<StreamingControlImpl<Item>>)
            new FilterPrice( maximum, minimum );
    }
    public static IComponent<StreamingControlImpl<Item>> CreateReviewRating(
        double rating) {
        return (IComponent<StreamingControlImpl<Item>>)new
            ReviewRating( rating );
    }
    public static IComponent<StreamingControlImpl<Item>> CreateOutput() {
        return (IComponent<StreamingControlImpl<Item>>)new Output();
    }
}
```

I've included abstract helper classes for SearchAmazon, ReviewRating, FilterPrice, and Output. When the implementations are manipulated with respect to the Chain type, the interface IComponent is exposed. The factory methods CreateReviewRating instantiate IComponent instance types and notice the use of a typecast to extract the IComponent interface.

And finally, the following source code searches for a television:

```
Chain< StreamingControlImpl< Item>> chain =
    new Chain< StreamingControlImpl<Item>>();
chain.AddLink( Factory.CreateSearchTV( "lcd" ) );
chain.AddLink( Factory.CreateFilterPrice( 1000, 2000 ) );
chain.AddLink(Factory.CreateReviewRating( 4.0 ) );
chain.AddLink( Factory.CreateOutput() );
StreamingControlImpl<Item> controldata = new StreamingControlImpl<Item>();
chain.Process( controldata );
```

Some Final Notes About the Pipes and Filters Pattern

The Pipes and Filters pattern seems very simple in concept, but complicated in implementation. The reality is that the complications are only apparent if the entire class diagram of the Pipes and Filters pattern is viewed as a whole.

The advantage patterns give you is that you don't see the individual types, but you see blocks of types. The blocks of types are implemented using .NET 2.0 Generics, through which one block can reference another without explicitly indicating the reference. Without Generics, the only way of creating black box types is to use the `Object` type as is done extensively by any .NET 1.1 collection class. When creating more complicated architectures, it's more difficult to use `Object` because you don't know what type is being referenced. Your brain can only hold so much information, and if that information isn't explicitly defined, the brain will forget.

Using Generics, it's easier to read a class diagram, even though the completed architecture diagram of Figure 4-5 seems complicated. The key in trying to understand Figure 4-5 isn't to look at Figure 4-5 as a whole, but in pieces. The essence of the Pipes and Filters pattern is shown in Figure 4-3, which only references the types `Chain`, `IComponent`, and `ControlData`. Subtract those types from Figure 4-5 and consider what you have left over. From the leftover pieces, subtract those from Figure 4-4, and consider what is left over. In each case, a block of functionality is subtracted. The point is that the diagram in Figure 4-5 can be organized as illustrated in Figure 4-6.

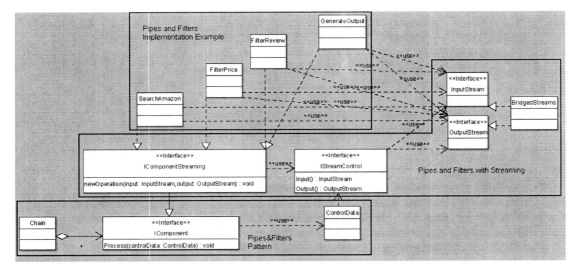

Figure 4-6. *Final Pipes and Filters pattern implementation that highlights three black boxes*

The diagram in Figure 4-6 is the same as the one in Figure 4-5, except that there are three boxes with text descriptors: Pipes and Filters Pattern, Pipes and Filters with Streaming, and Pipes and Filters Implementation Example. Each of these boxes demonstrates a single piece of abstract functionality that belongs to the Pipes and Filters pattern.

It has to be noted that this implementation of the Pipes and Filters pattern includes additional patterns such as Factory. This is very common, as larger patterns contain other patterns. From this point on, when looking at the patterns presented, don't just look at the class diagrams and try to figure out what the classes do. Pick out the blocks of types that represent the pattern, and consider how the patterns are assembled to solve a problem.

One last note about Figure 4-5: you might have realized that not all types were defined in that diagram. For example, the abstract base class `StreamingComponentBase` wasn't shown. This was done on purpose. Consider this: say that you are a house builder and you are looking at some plans. On the plans are the pipes, walls, bricks, etc. Not illustrated are the nails, concrete, electrical cabling, etc. This is because the abstract base classes like the nails are helper objects. They are part of the structure, but they live transparent lives in that everyone assumes that these pieces exist, but nobody explicitly references them. Adding every nail to a blueprint would make a blueprint more complicated, just like adding every helper object would make a UML diagram more complicated. Don't associate lack of reference in the UML diagram as being unimportant, because generally speaking, a modern-day house assembled with no nails results in a house that will very surely collapse.

This wraps up the discussion of the Pipes and Filters pattern. Let's move on to the next pattern I want to show you in this chapter: the Client-Dispatcher-Server pattern.

Client-Dispatcher-Server Pattern

In Chapter 3, you saw a simple plug-in factory. This factory worked, but with the side effect that any assembly that was loaded couldn't be unloaded. The plug-in factory was only capable of dealing with assemblies available on the local computer; it didn't have the capability to execute code on another computer. The simple plug-in factory could only deal with focused requirements.

In general, the Factory pattern isn't capable of dealing with complexity, even though it should. Remember, though, that the intent of the Factory pattern is to remove references so that the interface can be separated from the implementation. To make the Factory pattern work in more complex scenarios, another pattern has to be used—the Client-Dispatcher-Server pattern.[2] This new pattern is similar to the Factory pattern, but can deal with location and resolution issues.

The Client-Dispatcher-Server pattern addresses the resolution and location problems by introducing an intermediate that is responsible for establishing a connection between a client and a server. The intermediate is called the *dispatcher*. The pattern itself, like the Factory pattern, is relatively simple. Where the Client-Dispatcher-Server pattern differs from the Factory pattern is in the implementation. The Client-Dispatcher-Server pattern has more implementation details and is technologically specific, as it could involve network communications.

---

2. Frank Buschmann, et al., *Pattern-Oriented Software Architecture, Volume 1: A System of Patterns* (Indianapolis: Wiley Publishing, 1996), p. 323.

Defining the Client-Dispatcher-Server Pattern Architecture

The formal architecture of the Client-Dispatcher-Server pattern defines a client, server, and dispatcher. The client requests a server service from the dispatcher, and then uses the provided service. The server registers itself with the dispatcher and provides services to clients. The dispatcher is responsible for cross-referencing a service request from the client to a server. Having found a server, the dispatcher is responsible for instantiating the service.

In simple UML terms, the architecture is similar to what is shown in Figure 4-7.

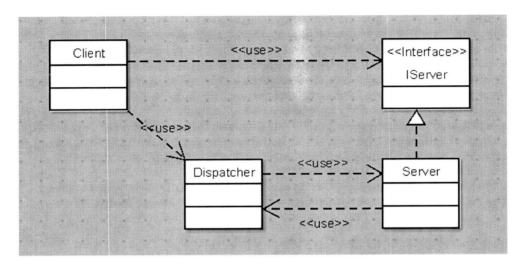

Figure 4-7. *UML architecture of Client-Dispatcher-Server pattern*

The Client uses both the Dispatcher and the interface IServer. The Server uses the Dispatcher to register itself, and the Dispatcher uses the Server when instantiating the type. The Dispatcher returns to the client the IServer interface. Note that the UML interface means either a .NET interface type or an abstract base class. However, as you'll see in the section "Understanding the Big Picture of AppDomains" later in this chapter, abstract base classes have major problems.

Before tackling the architecture and implementation of the Client-Dispatcher-Server pattern, let's take a look at the two dispatcher types: static dispatchers and dynamic dispatchers.

A Static Dispatcher Architecture

A static dispatcher is very similar to a plug-in architecture in that the assembly is loaded at runtime. Let's review the plug-in architecture and then compare it to a static Client-Dispatcher-Server pattern.

Plug-ins are dynamically loaded assemblies that implement a specific interface. In the context of the dispatcher, it means that the servers are plug-ins. The dispatcher manages the plug-ins through some resolution technique that associates an interface instance with a type. For example, if the type ExternalServer were implemented in the assembly ExternalServers.dll, then the dispatcher could be written as follows:

```
class Dispatcher {
    public type CreateInstance<type>( string assemblyPath, string @class) {
        Assembly assembly;
        assembly = Assembly.Load(
            AssemblyName.GetAssemblyName( assemblyPath ) );
        return (type)assembly.CreateInstance( @class);
    }
}

class Client {
    public void DoSomething() {
        IExternal obj =  CreateInstance<IExternal>(
            "ExternalServers.dll", "ExternalServer" );
        // Do something with obj
    }
}
```

The type Dispatcher has a single method, CreateInstance, which can dynamically load the assembly ExternalServers.dll and instantiate the type ExternalServer. The method Assembly.Load loads an assembly, and the method assembly.CreateInstance instantiates a type in the loaded assembly. The method CreateInstance uses Generics to typecast the Object type to the required type.

This solution of dynamically loading and instantiating a type works well, with one ramification: any loaded assembly can't be unloaded if the assembly changes. If the application were a client application in which the assembly doesn't change during execution, then the type Dispatcher is good enough. If the application were executing on the server side, then reloading a plug-in might be an issue. The string identifiers used in the method call CreateInstance<IExternal> are hard-coded.

One major additional feature of the Client-Dispatcher-Server pattern is that the dispatcher has to include functionality to perform resolution of an identifier to a type in an assembly. The Dispatcher type in the simple example assumed that the client would know the reference identifiers. The Dispatcher's added value was knowing the name of the path where the assembly and type resided.

From a pattern purists point of view, it could be argued that the simple example isn't an implementation of a dispatcher because the server didn't contact and register itself with Dispatcher. That is true, but here is where I tend to be more flexible about the exact behavior of the dispatcher. Having a server contact the dispatcher and then register itself is, in my opinion, one way of implementing a dispatcher. As you'll see demonstrated in later chapters, the Client-Dispatcher-Server pattern can implement and extend other patterns.

As a general rule of thumb, a dispatcher is responsible for resolving an identifier to a type and assembly. The resolution of the type and assembly can happen in one of the following ways:

- *Configuration file*: A configuration file is loaded and processed by the dispatcher. When a specific type needs to be instantiated, the dispatcher cross-references the requested type with the configuration information. The advantages of this approach are configuration of the application at runtime is possible, and you can use versioning information to load specific versions in specific contexts. The disadvantages of this approach are the administrator needs documentation from the developer on available plug-in implementations, and an improper configuration file can cause havoc when debugging a production issue.

- *Assembly directory*: Using a configuration file, a directory(s) is specified that contains a number of assemblies. The dispatcher reads the directory(s) and iterates the available assemblies. Each assembly has its type information extracted, which is then saved in a list. The list cross-references identifiers to types and assemblies whenever a type instantiation request is made. The advantages of this approach are minimal configuration information is needed since dynamic resolution occurs, and the application can heal itself if the appropriate version routines are kept. The disadvantages of this approach are loading and instantiation logic is hard-coded within the dispatcher, meaning a logic change requires an application restart; and the application developer has to know which plug-in implementation identifiers to use at development time.

- *Factory delegation*: For this solution, the assemblies are referenced as a directory or individually in a configuration file. The assemblies are dynamically loaded, but the type information isn't extracted. The dispatcher searches for a Factory pattern implementation that hooks itself to the dispatcher. When an instantiation request is made, the dispatcher delegates to the Factory pattern. The advantages of this approach are instantiation is delegated to the plug-in implementations, allowing the implementation to decide which logic to instantiate a type; and the micro-kernel or internal server does a delegation, allowing the assembly to handle its own versioning or identifier cross-reference. The disadvantages of this approach are each assembly must implement a standard type used as an entry point for type instantiation, and each assembly is responsible for figuring out which to instantiate, adding extra coding requirements for the developer.

- *Server registration*: For this solution, the dispatcher knows nothing, and it's the responsibility of the server to register its type information with the dispatcher. The problem with this approach is that some program has to start the servers and indicate where the dispatcher resides, which adds overhead. The advantage of this approach is that types can be switched dynamically whenever the server requires it. The other resolution techniques aren't quite as flexible, even though they are simpler.

Surveying all four of the resolution techniques reveals there is no single best way of performing a resolution, for each solution has its advantages and disadvantages. You have to decide for yourself which is the best solution for your situation.

A Dynamic Dispatcher Architecture

The scope of this chapter covers two resolution techniques: primitive name resolution as illustrated in the static dispatcher solution, and an assembly directory. The reason for the primitive dispatcher solution is that it's simple and it works. And remember from the Pipes and Filters pattern discussion, the objective is to create something simple and consider the architecture in terms of black boxes that fit together.

I demonstrate the assembly directory resolution technique because it's simple from a configuration point of view and essentially administers itself. One of the problems that has been growing in the Java programming community is the explosion of configuration files. In some frameworks, the complexity of the configuration file approaches the complexity of the implementation application. Configuration files were created to add flexibility to an application, and that concept can be taken too far. Hence, it's better for the application to make some assumptions. Remember, flexibility isn't about being able to do everything, but closing as few avenues as possible, making modifications less painful while implementation remains relatively simple.

At a technical level, a dynamic dispatcher architecture is very similar to a static dispatcher architecture. The dynamic dispatcher has the additional ability to unload an assembly. In implementation terms, unloading an assembly is more complicated because of the way .NET loads and unloads assemblies.

.NET uses *Application Domains* (AppDomains), which are containers for assemblies. To unload an assembly, you have to unload the AppDomain rather than the assembly itself. In .NET terms, an AppDomain is a construct, loosely defined, used to represent a process in .NET. The words "loosely defined" apply because an AppDomain is specific to .NET and represents a way of isolating assemblies, security descriptors, etc. In the early days of Java, when two Java applications were executing, each could see the static data of the other process. This is problematic because it meant that when two Java applications were using the same class with a static data member, each would see the same data. In .NET terms, this problem is solved using AppDomains.

AppDomains provide separate execution spaces for .NET assemblies so that a loaded assembly sees its own security descriptors, fault protection, and set of assemblies. When a loaded assembly attempts to make a cross-AppDomain call, it requires serialization and proxying. It isn't as simple as when an assembly calls another assembly within the same AppDomain.

In terms of the Client-Dispatcher-Server pattern, the AppDomain hierarchy is identical to what you see in Figure 4-8.

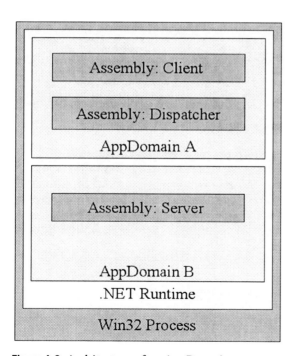

Figure 4-8. *Architecture of an AppDomain*

For the purposes of illustration, both AppDomains A and B reside in the same Win32 process. In an implementation, the AppDomains could reside in different processes or on different computers. The assemblies that represent the dispatcher and client server are hosted in AppDomain A. The server assemblies are hosted in AppDomain B. To reload the server assembly, AppDomain B is unloaded and the assemblies are reloaded. As a safety measure, each instance of the server's objects could be hosted in their own AppDomain. It's safer coding because if one server instance messes up its state, the other server instances aren't affected.

Now that you have an understanding of static and dynamic dispatchers, it's time to examine the Client-Dispatcher-Server pattern architecture.

Architecting the Client-Dispatcher-Server Pattern

The Client-Dispatcher-Server pattern is implemented using three architectural blocks. The first block is the base architecture, which is illustrated in Figure 4-9.

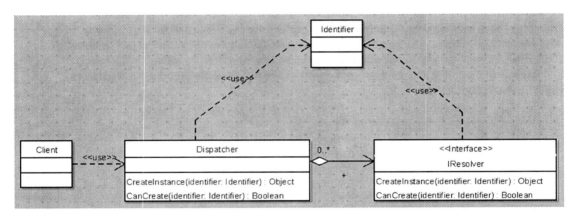

Figure 4-9. *UML architecture of the Client-Dispatcher-Server pattern*

The Client type uses the Dispatcher type, which has two methods: CanCreate and CreateInstance. The Dispatcher is a controller class that references a number of IResolver interface implementations. The purpose of the IResolver interface is to provide a mechanism whereby a type identifier can be converted into an object instance. The Dispatcher manages a collection of IResolver implementations, allowing servers to be registered and defined using multiple techniques. Both IResolver and Dispatcher use the type Identifier, which is a black box that makes type definition as flexible as possible.

Architecting the Resolver Type

In implementation terms, the IResolver type is defined as follows:

```
public interface IResolver<Identifier> {
    void Load();
    void Unload();
    bool CanCreate( Identifier identifier );
    ObjectType CreateInstance<ObjectType>( Identifier identifier );
}
```

The `IResolver` interface is a Generics-based interface that has two Generic parameters: `Identifier` and `ObjectType`. The Generic parameter `Identifier` refers to the type used to identify an assembly and type. The `Identifier` could be the .NET framework `Type` or a custom identifier. The Generic type `ObjectType` associated with the method `CreateInstance`, known as a *method-based Generic type*, represents the type that is being cast to. Usually, this will be an abstract base class or an interface. Using a Generic method saves a typecast, as an implementation of the `CreateInstance` method will perform the typecast.

The methods `Load` and `Unload` load and unload an `IResolver` implementation. The idea behind different `IResolver` implementations is to let the implementation determine how to instantiate assemblies, which will include the dynamic loading and unloading of assemblies, but these processes are instigated using the methods `Load` and `Unload`. This makes it possible for an `IResolver` implementation to reference multiple AppDomains, remoting-based objects, or even web services objects.

Architecting the Dispatcher Type

The `Dispatcher` type is defined as follows:

```
public abstract class Dispatcher<Identifier> {
    protected LinkedList<IResolver<Identifier>> _resolvers =
        new LinkedList<IResolver<Identifier>>();

    public abstract void Initialize();
    public abstract void Destroy();

    public void Load() {
        Initialize();
        foreach( IResolver resolver in _resolvers ) {
            resolver.Load();
        }
    }
    public void Unload() {
        foreach( IResolver resolver in _resolvers ) {
            resolver.Unload();
        }
        Destroy();
    }
    public ObjectType CreateInstance<ObjectType>( Identifier identifier ) {
        foreach( IResolver resolver in _resolvers ) {
            if( resolver.CanCreate( identifier ) ) {
                return resolver.CreateInstance<ObjectType>( identifier );
            }
        }
        return default( ObjectType );
    }
}
```

The implementation of the `Dispatcher` type is simple and follows the functionality defined previously in this chapter. The methods `Load` and `Unload` load and unload the `IResolver` implementations that most likely will load and unload AppDomains. The `CreateInstance` method instantiates a type. What is different is that no `Add` and `Remove` methods add or remove `IResolver` implementations. The different `IResolver` implementations are managed by the linked list variable `_resolvers`, but there is no way to add or remove `IResolver` implementations.

No `Add` or `Remove` methods are included because they aren't needed. `Dispatcher` is an abstract base class, and to instantiate the class, another class must subclass `Dispatcher`. The responsibility of the subclassed class is to add and remove `IResolver` implementations. A very simple example implementation could be as follows:

```
public class DispatcherImpl : Dispatcher<Identifier> {
    public DispatcherImpl( string applicationName ) {
        _resolvers.AddLast( new ResolverStaticAssemblies( applicationName ) );
    }
    public override void Initialize() {
    }
    public override void Destroy() {
    }
}
```

At first glance, it would appear the type `DispatcherImpl` is breaking multiple pattern rules by not using a factory to instantiate the type `ResolverStaticAssemblies`. Additionally, the `ResolverStaticAssemblies` instance is added to the `_resolvers` variables using hard-coded method calls. The reason the rules are violated is because the `DispatcherImpl` is deliberately a tightly knit implementation. In Chapter 3, I mentioned that sometimes overusing Generics makes code more complicated than less so. And often you are left with no choice but to write very specific code that uses specific instances. The type `DispatcherImpl` is one of those cases.

It isn't possible to define a dispatcher without having to fix the scope of the implementation. Think of it this way: the dispatcher executes in the context of a single AppDomain. This means whenever an `IResolver` implementation is loaded into the current AppDomain, it isn't possible to unload the `IResolver` implementation. When using a `Dispatcher` implementation, which is defined by Generic parameters, the subclassed type must specify the Generic parameters. This means the subclassed type has to have domain-specific knowledge about the `IResolver` implementations. Remember, to instantiate a resolver that uses directories, the directories have to be specified when the `IResolver` implementation is being instantiated. Even if server callbacks are used, some code somewhere has to start the ball rolling and establish the basic rules. Therefore, a `Dispatcher`-derived type has to know things, and it makes no sense trying to be general.

Of course, an argument can be made that the `DispatcherImpl` and `IResolver` implementations all execute in their own AppDomains so that a dynamic reload is possible. That is a solution, but it's also a complication, since the IResolver implementation will not be loaded very often. After all, the Client-Dispatcher-Server pattern is creating an infrastructure for dynamic reloading of objects. By adding the complication of more AppDomains and more dynamic capabilities, the Client-Dispatcher-Server pattern is being recursively embedded in itself—a solution that is asking for trouble.

Having said all this and made the case for breaking several pattern rules, I'll add you should break rules as infrequently as possible and only when necessary. And when you do break the rules, break them all in one spot so that it's easy to diagnose and fix problems. Also, realize that even though the type DispatcherImpl has knowledge about the IResolver implementations, external clients of DispatcherImpl use the Dispatcher type, meaning they will use the IResolver type. This has the end result that only one type has domain-specific knowledge.

This finishes the discussion on the architecture of Client-Dispatcher-Server. Next you'll see how to implement this pattern.

Implementing the Assembly Directory Resolver

An IResolver implementation is free to do what it pleases when cross-referencing an identifier with a type and assembly name. The only necessity is to fulfill the requirements of the IResolver interface. In most cases, this will mean manipulating multiple AppDomains.

Understanding the Big Picture of AppDomains

Using multiple AppDomains isn't as simple as it seems, but once explained, you'll see it's logical and understandable. As an illustration, let's look at a banking example. Don't concern yourself too much with the logic of the banking application, as that will be discussed in the section "Micro-Kernel Pattern." The banking application requires servers, as the servers implement accounts. The client doesn't interface with server-based accounts directly, but interacts with an interface or an abstract base class.

The definitions that are implemented by the servers are as follows:

```
public abstract class Account { }
public interface IAccount { }
```

For the time being, accept that there are two definitions that serve the same purpose, but are defined using either an abstract class or interface. The implementation of either definition is as follows:

```
internal class AbstractClassImpl : Account { }
internal class InterfaceImpl : IAccount { }
```

The objective of the dynamic dispatcher architecture is to be able to instantiate the types AbstractClassImpl or InterfaceImpl, and get in return the types Account or IAccount, respectively. The interfaces are defined in the definitions.dll assembly, and the implementations are defined in the implementations.dll assembly.

In simple terms, the way to instantiate the types is to create a new AppDomain using the method AppDomain.CreateDomain, and then instantiate the type using the method AppDomain.CreateInstanceAndUnwrap. Returned is a proxy instance to an object that is executing in another AppDomain.

What is a gotcha with AppDomains is the metadata. The definitions.dll assembly defines the interface metadata and needs to be loaded in the new and original AppDomains. The implementations.dll assembly only needs to be loaded in the new AppDomain. This means that implementations.dll can be unloaded and loaded again. What can't be reloaded is the definitions.dll. In programming terms, this means it's possible to introduce bug fixes and different implementations, but it isn't possible to change the definition signature without requiring the original AppDomain to be unloaded. Unloading the original AppDomain, generally speaking, means restarting an application.

Imagine running the client application, which calls the dispatcher, which in turn calls the server. The theory of what assemblies get loaded in which AppDomain needs to be tested. The method AppDomain.CurrentDomain.GetAssemblies returns the collection of loaded assemblies for the current AppDomain. Following is the output if the InterfaceImpl type is instantiated:

```
(Local Loaded Assemblies (
    (mscorlib, Version=2.0.0.0, Culture=neutral, PublicKeyToken=b77a5c561934e089)
    (nunit.core, Version=2.2.2.0, Culture=neutral, PublicKeyToken=96d09a1eb7f44a77)
    (nunit.core, Version=2.2.2.0, Culture=neutral, PublicKeyToken=96d09a1eb7f44a77)
    (nunit.util, Version=2.2.2.0, Culture=neutral, PublicKeyToken=null)
    (Chap04.Definitions, Version=1.0.1923.31719,
        Culture=neutral, PublicKeyToken=null)
    (nunit.framework, Version=2.2.2.0, Culture=neutral,
        PublicKeyToken=96d09a1eb7f44a77)
    (Devspace.Commons.Loader, Version=1.0.0.0, Culture=neutral, PublicKeyToken=null)
    (System, Version=2.0.0.0, Culture=neutral, PublicKeyToken=b77a5c561934e089)
    (System.Configuration, Version=2.0.0.0, Culture=neutral,
        PublicKeyToken=b03f5f7f11d50a3a)
    (System.Xml, Version=2.0.0.0, Culture=neutral, PublicKeyToken=b77a5c561934e089)
    (System.Deployment, Version=2.0.0.0, Culture=neutral,
        PublicKeyToken=b03f5f7f11d50a3a)
    (Devspace.Commons, Version=1.0.1923.30158, Culture=neutral, PublicKeyToken=null)
)
(Remote Loaded Assemblies ((Loaded Assemblies (
    (mscorlib, Version=2.0.0.0, Culture=neutral, PublicKeyToken=b77a5c561934e089)
    (System, Version=2.0.0.0, Culture=neutral, PublicKeyToken=b77a5c561934e089)
    (System.Drawing, Version=2.0.0.0, Culture=neutral,
        PublicKeyToken=b03f5f7f11d50a3a)
    (Devspace.Commons.Loader, Version=1.0.0.0, Culture=neutral, PublicKeyToken=null)
    (Chap04.Definitions, Version=1.0.0.0, Culture=neutral, PublicKeyToken=null)
    (Chap04.Implementations, Version=1.0.1923.31719,
        Culture=neutral, PublicKeyToken=null)
)
))
```

Consider the highlighted assembly references and notice how indeed the definitions.dll assembly is loaded in the original AppDomain. For the new AppDomain, both assemblies (definitions.dll and implementations.dll) are loaded. This is what was expected.

Where things become tricky is if the type AbstractClassImpl is instantiated, as the following loaded assembly output is generated:

```
(Local Loaded Assemblies (
    (mscorlib, Version=2.0.0.0, Culture=neutral, PublicKeyToken=b77a5c561934e089)
    (nunit.core, Version=2.2.2.0, Culture=neutral, PublicKeyToken=96d09a1eb7f44a77)
    (nunit.core, Version=2.2.2.0, Culture=neutral, PublicKeyToken=96d09a1eb7f44a77)
    (nunit.util, Version=2.2.2.0, Culture=neutral, PublicKeyToken=null)
```

```
    (Chap04.Definitions, Version=1.0.1923.31719,
        Culture=neutral, PublicKeyToken=null)
    (nunit.framework, Version=2.2.2.0, Culture=neutral,
        PublicKeyToken=96d09a1eb7f44a77)
    (Devspace.Commons.Loader, Version=1.0.0.0, Culture=neutral, PublicKeyToken=null)
    (System, Version=2.0.0.0, Culture=neutral, PublicKeyToken=b77a5c561934e089)
    (System.Configuration, Version=2.0.0.0, Culture=neutral,
        PublicKeyToken=b03f5f7f11d50a3a)
    (System.Xml, Version=2.0.0.0, Culture=neutral, PublicKeyToken=b77a5c561934e089)
    (System.Deployment, Version=2.0.0.0, Culture=neutral,
        PublicKeyToken=b03f5f7f11d50a3a)
    (Chap04.Implementations, Version=1.0.0.0, Culture=neutral,
        PublicKeyToken=null)
    (Devspace.Commons, Version=1.0.1923.30158, Culture=neutral, PublicKeyToken=null)
)
(Remote Loaded Assemblies ((Loaded Assemblies (
    (mscorlib, Version=2.0.0.0, Culture=neutral, PublicKeyToken=b77a5c561934e089)
    (System, Version=2.0.0.0, Culture=neutral, PublicKeyToken=b77a5c561934e089)
    (System.Drawing, Version=2.0.0.0, Culture=neutral,
        PublicKeyToken=b03f5f7f11d50a3a)
    (Devspace.Commons.Loader, Version=1.0.0.0, Culture=neutral, PublicKeyToken=null)
    (Chap04.Implementations, Version=1.0.0.0, Culture=neutral, PublicKeyToken=null)
    (Chap04.Definitions, Version=1.0.1923.31719, Culture=neutral,
        PublicKeyToken=null)
)
))
```

Notice in the highlighted output both assemblies are loaded in both AppDomains. This is because inheritance is used instead of interfaces. With inheritance, .NET loads the implementations.dll assembly because of the additional metadata it needs. When interfaces are used, the proxy only needs the interface signature, and doesn't care about the rest of the type's metadata. This means when defining plug-ins you need to use interfaces, as otherwise errors will be generated or assemblies loaded that shouldn't be.

Understanding the Details of AppDomains

In this section, I'll explain to you the details of implementing an IResolver that supports multiple AppDomains. When an application is loaded, a local AppDomain is created. The local AppDomain has a path reference and has preloaded the base assemblies. The path reference is used when resolving a type to an assembly. In the remote AppDomain, the local path probably can't be used because it refers to the local application, and the assemblies to be loaded are probably in another directory. To load a server in the remote AppDomain, the local path has to be modified to wherever the assemblies to be loaded are located. The remote AppDomain has to be created using a different set of parameters than those of the local AppDomain.

Following is the source code used to create a remote AppDomain:

```
public void Load( bool shadowCopyAll) {
    AppDomainSetup setup = new AppDomainSetup();

    setup.ApplicationBase = AppDomain.CurrentDomain.BaseDirectory;
    AssignPrivateBinPath( setup);
    AssignShawdowPath( setup, shadowCopyAll );
    setup.ApplicationName = _applicationName;

    _appDomain = AppDomain.CreateDomain( _applicationName, null, setup);

    Permissions.SetAppDomainPolicy( _appDomain);

    _remoteLoader = (RemoteLoader)_appDomain.CreateInstanceAndUnwrap(
        "devspace.commons.loader", "Devspace.Commons.Loader.RemoteLoader");
}
```

The type AppDomainSetup creates a new AppDomain that will be added to the collection of currently active AppDomains. When an AppDomain searches for a type or an assembly, the paths must be assigned. Two path properties can be assigned: ApplicationBase and PrivateBinPath. ApplicationBase accepts a single path and is the main directory of the AppDomain. For example, when the AppDomain loads the application configuration file, the main directory is searched.

The custom method AssignPrivateBinPath assigns the property PrivateBinPath. A custom method is used because the property PrivateBinPath can reference multiple paths where each path element is separated by a semicolon. The assigned paths can be either relative or absolute. If the path is relative, then concatenating the property ApplicationBase with the relative path creates an absolute path. If you are using Linux or OSX, a colon is required. Getting the value from the property System.IO.Path.PathSeperator retrieves the platform-specific separator.

The property ApplicationName identifies the AppDomain. This property should be assigned a unique value because when shadow copying is enabled, the ApplicationName represents a unique subdirectory. The method AssignShadowPath assigns the shadow and cache directories, which will be discussed next. Once the paths and application name have been assigned, it's possible to create an AppDomain using the method AppDomain.CreateDomain. The returned AppDomain instance represents the remote AppDomain that can be used to load assemblies that can be unloaded at a later point in time.

The following code creates an object:

```
public ObjectType CreateInstance<ObjectType>( Identifier identifier ) {
    if( identifier.DoesExist( Identifier.ID_type ) ) {
        string typeIdentifier = identifier[ Identifier.ID_type];
        string assemblyIdentifier =
            _remoteLoader.FindAssemblyForType( typeIdentifier );

        return (ObjectType)_appDomain.CreateInstanceAndUnwrap(
            assemblyIdentifier, typeIdentifier );
    }
    return default(ObjectType);
}
```

When the method _appDomain.CreateInstanceAndUnwrap is called, an assembly (devspace. commons.loader) is loaded in the remote AppDomain, and the type Devspace.Commons. Loader.RemoteLoader is instantiated. When a type is instantiated in a nonlocal AppDomain, it isn't the type Object that is returned, rather the type ObjectHandle. To access the underlying object instance, which is the proxy, the ObjectHandle type has to be unwrapped. Unwrapping calls the property ObjectHandler.Unwrap and returns the object instance.

Using Shadow Copying

Shadow copying is manipulated using three properties, although not all three are required. When an AppDomain loads an assembly, the assembly is locked for read access. The assembly is unlocked when the AppDomains that reference the assembly are unloaded, with one caveat: if a type such as Entry is defined and passed across AppDomain boundaries, the assembly has to be unloaded in all assemblies.

Replacing a locked assembly isn't possible, which makes it impossible to dynamically update an assembly. A solution would be to force the application to unload the assemblies, which are then updated before the assemblies are reloaded. Another solution is to use a shadow copy. When shadowing is enabled, the assembly is copied to a temporary neutral location before being loaded into an AppDomain. This makes it possible to overwrite the original assembly. The updated assembly is loaded when a new AppDomain requests the assembly. Already existing AppDomains won't be able to dynamically reload the assembly and must first be unloaded. Simply put, instead of exiting and restarting an application, the application can reload the assemblies while running.

Following is the source code that illustrates the implementation of AssignShadowPath used for active shadow copying:

```
protected virtual void AssignShawdowPath( AppDomainSetup setup,
    bool shawdowCopyAll ) {
    if( shawdowCopyAll ) {
        setup.ShadowCopyFiles = "true";
    }
    else {
        if( _shadowPaths.Count == 0) {
            return;
        }
        OperatingSystem os = System.Environment.OSVersion;
        string fullpath = "";
        if( (int)os.Platform == 128 ) {
            foreach( string path in _paths ) {
                fullpath += path + ":";
            }
        }
        else {
            foreach( string path in _paths ) {
                fullpath += path + ";";
            }
        }
```

```
            setup.ShadowCopyDirectories = fullpath;
        }
        if( _cacheDirectory.Length > 0 ) {
            setup.CachePath = _cacheDirectory;
        }
    }
}
```

In the implementation of the method AssignShadowPath, the three properties related to shadow copying are assigned depending on certain conditions. If the variable shadowCopyAll is true, then all assemblies should be shadow copied whenever an assembly is loaded. To activate this scenario, the property AppDomainSetup.ShadowCopyFiles is assigned to a string-based true value.

Another scenario is to only shadow copy assemblies located in specific directories. To do this, the property ShadowCopyFiles doesn't need to be assigned, but the property ShadowCopyDirectories is assigned to the paths that should be shadowed. For example, the directories referenced by the property PrivateBinPath could be shadowed, but the directory referenced by the property ApplicationBase couldn't. Or even a directory not referenced by either path properties could be shadowed. You would do this when you use the method LoadFrom to load a specific assembly located in a specific directory.

If shadowing is active, the .NET runtime needs to pick a location where the assembly is temporarily copied. The property AppDomainSetup.CachePath is concatenated with the property AppDomainSetup.ApplicationName, which specifies the root directory to where the shadowed assembly will be copied. The default is to copy the assembly to the directory %userprofile%\ local settings\application data\assembly concatenated with AppDomainSetup.ApplicationName.

Implementing a Web Service Resolver

Thus far, all of the resolver concepts presented consider the assembly and type locally installed. The reason why I haven't explicitly discussed a topic like .NET remoting is because calling across AppDomains requires using .NET remoting techniques. The only difference between calling across AppDomains and .NET remoting is that the instantiation of the .NET components when called across AppDomains doesn't use the .NET remoting calls. To implement a .NET remoting–capable resolver, a new IResolver implementation based on .NET channels needs to be created. Otherwise, the rules of interfaces and types apply for both cross-AppDomain method calling and .NET remoting calls.

Where things go awry is when the client attempts to call a web service. The problem isn't web services per se, rather how .NET 2.0 generates proxies. Consider the following interface as being a web service:

```
public interface ITestServiceSoap {
    string Echo(string a);
    int Add(int a, int b);
}
```

The web service ITestServiceSoap has two methods, Echo and Add. They are simple methods that echo a sent buffer and add two numbers together. The methods aren't important, and neither is the web service. What is important is to consider the interface as a web service that will be called.

To call a .NET web service, a proxy has to be generated. If you use Visual Studio, it includes wizards that do this automatically. Using the console, the following command generates a proxy:

```
$ wsdl http://jupiter:8008/1.1/webservice/TestService.asmx?page=wsdl
Microsoft (R) Web Services Description Language Utility
[Microsoft(R) .NET Framework, Version 2.0.41202.0]
Copyright (C) Microsoft Corporation. All rights reserved.


Writing file 'C:\cygwin\home\cgross\desktop\documents\active\
    oop-using-net-patterns\src\Chap04.Webservice\webservice\TestService.cs'.
```

The wsdl command converts a Web Services Description Language (WSDL) file into a proxy. A WSDL file is the equivalent of an interface in web-service-speak.

The generated wsdl file will appear similar to the following (please note that most of the file has been cut out to simplify the explanation):

```
[System.Diagnostics.DebuggerStepThroughAttribute()]
[System.ComponentModel.DesignerCategoryAttribute("code")]
[System.Web.Services.WebServiceBindingAttribute(
    Name="TestServiceSoap", Namespace="http://tempuri.org/")]
public partial class TestService :
    System.Web.Services.Protocols.SoapHttpClientProtocol {
}
```

The type TestService is a class, and this is a problem for the Client-Dispatcher-Server pattern, because it expects an interface or at least an abstract base class.

There is no magic hook to regenerate the code so that an interface is defined and referenced in the TestService type. The only solution is to run the wsdl generator twice as illustrated here:

```
$ wsdl /serverInterface
    http://jupiter:8008/1.1/webservice/TestService.asmx?page=wsdl
Microsoft (R) Web Services Description Language Utility
[Microsoft(R) .NET Framework, Version 2.0.41202.0]
Copyright (C) Microsoft Corporation. All rights reserved.


Writing file 'C:\cygwin\home\cgross\desktop\documents\active\
oop-using-net-patterns\src\Chap04.Webservice\webservice\
TestServiceInterfaces.cs'.
$ wsdl http://jupiter:8008/1.1/webservice/TestService.asmx?page=wsdl
Microsoft (R) Web Services Description Language Utility
[Microsoft(R) .NET Framework, Version 2.0.41202.0]
Copyright (C) Microsoft Corporation. All rights reserved.


Writing file 'C:\cygwin\home\cgross\desktop\documents\active\
oop-using-net-patterns\src\Chap04.Webservice\webservice\TestService.cs'.
```

In the first instance of running the wsdl command, the command-line option /serverInterface is used. This option generates a file that contains an interface that implements a web service on the server. The trick lies in taking the generated file, removing all of the attributes, and then subclassing the type `TestServiceInterface` in the type `TestService`. The resulting code will appear similar to the following:

```
[System.Diagnostics.DebuggerStepThroughAttribute()]
[System.ComponentModel.DesignerCategoryAttribute("code")]
[System.Web.Services.WebServiceBindingAttribute(
    Name="TestServiceSoap", Namespace="http://tempuri.org/")]
public partial class TestService :
    System.Web.Services.Protocols.SoapHttpClientProtocol, ITestServiceSoap {
}
```

Optionally, this redefined type is then encapsulated in a factory as illustrated by the following source code:

```
namespace Chap04.Webservice {
    public static class Factory {
        public static ITestServiceSoap Create() {
            TestService srvc = new TestService();
            return srvc;
        }
    }
}
```

The three pieces of code, `TestService`, `TestServiceInterface`, and `Chap04.WebService.Factory`, are compiled into an assembly. The assembly then behaves like any locally installed assembly, except when the contained type is called, the call is delegated to a remotely located web service implementation.

We've come to the end of this discussion of the Client-Dispatcher-Server pattern. Next up, I'll present one final structural pattern to round out this chapter: the Micro-Kernel pattern.

Micro-Kernel Pattern

The Micro-Kernel pattern[3] makes it possible for systems to adapt to changing requirements. The big picture idea of the Micro-Kernel pattern is to future-proof an application so that a change in the application won't require extensive recoding of the entire application. This pattern sounds promising, but has had a bad reputation because of how it has been used in the industry.

The Micro-Kernel pattern is usually associated with an operating system. For example, the original version of Windows NT had a micro-kernel architecture. The GNU Hurd operating system had a micro-kernel architecture. For many people, the original version of Windows NT and GNU Hurd aren't the best examples of how to properly implement a micro-kernel architecture, as both operating systems were slow.

Micro-kernels can be slow for operating systems because operating systems require that there be as few abstractions as possible. For an application, a micro-kernel isn't slow since applications tend to be based on abstraction. Architecting a micro-kernel can be difficult if the pattern isn't followed. The pattern has a certain degree of redundancy built in, which, when

---

3. *Pattern-Oriented Software Architecture, Volume 1: A System of Patterns*, p. 171.

not properly implemented, will make an implementation difficult. If the intent of the pattern is followed properly, then the micro-kernel is efficient, easy to maintain, and easy to extend.

In the upcoming sections, we'll take a closer look at the architecture for this pattern, followed by hiding and designing the micro-kernel, and implementing this pattern. Finally, I'll demonstrate how it all works in a simple banking application.

Architecture of the Micro-Kernel

The rules of the micro-kernel are fairly simple and can best be expressed using Figure 4-10.

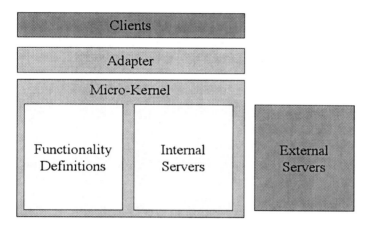

Figure 4-10. *Macro-level architecture of the Micro-Kernel pattern*

In Figure 4-10, you see four major functionalities: clients, adapter, micro-kernel, and external servers. The adapter is similar to the Adapter pattern presented in Chapter 5. For reference purposes, the adapter in this context has an additional functionality built in that borrows from the Façade pattern, which is discussed in Chapter 6. Within the micro-kernel box are two other boxes: functionality definitions and internal servers.

The clients of Figure 4-10 are the consumers of the micro-kernel. The consumers interact with the micro-kernel using only the functionality offered by the adapter. The client won't have detailed knowledge of the inner workings of the micro-kernel.

The micro-kernel defines the application logic and implements the infrastructure logic of the application. Defining the application means defining the interfaces, abstract base classes, and so on. Implementing the infrastructure logic of the application means to define how to load assemblies, process configuration information, and so on. The internal servers are the gopher classes for the micro-kernel. They are responsible for loading files, accessing the registry, retrieving GUI elements, and so on. The external servers implement the interfaces defined by the micro-kernel.

An explicit reference to internal servers and external servers is included. Internal servers are pieces of implemented functionality needed by the micro-kernel to carry out the business logic, but aren't part of the micro-kernel, as the internal server isn't directly related to the micro-kernel. Adding the internal server to the micro-kernel would bloat the kernel. The external servers are pieces of functionality used indirectly by the client though the micro-kernel, which serves as a middle entity.

In a nutshell, the idea of the micro-kernel is to create an architecture that can last for many application version numbers. What changes are the implementations of the individual pieces, but the contracts between the pieces remain for the large part identical. Important to realize is that each component can be changed independently without affecting the overall architecture. This is what makes the micro-kernel architecture so powerful and flexible.

Hiding the Details of the Micro-Kernel

Starting with a top-down analysis of the micro-kernel, the client interacts with the adapter, and the client has no detailed knowledge of the micro-kernel implementation. This is done on purpose: a micro-kernel, internal server, and external server implement some functionality. The functionality will use details such as lists, serialization, and association of types with each other. To make the micro-kernel do anything useful, you need to assemble the individual functionalities. This requires specific knowledge of the system, which the client shouldn't need. To understand this, consider the following source code:

```
class Math {
    public Decimal Addition( Decimal val1, Decimal val2 ) {
        return Decimal.Add( val1, val2 );
    }
}

class SimplerMath {
    public int Add( int val1, int val2 ) {
        Math math = new Math();

        return (int)(math.Addition( new Decimal( val1 ), new Decimal( val2 ) ));
    }
}
```

The class Math has a single method, Addition, which is used to add two numbers. I employ the type Decimal so that the method Addition is as useful in as many contexts as possible. The Decimal type is powerful in that it doesn't round off nor lose significant digits. The problem with the Decimal type, however, is that it isn't a native data type and requires additional knowledge on behalf of the coder.

To hide the complexities of the class SimplerMath, the method Add uses the native data type int. Using the SimplerMath type means using the Math type indirectly. The SimplerMath type provides a simpler-to-use interface and a bridge to the Math type.

This is one of the purposes of the adapter, in that it knows what the subsystem does and knows how to do it, so that the client doesn't need to know about it. Let me point out very quickly that the SimplerMath type isn't safe, as underflow and overflow situations could occur. And two floating-point numbers couldn't be added, as there are no methods available that can add use floating-point numbers. This ignores the purpose of the adapter, which is supposed to do the following:

- Hide the complexities of the micro-kernel.

- Hide micro-kernel dependencies.

- Provide a bridge between the client and the external servers and the micro-kernel.

The adapter is clever in that it knows how to piece together all of the external servers and how to call the micro-kernel. In effect, the adapter is the application programming interface (API) to the micro-kernel. The client only needs to know about the API.

Designing a Micro-Kernel

Implementing a micro-kernel isn't that simple because what might be considered as part of the micro-kernel might be an external or internal server, or even part of the adapter. The best way to understand how to design and implement a micro-kernel is to know the roles of each piece of the micro-kernel.

The micro-kernel will have to fulfill the following roles:

- Provide the basic access to the resources used by the internal servers, external servers, and emulators.

- Provide the framework that binds together the internal servers, external servers, and emulators.

- Provide the core functionality in abstract terms, meaning as few as possible actual implementations are created. Supplied are the definitions used by all of the other pieces.

When designing a micro-kernel, the key objective is to keep the kernel compact and focused; it should offer basic functionalities and delegate everything else. A micro-kernel should be updated as little as possible. In application design terms, the micro-kernel should always be using interfaces or abstract base classes.

The Bridge pattern and Micro-Kernel pattern do tie together, as the adapter uses the logic exposed by the external servers. Remember from Chapter 3 that the Bridge pattern focuses on a single aspect of the business logic, whereas the adapter focuses on the entire application.

The internal servers have to fulfill the following roles:

- Implement additional logic that isn't part of the micro-kernel.

- Encapsulate system specifics that are relevant to the micro-kernel.

The internal servers have a critical role to fulfill in that they are responsible for making the micro-kernel work properly. In a nutshell, the internal servers are gophers (they go get this and go get that) for the micro-kernel. For example, if the micro-kernel needs a configuration file, an internal server would supply that. Ideally, the internal server would provide a neutral interface so that a configuration file could be loaded from a local file or remote database. The micro-kernel shouldn't be aware where the data is loaded from, as the micro-kernel only cares about the configuration information.

Micro-kernels are also one of the ugliest pieces of code because they try to walk the thin line between abstraction and being too complex. Going back to the configuration file example, a coder could write an internal server that has the ability to read configuration information from any location using any storage engine. This might be attractive, but is useless if the configuration file will only ever be stored on the local hard disk. A well-implemented internal server provides a neutral interface to the micro-kernel without attempting to solve all programmatic ills related to the task.

And finally, the external servers have to fulfill the following role:

- Provide a programming interface used by the micro-kernel and adapter.

The external servers are simple to define as they only need to fulfill the role of doing the hard work that the micro-kernel, client, and adapter expect of them.

Micro-Kernel Implementation Details

The implementation of a micro-kernel starts with the definition of the logic that will be used by the other pieces of the Micro-Kernel pattern. Let's consider the following source code, which does nothing major, but is assembled as a micro-kernel would be:

```
namespace SimpleMicroKernel {
    interface IExternal {
        void DoSomething();
    }
    class ExternalServer : IExternal {
        public virtual void DoSomething() {
        }
    }

    class MicroKernel {
        public IExternal FindExternal() {
            return new ExternalServer();
        }
    }

    class Adapter {
        public void EasyDoSomething() {
            MicroKernel mk = new MicroKernel();
            IExternal external = new ExternalServer();
            external.DoSomething();
        }
    }
}
```

The only piece of the Micro-Kernel pattern that is missing is the internal server, which in this simple example wasn't needed. The interface IExternal is the contract between the adapter and the external server. The type ExternalServer implements the IExternal interface. The type MicroKernel has a single method, FindExternal, which acts like a Bridge pattern that instantiates an instance of ExternalServer. The type Adapter instantiates the MicroKernel type, retrieves an instance to IExternal, and calls the method DoSomething.

Building a Simple Banking Application

Having gone through the design of a micro-kernel and some practical implementation details, I'll construct a micro-kernel based on a business application need: a simple banking application that can manage accounts. The account must be flexible so different account types can be defined.

Defining the Interfaces

The first step in the design is to figure out the business application process, which means to design the interfaces used by the external servers. For this example, the following interfaces are defined:

```
namespace Definitions {
    public interface IAccount {
        void Add( Entry entry );
        Decimal Balance {
            get;
        }
    }
    public interface IClient {
        void Add( IAccount account );
        void Remove( IAccount account );
    }
}
```

Only two interfaces are necessary: IAccount and IClient. The IClient interface has only two methods: one that associates an account with a client and another that removes the account association. The IAccount interface has two methods: one adds entries, and the second is a property that finds the balance of the account.

The interface method IAccount.Add is structurally correct, but not correct in regard to business logic. Logically, the IAccount methods should be used to deposit or withdraw money, and therefore the business logic should be to have the methods Deposit or Withdraw. However, this isn't correct structurally because a bank doesn't understand the concept of a deposit or a withdrawal, as these are concepts known to the client. The bank sees an entry in the bank account that is either positive to indicate a deposit or negative to indicate a withdrawal. Fees are interesting in that they are based on the number of withdrawals or on each transaction, and again account for a minus value. The balance in the account is a summation of the entries. To be consistent, the micro-kernel employs methods to add entries, and the adapter uses those methods to deposit or withdraw money.

The Entry type that has been referenced but not defined represents a banking transaction and is as follows:

```
[Serializable]
public struct Entry {
    public readonly Decimal value;
    public readonly Decimal charges;
    public readonly string purpose;
    public readonly bool positive;
```

```
        public Entry( Decimal inpValue, Decimal inpCharges,
            string inpPurpose, bool inpPositive) {
            value = inpValue;
            charges = inpCharges;
            purpose = inpPurpose;
            positive = inpPositive;
        }
    }
```

Entry is defined as a value type using the struct keyword. A value type is used because the entry type is data based on a record. There are four public data members: value, charges, purpose, and positive. The data members aren't defined as properties because the data members are read-only and part of the value type. It's important to make the data members read-only so that the data type becomes immutable. The attribute Serializable is associated with the type Entry because it's required when making cross-AppDomain method calls.

Defining the Abstract Base Classes

The external servers expose interfaces and not base classes because of the metadata problem. There is still the need to define abstract base classes to implement helper classes. For the banking system, the abstract base class for the IAccount interface is defined as follows:

```
public abstract class Account : MarshalByRefObject {
    protected List< Entry> _entries = new List< Entry>();

    public virtual Decimal Balance {
        get {
            Decimal balance = new Decimal( 0);
            foreach( Entry entry in _entries) {
                if( entry.positive ) {
                    balance = Decimal.Add( balance, entry.value);
                }
                else {
                    balance = Decimal.Subtract( balance, entry.value);
                }
                balance = Decimal.Subtract( balance, entry.charges);

            return balance;
        }
    }
    public virtual void Add( Entry entry) {
        _entries.Add( entry);
    }
```

```
    public System.Collections.IEnumerator GetEnumerator() {
        foreach( Entry entry in _entries) {
            yield return entry;
        }
    }
}
```

The type Account derives from the type MarshalByRefObject, which is necessary if the type will be used to make a cross-AppDomain method call. The virtual methods Balance and Add are default implementations that manage bank account entries. The entries are stored in a Generics-based List type. The method GetEnumerator is a .NET 2.0 enhancement that iterates the bank account entries. All of the methods in the Account type are helper methods that make it simpler to define an account type.

Regarding the necessity of the Account type to derive from the MarshalByRefObject type: this requirement is only necessary if the external servers will be executed in a remote domain. The MarshalByRefObject type indicates to the .NET runtime that when a type instance is being referenced across AppDomains, the type shouldn't be serialized. In contrast, the type Entry has a Serializable attribute, indicating that when an object instance is passed across AppDomains, the object instance should be serialized and instantiated locally. Adding a Serializable attribute to the Account type would defeat the purpose of plug-ins, as it means that the Account type would be instantiated in the local AppDomain. When a reference is used, the .NET runtime creates a proxy that delegates any method calls into the remote AppDomain.

Creating a Micro-Kernel–Specific Resolver

The resolver used in the Micro-Kernel pattern is the Client-Dispatcher-Server pattern. The client, though, is the adapter, and the dispatcher is the micro-kernel. Therefore, the implementation is relatively simple, as the following illustrates:

```
public class Resolver :
    Devspace.Commons.Loader.Dispatcher<Devspace.Commons.Loader.Identifier> {
    Devspace.Commons.Loader.ResolverStaticAssemblies _resolverImpl;

    public override void Initialize() {
        _resolverImpl = new Devspace.Commons.Loader.ResolverStaticAssemblies(
            InternalServers.GeneralIdentifiers.ApplicationName );
        InternalServers.PathsResolver.AppendPaths( this );
    }
    public override void Destroy() {
    }
    internal void AppendPaths( string paths ) {
        _resolverImpl.AppendPath( paths );
        _resolverImpl = null;
    }
    public Resolver() {
    }
```

```
    public Definitions.IClient CreateClient() {
        return CreateInstance<Definitions.IClient>(
            new Devspace.Commons.Loader.Identifier(
                InternalServers.PathsResolver.ExternalServer,
                InternalServers.AssemblyIdentifierResolver.Client ) );
    }
    public Definitions.IAccount CreateAccount() {
        return CreateInstance<Definitions.IAccount>(
            new Devspace.Commons.Loader.Identifier(
                InternalServers.PathsResolver.ExternalServer,
                InternalServers.AssemblyIdentifierResolver.Account ) );
    }
}
```

The type Resolver subclasses the type Devspace.Commons.Loader.Dispatcher. At the end of the Client-Dispatcher-Server pattern discussion presented earlier, I mentioned how it was acceptable for any subclass of Dispatcher to not use factories, or interfaces, and so on. The Resolver type illustrates how specific a Dispatcher subclass can become. Consider the methods CreateClient and CreateAccount. Each creates an interface instance, but the controlling parameters of which assembly to call and the context is very specific. It's specific to the implementation of the micro-kernel, and there is no way that the Client-Dispatcher-Server pattern could ever figure it out—the permutations are simply too large.

In this example, the Resolver type is hard-coded with respect to the Dispatcher subclass, but is generic with respect to the Micro-Kernel pattern. This is because the assembly identifiers and type identifiers are managed by a set of classes in the InternalServers namespace. InternalServers references multiple types that know which paths to use and which identifiers to retrieve. The InternalServers namespace is identical to the internal servers of the Micro-Kernel pattern, and are responsible for figuring out where the configuration information is. The micro-kernel only references those configuration entries using properties or methods.

Implementing the External Servers

The external servers only need to implement the interfaces defined in the micro-kernel, IAccount and IClient, as in the following example:

```
internal class LocalAccountRemotable :
    Definitions.Account, Definitions.IAccount {
    public override void Add( Definitions.Entry entry ) {
        base.Add( entry );
    }
    public override Decimal Balance {
        get {
            return base.Balance;
        }
    }
}
```

```
internal class LocalClientRemotable :
    Definitions.Client, Definitions.IClient {
    public override void Add( Definitions.IAccount account ) {
        base.Add( account );
    }
    public override void Remove( Definitions.IAccount account ) {
        base.Remove( account );
    }
}
```

The types `LocalAccountRemotable` and `LocalClientRemotable` subclass their respective interfaces, but they also subclass the abstract base classes `Account` and `Client`. The subclassing of the abstract base classes, which is optional, is meant to simplify implementation of the interfaces. If you wanted to use your own abstract base classes instead, it would be entirely acceptable. However, you must remember to derive your external servers from `MarshalByRefObject`; otherwise, an error will result when calling the type across AppDomains. Notice in the interface method implementations of the types `LocalAccountRemotable` and `LocalClientRemotable` how the subclassed methods are called using the base reference. And one last item to note is the inclusion of the `internal` scope identifier, which prohibits using direct references for the types.

Implementing the Adapter

The last piece of the micro-kernel that needs to be implemented is the adapter. None of the pieces illustrated thus far have a has-a relationship, more an indirect uses-a relationship. The exceptions to this statement in the architecture are the micro-kernel and internal server pieces. The adapter ties everything together and presents an API that the client can use.

For the banking application, the adapter source code would be as follows:

```
public class Bank {
    Definitions.IAccount _account;
    public static Definitions.IClient CreateClient() {
        Implementations.Resolver resolver = new Implementations.Resolver();
        return resolver.CreateClient();
    }
    public static Definitions.IAccount CreateAccount( Definitions.IClient client ) {
        Implementations.Resolver resolver = new Implementations.Resolver();
        Definitions.IAccount account = resolver.CreateAccount();
        client.Add( account );
        return account;
    }
    public static Bank CreateBank() {
        return new Bank();
    }
    private Bank() {
    }
```

```
    public Definitions.IAccount ClientAccount {
        get {
            return _account;
        }
        set {
            _account = value;
        }
    }
    public void MakeDeposit( Decimal value ) {
        _account.Add( new Definitions.Entry( value,
            Implementations.ChargeCosts.GetDepositCharge(),
            "Default deposit", true ) );
    }
    public void MakeWithdrawal( Decimal value ) {
        _account.Add( new Definitions.Entry( value,
            Implementations.ChargeCosts.GetWithdrawalCharge(),
            "Default withdrawal", false ) );
    }
}
```

In a "big picture" sense, the Bank type is a self-contained type, which means that the client doesn't require extensive assembling of the necessary interfaces and types. The client of the type Bank only needs to call the appropriate methods. The Bank type is created using the method CreateBank, which is a simple factory. Notice how the constructor of the Bank type has a scope of private, making it impossible for any external client to instantiate.

The methods CreateClient and CreateAccount are like factories to create an individual client and account type. However, they aren't factories in the structural sense. They are methods used in the business process of creating a client and account. When an account is created using CreateAccount, a client interface reference has to be given. The implementations of the creation methods reference the Resolver type that is defined in the micro-kernel.

The property ClientAccount is the account that will be used when making deposits and withdrawals. For the implementations of the methods MakeDeposit and MakeWithdrawal, methods and definitions from the micro-kernel are assembled to carry out a business process.

Some Final Considerations for the Micro-Kernel Pattern

The micro-kernel is an extensive pattern that, when implemented, acts like a container for the external servers. This is the approach you should take when implementing your own micro-kernel. However, what you should never think about is turning your micro-kernel into a very sophisticated container that attempts to solve more complex issues like scalability. This is because many pieces of the micro-kernel use black boxes where the implementation details are delegated.

The best example of this is the Resolver type in the micro-kernel. Instead of implementing a new resolution mechanism, the Client-Dispatcher-Server pattern was plugged in. The resulting micro-kernel works, even though multiple patterns were combined. This is why you should never have grand plans when building your own container—it isn't necessary, nor desirable.

The Micro-Kernel pattern has clear distinctions of the responsibilities of each piece that makes up a complete micro-kernel. It's important to only implement the responsibilities required of each piece. For example, the adapter marries the micro-kernel with the external servers and carries out some business logic. The micro-kernel is kept small and focuses on structural issues of the application. The internal servers connect platform specifics with the micro-kernel. And the external servers process the bulk of the business logic. The reason for separating the various functionalities is to make it simpler to adapt the micro-kernel for future extensions. Doing so, you will be rewarded with a system that has future-proof capabilities built in.

Some Final Thoughts

Originally, when I came up with the outline for this chapter, I'd planned to discuss the patterns in this order: Micro-Kernel, Pipes and Filters, and Client-Dispatcher-Server. Off I went and implemented the Micro-Kernel pattern, and when I finished the application for this pattern, I realized very quickly that the order was wrong.

At that point, I had to take a step back and consider my next step. What triggered my realization of the wrong order was that the Resolver implemented for the Micro-Kernel pattern was in fact a prototype Client-Dispatcher-Server pattern implementation. I knew that if I continued following my original outline, you might realize that the examples contain multiple implementations of the same pattern. This could confuse you, and I would have to explain why I created two implementations that do nearly the same thing. I couldn't get around this problem without changing my approach.

After wrestling with this dilemma, I comprehended something more important about this chapter and patterns in general. The answer came by stepping back and thinking about what this book is trying to achieve. This book is about using patterns in real-life .NET applications. Here I preach that patterns are pluggable and the proof is in the pudding, which is if I am able to replace the Resolver code with the Client-Dispatcher-Server pattern without any complications. Because if I could not replace the code, it would mean patterns are nothing more than a bunch of buzzwords.

A funny thing happened. My new approach worked so effectively I even surprised myself. By default, I was putting black boxes in my pattern code, which means the old code could be ripped out easily and replaced with the Client-Dispatcher-Server implementation. The ramifications of the change resulted in altering only one class of the written micro-kernel, namely, the type Resolver, thereby proving that pluggable patterns in .NET do exist.

So the final consideration for this chapter isn't that these patterns work or are effective, rather that the magic of patterns lies in the ability to assemble them block by block. Thinking in grand frameworks is the wrong approach and makes an application fragile and hard to change. Of course, Generics, which were used extensively in this chapter, go a long way toward the goal of working productively with patterns.

CHAPTER 5

Implementing Component Groupings

Writing components is difficult because components have to reference other components. Creating a single component that doesn't use other components in the application other than the base .NET library is relatively simple and straightforward. Constructing an overall architecture when it's been sketched out is relatively straightforward as well. Where the fun begins is in the creating of a group of components that are related and reference each other to implement some application logic.

The problem with writing groups of components is that you start out and write well-thought-out components that reference other components. Then bug reports and feature requests trickle in. The initial grouping that looked good and worked now needs extensions and fixing. At that point, references are created that result in brittle code and make it difficult to extend and maintain the grouping of components.

This chapter is about managing a grouping of components and arranging them such that maintenance and writing extensions isn't difficult. The chapter starts out with a couple of object-oriented faux pas. Then the rest of the chapter implements a translation service that is split into two sections: the first section implements the basic translation service application, and the second section extends the basic translation service.

Two Traditional Object-Oriented Faux Pas

Sometimes certain things are said that aren't entirely true. Maybe they were true at the time when they were said, but times change and environment conditions change as well. Thus what was originally the truth turns out to be not entirely correct. The problem with these half-truths is that they make people feel guilty about acting on them or saying them without knowing the logic. If the logic is explained, very often people will do the right thing.

Did you know that Eskimo is the wrong word for people of the Canadian North, Greenland, and Alaska? The people of the north like to be called Inuit, as that is their proper name. Canadians adopted the new name very quickly, because a famous Canadian author associated the word *Eskimo* with the Indian translation "eaters of raw meat." The Indian translation is false,[1] or at least most think it's false. I suppose it's good that people have switched to calling the Inuit by

---

1. http://en.wikipedia.org/wiki/Eskimo, http://en.wikipedia.org/wiki/Inuit,
   http://www.answers.com/topic/eskimo

their proper name, but it's disappointing that it had to take a feeling of guilt to get people to change their habits. With respect to object-oriented development, many will harp on object design issues, but use the wrong arguments, thus making you feel guilty about something you should not have felt guilty about.

Properties and Controlling an Oven's Temperature

I recently read a book about patterns in which the author of that book considered properties evil and to be avoided at all times. That author isn't alone, as quite a few consider properties as non-object-oriented and to be avoided whenever possible. The reason why some people dislike properties is because properties reveal the internal implementation details of the type. And revealing the internal implementation of the type creates problems, even without the use of properties. Object-oriented programming dictates that the internal structure is never exposed externally, which is a good strategy because it allows the implementation to change without update issues.

The question, though, is whether properties should really be avoided at all costs. I'm going to go through an oven temperature problem, where the classical solution is to use a property, but explicitly for the purpose of illustration, this solution won't use properties. Let's say that I have an oven and want to monitor its temperature. The simplest way to monitor a temperature would be to create a property as illustrated by the following source code:

```
class Oven {
    private int _temperature;
    public int Temperature {
        get {
            return _temperature;
        }
        set {
            _temperature = value;
        }
    }
}
```

The class Oven exposes its temperature as the property Temperature, which is a direct reference to the variable _temperature. This means that the internal oven temperature implementation is directly tied to its external interface. The point of good object-oriented programming is to avoid this sort of programming, as it allows the implementation of a type to change without influencing the consumer of the type.

A better Oven implementation would be as follows:

```
class Oven {
    private int _temperature;

    public void SetTemperature( int temperature) {
        _temperature = temperature;
    }
    public bool IsPreHeated() {
        return false;
    }
}
```

In this implementation of Oven, the internal variable _temperature isn't tied to its external interface because there is no direct access using a property or a method. The property Temperature is replaced with the methods SetTemperature used to assign the temperature and IsPreHeated to indicate that the assigned temperature has been reached. This is a good object-oriented design, as you are telling the oven to take care of its own responsibilities.

So now suppose a client says, "I need the temperature to calculate statistics." For example, imagine a distillation process where the rate of increase of the temperature can't exceed one degree per minute. A developer might think that a temperature property is required, but it isn't, as .NET has the ability to define delegates. Consider the following example source code:

```
delegate void OnTemperature( int temperature);

class Oven {
    private int _temperature;
    OnTemperature _listeners;

    public void BroadcastTemperature() {
        _listeners( _temperature);
    }
    public void AddTemperatureListener( OnTemperature listener) {
        _listeners += listener;
    }
}
class Controller {
    public Controller( Oven oven) {
        oven.AddTemperatureListener(
            new OnTemperature( this.OnTemperature));
    }
        public void OnTemperature( int temperature) {
            Console.WriteLine( "Temperature (" + temperature + ")");
        }
}
```

Using delegates, the temperature of the oven isn't actively queried, but passively listened to. The listeners get a message of the current oven temperature. The object-oriented design rule of a type being responsible for its own data isn't violated, as the Oven has to generate the delegate message. The delegate OnTemperature is used to broadcast the temperature of the oven to all listeners who want to know. The method AddTemperatureListener adds a delegate instance to the list of listeners. The method BroadcastTemperature broadcasts the temperature.

It's important to realize that the BroadcastTemperature method is optional and an implementation detail. Maybe the class Oven executes using its own thread and periodically broadcasts a temperature. Maybe another class is responsible for polling the oven. In any case, the class Controller uses the Oven.AddTemperatureListener method to listen to the oven temperature.

The solution of using a delegate is elegant because Oven and Controller are loosely coupled, and it doesn't require the Controller to know about the implementation of the Oven class. So it would seem that not using properties is the better solution and hence properties are "evil." But the matter of the fact is that it ignores the big picture of how the temperature is actually retrieved.

In this example, it wasn't necessary to use a property, and the resulting design turned out elegant and maintainable. The problem is that the code is a wrapper for a property called `Temperature`. Look at the big picture and consider where the oven temperature comes from. Most likely the temperature comes from a device driver that interfaces with the oven. And that device driver exposes a property that represents the temperature oven. The reason why I make this assertion is that to generate an event in software, the state has to exist somewhere. And a state is represented as a property of something. In other words, the solution presented to you is a really nifty wrapper to a property.

A cynical reader could say, "Great, you managed to complicate something simple by adding pointless layers of abstraction." The layers aren't complications, because they decouple pieces of the application from each other. Imagine if the oven had two sensors, not just one. If a property were read directly, all of the code would have to be modified to read two properties. Worse yet, how do you combine the readings of two properties? Is it an average, lowest, or highest? You don't know as it's an application that must be implemented. Using the example of layers, the logic of a single or multiple temperature sensors is entirely encapsulated within the `Oven` class.

If I were involved in a code review, and somebody handed me a design for an oven with a property called `temperature`, I probably wouldn't accept the design, but depending on other conditions, might accept the design. Additionally, though it wasn't covered, the temperature shouldn't be a double value, but should be a type called `temperature`. This is a problem that can be spelled out in two words: Mars Lander. The Mars Lander failed because one team performed its calculation using imperial measurements, and the other team performed calculations using metric. As a result, the Mars Lander crashed. Hence the correct design would be a property or delegate where the temperature is exposed as type `Temperature`.

Overall though, using properties stops the developer from implementing separation of concerns. Separation of concerns is increasingly on the programmer's radar. Given the growing range of data access products and platforms, it's now essential to separate data producers from data consumers. The Observer pattern provides a simple but powerful model for achieving this crucial design goal.

Inheritance and the Fragile Base Class Problem

In many languages, one of the difficulties with inheritance is the fragile base class problem. In .NET, the fragile base class problem still exists, but only if the developer isn't careful. To understand the fragile base class problem, consider the following Java source code.[2] I'm not trying to pick on Java in this example. Other non-.NET languages have similar problems. I'm using Java because it's similar to C# and illustrates the problem without your having to figure out the semantics of the language. Also please note that the `Stack` class already exists in the .NET base class libraries and is used for illustrative purposes only.

```
class Stack extends ArrayList {
    private int topOfStack = 0;
    public void push( Object article) {
        add( topOfStack++, article);
    }
```

---

2. Allen Holub, *Holub on Patterns: Learning Design Patterns By Looking at Code* (Berkeley: Apress, 2004), p. 41.

```
    public Object pop() {
        return remove( --topOfStack);
    }
    public void pushMany( Object[] articles) {
        for( int i = 0; i < articles.length; ++i) {
            push( articles[ i]);
        }
    }
}
```

The Stack class exposes three methods: push, pop, and pushMany. What is important in this example is how the method pushMany has been implemented. In the implementation, the iteration of the elements results in the method push being repeatedly called. Now imagine a class that subclasses Stack and overloads some methods as illustrated by the following source code:

```
class MonitorableStack extends Stack {
    private int highWaterMark = 0;
    private int lowWaterMark = 0;
    public void push( Object o) {
        push( o);
        if( size() > highWaterMark) {
            highWaterMark = size();
        }
    }
    public Object pop() {
        Object poppedItem = pop();
        if( size() < lowWaterMark) {
            lowWaterMark = size();
        }
        return poppedItem;
    }
}
```

The class MonitorableStack subclasses the type Stack. The idea of the class MonitorableStack is to track the number of additions and removals from the stack. The solution used is to overload the methods pop and push. Then whenever the methods push, pop, and pushMany are called, the water marks are counted. This is illustrated by the following client code:

```
Stack cls = new MonitorableStack();
cls.pushMany( new Object[] { 1, 2});
```

The cls variable is a type instance of MonitorableStack, but downcast to the type Stack. When the methods pop and push are called, the overloaded methods of MonitorableStack are called. Now let's consider the following change to the base class Stack:

```
class Stack extends ArrayList {
    private int topOfStack = 0;

    public void push( Object article) {
        add( topOfStack++, article);
    }
    public Object pop() {
        return remove( --topOfStack);
    }
    public void pushMany( Object[] articles) {
        for( int i = 0; i < articles.length; ++i) {
            add( articles[ i]);
        }
    }
}
```

In this variation of the Stack class, the method pushMany doesn't call the push method. This change could be due to requirements, performance, or any other reason. This base class change results in the class MonitorableStack not functioning properly anymore. Going back to the client code, the overloaded push method isn't called, meaning that the watermarks aren't modified. This is the essence of the fragile base class problem, and why inheritance can be problematic. By changing the base class, higher-level functionality is impacted.

.NET knows about the fragile base class problem and has provided a solution that addresses the issue of overloading a method. In .NET, it isn't possible to just overload methods. .NET requires an explicit intention definition, and the following source code illustrates the same implementation that caused a fragile base class problem in Java:

```
class Stack : ArrayList {
    private int topOfStack = 0;
    public void Push( Object article) {
        this.Add( article);
        topOfStack ++;
    }
    public Object Pop() {
        Object retval = this[ --topOfStack];
        this.RemoveAt( topOfStack);
        return retval;
    }
    public void PushMany( Object[] articles) {
        foreach( Object item in articles) {
            Push( item);
        }
    }
}
```

```
class MonitorableStack : Stack {
    public int highWaterMark = 0;
    public int lowWaterMark = 0;

    public new void Push( Object item) {
        base.Push( item);
        if( this.Count > highWaterMark) {
            highWaterMark = this.Count;
        }
    }
    public new Object Pop() {
        Object popped = base.Pop();
        if( this.Count < lowWaterMark) {
            lowWaterMark = this.Count;
        }
        return popped;
    }
}
```

Notice in the .NET implementation how the MonitorableStack class methods Push and Pop have to use the attribute new. The attribute new indicates that the base class functionality should be ignored and a new functionality should be defined when the MonitorableStack type is used. Now let's consider the client code using the .NET implementation:

```
Stack cls = new MonitorableStack();
cls.PushMany( new Object[] { 1, 2});
```

The .NET implementation doesn't work like the Java implementation because of the way the methods Push and Pop were implemented. In .NET, when the instance cls is downcast to the base class Stack, calling Push or Pop will call the Push or Pop implementations of the base class. The methods Push and Pop aren't overloaded. This means when PushMany is called, the Stack implementation of Push is called, and not MonitorableStack.Push. Therefore, when the author of the base class Stack changes its implementation, the class MonitorableStack isn't impacted. This means there is no fragile base class problem.

Of course, this solution isn't ideal, as it doesn't solve the problem like the Java solution does. The technique was illustrated to show how .NET manages overloaded methods. To solve the problem like the Java solution, another keyword has to be used. The other keyword solves the problem to let the .NET code behave like the Java code, but you need to do so explicitly. To solve the actual problem, the following source code would be appropriate:

```
class Stack : ArrayList {
    private int topOfStack = 0;

    public virtual void Push( Object article) {
        this.Add( article);
        topOfStack ++;
    }
```

```
    public virtual Object Pop() {
        Object retval = this[ --topOfStack];
         this.RemoveAt( topOfStack);
        return retval;
    }
    public void PushMany( Object[] articles) {
        foreach( Object item in articles) {
            Push( item);
        }
    }
}

class MonitorableStack : Stack {
    public int highWaterMark = 0;
    public int lowWaterMark = 0;

    public override void Push( Object item) {
        base.Push( item);
        if( this.Count > highWaterMark) {
            highWaterMark = this.Count;
        }
    }
    public override Object Pop() {
        Object popped = base.Pop();
        if( this.Count < lowWaterMark) {
            lowWaterMark = this.Count;
        }
        return popped;
    }
}
```

In this variation of the solution, the keywords virtual and override are used, and the same result as the Java solution is generated. The clever reader will realize that the fragile base class problem exists in the exact same manner as in Java. Like in the Java example, if the Stack.PushMany method were modified not to use the Push method, the MonitorableStack class would cease to function properly. There is a big difference, though, in that in .NET, when you use the virtual keyword, it's explicitly meant that this method may be overridden. This means that if the method Stack.PushMany uses the Push method from version 1.0, it must do so after version 1.0 because the virtual keyword indicates that somebody will be overriding the default functionality.

Now that you've considered the potential pitfalls of properties and inheritance, let's move on to the creation of a basic translation program in our investigation of grouping components.

Sample Application: A Translation Program

Writing graphical user interface (GUI) applications can be complicated because of the nature of the application. It's tedious building a GUI, tedious making that GUI do something useful, and tedious making sure that the GUI is doing the right thing at the right time.

Everybody will recommend separating the GUI from the application logic. The idea sounds good, but is very hard to do effectively. Writing a modularized GUI application requires the implementation of several patterns. In this section, I walk you through an example GUI application, a translation program. We'll start with a "quick-and-dirty" implementation and move on to a pattern-based implementation that can be extended or ported to another platform without major problems.

Writing a Quick-and-Dirty Application

Let's start by building the translation application using "quick-and-dirty" techniques. The requirements are simple in that the application needs to be able to translate a text phrase from English to German. Using a tool that supports a GUI designer generates a user interface similar to what appears in Figure 5-1.

Figure 5-1. *Translation tool user interface*

The user interface has two textboxes. The user enters English text in the upper textbox that he or she wants to be translated and output in the lower textbox. The button executes the translation.

The translation service would be implemented as a class and be called from the GUI as illustrated by the following source code:

```
namespace Chap05.GenericGUI {
    public partial class BasicForm : Form {
        private Original.TranslateToGerman _translation =
            new Original.TranslateToGerman();

        public BasicForm() {
            InitializeComponent();
        }
```

```
        private void button1_Click( object sender, EventArgs e ) {
            textBox2.Text = _translation.Translate( textBox1.Text );
        }
    }
}
```

The class BasicForm uses .NET 2.0 techniques where it's partially defined using the partial keyword. The rest of the BasicForm implementation is beyond the scope of this book because it contains code generated to create the GUI illustrated in Figure 5-1.

The method button1_Click is an event handler that is called whenever the Translate button is clicked. The event handler instantiates the class TranslateToGerman, and then calls the method translation.Translate to translate the text.

The implementation of TranslateToGerman is defined as follows:

```
namespace Original {
    public class TranslateToGerman {
        public string Translate( string word ) {
            if( String.Compare( word, "Good Morning" ) == 0 ) {
                return "Guten Morgen";
            }
            else {
                return "Could not translate";
            }
        }
    }
}
```

The TranslateToGerman class is generally useless because it can only translate the text Good Morning. This is OK, because the implementation of the method Translate that performs the translation isn't the focus of this exercise. Having a simple implementation is acceptable because somebody else will implement a full translation service as defined by the class TranslateToGerman.

At this point, the application is complete, and the only remaining step is to implement the algorithms to translate the text. If you were the coder, you could feel happy about this code for the following reasons:

- The translation class TranslateToGerman is separate and not dependent on the BasicForm class, allowing the GUI developer to reuse the business logic of the TranslateToGerman class.

- The entire implementation is simple, making it easier to understand and test the application. An easy-to-understand application makes maintenance and writing extensions simpler.

From the source code, you can probably spot several reasons why you might not be happy with the implemented application. This doesn't negate the preceding reasons to be happy. What it means is that an application has been implemented using the most direct means possible. The direct means are object oriented, and more than that would not seem to be necessary.

One of the major reasons why this problem is difficult is because it's GUI code, which can very often be messy from an architectural point of view.

Refactoring Code

Instead of rewriting the example code, it's going to be refactored incrementally. *Refactoring* is the process of changing the source code without doing a rewrite of the source code. I'm also implementing the technique *refactoring to patterns*, which I'll discuss in more detail in Chapter 9. You'll want to refactor a code base for one of these four reasons:

- You want to add a feature, and it isn't possible without making changes.

- You want to fix a bug that affects other classes.

- You need to improve the design because there are hacks in a source code base that can become problematic in the future.

- You need to optimize resources because the application might be too slow or require too much memory.

The quick-and-dirty example needs to be refactored for the following reasons:

- There is no separation of intention and implementation of the class TranslateToGerman. Imagine if the application needed to support multiple languages.

- The application, while appearing simple, really isn't simple. The class TranslateToGerman requires some knowledge to use properly. That knowledge is embedded in the .NET form, where a value has to be extracted from one control, and then assigned to another control. If the application is ported to another platform, or used in another context, somebody has to take the time and inspect what the GUI code is doing.

- Testing the application is expensive because it's nearly impossible to write tests. For example, it's possible to write the tests for the class TranslateToGerman. What isn't testable using a simple script is whether the method button1_Click is implemented correctly. GUI-based tests are time consuming and difficult to decipher for correctness.

The example code will work and could be good enough for a beta or release candidate. It might even be good enough for version 1.0. One of the key concepts of refactoring to patterns is that you refactor when you need to. It's part of the overall test-driven development process.

Sometimes when code is refactored, the resulting source code is considered more complicated than the original source code. What is gained from the refactored code is testability, robustness, maintainability, and extendability. A major problem in the software industry is that the time to fix bugs and time required to extend an application isn't factored into the overall calculation. Consider the building of a bridge. If a bridge that was cheaper to build but more expensive to maintain were compared to a more expensive bridge that is cheaper to maintain, the engineer wouldn't blindly choose one over the other. The engineer would do an overall calculation and then consider the winner. Often software developers don't do this when they need to weigh the consequences of each.

Refactoring and Implementing a Bridge and Factory

Let's start the refactoring by fixing the class TranslateToGerman. The problem is that TranslateToGerman is used directly from the class BasicForm. This reference is hard coded and locks the client into translating English to German using the specific class TranslateToGerman. The pattern that TranslateToGerman will implement is the Bridge pattern, and therefore TranslateToGerman needs to implement an interface. The following source code defines the interface ITranslationServices that has the same method signature as the TranslateToGerman class:

```
public interface ITranslationServices {
    string Translate( string word );
}
```

The TranslateToGerman class is rewritten to implement the ITranslationServices interface as follows:

```
public class TranslateToGerman : ITranslationServices {
    public string Translate( string word ) {
        if( String.Compare( word, "Good Morning" ) == 0 ) {
            return "Guten Morgen";
        }
        else {
            return "Could not translate";
        }
    }
}
```

What is particularly effective about this single refactoring is that BasicForm doesn't need to be modified. The application does need to be recompiled. The semantics of the class have been preserved even if the original semantics aren't correct. This isn't always possible, but should be an objective. It isn't necessary to change the instantiation code in BasicForm, but it would be a good idea. TranslateToGerman uses an interface, and therefore a factory of some sort is called for. The quickest solution would be to create a simple factory within the context of the application. However, the quickest way isn't always the best. The best way is to use the Client-Dispatcher-Server pattern from Chapter 4 or the plug-in architecture from Chapter 3.

Whichever solution you choose to instantiate, TranslateToGerman depends on the context. The primary goal is to be able to update the language services without having to update the main GUI program. Both the Client-Dispatcher-Server pattern and plug-in architecture are viable alternatives. Since the GUI program is a client application that can be restarted, the plug-in architecture is probably a better solution, as it's compact and solves the problem. For the scope of this book, the Client-Dispatcher-Server pattern will be used, as that code is already written and tested.

So that the assembly can be dynamically loaded, the interface ITranslationService is moved out of the main application defined in an assembly called definitions.dll, and the class TranslateToGerman is also moved out of the main application and defined in an assembly called implementations.dll. The definitions.dll assembly is referenced both by the main application and the implementations.dll assembly. Also added to the definitions.dll assembly is the code that uses the Client-Dispatcher-Server pattern.

The rewritten `BasicForm` that uses the Client-Dispatcher-Server pattern is as follows:

```
namespace Chap05.GenericGUI {
    public partial class BasicForm : Form {
        private ITranslationServices _translation;
        private Loader _loader;

        public BasicForm() {
            InitializeComponent();
            _loader = new Loader();
            _loader.Load();
            _translation = _loader.CreateGermanTranslationDynamic();
        }

        private void button1_Click( object sender, EventArgs e ) {
            textBox2.Text = _translation.Translate( textBox1.Text );
        }
    }
}
```

The variable `_translation` is of type `ITranslation`, which is an interface instance of the type `TranslateToGerman`. The variable `_loader` references the type `Loader`, which, as illustrated in Chapter 4, is responsible for subclassing the Client-Dispatcher-Server pattern helper class `Dispatcher` and instantiating a type. The method `Loader.CreateGermanTranslationDynamic()` instantiates `TranslateToGerman` and passes to the client an `ITranslationServices` interface instance. The original Client-Dispatcher-Server pattern implementation didn't expose the method `CreateGermanTranslationDynamic`. The implementation of the `button1_Click` method remains identical.

When using the Client-Dispatcher-Server pattern from `BasicForm`, you will need to implement a thin-coded local context factory to hide the messiness of cross-referencing the correct assembly with the correct interface. Practically speaking, you don't want the `BasicForm` class to decide whether to use a configuration file or a directory to load a particular assembly.

Implementing the Mediator Pattern

GUI developers will consider the current user interface of the example and think to themselves that maybe a better way to do the translation is to do the translation dynamically. So instead of pushing a button to do a translation, the textbox text changed event is captured and will translate whatever the contents of the textbox are. The translation results are then output in the other textbox.

Implementing a Responsible Textbox

A possible way of doing a dynamic translation is to create a new textbox type that has built-in translation services. The new type is called `TranslationTextBox` and subclasses the type `System.Windows.Forms.Textbox`, which is defined as follows:

```
public class TranslationTextBox : System.Windows.Forms.TextBox {
    private System.Windows.Forms.TextBox _textBox;
    private ITranslationServices _translation;

    public TranslationTextBox(System.Windows.Forms.TextBox textbox) {
        _textBox = textbox;
    }
    protected override void OnTextChanged( EventArgs e) {
        _textBox.Text = _translation.Translate(this.Text);
    }
    public void AssignTranslation(ITranslationServices translation) {
        _translation = translation;
    }
}
```

The class TranslationTextBox subclasses the standard textbox System.Windows.
Forms.TextBox and has two private data members: _textBox and _translation. The two data
members are required because object-oriented programming means each object is responsible
for its own actions. In this case, this means the textbox is responsible for performing a translation and then assigning that value to another textbox, which is the data member _textBox.

The base class method OnTextChanged is overwritten so that whenever the contents of the
textbox change, a translation will be started. The translation code is identical to the translation
code written in the previous pattern for the method button1_Click. The method
AssignTranslation is added so that the ITranslationServices instance can be assigned to
TranslationTextBox, fulfilling the object-oriented requirement that a type is responsible for its
own actions.

Putting all of this together is a bit tricky because multiple changes have to be made. The
first change is to BasicForm because the form data member textbox1 has to be updated to use
the type TranslationText, and not the original textbox that was generated by the GUI designer.
The changes are illustrated as follows (note that many parts of the code have been deleted
for clarity):

```
namespace Chap05.GenericGUI {
    partial class BasicForm {
        private ITranslationServices _translation;
        private Loader _loader;

        public BasicForm() {
            InitializeComponent();
            _loader = new Loader();
            _loader.Load();
            _translation = _loader.CreateGermanTranslationDynamic();
            textBox1.AssignTranslation(_translation);
        }

        private System.ComponentModel.IContainer components = null;
```

```
    private void InitializeComponent() {
        this.button1 = new System.Windows.Forms.Button();
        this.textBox2 = new System.Windows.Forms.TextBox();
        this.textBox1 = new TranslationTextBox(this.textBox2);
        this.SuspendLayout();
    }

    private System.Windows.Forms.Button button1;
    private TranslationTextBox textBox1;
    private System.Windows.Forms.TextBox textBox2;
  }
}
```

When the GUI designer created `BasicForm`, the data member `textBox1` was defined to be of type `System.Windows.Forms.TextBox` and is updated to be `TranslationTextBox`. The method `InitializeComponent` needs to be altered to create the type `TranslationTextBox`, but the order of creation for `textBox1` and `textBox2` is reversed from the original. The reason is because the constructor of the `TranslationTextBox` requires the translation destination textbox. And finally, so that a translation does work in a constructor of `BasicForm`, the code is updated to assign the translation services to `textBox1` using the method `AssignTranslation`.

Stepping back and looking at the code, you can see that it's brittle. This common dilemma results from types needing to know about other types. Remember in Chapter 1 that one of the big problems in object-oriented applications is type referencing. When types reference too many other types, an application becomes brittle, and changes are very difficult to introduce. This application is starting to become brittle because of the simple desire to have text translated dynamically. Maybe this specific problem could have been avoided using a different programming strategy than what I presented. However, even a different programming strategy will encounter brittle code, as types will always reference other types.

To fix the brittle code problem, let's consider the architecture as a UML diagram (see Figure 5-2).

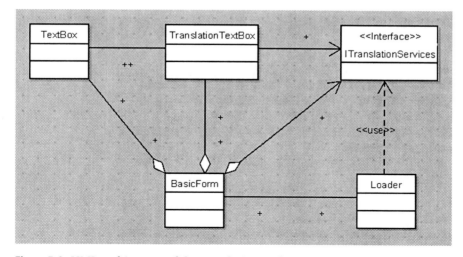

Figure 5-2. *UML architecture of the translation tool*

Taking a quick glance at Figure 5-2, it's obvious that the various references between the individual types are numerous and therefore are creating brittle code. The objective is to clean up the references.

Restructuring to Use the Mediator Pattern

When an application uses references extensively, one solution is to use a middle entity to manage the references and messages to the different entities. The Mediator pattern[3] allows you to avoid the problem of requiring types to hold an instance to other types. When implementing GUI applications, you'll use the Mediator pattern extensively.

A specialization of the Mediator pattern is the Relational Integrity Mediator pattern.[4] Languages like C# aren't meant to effectively manage references; in fact, programming languages do a very poor job of it. In contrast, languages such as Structured Query Language (SQL) do a remarkable job at managing references and constraints. To simplify managing references, a special type of mediator called a *relational mediator* is used. Like the standard mediator, it's used to manage collections of types that reference other types. More about this specialization of this pattern won't be discussed here, because it's beyond the scope of this book.

The Mediator pattern is created by default when you design a GUI. For example, when GUI elements such as buttons are added to a form, they are added as generic controls. The form manages children, and when updates are necessary, the form is responsible for informing the correct control at the correct time. When the child controls need to update other controls, they ask the form, which then gets the reference for the child. The child doesn't need to hold any references and can always ask for them dynamically.

The class `TranslationTextBox` can be simplified using the Mediator pattern by calling the parent form and asking for the textbox that needs to be updated, as in the following source code:

```
public class TranslationTextBox: System.Windows.Forms.TextBox {
    private ITranslationServices _translation;

    public TranslationTextBox() {
    }
    protected override void OnTextChanged( EventArgs e) {
        Form parent;
        TextBox othertextbox;

        parent = this.Parent as Form;
        othertextbox = parent.Controls[ "textbox2"] as TextBox;
        othertextbox.Text = _translation.Translate(this.Text);
    }
    public void AssignTranslation(ITranslationServices translation) {
        _translation = translation;
    }
}
```

3. Erich Gamma et al., *Design Patterns: Elements of Reusable Object-Oriented Software* (Boston: Addison-Wesley, 1995), p. 273.
4. Steven John Metsker, *Design Patterns in C#* (Boston: Addison-Wesley, 2004), p. 115.

Comparing this implementation of TranslationTextBox to the previous definition, notice how the data member _textbox isn't necessary. The constructor of TranslationTextBox is modified to not need any parameters. The form uses the Mediator pattern, and therefore if the TranslationTextBox needs the output textbox, it just asks the form. In the OnTextChanged method, the form is retrieved using the this.Parent property. Then the control is retrieved using the indexer parent.Controls["textbox2"]. The returned control is typecast to type TextBox. Twice types have been typecast (for example, as Form and as TextBox) to general .NET GUI-based types, and twice the typecast could have resulted in a cast exception. A cast exception didn't occur because the TranslationTextBox knew what it was asking for. This illustrates one aspect of the Mediator pattern: the individual clients managed by the mediator know about other clients in base type terms and know their identity. In the example, the identity was textbox2, but usually this would be an identifier associated with the functionality of the instance.

OnTextChanged is a classical implementation of the Mediator pattern because the child control is letting the parent container manage the references of other child controls. Then when the child control needs to access another control to display a message or perform some action, the parent container is asked. In terms of the Mediator pattern, the architecture would now appear similar to Figure 5-3.

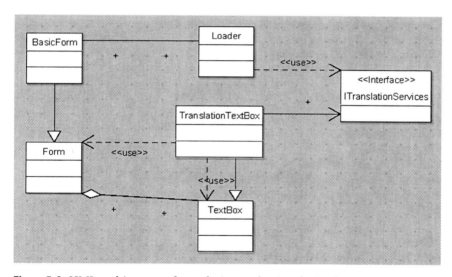

Figure 5-3. *UML architecture of translation tool using the Mediator pattern*

Notice the incremental improvement in Figure 5-3 in terms of a more organized and logical architecture. The referencing of all types by all types is gone and replaced with the referencing of types when necessary. The Mediator pattern is implemented by the types Form, BasicForm, TranslationTextBox, and TextBox. The types Form and BasicForm are the Mediator and ConcreteMediator, respectively. The TranslationTextBox doesn't use or know about the ConcreteMediator because that would violate the Mediator pattern and the separation of interface from implementation. The types TextBox and TranslationTextBox are colleagues and concrete colleagues, respectively.

The Mediator pattern is a collection container that has references to all of its children as colleagues. If one concrete colleague needs to reference another concrete colleague, it asks the mediator for a reference, and the concrete colleague is responsible for knowing which concrete colleague to ask for. In terms of the method `TranslateTextBox.OnTextChanged`, this meant knowing that the concrete colleague was called textbox2.

Looking at the overall architecture, you can see an improvement because now the Client-Dispatcher-Server, Bridge, and Mediator patterns are being used. However, in the process of using the Client-Dispatcher-Server pattern, the architecture has been slightly broken. Notice in Figure 5-3 how the `BasicForm` class references the `Loader`. This isn't necessary, as the `BasicForm` class doesn't care about the loading of the translation services. It's the `TranslationTextBox` class that cares about the loading of the translation services. The logical step is to move the `Loader` reference out of the `BasicForm` class and into the `TranslationTextBox` class as illustrated in the following modified source code:

```
public class TranslationTextBox: System.Windows.Forms.TextBox {
        private ITranslationServices _translation;
        private Loader _loader;

    public TranslationTextBox() {
        _loader = new Loader();
        _loader.Load();
        _translation = _loader.CreateGermanTranslationDynamic();
    }
    protected override void OnTextChanged( EventArgs e) {
        DoTranslation();
    }
    public void DoTranslation() {
        Form parent;
        TextBox othertextbox;

        parent = this.Parent as Form;
        othertextbox = parent.Controls["textbox2"] as TextBox;
        othertextbox.Text = _translation.Translate(this.Text);
    }
}
partial class BasicForm {
        private ITranslationServices _translation;
        private Loader _loader;

        public BasicForm() {
            InitializeComponent();
        }
        private void button1_Click( object sender, EventArgs e ) {
            textBox1.DoTranslation();
        }
        // Other stuff has been cut out for simplification
}
```

In this source code example, the types `TranslationTextBox` and `BasicForm` have been greatly simplified and cleaned up in terms of object-oriented design. The class `BasicForm` is no longer responsible for instantiating the language services and the assignment of the interface instance, as all that functionality has been delegated to the type `TranslationTextBox`. Again, this is classical object-oriented programming in that types are responsible for their own actions and data.

The class `TranslationTextBox` has an updated constructor that instantiates an `ITranslationServices` instance. And the method `AssignTranslation` is removed, since it isn't necessary. The method `DoTranslation` has been added to make it possible for another colleague to reference the `TranslationTextBox` and ask for a translation. An example of this is the `button1_Click` event that is illustrated in the `BasicForm` class.

Implementing the Template Pattern

The current translation services architecture does its job and is well structured, but there is still one problem in that the implementation is tied to the `System.Windows.Forms` architecture. The dream of all GUI designers is to create a platform-neutral UI. Many will say that we've attained that using the Web and Hypertext Markup Language (HTML). I'm not going to debate that comment, nor am I going to debate the merits of rich client/thin client, or anything along those lines. You should use whatever makes you happy and solves the problems efficiently and effectively. What I want to do is show you that it's possible to write GUI-neutral applications using the Template[5] pattern.

The Theory Behind the Template Pattern

There are people who need to use a UI toolkit like `System.Windows.Forms` who don't care about cross-platform support, and those people are interested in writing GUI code that isn't tied to a specific toolkit. What is common among all developers is to write an application that separates the GUI-specific code from the application logic. This is desirable because often a GUI changes, which means changing the application logic as well, if the application logic is embedded within the GUI. Developers don't want to have to change everything when either the application logic or GUI logic changes.

Ironically, one solution to this dilemma is to use a GUI toolkit that is portable across all platforms. The GUI toolkit then becomes part of the application logic. What makes this ironic is that the original problem of separating the GUI from the application still exists. A cross-platform GUI toolkit doesn't solve the separation of logic problem.

What is needed is a meaningful architecture that separates the GUI logic from the business logic. The solution to this problem is a combination of the Template pattern and the Adapter pattern. The purpose of the Template pattern is to provide a basis functionality that is completed by another type. A simplified form of the Template pattern has been used extensively thus far: helper types implemented using abstract base classes. Where the Template pattern distinguishes itself from a helper class is the requirement of the subclassing type to implement some additional functionality.

---

5. *Design Patterns: Elements of Reusable Object-Oriented Software*, p. 325.

Consider the following source code:

```
abstract class TemplateBaseClass {
    public abstract int Add( int num1, int num2);

    public int DoThreeNumberAdd(int num1, int num2, int num3) {
        return Add(num1, Add(num2, num3));
    }
}
```

The type `TemplateBaseClass` is defined as an abstract class with two methods that require a subclassing before the base class `TemplateBaseClass` can be used. The method `Add` is defined as abstract and must be implemented by any class that subclasses `TemplateBaseClass`. The method `DoThreeNumberAdd` uses the abstract method `Add` to add three numbers. As a result, the class `TemplateBaseClass` is saying I can provide the functionality to add three numbers, but somebody else has to provide the functionality to add two numbers.

The previous example is the classical implementation of the Template pattern, but there is another possibility, and it's illustrated as follows:

```
interface IIntMath {
    int Add(int num1, int num2);
}
class TemplateBaseClass< additiontype> where additiontype : IIntMath, new() {
    public int DoThreeNumberAdd(int num1, int num2, int num3) {
        IIntMath cls = new additiontype();
        return cls.Add(num1, cls.Add(num2, num3));
    }
}
```

The difference in this example is that instead of using an abstract class and method, .NET Generics and interfaces are used. The type `TemplateBaseClass` is defined as a class that uses Generics to specify required logic. The Generic parameter `additiontype` is constrained to implement the interface `IIntMath`, which is used by the method `DoThreeNumberAdd`.

Comparing the two solutions, each has its advantage and disadvantage. Using an abstract base class is useful when the required functionality is well defined and narrow in focus. Using Generics, it isn't necessary to subclass the type, thus creating a new type, and only requires the implementation of an interface. The interface implementation could be reused in other contexts.

Separating GUI Logic from Business Logic

The solution used to separate the GUI logic from the business logic is the Generics-based version of the Template pattern. The reason for using the Generics variation is flexibility. The flexibility stems from the ability to use constraints that specify an interface, and not a base class, thus enabling more flexibility for the interface implementations.

To understand the overall architecture, I'll be showing you a simplification of the logic used by the application. Implementing the entire application using the Template pattern would cause the discussion to focus on the numerous details instead of the main message of separating the GUI logic from the business logic.

Let's focus on a single aspect of the GUI. The translation application needs to transfer the contents of one textbox to another textbox. Using `System.Windows.Forms`, the following code transfers the content of one textbox to another textbox:

```
textbox1.Text = textbox2.Text;
```

The trouble with this solution is that it's specific to `System.Windows.Forms`. Also problematic is the embedding of the logic within the GUI, which is the crux of the problem when writing GUI applications. A cynic would comment that this approach is the only possible solution since a GUI component can't be abstracted. It's as if the impossible is being asked for. Yet, the rub is that writing GUIs in this fashion is wrong and needs to be altered. For example, how is the logic of transferring the data tested? Answer: somebody has to click some button, which means writing a GUI-based testing script. And if that button moves from one corner of the window to another corner, the GUI-based test script needs to be checked again. The better solution is to let some other routine do the transfer and have the GUI code define the source and destination control. A possible solution would be the following source code:

```
void TransferData( TextBox textbox1, TextBox textbox2);
```

This solution will work, but is specific to the `System.Windows.Forms` environment. Since we have .NET Generics, the solution is to use a Generic's defined method and let the implementation dictate what types to use. The rewritten method is defined as follows:

```
void TransferData<Control1, Control2>( Control1 ctrl1, Control2 ctrl2 )
```

Using Generics, the method `TransferData` can be used with any control types, or more simply put, any source types. `Control1` and `Control2` could be classes from an HTML form or database records. Based on this method, the following source is a complete implementation of the data transfer solution:

```
public class BusinessLogic< GUIAdapter> where GUIAdapter : IControlAdapter, new() {
    private IControlAdapter _adapter;

    public BusinessLogic() {
        _adapter = new GUIAdapter();
    }
    public virtual void TransferData<Control1, Control2>(
        Control1 src, Control2 dest ) {
        _adapter.SetValue( dest, _adapter.GetValue<Control1, string>( src ) );
    }
}
```

`BusinessLogic` is a Generics-based class that has a single generic parameter, `GUIAdapter`, that represents a GUI-based adapter, which will be discussed in the section "Implementing the Adapter Pattern." For the moment, consider the `GUIAdapter` type as a sort of bridge between the `BusinessLogic` class and the GUI toolkit.

The method `TransferData` accepts two parameters, which represent the controls to transfer the data from and to. In this example, the variable `src` is the source of the data, and the variable `dest` is the destination of the data. The data is transferred using the adapter methods `GetValue` and `SetValue`. The method `TransferData` is identical to the original GUI code:

```
textbox1.Text = textbox2.Text;
```

Looking at the original code and the new code, it would seem yet again a relatively simple implementation was complicated beyond reasonable measure. Yet this is incorrect, because with the new implementation, we have the ability to properly test the logic without resorting to GUI test scripts, and the ability to dynamically switch GUI toolkits or mix and match data sources. In the end, the result is a flexible and maintainable application.

Of course, this doesn't mean everything will need to use this architecture. There are instances when the code only relates to the GUI and doesn't contain any application logic. An example could be that when a button is pressed, another control will mark itself as busy. The key question that you must ask yourself is whether the action only affects the GUI, or whether the action affects the data managed by the application. If the answer is the latter, then you need to separate GUI logic from application logic.

Implementing the Translation Services

Applying Template pattern–based separation of GUI logic from application logic concepts to BusinessLogic and translation services means removing the application logic code from the TranslationTextBox type, and moving the functionality into another type. Following is the previously defined BusinessLogic class modified to perform a translation service using the Template pattern:

```
public class TranslationServices<GUIAdapter>
    where GUIAdapter: IControlAdapter, new() {
    private ITranslationServices _translation;
    private Loader _loader;
    private GUIAdapter _adapter;

    public TranslationServices() {
        _loader = new Loader();
        _loader.Load();
        _translation = _loader.CreateGermanTranslationDynamic();
        _adapter = new GUIAdapter();
    }
    public void DoTranslation<Control1, Control2>(Control1 src, Control2 dest) {
        _adapter.SetValue(dest,
            _translation.Translate(_adapter.GetValue<Control1, string>(src)));
    }
}
```

The class TranslationServices has a generic parameter, GUIAdapter, which is the functionality used to retrieve and assign GUI data values. _translation and _loader are the data members that have been removed from TranslationTextBox. The data member _adapter is of Generic type GUIAdapter and provides the interface to the GUI toolkit. The method DoTranslation accepts as a parameter the source and destination GUI elements.

Since some elements have been removed from TranslationTextBox, the modified class needs to be shown again:

```
public class TranslationTextBox:
    System.Windows.Forms.TextBox, Abstractions.IControlAdapter {

    public TranslationTextBox() {
    }
    protected override void OnTextChanged(EventArgs e) {
        DoTranslation();
    }
    public void DoTranslation() {
        Form parent;
        TextBox othertextbox;

        parent = this.Parent as Form;
        othertextbox = parent.Controls["textbox2"] as TextBox;

        Abstractions.TranslationServices<TranslationTextBox> srvc =
            new Abstractions.TranslationServices<TranslationTextBox>();
        srvc.DoTranslation( this, othertextbox);
    }
}
```

The class TranslationText implements the interface Abstractions.IControlAdapter, which is the GUI adapter mentioned previously, and will be explained in the next section. Removed from TranslationTextBox are the details to the translation services. Added to the method DoTranslation is the reference to the application logic class TranslationServices.

Now let's step back and look at the resulting architecture in UML terms as illustrated in Figure 5-4.

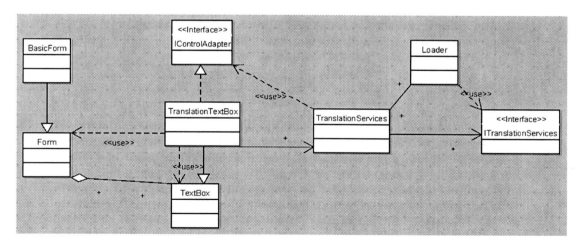

Figure 5-4. *UML architecture of the translation tool using the Template pattern*

As shown in the diagram, what has happened is that the `TranslationTextBox` class has separated the GUI logic (`BasicForm`, `Form`, and `TextBox`) from the application logic (`TranslationServices`, `Loader`, `ITranslationServices`). The class `TranslationTextBox` is the glue that holds both pieces together to perform a translation. When the GUI changes, the only class to update is `TranslationTextBox`, and when the application logic changes again, only class `TranslationTextBox` changes. At this point, it can be said that the tightly coupled application at the beginning has become loosely coupled. And all this has happened using a few design patterns and object-oriented design principles.

Implementing the Adapter Pattern

Now we come to the GUI adapter. I delayed the explanation until now because there are some specific problems addressed by the Adapter pattern that can't be explained in a single sentence or paragraph. Refer back to the interface `IControlAdapter` shown in Figure 5-4. This interface implements the Adapter pattern.[6] The general idea behind this pattern is to adapt one set of operating conditions to another. In technical terms, this means exposing a predefined interface to use another set of interfaces not directly related to the predefined interface. In simple terms, the Adapter pattern makes a square peg fit in a round hole.

Implementing an Adapter

Earlier in the section "Separating the GUI Logic from the Business Logic," you saw the following method:

```
void TransferData<Control1, Control2>( Control1 ctrl1, Control2 ctrl2 )
```

Let's say that this method is constrained to support types from the `System.Windows.Forms` namespace. The method implementation could then be written as follows:

```
class BusinessLogic {
    void TransferData<Control1, Control2>(Control1 ctrl1, Control2 ctrl2)
        where Control1: System.Windows.Forms.TextBox
        where Control2: System.Windows.Forms.TextBox {
        ctrl1.Text = ctrl2.Text;
    }
}
```

Some may comment that this example is trivial, as the parameters `ctrl1` and `ctrl2` could have been the type `TextBox` instead of types defined by Generics. A valid critique, but ignore this point, as the main thrust is to illustrate that the parameters are constrained. To make the method work, the parameters must be of a type that subclasses the type `TextBox`. Now imagine if the application is ported to another GUI toolkit like wx.NET (http://wxnet.sourceforge.net). The method `TransferData` wouldn't work as `TextCtrl` exists instead of `TextBox` and a `Value` property exists instead of a `Text` property. The method `TransferData` would need to be rewritten using different types, and that isn't an option. It would mean whenever the type changes so must the method, and that is a maintenance nightmare.

---

6. *Design Patterns: Elements of Reusable Object-Oriented Software*, p. 139.

Using the Adapter pattern, the method isn't rewritten, but a type is used to bridge between the two different types. In this case, the bridge would mimic the TextBox control, but redirect the methods to TextCtrl as illustrated by the following source code:

```
class WxToFormsAdapter: System.Windows.Forms.TextBox {
    wx.TextCtrl _ctrl = new wx.TextCtrl((wx.Window)null);

    public override string Text {
        get {
            return _ctrl.Value;
        }
        set {
            _ctrl.Value = value;
        }
    }
}
```

The type WxToFormsAdapter class subclasses the System.Windows.Forms.TextBox type. The data member _ctrl is the text control from the wx.NET GUI toolkit. The property Text, which represents the text contents of the control, is overloaded and redirected to the data member _ctrl.

This is the essence of the Adapter pattern. In a nutshell, the adapter is a type that implements an interface or subclasses a base class. In the implementation of the type, the methods of the exposed interface or subclass redirect the method calls to an existing implementation. An adapter doesn't need to be a method-to-method conversion. An adapter could include logic that makes use of multiple existing implementations. The important aspect of an adapter is that it exposes a predefined interface and uses existing implementations.

Implementing a GUI Adapter

The illustrated adapter WxToFormsAdapter works, but is kludgy because a wx.NET text control isn't a System.Windows.Forms.Textbox. A better approach is to consider the task at hand and then define an interface that serves as the basis of the Adapter pattern. The approach chosen is to consider the various controls as sources and sinks of data. The adapter interface needs methods to extract data and assign data. The adapter interface is defined as follows:

```
public interface IControlAdapter {
    returntype GetValue<ControlType, returntype>(ControlType control)
        where returntype: class;
    void SetValue<ControlType, type>(ControlType control, type value);
}
```

The method IControlAdapter.GetValue retrieves a value, and the method IControlAdapter.SetValue assigns a value. The interface IControlAdapter isn't defined using Generics, but the methods are. This is done on purpose to support any type of GUI control element. The interface must be able to arbitrarily support any control type, and having the IControlAdapter interface specify the type isn't useful. When using Generic parameters at the interface level, the specialization of the interface results in the support of a single type. This means if IControlAdapter is specialized to TextBox, then all methods must transform TextBox types.

Methods don't have these constraints, as you can see by revisiting the method implementation `TranslationServices.DoTranslation`:

```
public void DoTranslation<Control1, Control2>(Control1 src, Control2 dest) {
    _adapter.SetValue(dest,
        _translation.Translate(_adapter.GetValue<Control1, string>(src)));
}
```

The variable `_adapter` is an interface instance of `IControlAdapter`. The method `GetValue` retrieves the value of a control, and then assigns the value of the control using `SetValue`. Generic parameters are used at the method level to make it possible to use any data type. Of course, it goes without saying that when using Generics at the method level without constraints, you'll have to use typecasts.

Following is an implementation of `IControlAdapter` for the `System.Windows.Forms` namespace:

```
private class WindowsAdapter: Abstractions.IControlAdapter {
    public type GetValue<ControlType, type>(ControlType control) where type: class {
        if(control is TextBox) {
            TextBox cls = control as TextBox;
            return cls.Text as type;
        }
        return default(type);
    }
    public void SetValue<ControlType, type>(ControlType control, type value) {
        if(control is TextBox) {
            TextBox cls = control as TextBox;
            String strValue = value as String;
            cls.Text = strValue;
        }
    }
}
```

In the implementation of the `GetValue` and `SetValue` methods, notice how dynamic typecasting and type checking is used in the form of `is` and `as` statements. Using dynamic casting and dynamic checking allows the adapter implementation to check which kind of controls are being passed and then perform an appropriate action. For example, for the `GetValue` method in the case of a `TextBox`, it means retrieving the text contents. If the control were a check box, then it would mean retrieving a checked or unchecked value. The same sorts of rules apply for the `SetValue` method.

The value of the adapter is evident if a different toolkit needs to be implemented. In that case, the only requirement is to implement a new `IControlAdapter` implementation as illustrated by the following wx.NET example:

```
private class wxAdapter: Abstractions.IControlAdapter {
    public type GetValue<ControlType, type>(ControlType control) where type: class {
        if(control is TextCtrl) {
            TextCtrl cls = control as TextCtrl;
            return cls.Value as type;
        }
        return default(type);
    }

    public void SetValue<ControlType, type>(ControlType control, type value) {
        if(control is TextCtrl) {
            TextCtrl cls = control as TextCtrl;
            String strValue = value as String;
            cls.Value = strValue;
        }
    }
}
```

This time the methods GetValue and SetValue test the input controls with respect to the available wx.NET controls. The TranslationServices class doesn't care which adapter is used and will perform the task required of it.

Implementing an NUnit Adapter

Where the adapter becomes a necessity is when testing GUI. Traditionally, the GUI is hard to test, and complex scripts have to be written. Worse is if the GUI changes, slightly invalidating all of the scripts. With the new translation services architecture that has been defined, the GUI has no functionality other than calling the appropriate method with the appropriate parameters on the TranslationServices classes. To test the application logic, the only necessity is to implement an IControlAdapter-derived implementation. Following is an example IControlAdapter-derived type that is compatible with an NUnit test:

```
internal class PropertyKeeper {
    public string Value;
}

internal class NUnitAdapter: Abstractions.IControlAdapter {
    public type GetValue<ControlType, type>(ControlType control) where type: class {
        PropertyKeeper cls = control as PropertyKeeper;
        return cls.Value as type;
    }

    public void SetValue<ControlType, type>(ControlType control, type value) {
        PropertyKeeper cls = control as PropertyKeeper;
        cls.Value = value as string;
    }
}
```

The class PropertyKeeper is a generic holder class that acts as a control. Even though PropertyKeeper has nothing to do with a GUI element, using .NET Generics it doesn't matter, as TranslationServices uses the type as black boxes. So even though the generic parameters ControlType are labeled as control elements, they don't need to be. The class NUnitAdapter implements the IControlAdapter interface and manipulates the properties of the PropertyKeeper that is instantiated by the NUnit test.

The NUnit test code is implemented as follows:

```
[TestFixture]
public class TestBusinessLogic {
    [Test]
    public void TestTranslation() {
        PropertyKeeper src = new PropertyKeeper();
        PropertyKeeper dest = new PropertyKeeper();

        src.Value = "Good Morning";
        Abstractions.TranslationServices<NUnitAdapter> srvc =
            new Abstractions.TranslationServices<NUnitAdapter>();
        srvc.DoTranslation(src, dest);
        Assert.AreEqual("Guten Morgen", dest.Value);
    }
}
```

Compare the NUnit test method TestTranslation to the code in the method TranslationTextBox.OnTextChanged. The methods are nearly identical in implementation terms, where the exceptions are the types PropertyKeeper and System.Windows.Forms.TextBox. This is good, because it means the tests can reflect closely how the GUI calls the application logic. And that means the overall application can be tested effectively.

Some Final Notes About the Application

The translation application has been dissected and restructured to use multiple patterns. If you consider the incrementing complexity from the initial application to the resulting architecture, the question that must be asked is, Why do this? The answer is flexibility and testability. The initial code can't be easily tested, nor easily extended. Even though the translation application is simple, most applications aren't. That means being able to test and extend are important attributes that can make or break an application.

The application used Generic types extensively to illustrate how powerful it is to write code that uses black boxes that are manipulated by an adapter. Because of the Generic types, no type information is lost at the developer level, as using the Object type requires the developer to think about what type is being passed around. As illustrated, the type could be System. Windows.Forms.TextBox, or a wx.TextCtrl, or NUnit PropertyKeeper. It doesn't matter, as the adapter knows what the type is and how to process the type.

Moving on, I'll show you how to extend this translation application in the next section.

Adding Multiple Languages to the Application

The translation application as it stands solves the problem of translating a text from English to German. Let's call this version 1.1; remember that version 1.0 was the original quick-and-dirty implementation. A customer request has come in and the application has to be able to translate to other languages. It has been decided to add this feature and call it version 1.5.

The question, though, is how to implement the support of multiple languages. There is the issue of which languages to support, whether to support dynamic translation into multiple languages, and so on. As the developer, you realize that things could become complex again and want to implement the feature using patterns. Confronted with these new requirements, you will want to use patterns, and you know that `ITranslationServices` will need to be implemented for the multiple languages. The main question is how to wire everything together.

This section of the chapter will illustrate how confusing patterns sometimes can be. Many patterns from an implementation point of view look similar, even though their purpose isn't. What will happen in this section are two things: I outline six potential pattern solutions to implement multiple languages, and then I select of one of the patterns and present the reasons why. Here I attempt to model the problems of the real-life developer who has to make choices.

Look Up: Is It a Decorator, Is It a Composite?

Thus far, in all of the chapters, the patterns and their solutions are very obvious, but for this section, six similar, technically implemented patterns are illustrated: Decorator, Composite, Chain of Responsibility, Strategy, State, and Command. In a nutshell, all six patterns expose an interface that a client uses to execute some logic. Hiding behind the interface can be single or multiple instances.

To understand this problem of not knowing what a pattern does, even though its technical implementation looks similar to other patterns, let's look at two definitions of two patterns. From the book *Design Patterns: Elements of Reusable Object-Oriented Software*, the State and Strategy patterns are defined as follows:

- *State*: Allows an object to alter its behavior when its internal state changes. The object will appear to change its class.

- *Strategy*: Defines a family of algorithms, encapsulates each one, and makes them interchangeable. Strategy lets the algorithm vary independently from clients that use it.

Thinking about the two explanations, the conclusion is that a client will use a class that will change behavior without having to tell the client that the behavior has changed. In other words, the State pattern and the Strategy pattern are the same thing, and looking at the UML diagrams in *Design Patterns: Elements of Reusable Object-Oriented Software* won't help that much, as they appear similar. And yet, in the book they are described as two separate patterns.

The problem is that the State pattern and the Strategy pattern illustrate how problematic learning patterns can be. When you learn patterns, many patterns will appear similar, and yet have different names. The problem of the separate patterns for State and Strategy isn't the pattern, but the wording and relationship. Consider the following modified definitions of each pattern:

- *Strategy*: The Strategy pattern uses the Bridge pattern in combination with a controller to define a generic solution. Associated with the controller is a family of algorithms, but assigned by the client is a specific algorithm that is used by the controller. The controller doesn't change behavior whenever the algorithm is changed and isn't aware that a change has occurred.

- *State*: This is a specialized form of the Strategy pattern where the client for the most part doesn't control the selection of algorithm. The client may define an initial algorithm to use and call that an initial algorithm state. As a client makes repeated use of the interface algorithm, state changes occur, and this results in changing of the algorithm implementations without the knowledge of the client.

I think using these explanations, the purpose of each pattern is more obvious, because a context is established including any other pattern that is used. Confusion when learning patterns is common, and I suggest you don't get too worried about it.

So with no further ado, let's go through the six patterns used to implement Version 1.5.

Implementing the Chain of Responsibility Pattern

The purpose of the Chain of Responsibility[7] pattern is to allow a client to make a request, but have it processed by the appropriate handlers. In UML terms, the Chain of Responsibility pattern is defined as shown in Figure 5-5.

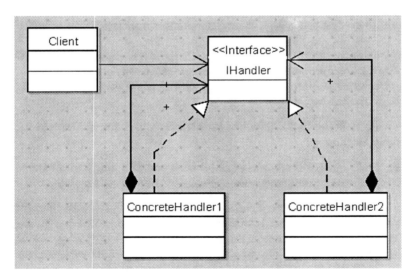

Figure 5-5. *UML definition of the Chain of Responsibility pattern*

The Chain of Responsibility pattern is implemented using an interface that a class implements. The various implementations are linked together in some type of list structure. When the client wants some information processed, a call is made to the front of the list or the first

---

7. *Design Patterns: Elements of Reusable Object-Oriented Software*, p. 223.

interface instance. The first interface instance can decide to process the request or hand it off to another interface instance that may or may not process the request. This course of decision, processing, or delegation continues until somebody has processed the request or no more interface implementation instances are left. The client will know whether the request has been handled or not by the Boolean return value that the client receives.

Based on the diagram in Figure 5-5, a classical implementation of the IHandler interface would be as follows:

```
interface IContext {
}
interface IHandler {
    bool HandleRequest( IContext context);
}
```

The IHandler interface has a single method, HandleRequest, which has a single parameter, IContext. The use of a parameter is purely optional, and there could be multiple parameters. If parameters are specified, they need not be the type IContext, they could be Generic types or some other type that refers to the context of the request. If no parameters are specified, the contextual information could be provided using a singleton (an object-oriented global variable), but it's better to use a parameter, as a parameter occurs per request, involving fewer concurrency issues.

Assuming that the IContext interface is used, then the following source code represents an implementation of the Chain of Responsibility pattern:

```
class ContextForHandler1: IContext {
}
class ContextForHandler2: IContext {
}
class UnknownContext: IContext {
}

class ConcreteHandler1: IHandler {
    IHandler _next;

    public ConcreteHandler1(IHandler next) {
        _next = next;
    }
    public bool HandleRequest(IContext context) {
        if(context is ContextForHandler1) {
            return true;
        }
        else {
            return _next.HandleRequest(context);
        }
    }
}
```

```
class ConcreteHandler2: IHandler {
    public bool HandleRequest(IContext context) {
        if(context is ContextForHandler2) {
            return true;
        }
        else {
            return false;
        }
    }
}
```

The classes ConcreteHandler1 and ConcreteHandler2 are implementations that will process a request. Look at how the constructor of ConcreteHandler1 references another IHandler implementation, whereas ConcreteHandler2 doesn't. This means that when the concrete handlers are linked together, ConcreteHandler2 will reference another concrete handler using the IContext interface. In the example code, this would mean ConcreteHandler1, but doesn't have to. In fact, the different concrete handlers don't need to be related in functionality. If the concrete handlers process e-mail requests, there is no reason why a concrete handler for HTTP requests could not be part of the list. Looking at the implementations of each HandleRequest method, the logic is to process it, hand the request off to another implementation, or return a false answer indicating that it wasn't processed.

Notice how ConcreteHandler1 and ConcreteHandler2 decide to process the request based on the type of the IContext implementation. This is very common for a Chain of Responsibility implementation. But the processing request logic can be triggered in other ways, such as a property on the context or a condition on a singleton. The trigger can be whatever the developer needs, but it should be request related and not a configuration item.

Following is the test code that illustrates how the Chain of Responsibility pattern is used:

```
[TestFixture]
public class TestChainOfResponsibility {
    [Test]
    public void Test() {
        ConcreteHandler1 handler = newConcreteHandler1( new ConcreteHandler2());

        ContextForHandler1 context1 = new ContextForHandler1();
        ContextForHandler2 context2 = new ContextForHandler2();
        UnknownContext context3 = new UnknownContext();

        Assert.IsTrue(handler.HandleRequest(context1));
        Assert.IsTrue(handler.HandleRequest(context2));
        Assert.IsFalse(handler.HandleRequest(context3));
    }
}
```

In the source code, the structure of the concrete handlers is predefined before the requests are made. The order of the instances in the list is important, as otherwise certain steps might be missed or processed out of order.

Another way of implementing the Chain of Responsibility pattern is to use delegates in place of the interface, as illustrated by the following example:

```
delegate bool HandleRequest<ContextType>(ContextType context);
```

The delegate HandleRequest is defined as a Generic type where the delegate parameter represents the contextual information about the request. Very quickly it should be apparent that delegates by themselves can't be used to implement the Chain of Responsibility pattern. The problem with delegates is that when you call a list of delegates, they are all called, and processing is stopped only when there are no more delegates. This is entirely undesirable and doesn't implement the Chain of Responsibility pattern.

Delegates, though, are very useful and would be an ideal solution for the Chain of Responsibility pattern. To make delegates useful for this pattern, you have to implement the Proxy pattern. For simplicity of discussion and visualization, consider the Proxy pattern as an implementation of the Adapter pattern (the Proxy pattern will be discussed in more detail in Chapter 6).

Following is the source code that implements the proxy:

```
class HandlerProxy<ContextType> {
    private HandleRequest<ContextType> _handlers;
    private HandleRequest<ContextType> _localHandler;

    public HandleRequest<ContextType> AddHandler(
        HandleRequest<ContextType> handler) {
        if(_localHandler == null) {
            _localHandler = new HandleRequest<ContextType>(this.LocalHandleRequest);
        }
        _handlers += handler;
        return _localHandler;
    }
    private bool LocalHandleRequest(ContextType context) {
        Delegate[] handlers = _handlers.GetInvocationList();

        for(int c1 = 0; c1 < handlers.Length; c1++) {
            if((bool)handlers[c1].DynamicInvoke(new Object[] { context })) {
                return true;
            }
        }
        return false;
    }
}
```

The class HandlerProxy is a Generic type, as it must expose a method with the same signature as the delegate HandleRequest. The class HandlerProxy has two delegate data members: _handlers and _localHandler. The purpose of the data member _localHandler is to represent the handler that the client calls, which serves as the proxy to the other delegates. The data member _localHandler is a delegate for the method LocalHandleRequest. The data member _handlers represents the handlers that are called by the proxy. The handlers are added using the method AddHandler.

The implementation of the LocalHandleRequest method makes use of the knowledge that delegates, when they are compiled, are classes that derive from the type Delegate. Using the method Delegate.GetInvocationList, an array of delegates is returned. Remember that a delegate instance can refer to a collection of delegates. Then the delegates are iterated and invoked dynamically using the method DynamicInvoke, which is a method called using an array of Object type instances. Then as each delegate is invoked, a test is made for whether the delegate processed the request or not. If a delegate did process the request, the iteration stops and a return value of true is generated.

Putting all of this together, the following source code represents a request made using the HandleRequest:

```
HandleRequest<IContext> CreateHandlers() {
    ConcreteHandler cls = new ConcreteHandler();
    HandleRequest<IContext> handlers;

    HandlerAdapter<IContext> adapter = new HandlerAdapter< IContext>();

    adapter.AddHandler(new HandleRequest< IContext>(cls.HandleRequest2));
    handlers = adapter.AddHandler(
        new HandleRequest< IContext>(cls.HandleRequest3));
    return handlers;
}
[Test]
public void TestDelegate() {
    HandleRequest<ChainOfResponsibility.IContext> handlers = CreateHandlers();

    ContextForHandler1 context1 = new ContextForHandler1();
    ContextForHandler2 context2 = new ContextForHandler2();
    UnknownContext context3 = new UnknownContext();

    Assert.IsTrue(handlers( context1));
    Assert.IsTrue(handlers( context2));
    Assert.IsFalse(handlers(context3));
}
```

What is interesting about this source code example is that the handlers are created using types that are declared only in a single method. The caller of the method CreateHandlers only receives an instance of the HandlerRequest<IContext> delegate.

The class ConcreteHandler implements two methods used by the Chain of Responsibility pattern. What is interesting about this approach, in contrast to the classical interface approach, is that a class can implement multiple delegate instances. The client will be none the wiser regarding how many classes are used to process the request. The Chain of Responsibility pattern has the following distinguishing attributes:

- The structuring of the IHandler implementations is relevant to the processing order.

- An IHandler implementation either processes the request or delegates the request for processing elsewhere.

- An IHandler implementation doesn't need to be related to another IHandler implementation.

- The structuring of the IHandler implementations must not be a single linear order, but could be hierarchical where only certain portions of the tree will process the request.

- Not every IHandler implementation should process a request, and most likely only one implementation will process the request before exiting the iteration.

- Which IHandler implementation should perform the processing is based on the contextual information, and not a state that is defined externally. The only exception is if the contextual information is stored externally. The main idea isn't to use a configuration item to define which handler processes a request.

Implementing the Command Pattern

The purpose of the Command pattern[8] is to make it possible to encapsulate a request as a command that can be executed at some later point in time. Multiple commands are linked together in a list to replicate a state. For example, to implement undo or redo operations in an application, you need the Command pattern. The UML diagram of the Command pattern is illustrated in Figure 5-6.

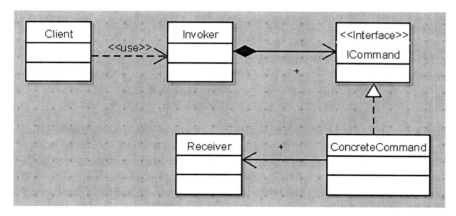

Figure 5-6. *UML implementation of the Command pattern*

The Command pattern has four main pieces: Invoker, ICommand, ConcreteCommand, and Receiver. The Invoker is typically a class that manages a collection of ICommand implementations, and when asked will execute them in a serial fashion. The ICommand interface will typically have a single method, Execute, to execute its own state. The class ConcreteCommand implements the ICommand interface and references a class called Receiver. Receiver could also be called a context, but that might be confused with the Chain of Responsibility pattern. The idea of a Receiver class is to provide an entry point to the infrastructure that ConcreteCommand can manipulate. Unlike the Chain of Responsibility pattern, the context used by the ConcreteCommand

---

8. *Design Patterns: Elements of Reusable Object-Oriented Software*, p. 233.

doesn't contain state used by the ConcreteCommand. All of the state that ConcreteCommand needs is contained within ConcreteCommand. When ConcreteCommand is persisted and re-created, all of the state needed is persisted and re-created.

Following is an example interface definition for ICommand:

```
public interface ICommand<Receiver> {
    void Execute( Receiver receiver);
}
```

The interface ICommand uses Generics to define the Receiver type. In this example of defining the ICommand interface, there is the single method, Execute. The Invoker will call Execute, which then causes ICommand to execute its contained state. An example implementation of ICommand is as follows:

```
public class CommandReceiver {
    public void Output(String buffer) {
        Console.WriteLine(buffer);
    }
}
[Serializable]
public class Operation : ICommand< CommandReceiver> {
    private string _data;
    public Operation(string data) {
        _data = data;
    }
    public void Execute(CommandReceiver output) {
        output.Output( "My Data (" + _data + ")");
    }
}
```

The class Operation implements the ICommand interface and uses the CommandReceiver class as a Receiver type. The constructor to Operation has a single string parameter that represents the state of the class. The state doesn't have to be assigned using the constructor, but could be assigned using methods and properties, or through the Memento pattern discussed in Chapter 8. The methods used to assign the state shouldn't be part of the ICommand interface. The method Execute executes the logic of Operation class, which is to output the state using the Receiver-supplied method CommandReceiver.Output.

If additional methods are assigned to the ICommand interface, then they must relate to the process of executing the command state, such as Initialize and Destroy. The method Initialize would be used to prepare the state of the command. The method Destroy would be used to tear down the state of the command. An example of setting up the state is the preparation of a database connection. Remember that commands can be used as macros in an application to carry out nonprogrammatically specified logic. Notice in the declaration of the Operation class the Serializable attribute is used. This is important because most likely the ICommand implementations will be serialized to a hard disk or network for later referral.

To create a list of commands, it's necessary to execute an Invoker, which is defined as follows:

```
class Invoker< Receiver> {
    private List<ICommand< Receiver>> _commands =
        new List<ICommand<Receiver>>();
    public void Add( ICommand<Receiver> command) {
        _commands.Add(command);
    }
    public void Run( Receiver receiver) {
        foreach(ICommand<Receiver> command in _commands) {
            command.Execute(receiver);
        }
    }
}
```

The Invoker class has two methods: Add and Run. The Add method adds additional ICommand implementations to a list. The Run method iterates the ICommand implementations and executes each one of them. The Run method has a single parameter, which is the Receiver type that will be passed to each ICommand implementation. The Invoker class in this example doesn't implement any serialization routines, because I want to hold off discussing serialization in detail until Chapter 8, which is where the Invoker class will be extended to include serialization.

Putting it all together, the client source code would be as follows.

```
Invoker< CommandReceiver> macro = new Invoker< CommandReceiver>();

macro.Add( new Operation( "First"));
macro.Add( new Operation("Second"));
macro.Run( new CommandReceiver());
```

The variable macro references an Invoker instance. Using the Add method, operations are added, and then the commands are executed using the Run statement. The client is responsible for providing the initial state of the command object and providing a receiver. Once the state has been assigned, then it shouldn't be modified or adapted. If a modified command chain is required, then clone the original and modify the cloned elements. Any other type of interaction isn't allowed and would break the intent of the Command pattern.

The Command pattern can be implemented using delegates, but only for transient lists that don't need serialization, initialization, or destruction. The problem with using delegates is that only the Run method can be implemented. For most Command pattern implementations, you need the Initialize and Destroy methods. When using delegates, a typecast is necessary to perform serialization, initialization, or destruction. And if a typecast is necessary, there is no advantage to delegates, and an interface can be used.

The Command pattern has the following distinguishing attributes:

• The ICommand implementations have an assigned state that isn't manipulated by external classes. Once assigned, the state of the ICommand implementation is essentially read-only and typically not altered.

• An external type that is called an Invoker manages the ICommand implementations as a single collection. It's possible to create a proxy that converts an ICommand interface to reference another Invoker that executes another list of ICommand implementations.

- The ICommand implementations interact with the external environment using the Receiver type. Any other interaction should be avoided, as it could lead to a referencing nightmare.

- The ICommand implementations are read only once they have been assigned, and if the state needs to be modified, an ICommand implementation is cloned.

- The Invoker class is responsible for managing the collection of ICommand implementations, including serialization.

Implementing the Composite Pattern

The purpose of the Composite pattern[9] is to define a structure of objects in a hierarchy, where some objects are containers, and others are leaves. The UML diagram of the Composite pattern is illustrated in Figure 5-7.

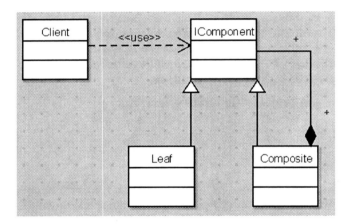

Figure 5-7. *UML implementation of the Composite pattern*

The UML diagram for the Composite pattern looks similar to that of the Chain of Responsibility or Command pattern, and from a high-level perspective it is. There are two main features that compromise a Composite pattern implementation: dynamic storage of data occurs in a hierarchical structure, and the implementations don't process requests.

The Composite pattern is implemented using either interfaces or abstract base classes. Using delegates isn't recommended because a typical Composite pattern base type has multiple methods. The simplest way to illustrate a Composite pattern is to implement a storage system. For example, on the UNIX operating system, the storage system is defined by a hierarchy of nodes, where individual nodes can be directories or files. Following is the definition of the base INode abstract class:

---

9. *Design Patterns: Elements of Reusable Object-Oriented Software*, p. 163.

```
public abstract class Node {
    protected string _name;

    public INode( string name) {
        _name = name;
    }
    public virtual void Add( INode node) {
        Console.WriteLine( "Not implemented");
    }
    public abstract void Display();
}
```

With respect to Figure 5-7, Node represents IComponent. In the definition of Node, multiple ideas are wrapped in one. The method Add is considered a structural method that manipulates the hierarchy. In the example, you see only one structural method, but there could be multiple methods such as add, delete, move, etc. Of course, the number of methods should be limited to the absolute essentials. The method Display is an application logic method, as it references some type of logic that should be performed on the element, and if the element is a container, then the logic applies to all of the contained elements.

For organization purposes, it's acceptable to create a lowest-common-denominator interface that contains all structural methods, and then create an interface that derives from the structural interface and contains all of the application logic methods. What isn't recommended is to create a helper class that implements some base operations of the interfaces. The Composite pattern interface contains methods that not all implementations need, and therefore providing an implementation would be wrong, as that would be adding functionality to an implementation that doesn't want it. For example, implementing the Add method for a File type would be meaningless, as a file can't contain other nodes.

Following is the implementation of the Directory type:

```
public class Directory : Node {
    private List<Node> _entries = new List<Node>();
    public Directory( string name) : base( name) { }

    public override void Add( Node node) {
        _entries.Add( node);
    }
    public override void Display() {
        Console.WriteLine( "Node : {0}", _name);
        foreach( Node node in _entries) {
            node.DumpContents();
        }
    }
}
```

The Directory type is considered a container for other Node data types, which are stored in the _entries data member. With respect to Figure 5-6, Directory represents Composite. Notice how the _entries data member isn't stored in Node. This is because a typical Composite pattern implementation has multiple types that, while related, aren't identical in implementation and share very little functionality, other than the requirement to implement an interface.

The constructor of Directory requires a single parameter that represents the name of the directory, which is stored in the Node base class. Storing the identifier in the base class is useful, because every implementation will have an identifier. The method Display outputs the name of the directory and displays the name of all items referenced by the Directory. Iterating and delegating a method call is very common in the Composite pattern.

Following is an implementation of the File type:

```
public class File : Node {
    public File( string name) : base( name) { }

    public override void Display() {
        Console.WriteLine( "Name of file is " + _name);
    }
}
```

The implementation of the File type is simpler, and with respect to Figure 5-7, File represents Leaf. The File type only implements the Display method, which is usual, as the Leaf types only implement the application logic and not the structural.

It should be noted that the Composite pattern doesn't use the Mediator or Relational Mediator pattern when associating IComponent implementations. In theory, there is nothing to say against using the Mediator pattern, though it would complicate the Composite pattern implementation. A potential reason to use the Mediator pattern would be if there are multiple hierarchical data trees that have complex referencing. The XML Document Object Model might be a good example of where a Composite pattern should be combined with a Mediator pattern, because the XML DOM has a very flexible hierarchical data structure in which DOM elements are moved from document to document.

The Composite pattern has the following distinguishing attributes:

- The hierarchy of the IComponent implementations is dynamic.

- The IComponent implementations aren't used to process data, but to store data.

- The IComponent interface defines a lowest common denominator of a hierarchical data structure that includes structural and application logic methods. When a method doesn't apply to the implementation, it should do nothing. If exceptions must be thrown, then they are thrown only on structural methods, and not application logic, as all application logic methods should act similarly.

- The IComponent interface can have as many methods as needed, but they must include methods to manipulate the hierarchical data structure.

- There are two major types of IComponent implementations: containers that reference other IComponents, and IComponents that represent some state.

Implementing the Decorator Pattern

The purpose of the Decorator pattern[10] is to be able to add functionality dynamically to an object, making it appear as if the object used inheritance. The UML diagram of the Decorator pattern is illustrated in Figure 5-8.

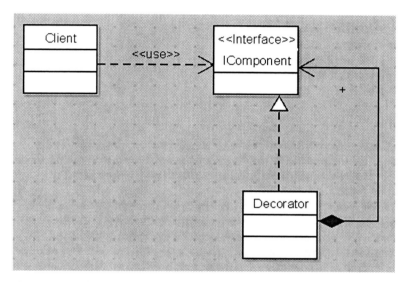

Figure 5-8. *UML implementation of the Decorator pattern*

Yet again, this UML diagram looks strikingly similar to those of the Chain of Responsibility and Composite patterns. The Decorator pattern is different in that it uses all child nodes to process data, and the data structure can be created dynamically on the fly.

The Decorator pattern can be realized using interfaces, abstract base classes, or even delegates as illustrated in the Chain of Responsibility pattern. If an interface or an abstract base class is used, you can define multiple methods. The different methods must be related, and all application logic related. This means that there should be no structural methods in the base type.

To illustrate the Decorator pattern, consider the creation of a burger. A burger is essentially a bun, some meat, and other stuff. There can be cheeseburgers or regular hamburgers. All of the items that make up a burger are ingredients, and that would be the base interface of a Decorator implementation. Following is the base interface definition called `Ingredient`:

```
public interface Ingredient {
    String GetIdentifier();
}
```

The base type `Ingredient` doesn't contain any methods that relate to organization of the `Ingredient` implementations. The only method, `GetIdentifier`, relates to retrieving all of the ingredients of the chain. It's assumed that when one method of the `Ingredient` interface is called, that method invocation will be delegated to all of the other `Ingredient` implementations.

---

10. *Design Patterns: Elements of Reusable Object-Oriented Software*, p. 175.

The different implementations of the Decorator pattern are related and as a whole form a grouping. This is useful to know because it enables the definition of a helper class to do some of the heavy lifting as illustrated by the following source code:

```
public abstract class Decorator : Ingredient {
    protected Ingredient _nextIngredient;

    public Decorator( Ingredient ingredient) {
        _nextIngredient = ingredient;
    }
    public virtual String GetIdentifier() {
        return _nextIngredient.GetIdentifier();
    }
}
```

The abstract base class Decorator implements a default constructor that manages the next Ingredient reference. The method GetIdentifier provides a mechanism to call the next Ingredient. The Decorator type provides a default implementation or a helper class for all Ingredient implementations.

The link to the next ingredient could have been managed by a proxy as illustrated by the delegate-based Chain of Responsibility pattern. That approach isn't advisable, as the Decorator pattern is intended to be a self-contained grouping that can be dynamically modified. If a container manages the individual elements, then the individual elements would need to know about the container and its siblings. The end result would be an overly complicated hierarchy that would need to include the Mediator pattern to manage the individual references.

Following is the source code that illustrates how the individual ingredients are implemented:

```
public class Bun : Ingredient {
    private String _description = "bun";

    public Bun() {
    }
    public String GetIdentifier() {
        return _description;
    }
}

public class Lettuce : Decorator {
    private String _description = "lettuce";

    public Lettuce( Ingredient component) : base (component) {
    }
    public override String GetIdentifier() {
        return _nextIngredient.GetIdentifier() + " " + _description;
    }
}
```

```
public class Cheese : Decorator {
    private String _description = "cheese";

    public Cheese( Ingredient component) : base( component) {
    }
    public override String GetIdentifier() {
        return _ nextIngredient.GetIdentifier() + " " + _description;
    }
}

public class Meat : Decorator {
    private String _description = "meat";

    public Meat( Ingredient component) : base( component) {
    }

    public override String GetIdentifier() {
        return _nextIngredient.GetIdentifier() + " " + _description;
    }
}
```

The individual Ingredient implementations derive from the Decorator type, except for the Bun class. This is because the decorator has a complication in how it's created. Each ingredient references another ingredient, which is the default implementation technique as defined by the Decorator abstract base class. Where the default implementation technique can't be used is at the end of the list, since the end of the list doesn't have another ingredient.

To understand the problem of the end of the list, consider the following source code, which illustrates programmatically how to create a hamburger:

```
Ingredient hamburger = new Meat( new Lettuce( new Bun()));
```

The hamburger is created by successively instantiating an ingredient and passing that instance to the constructor of another ingredient. Since Bun is the end of the list, there is no class to pass in. Of course, an option would be to pass in a null value to indicate an end of list. However, doing that is a hack on a hack. The Decorator pattern is very useful because it provides a neutral interface to what a client considers as a single object. In effect, it's as if a class has its functionality extended.

The downside to the Decorator pattern is the instantiation and organization of the individual elements. When creating the hamburger, the new statement was used. Going back to Chapter 3 and the Factory pattern, recall that I explicitly said this is a bad idea, because it locks down the implementation. A better idea is to use the Builder pattern to preconstruct specific configurations of hamburgers. If the structure of the Decorator pattern is to change dynamically, then the Builder pattern implementation that created the structure initially should have methods to dynamically modify the structure. It isn't recommended that the structure be manipulated and created by multiple Builder or Factory patterns. Doing so will complicate the bookkeeping of the references, causing maintenance and extension problems.

The Decorator pattern has the following distinguishing attributes:

- The linear list of IComponent implementations is dynamic and can be altered at runtime.

- The linear list of IComponent implementations is a grouping of similar types. For example, you would never create a list of objects where some parts are from planes and other parts from a hamburger.

- IComponent implementations manage their own referencing, where the referencing methods (for example, Add, Remove, etc.) are preferably defined in an abstract base class. The abstract base class is known to all IComponent implementations, and therefore a typecast is acceptable, even though the abstract base class won't be exposed publicly.

- IComponent implementations may and can manage a state and operate on an external state.

Implementing the State Pattern

As defined previously, the purpose of the State pattern is to make it possible to dynamically select an algorithm without the intervention of the client. The UML diagram for the State pattern is shown in Figure 5-9.

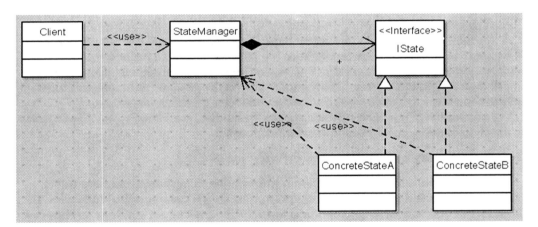

Figure 5-9. *UML definition of the the State pattern*

The State pattern has some Mediator pattern aspects to it. The StateManager class manages the references to the individual ConcreteState (A and B) implementations. When the client attempts to call the ConcreteState implementations, either a direct method call or an indirect method call can be made. The StateManager, not the client, manages the switching of the state implementation.

To get an idea of how the State pattern manages state, let's consider a simple example of switching a light on using a single button light switch. If the light is on, then touching the switch will turn the light off, and if the light is off, then the light is switched off. Each state is an individual instance that is wired together to make a light. The base interface would be the state of the light and is defined as follows:

```
public interface ILightState {
    bool IsLightOn {
        get;
    }
    void TouchButton();
}
```

The interface ILightState defines one method and one property. The method TouchButton is responsible for changing the state of the light switch. The property IsLightOn defines the state of the light and whether it's on or off. In this simple method, there are two types of methods. The property IsLightOn is an application logic method, which would be called by the client to perform some sort of processing. In this example, there is very little processing, and a state is returned.

What is problematic is the method TouchButton, as it's structural and is responsible for changing the state of the light. The problem is, who changes the state? Each state is an individual instance, which means that to change state, one state must reference another state from somewhere. The TouchButton method is defined as part of the interface, which means that individual state manages the next state. But is that optimal? Remember from object-oriented principles, each object is responsible for its own actions and data. When manipulating state, this principle is problematic, as either an über object knows about all the implementations or the clients know about each other using the Mediator pattern.

To illustrate each solution, let's first consider the use of an über object, which in terms of the State pattern is the StateManager class. An example implementation is defined as follows:

```
public class StateManager {
    private ILightState _onLight = new LightStateOn();
    private ILightState _offLight = new LightStateOff();
    private ILightState _current = _offLight;

    public ILightState LightState {
        get { return _current; }
    }
    public void TouchButton() {
        if(_current.IsLightOn) {
            _current = _offLight;
        }
        else {
            _current = _onLight;
        }
    }
}
```

When using the State pattern, you must define a default state, which in the sample is the off light (_offLight). It isn't advisable to assign the current state as being a null object, because that isn't what happens in reality. In reality, there is always a state, and that must be defined. Using a null object state results in an inconsistent state where the State manager has to be initialized before use.

The StateManager class exposes the property LightState to indicate the current state, which is a reference to the data member _current. The data member _current represents either an on light state or off light state. The data member _current will reference one of the state implementations: _onLight, which is LightStateOn to indicate a light that is on; or _offLight, which is LightStateOff to indicate a light that is off.

The method TouchButton would assign the current light state reference based on the current state of the light. The method TouchButton is considered a structural method as it modifies the data member _current. If the light is on, then the light state will be assigned to _offLight, and if off, then the light state will be assigned a value of _onLight. When using an über object, you don't need structural methods in the ILightStateButton interface.

The trouble with this approach is that the StateManager has to be aware of what the ILightState implementations do. In the simple example of a light switch with on or off states, this isn't a problem. Imagine the scenario where there are multiple states to check. Imagine the complexity of the TouchButton method implementation that has multiple ifs and selects. It could very easily happen that a specific state is missed, and therefore a bug is introduced into the application. Additionally, it isn't possible to add a state dynamically, because that would mean modifying the StateManager code.

Another approach to the state problem is to let the individual states determine what the next state is. This is where the Mediator pattern is applied, as illustrated by the following StateManager implementation:

```
public class StateManager {
    private ILightState _onLight;
    private ILightState _offLight;
    private ILightState _current;

    public StateManager() {
        _onLight = new LightStateOn(this);
        _offLight = new LightStateOff(this);
        _current = _offLight;
    }

    public ILightState LightState {
        get { return _current; }
        set { _current = value; }
    }

    public ILightState this[string state] {
        get {
            if(String.Compare("on", state) == 0) {
                return _onLight;
            }
            else if(String.Compare("off", state) == 0) {
                return _offLight;
            }
            throw new NotSupportedException();
        }
    }
}
```

In this implementation, the StateManager has a constructor that initializes the LightStateOn and LightStateOff types and very importantly defines a default state of the light being off. Passed to each state implementation is the parent parameter, which is the this reference or the instance of the StateManager. The property LightState has implemented the set method, allowing the assignment of the current state. The method with the this reference is an indexer that retrieves a specific state. Notice in this implementation of StateManager the lack of a TouchButton method. This is because the ILightState interface implements the method. The client would manipulate the StateManager as follows:

```
StateManager manager = new StateManager();
manager.LightState.TouchButton(); //Light is turned off
manager.LightState.TouchButton(); //Light is turned on
```

The client references the current state and calls the TouchButton method. When the TouchButton method is called, the client would ask the parent for a state and then assign the next state. This strategy is illustrated by the following LightStateOn and LightStateOff implementations:

```
public class LightStateOn : ILightState {
    StateManager _parent;
    public LightStateOn(StateManager2 parent) {
        _parent = parent;
    }
    public bool IsLightOn {
        get { return true; }
    }
    public void TouchButton() {
        _parent.LightState = _parent["off"];
    }
}

public class LightStateOff : ILightState {
    StateManager _parent;
    public LightStateOff(StateManager2 parent) {
        _parent = parent;
    }
    public bool IsLightOn {
        get { return false; }
    }
    public void TouchButton() {
        _parent.LightState = _parent["on"];
    }
}
```

The Mediator pattern implementation is necessary, as the individual ILightState implementations need to reference other ILightState implementations to indicate a state change. In the TouchButton methods, the _parent.LightState is assigned a state determined by the implementation.

In the approach where the `ILightState` implementations determine the next state, the solution is considered more traditionally object oriented, as the implementations manage their own responsibilities. The downside is complexity, as the `StateManager` must expose all states and allow external access for state assignment. This could be a problem, because it means that a client or `ILightState` implementation could manipulate the state and violate the application logic used to determine the correct state.

The rules for determining which approach to use are as follows:

- If the states are well defined and the conditions to the corresponding state are well defined, then letting the `StateManager` class assign the state is better.

- If the states are difficult to understand or to determine and prone to misuse, then the `StateManager` class assigns the current state.

- If the state conditions and numbers of states constantly change, then the `ILightState` implementations should manage the current state.

- If you want the flexibility to have states be determined dynamically using configuration entries and are willing to invest in coding a secure `StateManager`, then let the `ILightState` implementations determine the current state.

The State pattern has the following distinguishing attributes:

- The client doesn't know which `IState` implementation is used and assumes that the `StateManager` has chosen correctly.

- The `StateManager` can manage the states however it pleases (for example, through collection, hard-coded data members, etc.). The `StateManager` must be able to cross-reference an identifier for a state with a state. If an entirely generic `StateManager` is desired, the state identifier could be added to the `IState` interface as a property that the `StateManager` iterates when asked for a specific state implementation. It isn't the responsibility of the `IState` implementation nor the client to find a state implementation for a specific identifier.

- The individual `IState` implementations belong to a single grouping. It isn't possible to contain a state for turning a light bulb on and for sending e-mail to a client.

- The individual `IState` implementations relate to states of an object and not an object. For example, even though the light switch controlled a light bulb, there was neither a light bulb object nor a light switch object. Instead, there was a state manager that managed a light bulb state. This means the State pattern is useful for problems that involve state.

- The state of an individual `IState` implementation is defined at compile time, and not defined at runtime.

Implementing the Strategy Pattern

As defined previously, the Strategy pattern enables an object to alter its behavior when its internal state changes. The UML diagram for the Strategy pattern is shown in Figure 5-10.

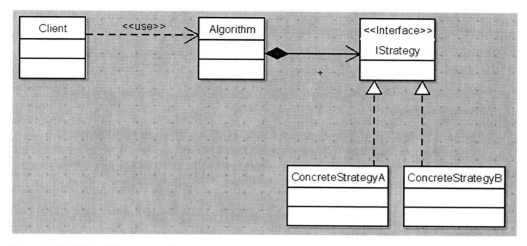

Figure 5-10. *UML definition of the Strategy pattern*

In Figure 5-10, the Strategy pattern is similar to the State pattern from an architectural point of view, but the intent is entirely different. Unlike the State pattern, the `Algorithm` class doesn't manage state, but represents an algorithm that uses one or more `IStrategy` implementations. The `IStrategy` implementation isn't managed by the `Algorithm` class, but assigned by the client.

Following is a very simple example of the Strategy pattern:

```
interface IStrategy { }

class ConcreateStrategyA: IStrategy { }
class ConcreateStrategyB: IStrategy { }

class Algorithm {
    private IStrategy _strategy;

    public void SetStrategy(IStrategy strategy) {
        _strategy = strategy;
    }

    public void ApplicationLogic() {
        // do something with _strategy
    }
}
```

The `IStrategy` interface instance is assigned using the method `Algorithm.SetStrategy`. The method `SetStrategy` is called by the client, which means that the client must know about the general intent of the internal workings of the `Algorithm` class. The method `Algorithm.ApplicationLogic` will use the assigned `IStrategy` implementation to execute its logic.

The Strategy pattern has the following distinguishing attributes:

- The client does need to know about the general workings of the various `IStrategy` implementations and the workings of the `Algorithm` class.

- The `Algorithm` class doesn't know about the different `IStrategy` implementations, and only knows the `IStrategy` interface.

- The individual `IStrategy` implementations may or may not contain state related to the operations.

- The individual `IStrategy` implementations don't know about the workings of the `Algorithm` class. The `Algorithm` class won't directly reference the `IStrategy` implementations (other than the pattern-defined references), and the `IStrategy` implementations won't directly reference the `Algorithm` class instance.

Implementing Dynamic Selection of Language Translation

Having illustrated the different patterns, the question is which pattern should be applied to solve the problem of implementing a dynamic selection of the language used for translation. When confronted with a problem, you follow these steps:

1. Define the problem to be solved and consider what the important attributes are.

2. Pick the patterns that you think apply.

3. From the selected patterns, define the distinguishing attributes. This means pick out the attributes of the patterns that separate them from the other selected patterns.

4. Then take those attributes and compare them to the attributes you need to solve the problem.

Having defined the problem and the patterns, let's start figuring out which pattern could be used and why. First, let's eliminate the patterns that don't apply and I'll explain why. Note that the explanation of why a pattern doesn't apply is as important as explaining why a pattern does apply. When a pattern isn't used, there should be a clear reason why not.

- *Command pattern*: Doesn't apply because the Command pattern is generally used for executing a number of steps after they have already been completed. The caller gives the state, and thus this single aspect negates the use of this pattern.

- *Composite pattern*: Doesn't apply because there is no hierarchical storage of objects. The requirement is to perform a single translation of a single phrase that is given by the request.

- *Decorator pattern*: Doesn't apply because the text isn't translated multiple times. The text is translated using a single language. The only exception is if concurrent translations were to be executed. For example, if you want to convert a text into five different languages at once for every request, then a Decorator pattern might be useful, as the list of languages could represent the five different languages.

Three patterns were removed as being obviously incorrect, but the three left over are potential solutions. From the three, two are close solutions, but not close enough, as I explain here:

- *State pattern*: The State pattern could apply, but there is a problem in that translating languages doesn't involve shifting from one language to another language. For example, the translation service wouldn't expect to have the first text translated into German and the second text translated into Japanese. The choice of translation is determined by the client, and therefore this pattern isn't applicable.

- *Strategy pattern*: The strategy pattern does apply and would work. In fact, the strategy pattern would be a natural fit. Going back to the original definition of the TranslationServices class, it represents the Algorithm class. This means that the client that consumes the TranslationServices class would have to define the language to use for translation. The reason why I didn't choose this approach relates to Figure 5-4 and Figure 5-3. In Figure 5-3, the Loader class is contained in the Form class. Then in Figure 5-4, the Loader is contained in the TranslationServices class. If the Strategy pattern were used, then the Loader class would have to be moved back to the Form class or more appropriately to the TranslationTextBox class. Remember that the TranslationServices type represents the State pattern–defined Algorithm type, and therefore the client must define the translation. This means the GUI must contain application logic on which language to choose, meaning it must know, instantiate, and assign the language type. This is what we want to avoid because it violates separating GUI logic from application logic.

The solution is to use the Chain of Responsibility pattern, because a configuration file could define all possible languages that would be loaded. The TranslationServices would expose a collection of available languages as a series of identifiers. Then the GUI would select a language that would be used to translate the text. The Loader class would be converted from a simple Client-Dispatcher-Server pattern to also take advantage of the Chain of Responsibility and implement the ITranslationServices interface.

The new and final architecture that allows a dynamic selection of the language is illustrated in Figure 5-11.

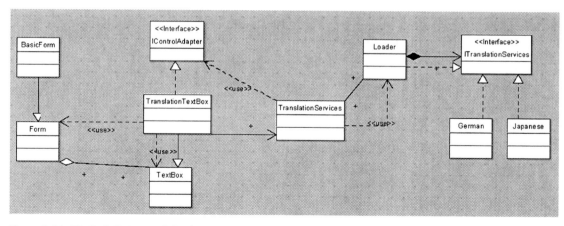

Figure 5-11. *UML definition of the final translation services architecture*

The Chain of Responsibility pattern is implemented using delegates because the Loader class is serving the dual purpose of implementing the Client-Dispatcher-Server pattern and the

Chain of Responsibility pattern. The exact details are beyond the scope of this book, as the reasons have already been explained. However, for those interested in the sources, please download the source code associated with this book at the Apress web site (`http://www.apress.com`).

Some Final Thoughts

The purpose of this chapter was to illustrate a real-life scenario of applying patterns to a problem. The beginning of the chapter illustrated a sample application. The application was refactored to add patterns. The added patterns resulted in a solution that is maintainable, flexible, and extendable. Yet the patterns didn't introduce a large framework; instead, the patterns modularized and compartmentalized the application. The modularized application was GUI based and could be tested using test scripts that didn't employ GUI test scripts, making it cheaper and more efficient to ensure the quality of an application.

And finally, the application was extended to include new functionality. Instead of refactoring, several patterns were explored as candidates for solving a specific problem. Outlined was the decision process of which pattern applied and which didn't.

Throughout the chapter, I've attempted to use object-oriented principles. Not all object-oriented principles are wrong, but many need to be extended to include modern development practices. Sometimes the resulting code is more complex, but the result is code that is modular. I feel we tend forget that there is modular programming, which is as important as writing reusable code. Each technique has its use, and neither one or the other is more important.

CHAPTER 6

■■■

Writing Algorithms

Let's say that you're writing an application. Everything is going well. You've created and verified the use cases, and you've designed, verified, and implemented the initial architecture. Then it becomes necessary to write code that does something, and that's when the problems creep in. This slow creep of problems, due to the inevitable trade-offs and the very act of writing code, is a natural part of the design process; it can't be avoided, because a decision that looked good at the time could prove very bad in hindsight. Sometimes you have to make a mistake in the first place to recognize that it was a mistake.

This chapter is about writing the guts of your application using patterns that make it simpler to implement the various algorithms to get the application to do something. Specifically, this chapter focuses on how to ensure consistency in your application logic. Your application will exhibit problem creep, but using the patterns and ideas in this chapter, you can isolate problem creep enough to refactor and sanitize your application.

The patterns defined in this chapter illustrate how to mimic other interfaces without the client knowing the difference. Using these patterns, it's possible to create a modularization that kicks off other algorithms. These other algorithms aren't part of the mimicked implementations, rather they control the mimicked implementations. *Functors*, which I introduce in this chapter, are often used to kicked off other algorithms. You'll see that functors are an essential part of the development process when writing consistent applications. Traditionally, functors manage collections, but they can be used in other contexts. Here you'll get a chance to explore the different kinds of functors, some of which perform verification operations, and others that perform transformation operations.

Impersonating Functionality Without Modifications

As you may recall from the last chapter, you can use the Decorator pattern to chain together multiple implementations of a single interface to solve a common problem. Specifically, the Decorator pattern example I presented demonstrated the creation of a hamburger, where each interface implementation represented an ingredient of the hamburger. The Proxy pattern, which I explain in this section, is similar to the Decorator pattern in that both attempt to offer functionality without altering the source code of the other implementations.

However, unlike the Decorator pattern, individual implementations of the Proxy pattern don't work together. The best way to understand this concept is to consider a collection. Imagine for the moment that collections were not thread safe. And imagine writing an application that didn't use threads that happened to use an unsafe collection. Now imagine taking that application and adding threads. The collection won't work with multiple threads because it was never meant to be used in a multithreaded context. In this case, you face the challenge of either not using multiple threads or rewriting the collection class.

Another solution that illustrates the Proxy pattern is to create an implementation with the same interface as the collection has. In the new implementation, the existing collection is encapsulated, and the methods of the interface are implemented. The client gets a reference to the new implementation, not the original collection. Then whenever a client calls a collection method, the new implementation synchronizes access and delegates the call to the encapsulated method.

Now that you know a little about the Proxy pattern, let's see how you'd go about using it.

Implementing the Proxy Pattern

The essence of the Proxy pattern[1] is to provide a surrogate or a placeholder for another class that manages the access and control of just that class. Figure 6-1 illustrates the Proxy pattern in UML terms.

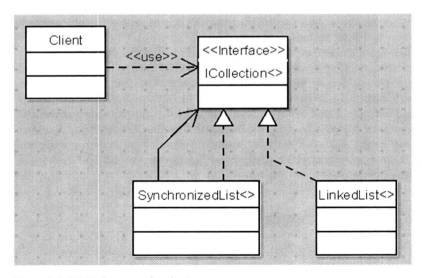

Figure 6-1. *UML diagram for the Proxy pattern*

As you can see in this diagram, Client interacts with the interface ICollection, which is implemented by both the LinkedList and SynchronizedList types. Because LinkedList is from the .NET library API, it can't be changed in functionality. Attempting to do so isn't appropriate, as LinkedList is managed by Microsoft. Therefore, the only possible option is to use the Proxy

---

1. Erich Gamma et al., *Design Patterns: Elements of Reusable Object-Oriented Software* (Boston: Addison-Wesley, 1995), p. 207.

pattern. The class SynchronizedList implements the ICollection interface and references a parent ICollection implementation. The parent reference is responsible for doing all the heavy lifting of managing the collection items.

In code terms, you implement the SynchronizedList as follows (note that for clarity not all of the code is shown):

```
class SynchronizedList<type>: ICollection<type> {
    private ICollection<type> _parent;

    public SynchronizedList(ICollection<type> parent) {
        _parent = parent;
    }

    public void Add(type item) {
        lock(this) {
            _parent.Add(item);
        }
    }
}
```

The class SynchronizedList<> uses Generics like the interface ICollection that it implements. What is distinctive about the SynchronizedList class is the constructor and the data member _parent. The constructor SynchronizedList<> requires as a parameter the parent ICollection implementation that will receive all delegated method calls. The implementation of the method Add does two things: perform the added value of the proxy and call the parent implementation. All methods that implement the Proxy pattern will do the same as the Add method. One caveat: the logic of the implementation might do different things depending on the method call, but if accepted the method call will always be delegated. It isn't acceptable for the Proxy pattern to act like the parent that the pattern implements. Doing that would be redundant and create consistency problems.

Also extremely important is that the Proxy pattern encapsulates the parent implementation and doesn't expose the parent functionality directly. For example, in the implementation of the SynchronizedList<> class, the data member _parent can only be assigned via the constructor, ensuring a consistent Proxy pattern implementation.

From the client perspective, the way to use the synchronized collection is as follows:

```
ICollection<string> collection = ➡
new SynchronizedList<string>(new LinkedList<string>());
```

The variable collection is of the type ICollection<>, which refers to the SynchronizedList<> type. And the SynchronizedList<> type refers to the LinkedList<> type. The variable collection must be an interface reference, rather than a direct reference to the class like the one you see in this example:

```
LinkedList<string> collection = new LinkedList<string>();
```

I include this direct reference example because very often developers will use the types directly when using collections, even though this is incorrect. Using the type makes it impossible to use the Proxy pattern. And frankly, it violates the original intention of the Bridge pattern.

Enhancing Types Using Functors

The Proxy pattern is useful when you want to modify the functionality of a type without the blessing or cooperation of that type. SynchronizedList<> illustrates how synchronization capabilities can be added without having to change the type. In contrast, the various interface implementations of the Decorator pattern cooperate to solve a problem.

Enhancing types through the Proxy pattern can be very useful. The previous example illustrated synchronization, but in the developer community the Proxy pattern is implemented in conjunction with *functors*.[2] The purpose of a functor is to perform a mapping from one domain to another or to perform an operation or function. Functors are traditionally mathematically based, but need not be.

You want to use functors because they make it possible to attach standard logic to another type using a predefined construct. For example, when used by collections, Generics validate the type, but do not validate whether the contents of the type are correct. You use a predicate functor to validate the contents of the type.

The most common functor types are defined as follows:

- *Comparer*: Accepts two objects and performs a comparison between the two. The return value is an integer, which represents whether one object is equal, less than, or greater than the other.

- *Closure*: Accepts a single object and performs some logic. No value is returned.

- *Predicate*: Accepts a single value and performs some logic. A true value indicates that the predicate logic triggered, and a false value means that the predicate logic didn't trigger.

- *Transformer*: Accepts a single value and performs a transformation that results in either a new type being generated or the original type being transformed.

Let's take a closer look at these common functor types.

Adding Comparer Capabilities

The IComparable interface, shown in the following example, is defined in the .NET base classes:

```
public interface IComparable {
    int CompareTo(object obj);
}
```

The IComparable interface has a single method, CompareTo, that represents the object instance to compare to. The IComparable interface works if the object that performs the testing implements this interface. The problem with this approach is if the objects to be compared don't have IComparable implemented, then the comparer functor won't work. It's similar to the Decorator pattern, where all implementations concerned have to cooperate.

From the .NET base classes, another interface, IComparer, can be used to compare two objects and is defined as follows:

---

2. http://en.wikipedia.org/wiki/Functor, http://dictionary.reference.com/search?q=functor

```
public interface IComparer {
    int Compare(object x, object y);
}
```

IComparer has a single method with two parameters representing the objects to be compared. The advantage of the IComparer interface is that the objects to be tested don't have to implement any additional functionality.

For the scope of this pattern, and the rest of this book, examples will include a delegate, not an interface. The advantage of a delegate is that it can be implemented using C# 2.0 anonymous methods or any method of a class, whereas an interface must be implemented and then instantiated. If necessary, you can apply the Adapter pattern (which I discussed in Chapter 5) to convert the delegate into an interface. The IComparer interface defined in terms of a delegate is as follows:

```
public delegate int DelegateComparer< type1, type2>( type1 obj1, type2 obj2);
```

The delegate DelegateComparer<> is defined using a template, making it type safe, and returns an int value indicating the results of a comparison. The two parameters are the object instances to compare.

To give you a clearer idea of how the comparer delegate works, let's see how to create a program that generates a flight ticket.

Creating a Flight Ticket Application

For this flight ticket example, assume a flight ticket is defined in terms of individual flight legs. Consider the following interface definition used to define one leg of a flight:

```
interface IFlight {
    string Origin { get; set; }
    string Destination { get; set;}
    IFlight NextLeg { get; set; }
}
```

The interface IFlight has three properties: two strings and a reference to IFlight. The individual flight legs can be managed either using an individual instance that references another instance or as a collection of flight legs. The property NextLeg represents a leg in a flight, and therefore no collection is required. The interface IFlight has been reduced to the essentials to illustrate how you employ a comparer functor. The comparer functor is used by the property NextLeg to ensure that the property isn't assigned the same leg twice, as it would be very silly to fly to the same destination at the same time.

You may think that it's better to have a collection of flight legs rather than one flight leg referencing another flight leg, but this depends on the nature of the application. And in this case, I'm trying to illustrate that the delegate DelegateComparer<> can also be applied in contexts where there is no collection. Now that you are aware of functors, you may realize that most of the time other documentation or other books will illustrate them solely in the context of a collection. This isn't, and shouldn't be, the only way to use functors. Functors are little black boxes that carry out a specific piece of logic. Remember from previous chapters that you want little black boxes throughout your entire code.

Managing the Flight Legs Using Object.Equals

Let's see how you might approach managing flight leg information without a functor to get a firm understanding of why a functor is useful. The constraint for NextLeg is that it shouldn't reference an identical leg. As an example, a class named Flight implements the IFlight interface, and an abbreviated class declaration appears as follows:

```
class Flight : IFlight {
    IFlight _nextLeg;
    public IFlight NextLeg {
        get {
            return _nextLeg;
        }
        set {
            if( !value.Equals( this)) {
                _nextLeg = value;
            }
        }
    }
}
```

Notice the property NextLeg in the Flight implementation. In the set part of the property, the method value.Equals is called. The return value from value.Equals should be a comparison of the values of the data members. The value returned from value.Equals in this case is incorrect because the comparison is based on the reference information and not the data members of Flight. To have Equals return a correct value, you have to implement the Equals method. And if the Equals method is implemented, the GetHashCode method also has to be implemented.

The return value of the method GetHashCode uniquely identifies an object with a certain state. If two different object instances contain the same state, then the GetHashCode method will return the same value. This carries over into the Equals method in that two objects that contain the same state are equal to each other. Implementing a hash code is a difficult task best delegated to a helper class that does the heavy lifting. The book *Effective Java Programming Language Guide*[3] outlines this robust technique:

1. Store some constant nonzero value, for example, 17, in a variable.

2. For each data member of the type, perform a mathematical operation that results in int values that are successively multiplied and added, where the operation is specific to the type and defined as follows:

   • bool: If true return 0; otherwise return 1.

   • byte, char, short, or int: Return the value of the type.

   • long: Return (int)(f ^ (f >>> 32).

   • float: Return Convert.ToInt32 of the value.

---

3. Joshua Bloch, *Effective Java Programming Language Guide* (Boston: Addison-Wesley, 2001), p. 38.

- object: Return the value generated by calling object.GetHashCode.

- array: Iterate and treat each element individually.

The rules are implementing in a class called HashCodeAutomater, which is illustrated as follows in abbreviated form:

```
public class HashCodeAutomater{
    private readonly int _constant;
    private int _runningTotal;

    public HashCodeAutomater() {
        _constant = 37;
        _runningTotal = 17;
    }

    public HashCodeAutomater AppendSuper(int superHashCode) {
        _runningTotal = _runningTotal * _runningTotal + superHashCode;
        return this;
    }

    public HashCodeAutomater Append( Object obj) {
        if (obj == null) {
            _runningTotal = _runningTotal * _constant;

        } else {
            if( obj.GetType().IsArray == false) {
                _runningTotal = _runningTotal * _runningTotal + obj.GetHashCode();

            } else {
                if (obj is long[]) {
                    Append((long[]) obj);
                }
                // Other tests have been removed for clarity
                else {
                    // Not an array of primitives
                    Append((Object[]) obj);
                }
            }
        }
        return this;
    }

    public HashCodeAutomater Append(long value) {
        _runningTotal = _runningTotal * _constant + ((int) (value ^ (value >> 32)));
        return this;
    }
```

```
    public HashCodeAutomater Append(long[] array) {
        if (array == null) {
            _runningTotal = _runningTotal * _constant;
        }
        else {
            for (int i = 0; i < array.Length; i++) {
                Append(array[i]);
            }
        }
        return this;
    }
    public HashCodeAutomater Append(Object[] array) {
        if (array == null) {
            _runningTotal = _runningTotal * _constant;
        }
        else {
            for (int i = 0; i < array.Length; i++) {
                Append(array[i]);
            }
        }
        return this;
    }
    public int toHashCode() {
        return _runningTotal;
    }
}
```

The different implementations of the method Append in this example belong to a single grouping for a single data type, which happens to be the data type long. For example, notice the Append method that accepts a long type and long array. In the full implementation of HashCodeAutomater, there would be an Append method for the short type and the short array, and all of the other data types. No specific group implementation for the string type exists, because it's treated like an object that has its own hash code calculation implementation.

Notice in the implementations of the Append methods how a calculation is performed and then added to the data member _runningTotal. The return value is a this reference so that the methods can be chained together. This allows a client to use the HashCodeAutomater class as illustrated by the following GetHashCode implementation:

```
class HashcodeExample {
    public int value;
    public string buffer;

    public HashcodeExample( int val, string buf) {
        value = val;
        buffer = buf;
    }
```

```
public override int GetHashCode() {
    return new HashCodeAutomater()
        .Append( value)
        .Append( buffer).toHashCode();
}
}
```

The implementation of HashcodeExample includes two data members, value and buffer. These data members make up the state of the class. Not all data members are used when calculating the hash code value of a class instance. For example, if HashcodeExample has a data member that references a database connection, it shouldn't be used when calculating the hash code, because the database connection is used to get state, and doesn't influence the state. It's a means-to-an-end sort of object.

Once you've created the GetHashCode method, you can implement the Equals method as follows:

```
public override bool Equals( Object obj) {
    return (obj.GetHashCode() == this.GetHashCode());
}
```

It's perfectly acceptable to use the GetHashCode method because it validates content, which is what the method Equals expects. Note that if you implement the Equals method, but not the GetHashCode method, the .NET compiler will generate a warning that you should implement the GetHashCode method.

The Problem of Validation

Although the example of validating the next leg without functors and adding the validation to the property NextLeg works, it doesn't represent a correct solution. The problem is that the validation is carried out in the context of the class. Classical object-oriented design dictates that this is the approach to use. However, if any other type of validation is required, the validation code will have to be updated by changing the source code of the type. This makes validation a maintenance issue.

In Chapter 5, you saw how patterns can separate the GUI logic from the application logic. That concept needs to be extended so that validation logic is separated from the class. The class might consume validation logic, but doesn't define what the validation logic is. This approach still adheres to the classical object-oriented design rule in which the object is responsible for performing the validation, but doesn't need to know the exact implementation of the validation. Imagine the following: you are writing the code for the flight ticket program and release version 1.0. For version 1.1, it has been decided that the flight legs won't be referenced in Flight, but in a class called Ticket, which references a list of IFlight interface instances. The validation logic will have to be transferred from the Flight implementation to the Ticket implementation.

Here's an abbreviated implementation of Ticket in which the validation logic is moved:

```
class FlightAlreadyPresentException : Exception {
 }
class Ticket {
    private IList< IFlight> _flightLegs = new List< IFlight>();

    public void AddLeg( IFlight leg) {
        foreach( IFlight flight in _flightLegs) {
            if( flight.Equals( leg)) {
                throw new FlightAlreadyPresentException();
            }
        }
        _flightLegs.Add( leg);
    }
}
```

The class Ticket has a method called AddLeg in which the flight legs are iterated and tested for equality. If the flight leg to be added is equal to an already existing flight leg, then an exception is thrown. Otherwise, the flight leg is added to the list _flightlegs.

The problem is that the application logic had to be moved from one type to another. In the example, the logic is based on calling the method Equals with the correct parameters. Imagine if the logic were more complicated, and more code had to be copied or moved. This results in maintenance issues because validation logic exists in multiple places. In this example, the maintenance issues aren't as grave, since most likely the property Flight.NextLeg would be deleted from the interface. But then you have a design dilemma in that interfaces are supposed to be immutable, and therefore the method Flight.NextLeg needs to remain in place. The property can be deprecated, but the bigger problem is that you have validation logic in multiple places coded to fit the situation. Separating the validation from the implementation into a single method call makes it possible to use the same validation code in the method AddLeg and property NextLeg.

Making the Case for Functors and Validating a Flight Leg

Validation can be separated from the object using functors and the Proxy pattern. What makes functors so useful is that they can be reused in multiple contexts. Regardless of whether the functor is used for validation, transformation, or additional operations, separating the logic ensures consistency.

Figure 6-2 illustrates the combination of the Proxy pattern and functors in the context of the original Flight class.

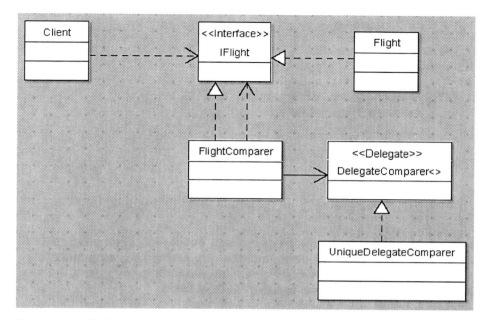

Figure 6-2. *UML diagram for functor-enabled proxy*

The class FlightComparer demonstrates the Proxy pattern, in that it implements the IFlight interface and references a parent IFlight interface implementation. The parent IFlight implementation is the previously defined Flight class minus the NextLeg property validation. FlightComparer doesn't employ a functor, but references and uses the functor DelegateComparer. The FlightComparer class has the role of calling DelegateComparer and, depending on the result, passing the method call to the parent IFlight implementation. The role of the FlightComparer class has turned into delegation of validation and execution. Following is an example of the FlightComparer class (note that the implementation of the Origin and String properties have been omitted for clarity):

```
class FlightComparer : IFlight {
    IFlight _parent;
    DelegateComparer< IFlight, IFlight> _delegateComparer;

    public FlightComparer(➥
 IFlight parent, DelegateComparer< IFlight, IFlight> delg) {
        _delegateComparer = delg;
        _parent = parent;
    }
```

```
    public IFlight NextLeg {
        get {
            return _parent.NextLeg;
        }
        set {
            if( _delegateComper( _parent, value) != 0) {
                _parent.NextLeg = value;
            }
            else {
                throw new ComparerEvaluationException();
            }
        }
    }
}
```

The constructor of FlightComparer requires two parents, the parent IFlight implementation and a DelegateComparer delegate implementation. In the property NextLeg, the get part calls the delegate _delegateComparer. If the delegate returns a nonzero value, the _parent.NextLeg data member can be assigned; otherwise an exception is generated.

This example illustrates how the logic of validation isn't part of the original class. Validation has been removed from the Flight class, and if Flight is instantiated, then an inconsistent hierarchy can be created—it's enough to make you wince. Remember that Flight implements an interface, and that the interface is defined as having public scope, whereas the implementation has internal scope. Therefore, a factory is required to instantiate Flight. And if a factory is required, then the factory can implement the Builder pattern that instantiates both classes as illustrated by the following example:

```
IFlight FlightBuilder() {
    return new FlightComparer( new Flight(),
        delegate( IFlight flight1, IFlight flight2) {
            if( flight1.Equals( flight2)) {
                return 0;
            }
            else {
                return -1;
            }
        });
}
```

The method FlightBuilder instantiates the type FlightComparer and passes in as the first parameter for the constructor a new Flight instance. The second constructor is unique in that it's a delegate. Instead of declaring a class with a method for the second parameter, an anonymous method is created, which performs the validation. An anonymous method is ideal because functors will be defined as delegates. The returned IFlight instance will have the correct hierarchy, and since FlightComparer doesn't allow access to the Flight instance, there is no chance that the client can bypass FlightComparer and corrupt the data.

If, however, you're still uncomfortable with the use of the Proxy pattern, it's technically possible to use the Flight class and have the property NextLeg use the delegate DelegateComparer directly. A proxy is advised because it makes it simpler to maintain and extend an application. I should also point out that from the client perspective the difference between the Factory or Builder pattern is zero, hence using a proxy is entirely acceptable.

Now that you've had a taste of what the comparer can do, let's see how it works in manipulating collections.

Creating a Generic Functor Architecture for Collections

Functors are often used when manipulating collections. For example, maybe you want to compare values and have a collection sorted whenever an element is added to that collection. Or maybe you only want to be able to find objects that have certain properties constrained to certain values. DelegateComparer isn't a static implementation in that it can compare different types according to different criteria. DelegateComparer could validate whether the age of a person is greater than that of another person. These types of sorting, arranging, and filtering are typically implemented as unique collection types: LinkedList, Stack, Queue, and so on. A functor can offer more functionality, but uses standard collection types.

Figure 6-3 shows the UML functor architecture for collections.

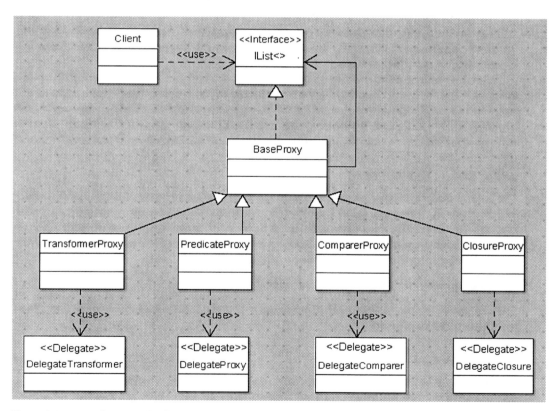

Figure 6-3. *UML diagram for functor-enabled collections*

`IList<>` is the base interface used for defining all functor proxies. This interface extends the `ICollection<>`, `IEnumerable<>`, and `IEnumerable` interfaces. `BaseProxy<>` is an abstract base class that provides a default implementation for the `IList<>` interface. The default action for `BaseProxy<>` is to proxy all requests to the parent `ICollection<>` implementation. The classes `TransformerProxy<>`, `PredicateProxy<>`, `ComparerProxy<>`, and `ClosureProxy<>` represent the implementations of the various functors.

When defining a proxy that uses functors, the prime consideration is what functionality the functor will override. A collection has many operations, such as adding, deleting, and retrieving elements. A very popular use of functors is to execute the functor when adding elements to a collection. However, there is nothing that says that a functor can't override the operations that remove elements. But it's very important never to create proxies that will call a functor when adding and removing elements. This is because the default method signature of the functors don't know what the operation is. The preferred approach is to create a proxy for each grouping of operations and then combine multiple proxies.

This Looks and Feels Like the Decorator Pattern

You may have noticed that the combination of functors with the Proxy pattern seems to result in a Decorator pattern. Although the architecture is very similar to a Decorator pattern, what is different is how the interfaces are instantiated and manipulated. In the case of the functors and the Proxy pattern, the client has no direct access to the underlying parent collection. All access is controlled by the Proxy pattern.

The Decorator pattern is different in that a client can access any element in the chain of elements created by the Decorator pattern. And more often than not, the Decorator pattern decorates a single method or subset of the full functionality offered by the implementation. So in a nutshell, the difference between a Proxy and Decorator pattern is that the Proxy pattern controls all access to the underlying implementation, and the Decorator pattern doesn't care.

Adding Closure Capabilities

The idea behind the closure functor is to be able to add an extra processing step when a specific logic is executed. For example, let's say that for a collection it's necessary to assign a parent-child relationship. When an object is added to a collection, a closure functor would assign the parent to the child object. You could also use a closure functor to perform logging operations.

Following is the definition of the closure delegate:

```
public delegate void DelegateClosure< type>( type input);
```

The delegate `DelegateClosure<>` uses Generics to define the `input` parameter, which represents the object to be manipulated.

Adding Predicate Capabilities

Predicate functors in some ways are similar to comparer functors when testing an object for a go or no-go condition. The difference is that predicate functors return either a true or false value. You use a predicate functor to test an object to see if it meets certain conditions.

Following is the definition of the delegate for the predicate functor:

```
public delegate bool DelegatePredicate< type>( type input);
```

DelegatePredicate uses Generics to define the type that will be tested and has a single parameter. An implementation performs some operations on the type and returns either a true or false value.

Unlike other functors, predicate functors are usually chained together using Boolean operators such as and, or, and not to perform more sophisticated tests. For example, consider the following Boolean and functor implementation:

```
public class PredicateAndFunctor< type> {
    DelegatePredicate<type> _predicates;
    public PredicateAndFunctor( DelegatePredicate<type>[] functors) {
        foreach( DelegatePredicate< type> functor in functors) {
            _predicates += functor;
        }
    }

    private bool PredicateFunction( type obj) {
        foreach( Delegate delg in _predicates.GetInvocationList()) {
            if( !delg( obj)) {
                return false;
            }
        }
        return true;
    }
    static DelegatePredicate< type> CreateInstance(
        DelegatePredicate< type>[] functors) {
        return new DelegatePredicate< type>(
            new PredicateAndFunctor< type>( functors).PredicateFunction);
    }
}
```

The class PredicateAndFunctor<> has a private data member _predicates, which represents an array of child predicates that will be and'ed together. If any of the child predicates return false, then PredicateAndFunctor<> will return false. The method PredicateFunction is the delegate implementation that iterates and calls in successive fashion the delegates contained within the _predicates data member.

Earlier an anonymous method was used to create the flight comparer delegate. Because PredicateAndFunctor<> has state, a class instance is needed, and the static method CreateInstance is used to instantiate the type, which in turn creates the delegate DelegatePredicate.

Adding Transformation Capabilities

Another type of functor is the transformation functor. The transformation functor takes as a parameter one type, and returns another type that represents the original type using the new type. The big-picture idea behind a transformation functor is to make it possible for a user to continue using one type that will be converted dynamically into another type. As an example, the transformation functor is useful in the context of integrating a new system with legacy objects and vice versa.

Following is the delegate definition of the transformation functor:

```
public delegate outType DelegateTransformer<inpType, outType>(inpType input);
```

The delegate DelegateTransformer<> is a generic type with two parameters: the type inpType is the input, and the type outType is the output that the input is converted into.

Now that you have a general understanding of functors, let's take a detailed look at how they work by walking through the creation of an example program, a simplified movie ticket application.

Building a Movie Ticket Application

Functors are easy to explain, and providing a reason for using them isn't difficult. What's more difficult is actually using them, which can be awkward if you're new to functors. What makes them awkward is the separation of functionality between the functor and the type being managed. It isn't easy for a programmer to write an object that includes no validation code.

An example application of a functor is to preprocess collection elements before they are added to the collection. Using traditional programming techniques, code would preprocess the element before adding it to a collection. With a functor, the client doesn't need to preprocess the element, and you'll see an example of this in the movie ticket application developed in the following text. It's a simple application, nowhere near complete, but it illustrates the details of using a functor, interface, and implementation as a single solution.

Starting with the Basics

The ticketing application will start with the basics and incrementally incorporate more complicated logic. The heart of the ticketing system is Ticket, which represents a movie ticket and is defined as follows:

```
public class Ticket {
    private double _price;
    private int _age;

    public Ticket( double price, int age) {
        _price = price;
        _age = age;
    }

    public virtual double Price {
        get {
            return _price;
        }
    }
    public virtual int Age {
        get {
            return _age;
        }
    }
}
```

Ticket only has two data members, _age and _price, which represent the age of the movie-goer and price of the ticket. _age and _price are defined when Ticket is instantiated. The values of _age and _price are retrieved using the properties Age and Price, respectively.

Calculating Ticket Sales

When selling movie tickets, ticket sales constitute an important statistic, as they indicate the popularity and success of a movie. In a traditional programming approach, ticket sales are calculated by iterating a collection of Tickets. The total would be generated each time a ticket sales total is requested. Another approach would be to use a closure functor, as shown in the following source code for calculating the total sales of a movie:

```
public class TicketsBuilder {
    private class StatisticsCounter {
        private double _runningTotal;
        public StatisticsCounter() {
            _runningTotal = 0.0;
        }
        public void ClosureMethod( Ticket ticket) {
            _runningTotal += ticket.Price;
        }
    }
    public static IList<Ticket> CreateCollection() {
        return new Devspace.Commons.Collections.ClosureAddProxy< Ticket>(
            new List< Ticket>(),
            new Devspace.Commons.Functors.DelegateClosure< Ticket>(
                new StatisticsCounter().ClosureMethod));
    }
}
```

TicketsBuilder is a class that has a method, CreateCollection, that creates an IList<> instance. The method CreateCollection instantiates the type ClosureAddProxy<>, which implements the Proxy pattern for the closure functor. The parent collection for ClosureAddProxy<> is List<>. The delegate used for the closure functor is StatisticsCounter.ClosureMethod.

Like in the comparer functor example, every time an element is added to the returned IList<> instance, DelegateAddClosure<> will call the closure delegate. Each time the closure delegate method StatisticsCounter.ClosureMethod is called, the input price is added to the total ticket sales.

The class StatisticsCounter.ClosureMethod has a problem in that it isn't entirely accurate. Imagine the scenario where a person buys a ticket and then asks for his or her money back or decides to watch a different movie. The ticket would need to be removed from the collection, and the total sales variable, _runningTotal, would need to be decremented by the price of the removed ticket. Even if it's impossible to get money back, it isn't possible to use such logic for all applications. The problem of the corrupted data needs to be solved. The reason why ticket sales can only be incremented is because ClosureAddProxy overrides the methods that add elements to the collection.

The solution is to use a closure delegate that overrides the remove element methods. As I mentioned earlier, even though it's tempting to merge add and remove closure proxies, I don't recommend it. When an add closure method is called, it doesn't know it's being called because of an add element operation. To have the closure functor know which operation is currently underway, a direction parameter would have to be added to the closure functor delegate. And that is a very bad idea, because it locks the delegate into certain operations.

Following is an example of two closure functors implementing the add and remove element methods:

```
public class TicketsBuilder {
    private class StatisticsCounter {
        private double _runningTotal;
        public StatisticsCounter() {
            _runningTotal = 0.0;
        }
        public void ClosureAddMethod( Ticket ticket) {
            _runningTotal += ticket.Price;
        }
        public void ClosureRemoveMethod( Ticket ticket) {
            _runningTotal -= ticket.Price;
        }
    }
    public static IList<Ticket> CreateCollection() {
        StatisticsCounter cls = new StatisticsCounter();
        IList<Ticket> parent = new ClosureAddProxy< Ticket>(
            new List< Ticket>(),
            new DelegateClosure< Ticket>( cls.ClosureAddMethod));
        return new ClosureRemoveProxy<Ticket>( parent,
            new DelegateClosure< Ticket>( cls.ClosureRemoveMethod));
    }
}
```

In this modified implementation of TicketsBuilder, StatisticsCounter has two closure methods: ClosureAddMethod and ClosureRemoveMethod. The method ClosureAddMethod increments the ticket sales, and the method ClosureRemoveMethod decrements ticket sales. The method CreateCollection is modified to create two closure proxies: ClosureAddProxy and ClosureRemoveProxy. The appropriate closure method is associated to each proxy.

Reading Ticket Sales Data

The code for calculating the grand total for the ticket sales works. But there is a very big problem in that no client can ever retrieve the value of the ticket sales. TicketBuilder creates an instance of StatisticsCounter, but the instance of StatisticsCounter isn't saved for reference. In other words, statistics are being generated, but no client has access to those values.

The simplest solution for the ticket sales total problem is to create a property called RunningTotal. But where should this property be created? Associating RunningTotal with TicketBuilder is a shortcut as TicketBuilder instantiates object hierarchies only. Associating RunningTotal with the IList<> instance would work, but is kludgy, as the consumer of IList<> has to know that the RunningTotal property exists. This would bind the consumer of IList<> to the closure functors, which is also not part of the overall design.

Recall from the oven monitoring example back in Chapter 5 how it was possible to get the temperature of the oven using a callback. In that example, it seemed simpler to create a property that referenced the temperature. This time though, a property is neither desirable nor possible, since it would create impractical interface bindings. And remember, the idea of a proxy is to make the client think it's using the actual implementation. Adding a property isn't possible. If in Chapter 5 the argument against properties seemed weak, now you should be convinced otherwise.

Implementing the Observer Pattern

The solution to the ticket sales problem is to use the Observer pattern.[4] Implementing the Observer pattern is easy because it's a delegate in .NET. The oven temperature example in Chapter 5 used the Observer pattern. It's possible to use .NET events, but in this example, they complicate the solution. The theory of the Observer pattern is to allow a client to be informed of data changes via an indirect callback mechanism identical to a publish and subscribe process.

The event that will be generated is defined by the following delegate:

```
public delegate void RunningTotalBroadcast( double runningTotal);
```

RunningTotalBroadcast has a single parameter, which represents the running total of all ticket sales. Every client that is interested in ticket sales defines a delegate and informs StatisticsCounter. It's important to realize that the delegate sends the running total, and not the value of an individual ticket sale. Broadcasting the running total means that the publisher keeps the current state, and not the subscriber of the data, which is often, but not always, the case.

The following source code represents the modified TicketBuilder that uses delegates to broadcast the running total:

```
public class TicketsBuilder {
    private class StatisticsCounter {
        private double _runningTotal;
        private RunningTotalBroadcast _delegateRunningTotal;

        public StatisticsCounter(RunningTotalBroadcast delegateRunningTotal) {
            _runningTotal = 0.0;
            _delegateRunningTotal = delegateRunningTotal;
        }
        public void ClosureAddMethod(Ticket ticket) {
            _runningTotal += ticket.Price;
            _delegateRunningTotal(_runningTotal);
        }
        public void ClosureRemoveMethod( Ticket ticket) {
            _runningTotal -= ticket.Price;
            _delegateRunningTotal( _runningTotal);
        }
    }
    public static IList<Ticket> ➦
```

---

4. *Design Patterns: Elements of Reusable Object-Oriented Software*, p. 293.

```
CreateCollection(RunningTotalBroadcast runningTotal) {
        StatisticsCounter cls = new StatisticsCounter( runningTotal);
        IList<Ticket> parent = new ClosureAddProxy< Ticket>(
            new List< Ticket>(),
            new DelegateClosure< Ticket>( cls.ClosureAddMethod));
        return new ClosureRemoveProxy<Ticket>( parent,
            new DelegateClosure< Ticket>( cls.ClosureRemoveMethod));
    }
}
```

The method `TicketBuilder.CreateCollection` has been modified to require a parameter. The parameter `runningTotal` is a delegate that is passed to `StatisticsCounter` and is called whenever the methods `ClosureAddMethod` and `ClosureRemoveMethod` are called.

Next, let's look at a test method that illustrates how to add tickets:

```
[TestFixture]
public class TestMovie {
    private void RunningTotalMethod(double runningTotal) {
        Console.WriteLine("Running Total " + runningTotal);
    }
    [Test]
    public void TestCallback() {
        IList<Cinema.Ticket> list =
            Cinema.Implementations.TicketsBuilder.CreateCollection(
            new Cinema.RunningTotalBroadcast( this.RunningTotalMethod));
        list.Add(new Cinema.Ticket(10.0, 12));
        list.Add(new Cinema.Ticket(10.0, 12));
        list.RemoveAt( 1);
    }
}
```

The method `TestCallback` instantiates the `IList<>` variable `list` using the method `TicketsBuilder.CreateCollection`. The method `RunningTotalMethod` is a callback that receives the updates whenever a ticket is added to the collection. When an update is received, `RunningTotalMethod` displays the ticket sales running total.

What is important about the `TestCallback` method is that the client only interacts with an `IList<>` type. Therefore, whenever the methods `Add` or `RemoveAt` are called, the closure functors react and process the data. The client only needs to understand the `IList<>` interface and the events that are propagated.

The Ramifications of Using an Observer Pattern for Ticket Sales

The Observer pattern as it has been implemented is great for informing the client of the newest ticket sales. However, this results in the ticket sales data being maintained in two separate locations. Contrast this to the approach where the total ticket sales are calculated on the fly and the only state is the collection of tickets.

Using the Observer pattern, there are two states, running total and tickets in the collection. The proxy needs to keep the two states in sync, which generally isn't a problem since the proxy manages both states. A data corruption is only possible if the proxy doesn't do its job properly.

The Problem of Using Null

Let's look a bit closer at the method TicketBuilder.CreateCollection. In the last iteration, a delegate was required to implement the Observer pattern. The method TicketBuilder. CreateCollection requires a delegate because the constructor of the class StatisticsCounter requires it. Let's say that you don't care about the statistics. In this case, it's tedious to define a delegate for something you don't need or want to provide.

The simplest solution is to modify the TicketBuilder.CreateCollection to include a method that doesn't require a delegate. This would then mean the StatisticsCounter class would have to provide a constructor without parameters. Implementing both changes isn't complicated, and the structure without implementations of the classes would appear as follows:

```
public class TicketsBuilder {
    private class StatisticsCounter {
        private double _runningTotal;
        private RunningTotalBroadcast _delegateRunningTotal;

        public StatisticsCounter() {
        }
        public StatisticsCounter(RunningTotalBroadcast delegateRunningTotal) {
        }
        public void ClosureAddMethod(Ticket ticket) {
        }
        public void ClosureRemoveMethod( Ticket ticket) {
        }
    }
    public static IList<Ticket> CreateCollection() {
    }
    public static IList<Ticket> ➥
CreateCollection(RunningTotalBroadcast runningTotal) {
    }
}
```

Looking at the implementation of StatisticsCounter and TicketsBuilder, it's obvious that implementing all methods would require a copy-and-paste operation from the other method. Such is the case for the CreateCollection methods, for which the code would have to instantiate an IList<> implementation. Ideally, it would be better if one CreateCollection method called the other CreateCollection method, as in this example:

```
    public static IList<Ticket> CreateCollection() {
        CreateCollection( null);
    }
    public static IList<Ticket>➥
 CreateCollection(RunningTotalBroadcast runningTotal) {
    }
```

The proposed solution will work, and it means that the StatisticsCounter class would not require any changes. However, it does require that the StatisticsCounter constructor may be called with a null value. And that brings up the recommendation originally presented in Chapter 2: null values should be used as little as possible since they don't indicate a consistent state.

Using the Null Object Pattern

The Null Object pattern[5] addresses the issue of not wanting to use null values. As outlined in Chapter 3, null values cause developers to have to check for valid conditions, empty conditions, and null conditions. For a large percentage of applications, empty conditions and null conditions are the same thing. Yet when writing code, both conditions need to be accounted for, causing more complex logic. A Null Object pattern is a specialization of the Proxy pattern in which the surrogate has no implemented functionality. You can employ the Null Object pattern if there is a base type, and that base type is defined using either an interface or base class.

It's possible to use the Null Object pattern when the client does want to receive statistics information. For the movie ticket application, you need to implement the delegate RunningTotalBroadcast as follows:

```
public class NullRunningTotalBroadcast {
    static void NothingRunningTotalBroadcast( double runningTotal) {
    }
    public static RunningTotalBroadcast GetInstance() {
        return new RunningTotalBroadcast( NothingRunningTotalBroadcast);
    }
}
```

NullRunningTotalBroadcast has declared two static methods. The method NothingRunningTotalBroadcast is the delegate for RunningTotalBroadcast. The method GetInstance retrieves a delegate instance that can be used by TicketBuilder.

Following is the rewritten client code that uses the Null Object implementation:

```
IList<Cinema.Ticket> list = Cinema.Implementations.TicketsBuilder.CreateCollection(
    Cinema.NullRunningTotalBroadcast.GetInstance());
list.Add(new Cinema.Ticket(10.0, 12));
list.Add(new Cinema.Ticket(10.0, 12));
list.RemoveAt( 1);
```

The CreateCollection method receives as a parameter the result from NullRunning➥TotalBroadcast.GetInstance(), which is a delegate that does nothing. The client code illustrates how it's possible to use the existing types and methods, and yet implement new logic.

A Null Object Isn't Always a Null Object

The example Null Object delegate is implemented as a method that does nothing. The question is whether that is the desired behavior. Instead of doing nothing, another option is to throw an exception when any statistic is generated. Throwing an exception, as in the case of the statistics example, would be incorrect because that wasn't the purpose of the Null Object pattern implementation. With the Null Object pattern there is no clear answer as to what is a correct behavior. The Null Object pattern is one of the few patterns that changes its implementation depending on the context it's used in.

---

5. Robert C. Martin, et al., *Pattern Languages of Program Design 3* (Boston: Addison-Wesley, 1997), p. 5.

The Null Object pattern can execute two actions. The first is to act silently as a pass-through and do nothing. When nothing happens, then the Null Object pattern is used as a placeholder to avoid having to write additional code that deals with null or empty conditions. In this implementation, the Null Object pattern could even be used as a mock object when writing NUnit test code.

The second action is to generate an exception. An exception should be generated when the implementation shouldn't be called. For example, imagine implementing a security system where certain pieces of functionality aren't available. Using the Null Object pattern as a pass-through would confuse the system, whereas if an exception is generated, an error message could be raised. Another reason to generate an exception is when certain pieces of an application shouldn't be using some components because they have been deprecated.

To understand more clearly when you should employ which action, let's see how the Null Object pattern should work with the Decorator and Proxy patterns. If the Decorator pattern has been implemented, then a Null Object implementation should use the pass-through strategy, the reason being the individual elements in the Decorator have the option to do something. In contrast, when used in the context of the Proxy pattern, the Null Object implementation should generate an exception.

Another context in which the Null Object pattern is useful is in the defining of empty iterators as outlined by the following source code:

```
public class NullEnumerator< type> : IEnumerator< type> {
    public bool MoveNext() {
        return false;
    }
    public void Reset() {
    }
    public void Dispose() {
    }
    public type Current {
        get {
            return default( type);
        }
    }
    object System.Collections.IEnumerator.Current {
        get {
            return default( type);
        }
    }
}


public class NullIterator< type> : IEnumerable< type> {
    public IEnumerator<type> GetEnumerator() {
        return new NullEnumerator< type>();
    }
    System.Collections.IEnumerator System.Collections.IEnumerable.GetEnumerator() {
        return new NullEnumerator< type>();
    }
}
```

NullIterator<> implements the IEnumerable<> interface, which defines a base class that in turn defines an empty iterator. NullEmumerator<> is used as an empty iterator. NullEnumerator<> is an implementation that can be used by a class to return Null Object iterator implementation.

The following testing code illustrates how to use a Null Object iterator:

```
[TestFixture]
public class TestEmptyIterator {
    public class EmptyIterator  {
        public IEnumerator<string> GetEnumerator() {
            return new NullEnumerator< string>();
        }
    }

    [Test]
    public void TestNonIterable() {
        EmptyIterator iter = new EmptyIterator();
        foreach( string element in iter) {
            NUnit.Framework.Assert.Fail( "Should never be reached");
        }
    }
}
```

The inner class EmptyIterator exposes a single method, GetEnumerator, which returns an instance of type NullEnumerator<>. In the method TestNonIterable, the inner class EmptyIterator is instantiated and then iterated using the foreach loop.

The power of this approach is that a user-defined object that references a user-defined collection of objects can be iterated even if the collection of objects doesn't exist. There is no need to check for a null condition for a user-defined collection. Note that if the collection references a type from the .NET collection implementation library, it's possible to use a foreach loop on empty collections.

A Simpler Way to Buy Tickets: Using the Façade Pattern

For the Observer pattern, the NUnit test code requires the definition of a delegate, the instantiation of the IList<> instance, and knowing how to use the TicketBuilder class. These are three things that the client needs to know about. For more complicated systems, the client programmer will often need to understand the inner workings of the application. This isn't always a good idea, because when the inner workings are updated, the application might become more complicated. In such cases, it would be simpler to instantiate a class and use those methods. After all, all we are trying to do is create a movie ticket application and calculate the running total.

The Façade Pattern in Theory and in Practice

The Façade pattern[6] simplifies and provides uniform access to an underlying architecture. The main objective of the Façade pattern is to reduce complexity. The Façade pattern has similarities to the Adapter and Proxy patterns, with some very specific differences. First, it doesn't implement a predefined interface. This doesn't mean that the Façade pattern doesn't implement an interface, it's just that the Façade pattern might define its own interface.

Additionally, the Façade pattern is different from all other patterns in that there may or may not be an interface or base class. If there is an interface or base class, then there might be a single implementation of any derived classes. In a nutshell, the Façade pattern implementation is very specific to the problem it solves.

To illustrate a sample implementation of the Façade pattern, let's simplify the movie ticket application:

```
public class TicketsFacade {
    private double _runningTotal;
    private IList<Ticket> _tickets;

    public TicketsFacade() {
        _tickets = CreateCollection();
    }
    public void Add(Ticket ticket) {
        _tickets.Add(ticket);
    }
    public double RunningTotal {
        get {
            return _runningTotal;
        }
    }
    private IList<Ticket> CreateCollection() {
        return TicketsBuilder.CreateCollection(
            new RunningTotalBroadcast(this.RunningTotalMethod));
    }

    private void RunningTotalMethod(double value) {
        _runningTotal = value;
    }
}
```

TicketsFacade is basically the same as the code that tests the classes IList<> and TicketsBuilder. The class TicketsFacade is fairly ordinary but contains the following important features:

- TicketsFacade is a class that won't be instantiated by a Factory pattern, but instantiated directly.

---

6. *Design Patterns: Elements of Reusable Object-Oriented Software*, p. 185.

- The method `RunningTotalMethod` is the delegate for `RunningTotalBroadcast` and receives updates of the running total.

- The `IList<>` interface isn't exposed to the client. This is a controversial detail because it requires including add and remove collection methods to `TicketsFacade`. Alternatively, a Façade implementation could have exposed the `IList<>` interface, as it's a general interface and isn't required as a handle to any other Façade type method. This means any interface instance or base class reference returns to the client, and the owner of the returned data is and remains the Façade implementation.

- The `RunningTotal` property is exposed and is callable by the client to determine what the current running total is. If the Façade implementation exposes a property that represents a state, then the Façade implementation must be the manager and owner of the state. The management of the state can't be delegated to the client.

What is important to remember when implementing the Façade pattern is that the Façade implementation is the owner and manager of state, references, and anything else. The client only sees an easy-to-use class with methods and properties that makes it simpler for it to realize the solution to the problem.

Another Façade Example: Organizing Books

Another use of the Façade pattern is in the realization of the *agent class*. The agent class isn't an agent in the sense of spying or artificial intelligence, rather the agent class helps to get something done. In this instance, the Façade pattern could be considered a sort of über class.

This problem is best illustrated by riddle posed at OOPSLA:[7]

On an object-oriented farm, there is an object-oriented cow with some object-oriented milk. Should the object-oriented cow send the object-oriented milk the uncow yourself message, or should the object-oriented milk send the object-oriented cow the unmilk yourself message?

The posed riddle is asking who does what to whom. Does the cow say to the milk, "Here you go," or does the milk say to the cow, "Give me what you have"? An identical problem would be the book and the bookshelf. There is a book and a shelf. Does the book put itself on the shelf, or does the shelf associate itself with the book? The question posed in coding terms would be as follows:

```
class Book {
    public void AssignShelf( Shelf shelf) {

    }
}
class Shelf {
    public void AssignBook( Book book) {

    }
}
```

---

7. Meiler Page-Jones, OOPSLA, 1987.

In the example, Book has an AssignShelf method, and Shelf has an AssignBook method, and the coder would look at this and say, "Hey, no problem. Both methods stay." Yet there is a problem because the dilemma of who assigns whom isn't solved. Let's look at the code again, except with the methods filled in:

```
class Book {
    Shelf _shelf;
    public void AssignShelf( Shelf shelf) {
        _shelf = shelf;
        _shelf.AssignBook( this);
    }
}
class Shelf {
    List< Book> _books;
    public void AssignBook( Book book) {
        _books.Add( book);
        book.AssignShelf( this);
    }
}
```

Now the problem is evident because if either the method AssignShelf or AssignBook is called, with the method implementations the other appropriate method is called. A recursive loop has been created where Book calls Shelf, which calls Book, which calls Shelf, and so on. A quick way to stop this is to cancel one of the implementation method calls. However, which one should be canceled? Should the client call AssignShelf, which calls AssignBook, or vice versa?

The problem is that Book and Shelf are acting as a team without the intervention of some other type. This is object-oriented design in its rawest form and what we desire. Yet it makes development awkward because we don't know which type to use to instantiate the calling sequence. The answer is that there is no single answer. It depends on the context and often on the flip of a coin. You may wonder what all of this writing is about if you're one of those who would never do this in the first place, a programmer who would create some other type that assigns the book to a shelf. Well, that is the solution, and it neatly avoided the main problem, which is to stick to object-oriented design principles.

The additional third type understands both Book and Shelf and complicates the architecture. Yet that is our only solution, and the other type is an über type that understands what a Book and Shelf is and knows what to do with them. This über type could be called Librarian and implements the Façade pattern. It makes a complex situation simpler. Über types aren't always necessary, because sometimes the client can manage the complexity it hides, or it can be refactored among the individual participating types.

Going back to the section "The Façade Pattern in Theory and in Practice," you can see the class TicketFacade acted like an über object, but wasn't, because TicketFacade didn't contain any complex application logic. The class only made manipulating the Ticket and IList<> types simpler. When the Façade pattern acts like an agent, it employs specific application logic. To illustrate the difference, consider the case in which Librarian sorts the order of books before shelving them. The sort order is part of Librarian, and not part of the participating classes.

Another reason to use an agent is when you need some logic performed that will only be used in that one specific context. In that one specific context, using interfaces, base classes, and factories complicates the solution unnecessarily.

This raises the question of when is a façade an agent, and when is it a simple façade. The answer is that a façade is an agent when it has no choice. The Façade pattern should be used as little as possible as an agent because it's too easy to add a little logic to one class, and a little logic to another class. After those scattered little changes, an application will become hard to maintain and extend.

Managing Extensions Using Polymorphism

When a single class implements a single interface, the code is easy to understand and manage. The client that consumes the interface doesn't have to worry about anything, because the implemented functionality is contained within the interface. Now imagine the situation when two different versions of an interface have to be consumed. Does that mean a client has to instantiate two different interface instances? Or how about the situation when a client needs to access multiple functionalities? Does that require multiple interface instances?

Polymorphism is the ability to process objects differently depending on the context. The Extension pattern[8] makes it possible to define polymorphism in multiple forms and enables you to add functionality without having to necessarily modify the already existing functionality. You might be thinking, "But hey, what about the Decorator pattern?" The answer is that the Extension pattern doesn't preclude the Decorator pattern, the Strategy pattern, the State pattern, or any other pattern. What the Extension pattern does is provide a mechanism to implement the Decorator pattern.

The Extension pattern comprises two variations, the Static Extension pattern and the Dynamic Extension pattern, both of which we'll look at in the following text.

Implementing the Static Extension Pattern

The simplest version of the Extension pattern is the Static Extension pattern. The Static Extension pattern is implemented using interfaces. This has the benefit of being able to extend the functionality of an implementation by attaching multiple interfaces as illustrated by the following example:

```
public interface IBase1 {
}
public interface IBase2 {
}
public class Implementation : IBase1, IBase2 {
}
```

The class Implementation has implemented the interfaces IBase1 and IBase2. Granted the interfaces have no methods, but the overall idea is illustrated. For example, if IBase1 is the original, then when Implementation implements IBase2, the implementation of IBase1 doesn't need to be modified.

In UML terms, the Static Extension pattern is identical to what you see in Figure 6-4.

---

8. James O. Coplien and Douglas C. Schmidt, *Pattern Languages of Program Design* (Boston: Addison-Wesley, 1995), p. 81.

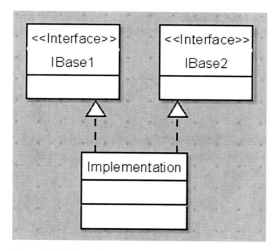

Figure 6-4. *UML diagram that illustrates two interfaces implemented by a single class*

The Static Extension pattern is a fundamental part of the C# programming language, and you probably haven't even realized that you were using it. The following test code illustrates how an interface can be tested for existence:

```
[TestFixture]
public class TestExtensions {
    [Test]
    public void TestStaticExtension() {
        IBase1 extension = new Implementation ();

        Assert.IsTrue( extension is IBase2);
    }
}
```

The test code method TestStaticExtension instantiates the class Implementation and assigns it to a variable of type IBase1. The Static Extension pattern occurs when Assert is tested for the existence of the IBase2 interface, even though the variable references the type IBase1. The Assert.IsTrue method doesn't fail and indicates that indeed the variable extension can be converted to the type IBase2. What is happening is that the .NET runtime is capable of doing a conversion to IBase2 because the implementation of IBase1 is the class Implementation, which also implements IBase2.

Associating a Single Method to Multiple Interfaces

Now let's complicate the scenario by having both IBase1 and IBase2 define the same method:

```
public interface IBase1 {
    int Value();
}
public interface IBase2 {
    int Value();
}
```

Both interfaces define the method Value, which has an int return value. The simplest way to implement the interfaces is illustrated by the following class declaration:

```
public class ImplementationBoth : IBase1, IBase2 {
    public int Value() {
        return 1;
    }
}
```

ImplementationBoth implements both IBase1 and IBase2, and the method implemented by both interfaces is Value. The following test code illustrates that when IBase1.Value and IBase2.Value are called, the value of 1 is returned:

```
[TestFixture]
public class TestExtensions {
    [Test]
    public void TestStaticExtension() {
        IBase1 base1 = new ImplementationBoth();
        IBase2 base2 = base1 as IBase2;

        Assert.AreEqual( 1, base1.Value());
        Assert.AreEqual( 1, base2.Value());
    }
}
```

The method TestStaticExtension instantiates the type ImplementationBoth and is assigned to base1, which is the type IBase1. Then the variable base2 is assigned using a typecast defined by the statement base1 as IBase2. The Assert tests illustrate that regardless of whether the Value method is called from IBase1 or IBase2, the same value of 1 is returned.

If you aren't familiar with the as statement, note that it doesn't generate an exception if the interface can't be cast. If the interface can't be cast to the type, then the variable will have a value of null. To generate a cast exception, the cast (IBase2)base would have to be used.

Let's step back and consider what has happened. Imagine a class has to implement a new interface in your application. The new interface has some methods that are identical to the old interface and some methods that are unique to the new interface. For those methods that are identical to the old interface, the same method will be called.

Associating Multiple Same-Named Methods to Multiple Interfaces

Only allowing one method to implement multiple interface methods doesn't make sense for the Extension pattern, because the focus of the Extension pattern is to allow extensions to already existing types. This means if an interface method has been implemented, but a new implementation needs to be added to an already existing type, there is a problem. C# has a solution in that methods can be defined to implement specific methods to specific interfaces as in the following source code:

```
public class ImplementationBothSeparate : IBase1, IBase2 {
    public int Value() {
        return 0;
    }
    int IBase1.Value() {
        return 1;
    }
    int IBase2.Value() {
        return 2;
    }
}
```

ImplementationBothSeparate has three implementations of the method Value. The first version of the method Value is the method used when the variable type is ImplementationBothSeparate. The second version of the method Value is prefixed with the identifier IBase1, which indicates that this method is used when the instance of ImplementationBothSeparate is cast to IBase1. The third and last version is associated with the interface IBase2.

To illustrate how this works, consider the following test code:

```
[TestFixture]
public class TestExtensions {
    [Test]
    public void TestDoubleStaticExtension() {
        ImplementationBothSeparate cls = new mplementationBothSeparate();
        IBase1 base1 = cls;
        IBase2 base2 = base1 as IBase2;

        Assert.AreEqual( 0, cls.Value());
        Assert.AreEqual( 1, base1.Value());
        Assert.AreEqual( 2, base2.Value());
    }
}
```

The variable cls is type ImplementationBothSeparate, variable base1 is type IBase1, and variable base2 is type IBase2. There were three different Value method implementations, and each is associated with a different interface, which is illustrated by the Assert method calls. In the case of the cls variable, the value 0 is returned, base1 returns a value of 1, and base2 returns a value of 2.

What this demonstrates is that it's possible to fine-tune which method is associated with which interface. Whenever a method is associated with a specific interface, the scope modifier of the method must not be public. It's also not possible from an external method to call an interface-associated method. To call an interface-associated method, you need to cast the instance to the associated interface.

In the example, the Value methods are tuned for each subclassed interface. It's possible to specify only one method for one interface, and not the other, for example, IBase1 and not IBase2. If that happens, then the unimplemented interface method will default to the Value method that is associated with the type ImplementationBothSeparate.

Using Inheritance with Multiple Methods and Multiple Interfaces

Another way to implement an interface isn't to add the interface to the class, but to subclass the original class, and then implement the interface. Figure 6-5 shows the UML diagram of this hierarchy.

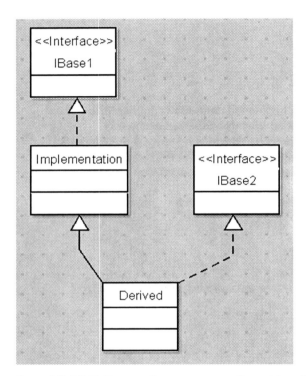

Figure 6-5. *UML diagram for a more complicated interface and class hierarchy*

In code terms, the UML diagram translates as follows:

```
public class Implementation : IBase1 {
    public int Value() {
        return 1;
    }
}

public class Derived : Implementation, IBase2 {
    public new int Value() {
        return 2;
    }
}
```

`Implementation` implements the interface `IBase1` and represents a version 1.0 component. The class `Derived` implements the new interface `IBase2`, and subclasses `Implementation`.

In both Implementation and Derived are the Value method implementations. Consider the test code to understand which method is called when:

```
[TestFixture]
public class TestExtensions {
    [Test]
    public void TestDoubleInherited() {
        Implementation cls = new Derived();
        IBase1 base1 = cls;
        Assert.AreEqual( 1, cls.Value());
        IBase2 base2 = base1 as IBase2;
        Assert.AreEqual( 2, base2.Value());
    }
}
```

The variable cls is of the type Implementation, but references the type Derived. This means that the variable cls references a downcast type. The typecast of cls to base1 is a natural one because Implementation implements the interface IBase. Assert.AreEqual tests whether the return value of 1 is generated, which means that the Implementation.Value method was called. Then the base1 variable is cast to IBase2, which means that the .NET runtime performs an upcast from Implementation to Derived. This is possible because Derived implements IBase2. If this cast wasn't possible for the example code, the variable base2 would have a null value. This is why it's important to test for castability using the is the statement if you don't know whether or not an interface is supported.

Let's consider the same implementation code, but this time declare the Value methods as virtual:

```
public class Implementation : IBase1 {
    public virtual int Value() {
        return 1;
    }
}
public class Derived : Implementation, IBase2 {
    public override int Value() {
        return 2;
    }

}
```

Running the same test code, the answer will be different, because regardless of which interface is called, the answer will be 2.

What is important to notice is that the .NET runtime knows which method to use for which interface, and the implementation can tune this process. The client doesn't have to do any complicated work to make the cast work.

Implementing the Dynamic Extension Pattern

When you require more flexibility, namely a noninvasive way to define an extension, you need the Dynamic Extension pattern. The difference between the Dynamic Extension pattern and the Static Extension pattern is that the Dynamic Extension pattern object requires the implementation of a standard interface that can be used to navigate other interfaces.

An Example of What Doesn't Work

Ideally, you would be able to overload a conversion method and let the .NET runtime perform the conversion. Consider the following attempt at dynamic conversion:

```
public class UserDefinedCasts {
    public static implicit operator IBase1(UserDefinedCasts impl) {
    }
}
```

The code as it's written says that the class UserDefinedCasts implements a method where the type UserDefinedCasts can be converted to the interface IBase1. Unfortunately, this doesn't compile. Type conversions are only possible between classes and structs. You can't enable a type conversion to an interface, which essentially makes this technique not applicable to the Extensions pattern.

Implementing the Dynamic Extension Architecture

In the dynamic approach, it's possible to string together different implementations and have the user retrieve the extension using an indirect typecast. The UML diagram in Figure 6-6 illustrates how to implement the Dynamic Extension pattern.

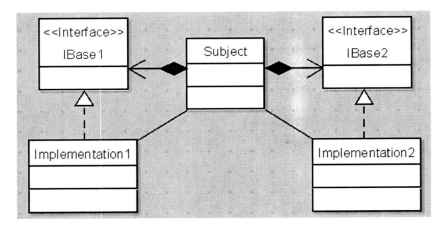

Figure 6-6. *UML diagram for the Dynamic Extension pattern*

When the Dynamic Extension pattern is used, there are multiple implementations that can take advantage of single or multiple interfaces. The different implementations are grouped together using another class called Subject. Subject is a collection of implementations. For example, Implementation2 contains an instance of Subject, which contains a collection of interface implementations, IBase1 and IBase2. It's important to realize that Subject can only reference a single interface implementation of IBase1 and IBase2, just like the Static Extension pattern.

The class Subject implements the IExtension and ISubject interfaces, which are defined as follows:

```
public interface ISubject {
    type GetExtension< type>() where type: class;
}

public interface IExtendedSubject : ISubject {
    void AddExtension< type>( type extension) where type: class;
    void RemoveExtension< type>( type extension) where type: class;
}
```

The interface ISubject has a single method, GetExtension<>, which returns the type being requested. Consider this: because it isn't possible to use C# type conversions with interfaces, each class that supports the Dynamic Extension pattern has to implement the ISubject interface, which is used to perform something similar to, but not quite the same as, a typecast—this is more of a query for the ISubject interface to let the method GetExtension get the right interface implementation.

The interface IExtendedSubject has two additional methods, AddExtension<> and RemoveExtension<>. These methods are used to build the list of interface implementations that can be queried for. This makes it appear that the Dynamic Extension pattern is identical to the Mediator pattern from Chapter 5 because both have a manager of implementations. The difference is that the manager for the Dynamic Extension pattern isn't a container and isn't visible to the client. The client only sees the ISubject interface and lets the peer of Subject retrieve the correct interface implementation.

The IExtended interface is implemented by the Subject class and is responsible for retrieving the correct interface implementation from the type. Following is the implementation of the Subject class:

```
public sealed class Subject : IExtendedSubject {
    bool InterfaceFilter(Type typeObj, Object criteriaObj) {
        return (typeObj.ToString() == criteriaObj.ToString());
    }
    bool DidImplement(string @interface, Type targetType) {
        TypeFilter interfaceFilter = new TypeFilter(InterfaceFilter);
        Type[] interfaces = targetType.FindInterfaces( interfaceFilter, @interface);
        return (interfaces.Length > 0);
    }

    ArrayList _list = new ArrayList();

    public type GetExtension< type>() where type: class{
        foreach( Object obj in _list) {
            if( DidImplement( typeof( type).FullName, obj.GetType())) {
                return obj as type;
            }
        }
        return null;
    }
```

```
    public void AddExtension< type>( type extension) where type: class{
        if( extension == null) {
            throw new NotSupportedException();
        }
        _list.Add( extension);
    }
    public void RemoveExtension< type>( type extension) where type: class{
        for( int c1 = 0; c1 < _list.Count; c1 ++) {
            if( Object.ReferenceEquals( _list[ c1], extension)) {
                _list.RemoveAt( c1);
            }
        }
    }
}
```

Here the individual implementations are stored in the data member _list, which is of the type ArrayList. The type ArrayList is used because different types are stored in one list, where the lowest common denominator is Object. The method AddExtension<> adds an implementation to the collection of implementations.

The method RemoveExtension removes an extension, but notice how an extension is removed, paying particular attention to the method Object.ReferenceEquals. ArrayList has a Remove method that can remove an object from the collection, but typically the method uses Equals to test for equality of two object instances. This isn't the best way because Equals does a class instance state comparison and doesn't perform a reference equality comparison. Using the method Object.ReferenceEquals, it's possible to test whether two object instances are the same reference. If two object instance references are identical, then the first instance is removed using the RemoveAt method, hence the use of a for loop and not foreach.

The method GetExtension retrieves an extension based on the generic parameter type. The method DidImplement retrieves the generic parameter type's name and tests whether it has been implemented by the variable obj. It isn't possible to use the notation obj is type in the if statement, because it doesn't always work. The method DidImplement uses .NET reflection and tests whether somewhere in the hierarchy of the variable obj the type, which is an interface, has been implemented. If so, then the object instance is returned.

Diving into Code

Going back to Figure 6-6, notice the classes Implementation1 and Implementation2 need to be defined, and they need to use Subject to implement the dynamic extensions. Following are the definitions of the implementation classes:

```
public class Implementation1 : IBase1, ISubject {
    Subject _subject;
    public Implementation1( Subject subject) {
        _subject = subject;
    }
    public type GetExtension< type>() where type: class {
        return _subject.GetExtension< type>();
    }
```

```
        public int Value() {
            return 1;
        }
}
public class Implementation2 : IBase2, ISubject {
    Subject _subject;
    public Implementation2( Subject subject) {
        _subject = subject;
    }
    public type GetExtension< type>()  where type: class{
        return _subject.GetExtension< type>();
    }
    public int Value() {
        return 2;
    }
}
```

Implementation1 implements both IBase1 and ISubject. The implementation of IBase1 is obvious, since that is the interface that will be cast to. The implementation of ISubject is required, because if a client has a reference to the IBase1 interface, it will typecast to ISubject and use the method GetExtension to retrieve the interface instance that is needed. The same sort of implementation logic applies to Implementation2.

In the example, both Implementation1 and Implementation2 have constructors with a parameter of type Subject. This is done on purpose so that when either Implementation1 or Implementation2 is instantiated, they are associated with a Subject instance that will chain together Implementation1 and Implementation2.

The last step is to use the Factory pattern to instantiate both types and link them together:

```
class Factory {
    public static IBase1 CreateInstance() {
        Subject main = new Subject();

        Implementation1 impl1 = new Implementation1( main);
        Implementation2 impl2 = new Implementation2( main);

        main.AddExtension( impl1 as IBase1);
        main.AddExtension( impl2 as IBase2);
        return impl1;
    }
}
```

Factory has a single method, CreateInstance, which returns an interface instance of type IBase1. In the implementation of CreateInstance, the first step is to instantiate Subject because it's the class that binds together all of the implementations. Then the different implementations (impl1 and impl2) are instantiated and the Subject instance passed to them. At this point, both impl1 and impl2 have been instantiated and are valid instances, but they aren't linked together. This means if a client has a reference to IBase1, which is impl1, and attempts to get the extension instance impl2, which is IBase2, a null value is returned. Therefore, as a last step, the method AddExtension of Subject is called, and the implementation instances impl1 and impl2 are added.

The last step would be to call the Factory.CreateInstance method and use both the IBase1 and IBase2 interface instances. Following is a simple example of the NUnit test code for this step:

```
[TestFixture]
public class TestDynamicExtensions {
    [Test]
    public void TestSimple() {
        IBase1 base1 = Factory.CreateInstance();
        IBase2 base2 = ((ISubject)base1).GetExtension< IBase2>();
        Assert.IsNotNull( base2);
        Assert.AreEqual( 2, base2.Value());
        base1 = ((ISubject)base2).GetExtension< Extensions.IBase1>();
        Assert.IsNotNull( base1);
        Assert.AreEqual( 1, base1.Value());
    }
}
```

The variable base1 is instantiated and is type IBase1, which means it's the implementation instance of Implementation1. Then in the next line where base2 is assigned, a typecast to ISubject is performed with a GetExtension method call to retrieve an instance of IBase2. The variable base2 will reference the implementation instance Implementation2. Unlike the Static Extension pattern example, the references of base1 and base2 won't be identical. However, the client using base1 and base2 doesn't know that. Several lines down the GetExtension method is called again to illustrate how it's possible to retrieve the IBase1 implementation instance from the IBase2 implementation instance.

Extensions, Typecasting, and What It All Means

The Extension pattern, whether static or dynamic, illustrates polymorphism using interfaces. The idea is to allow a client to reference an interface instance, and from that interface instance reference other functionality. In .NET, the System.Windows.Forms and ASP.NET classes use this capability in multiple places. Polymorphism makes it possible to use the same interfaces and groupings of interfaces in different contexts.

Though the static implementation is simpler than the dynamic implementation, the dynamic implementation can exhibit dynamic polymorphism where a configuration file or some other logic determines which interfaces and implementations belong together. It's also important to realize that the Factory pattern was used for creating the dynamic extension, because the dynamic extension represents an instance of one object. At least the dynamic extension gives this impression to the client.

One little annoying aspect of the Extension pattern is that the way to retrieve the interface instance using the static implementation isn't identical to that for the dynamic implementation. A solution is to use the following static class method:

```
public static returntype Cast< inputtype, returntype>( inputtype input)
    where inputtype: class where returntype: class {
    if( input is returntype) {
        return input as returntype;
    }
    return ((ISubject)input).GetExtension< returntype>();
}
```

Cast is a generic method that has an input type and return type. The input type represents the object instance to be cast. In the implementation of the method, the first attempt determines whether the return type is implemented using the Static Extension pattern. If so, then that instance is returned. Otherwise, it's assumed a Dynamic Extension pattern has been implemented, and it casts to the ISubject interface and calls the GetExtension method to retrieve the return type. Then when the client uses the Cast method, it won't know or care how polymorphism is implemented.

Looping Through Your Data Using the Iterator Pattern

In your coding, you have probably already encountered the foreach operator. However, you might not have known that you were using the Iterator pattern when employing foreach. With the release of .NET 2.0, an interesting new mechanism has been added to make it possible to easily implement the Iterator pattern.

Implementing the Iterator Pattern Using C# 2.0

Originally, when using the Iterator pattern for anything that wasn't collection based, the IEnumerator interface had to be implemented. The IEnumerator interface isn't complicated, but it's extra work. With the release of C# 2.0, the yield statement makes everything simpler.

Consider the following simple example of iterating through a hard-coded list of three numbers:

```
class ExampleIterator : IEnumerable {
    public IEnumerator GetEnumerator() {
        yield return 1;
        yield return 2;
        yield return 3;
    }
}
```

In the method GetEnumerator are three return statements prefixed with the yield statement. The yield statement is an easy way of indicating to the client to return the data caller of the GetEnumerator implementation. Take a look at the following code that iterates the data in ExampleIterator:

```
ExampleIterator iter = new ExampleIterator();
foreach( int number in iter) {
    Console.WriteLine( "Number (" + number + ")");
}
```

Let's step through this and the previous code example and highlight what happens:

1. The variable `iter` is assigned an instance of `ExampleIter`.

2. The `foreach` loop starts, asks for the `IEnumerable` interface, and calls the `GetEnumerator` method.

3. The `ExampleIterator.GetEnumerator` method encounters a `yield` statement and returns the value 1. But before returning from the method, a *bookmark* is made to where execution returned control.

4. In the `foreach` loop, the .NET runtime assigns the variable `number` the value of 1.

5. The loop executes and calls the method `Console.WriteLine`.

6. A new loop is started, and the bookmark in the `GetEnumerator` method is the starting point of the next execution.

7. Then another `yield` statement is encountered, and the value of 2 is returned.

8. Another `foreach` loop occurs, and this bookmarking and looping occurs until there are no more yields.

The way that the `GetEnumerator` method is implemented, it shouldn't work. Remove the `yield` statements, and the C# compiler will complain that it can't convert the numbers 1, 2, or 3 to type `IEnumerator`. The `yield` statements make it possible to return 1, 2, or 3.

Using Functors in an Iterator

In previous sections of this chapter, I discussed functors in conjunction with the Proxy pattern. But a functor can be extremely useful in the context of an iterator. For example, imagine wanting to iterate a set of data, but only wanting a subset of data.

Consider the following class, which manages a list of integer values:

```
class IntegerData : IEnumerable {
    private IList< int> _list = new List< int>();
    private DelegatePredicate< int> _predicate;

    public IntegerData( DelegatePredicate< int> predicate) {
        _predicate = predicate;
    }
    public void Add( int value) {
        _list.Add( value);
    }
```

```
public IEnumerator GetEnumerator() {
    foreach( int value in _list) {
        if( _predicate( value)) {
            yield return value;
        }
    }
}
}
```

The class `IntegerData` implements the `IEnumerable` method, which requires implementation of the `GetEnumerator` method. The constructor has a single parameter that represents the predicate delegate `DelegatePredicate`. The method `Add` adds integer values to the collection data member `_list`.

The `GetEnumerator` method deserves closer attention in that instead of just returning the value of `_list.GetEnumerator`, the list is iterated using a `foreach` loop. Then the predicate `_predicate` is called, and if a value of true is returned, the `yield` statement returns the variable value to the client.

Here is an example of client code that provides a predicate delegate:

```
IntegerData data = new IntegerData(
    delegate( int value) {
        if( value > 10) {
            return true;
        }
        else {
            return false;
        }
    });

data.Add( 1);
data.Add( 5);
data.Add( 15);
data.Add( 20);

foreach( int number in data) {
    Console.WriteLine( "Number " + number);
}
```

The `IntegerData` constructor parameter in this example is an anonymous delegate method that represents the predicate delegate. The logic is simple in that the predicate returns true if the value is greater than 10. The method `Add` is called four times when two values are greater than 10 and two are less than 10. When the `foreach` loop is started, the predicate is called, and there will only be two values generated, 15 and 20.

This example illustrates the power of `yield` in that algorithms can be executed that will determine what the collection value is. With this change in the Iterator pattern implementation, a collection isn't a collection anymore. Instead, the `foreach` construct should be considered as being able to iterate a set of data, where the set may represent real or generated values.

Some Final Thoughts

Making the code do something useful is the hard part of an application. This isn't to say that creating the proper skeleton is simple. It's just that writing the details shows whether or not the application is actually working. It's like building a house in that it's easy to see the walls and consider the house as a house. However, a house doesn't become a home until the walls are painted and the floor laid. And until a house becomes a home, it has less value, typically a bit more than the property value.

Writing the details of an application is known as implementing algorithms, some of which solve serialization or efficiency problems. In this chapter, you learned about modularizing algorithms. In most cases, when implementing the details of an application, you just write the code. But in fact, modularization and interfaces don't stop at some higher-level architecture. Modularization continues right down to the algorithm level, even though the modular pieces have module scope, not application scope.

One way to modularize algorithms is to use functors. This chapter covered four types of functors, but you could define more. The four functors discussed represent the most common types. Functors are very important because they make it possible to implement algorithms that can be reused in multiple contexts. If you have never used a functor and are skeptical, try them—you will be pleasantly surprised.

CHAPTER 7

■■■

Efficient Code

What is "efficient code"? Is it code that is fast? Or is it code that is well written and documented? Or is it code that is easy to understand and maintain? The issue of efficiency is very subjective, as it doesn't mean the same thing to all people. This chapter doesn't attempt to provide a philosophical basis for what efficient code is. For the scope of this book, the notion of efficient code represents code that solves a particular problem related to performance as elegantly as possible. This may result in code that is more complicated and at first glance appears to consume more resources.

In this chapter, the techniques presented involve immutable classes and how they can be used to write more efficient code. In those situations where multiple things have to occur concurrently, you'll learn how to apply threads and synchronization, which I also discuss in this chapter.

Immutable Classes Are Efficient Classes

The meaning for immutable is to "not be subject or susceptible to change."[1] In layman terms, immutable means cast in stone. In programming terms, it means once assigned and defined, there can be no change. Specifically, the string class is immutable. Once a string variable has been assigned, the variable contents can't be modified. There is no way to call a method or property of a string class instance to modify a single byte of the data. In coding terms, it means .NET properties have a get part, but no set part.

Immutability is an interesting concept in that we mostly write code that isn't immutable. We write applications in which the state of the object can be modified and generally ignore immutability. In fact, thus far I'm guilty of not considering immutable code. Immutable code isn't a cure-all, but immutable classes have many advantages, with the two biggest being consistency and scalability, which we'll explore in this part of the chapter along with some rules of thumb for using these classes.

Immutable classes don't constitute a pattern per se because immutability has been around for a long time. However, many websites (such as http://www.developer.com/java/other/ article.php/10936_617931_2 and http://www.mindspring.com/~mgrand/pattern_synopses. htm#Immutable) refer to the immutable class as a pattern, as it should be.

---

1. http://dictionary.reference.com/search?q=immutable

Why Immutable Classes Are Consistent

Immutable classes are consistent because they avoid the problem of having their consistency corrupted by inappropriate manipulations. Let's consider the classical object-oriented problem of creating shapes, specifically the issue of rectangles and squares. The question is whether a square subclasses a rectangle or a rectangle subclasses a square.

An Inconsistent Square Subclasses a Rectangle

To start, let's say we define a rectangle as a base class as illustrated by the following example:

```
class Rectangle {
    private long _length, _width;

    public Rectangle( long length, long width) {
        _length = length;
        _width = width;
    }
    public virtual long Length {
        get {
            return _length;
        }
        set {
            _length = value;
        }
    }
    public virtual long Width {
        get {
            return _width;
        }
        set {
            _width = value;
        }
    }
}
```

The class Rectangle has a constructor with two parameters that represent length and width. Two properties, Length, and Width, are the length and width of the rectangle, respectively. As in a typical coding scenario, the properties can be retrieved and assigned, meaning that they are read-write.

A square is a specialized form of rectangle for which the length and width happen to be equal. Using the previously defined Rectangle as a base class, the Square could be defined as follows:

```
class Square : Rectangle {
    public Square( long width) : base( width, width) {
    }
}
```

To define a square, the class Square only needs to redefine the base class Rectangle constructor to have a single parameter representing the dimensions. The constructor calls the base constructor and passes the same dimension to the length and width. When Square is instantiated, the type will have the correct dimensions, and it would seem all's well in this object-oriented design.

All isn't well, however, because a major design flaw exists, which the following test code illustrates:

```
[TestFixture]
public class TestShapes {
    [Test]
    public void TestConsistencyProblems() {
        Square square = newSquare( 10);
        Rectangle squarishRectangle = square;

        squarishRectangle.Length = 20;
        Assert.AreNotEqual( square.Length, square.Width);
    }
}
```

The variable square references a square with dimensions of 10 units. The variable square is downcast to the variable squarishRectangle, which is of the type Rectangle. Where the consistency problem occurs is when the squarishRectangle.Length property is assigned a value of 20. Even though it's legal to reassign the property, it isn't consistent with the requirements of the type Square. The Assert.AreNotEqual illustrates how the dimensions of the square are inconsistent and therefore not a square anymore.

The problem is that polymorphism has caused consistency violations. One solution to make the Square consistent is the following source code:

```
class Square : Rectangle {
    public Square( long width) : base( width, width) {

    }
    public override long Length {
        get {
            return base.Length;
        }
        set {
            base.Length = value;
            base.Width = value;
        }
    }
    public override long Width {
        get {
            return base.Width;
        }
```

```
        set {
            base.Length = value;
            base.Width = value;
        }
    }
}
```

In the new implementation, Square overrides the properties Length and Width. If the same client test code is used whenever Length or Width is assigned, the property called is from Square. Within the implementation of Square's Length and Width, the base class Rectangle's Length and Width properties are assigned the same value. This means that a square will always be a square, and the consistency is upheld. However, there is a price for this consistency, and that is complexity, because both Rectangle and Square must implement all methods. It really begs the question of why use inheritance in the first place.

A Consistent Rectangle Subclasses a Square

Another solution is to define the Rectangle as a type that subclasses Square, which is defined as follows:

```
class Square {
    private long _width;

    public Square( long width)  {
        _width = width;
    }
    public virtual long Width {
        get {
            return _width;
        }
        set {
            _width = value;
        }
    }
}

class Rectangle : Square {
    private long _length;

    public Rectangle( long length, long width) : base(width) {
        _length = length;
    }
    public virtual long Length {
        get {
            return _length;
        }
```

```
        set {
            _length = value;
        }
    }
}
```

The base class is Square, and it defines the property Width, which represents the length and width of a Square. The class Rectangle subclasses Square and adds the missing dimension, which is Length. In this case, the hierarchy is consistent, and there can never be the situation where a Square becomes inconsistent.

Following is some test code that shows how to use Square and Rectangle:

```
[TestFixture]
public class TestShapes {
    void TestSquare( Square square) {
        square.Width = 10;
    }
    [Test]
    public void TestSubclass() {
        Rectangle rectangle = new Rectangle( 30, 30);
        long oldLength = rectangle.Length;
        TestSquare( rectangle);
        Assert.AreEqual( oldLength, rectangle.Length);
    }
}
```

In the test code, the method TestSubclass instantiates Rectangle. Prior to calling the method TestSquare, the length of Rectangle is stored. When the method TestSquare is called, the property Width is modified. After the call to TestSquare, the following Assert.AreEqual call tests to ensure that the length of the rectangle equals oldLength. If, on the other hand, the Width property of the Rectangle is modified, then when a downcast to Square is made, the dimensions of the Square will still be consistent.

This solution is correct from an object-oriented perspective because each type is responsible for its own data. Yet you may have a nagging feeling that this solution feels strange. The reason why you might feel this solution is weird is because it goes against typical thinking, which is that a square has a length and width, and they happen to be equal. So from this thinking a Square subclasses Rectangle. But from an object-oriented perspective, it should be the reverse. This is what often makes object-oriented design so difficult.

Consistency Isn't Always Clearly Defined

The last solution that was presented was correct, and it fits into an object-oriented architecture. As discussed, there is a nagging feeling that the object-oriented design is wrong. A subtle difference arises because of the object-oriented design using inheritance.

You decide to use both Square and Rectangle. You believe in the viability of patterns, and search for the factories for either Square or Rectangle. Yet you search with some misgiving, as there is no factory because having a factory in this case doesn't make sense. Remember, a factory exposes an interface or base class while hiding the implementation. In the object-oriented solution, there is no base class and no interface. The base class Square doesn't expose all of the members that Rectangle exposes. This goes back to the reason that Square is base functionality, and a Rectangle extends that functionality. In other words, the example defines a consistent inheritance structure that doesn't fit cleanly into a pattern-oriented world.

The problem isn't object-oriented design, nor is it inheritance, but the original assumption that we think a square is a shape with two dimensions: length and width. What is necessary isn't an inheritance structure, but the use of an object-oriented structure that dovetails into our thinking. Namely, we have two shapes, with a length and width, and the base class shouldn't be a square or rectangle, but an interface that is defined as follows:

```
interface IShape {
    long Length {
        get; set;
    }
    long Width {
        get; set;
    }
}
```

The interface IShape doesn't indicate whether it's a rectangle or a square, but defines some implementation that has both a Length and Width. The implementation will determine if it's a square or rectangle, which implements the constraints. An example implementation of both Square and Rectangle is as follows:

```
class Rectangle : IShape {
    private long _width;
    private long _length;

    public Rectangle( long width) {
        _width = width;
    }
    public virtual long Width {
        get {
            return _width;
        }
        set {
            _width = value;
        }
    }
    public virtual long Length {
        get {
            return _length;
        }
        set {
            _length = value;
        }
    }
}
```

```
class Square : IShape {
    private long _width;

    public Square( long width) {
        _width = width;
    }
    public virtual long Length {
        get {
            return _width;
        }
        set {
            _width = value;
        }
    }
    public virtual long Width {
        get {
            return _width;
        }
        set {
            _width = value;
        }
    }
}
```

This time Square and Rectangle do the right things, and there are no consistency problems. Square exposes the properties Length and Width, but the implementation only contains one data member, _width. Neither Square nor Rectangle share any implementation details and can be instantiated using the Factory pattern. This solution is object-oriented, pattern compatible, and consistent.

Consistency Is Easy to Implement

Thinking about the last solution to Rectangle and Square, let's take a step back and consider the big picture. First, would there ever be another shape that can be defined using a length and width? Most likely not, because it illustrates that shapes in general don't relate to each other and have unique descriptions. For example, a circle is defined by its diameter, the lengths of the three sides define a triangle, and a parallelogram is defined by length, width, and angle. In a nutshell, trying to define shapes using a generic base class is futile, and the object-oriented solution where Rectangle subclasses the Square is acceptable.

Having said all that, there is still another option. After all, shapes are related (for example, square, rectangle, and parallelogram), and using inheritance that has a common base class would be useful for programming purposes. The solution is to make all shapes immutable in that once the dimensions have been assigned, they can't be modified. Following is an example of the immutable square and rectangle implementation (note it would have been better to use parallelogram as a base class, but that is beyond the scope of discussion):

```
class Rectangle {
    private readonly long _length, _width;

    public Rectangle( long length, long width) {
        _length = length;
        _width = width;
    }
    public virtual long Length {
        get {
            return _length;
        }
    }
    public virtual long Width {
        get {
            return _width;
        }
    }
}

class Square : Rectangle {
    public Square( long width) : base( width, width) {

    }
}
```

The properties Length and Width are missing the set keyword, meaning that neither the Square nor Rectangle can be modified. Therefore, when downcasting a Square to a Rectangle, the end user happens to reference a rectangle, which happens to have the same length and width. The consumer of the Rectangle doesn't care because a rectangle can have a length and width that are identical. And when the consumer references a Square, it still has a shape that has an equal length and width.

The result from making the inheritance hierarchy immutable is that all pieces of the hierarchy make sense. No information is missing, and the hierarchy is always consistent. In a nutshell, this is the best solution in terms of patterns, object-oriented design, and consistency. Additionally, this solution is better than an interface-based solution because it's compact and the classes being discussed are data classes. The importance here of data classes lies in their containing data, not in the operations they possess.

Why Immutable Class Are Scalable

Scalability is achieved by being able to execute a program using multiple threads. Of course, it could be argued, when you have a single processor, then multiple threads don't make an individual application faster. With the release of CPUs that contain multiple cores (a CPU within a CPU), multiple threads will increase the scalability of an application. When using multiple threads in an application, it's necessary to synchronize access to data.

Synchronizing access to data means to allow only a single thread the ability to modify a piece of data. Synchronization doesn't happen automatically, but is added by the developer in the form of method calls, or keywords. The trouble with synchronization can easily be compared to that of using traffic lights. When using traffic lights, traffic is interrupted because cars have to stop when the lights are red. This causes an abrupt behavior to traffic flow, and if badly designed, causes traffic to deadlock. However, if traffic lights are planned effectively, for example, using the so-called green wave (where lights are synchronized to green to allow fairly free flow of vehicles), then traffic will be smoother. This is the challenge for programmers when using synchronization.

A Simple Example of Synchronization

The simplest of all synchronization techniques is to use the lock keyword. The lock keyword synchronizes access to a block of code as illustrated by the following example:

```
class ConcurrentAccess {
    private int _a;

    public void AssignVariable( int a) {
        lock( this) {
            _a = a;
        }
    }
}
```

Here the method AssignVariable includes the keyword lock, which has a single parameter, this. This results in a synchronization block being defined between the curly brackets. A single thread will only execute code between the curly brackets. Other threads will have to wait until the single thread exits the code block. Synchronization is relative to the parameter associated with the lock keyword. Consider the following source code:

```
class ConcurrentAccess {
    private int _a;

    public void AssignVariable( int a) {
        lock( this) {
            _a = a;
        }
    }
    public void AssignAndIncrement( int a) {
        lock( this) {
            _a = a;
            _a ++;
        }
    }
}
```

In this modified implementation, an additional method, AssignAndIncrement, was added that also used the lock keyword. Notice how both lock examples use as a parameter this. This means that regardless of which method is called, the code bounded by the lock keyword will only ever have a single thread accessing the data. This is absolutely vital, because it would be entirely undesirable to have two threads assigning the variable _a.

Now it should become obvious what is problematic is that threads might have to wait excessively to manipulate the data. Or worse, the code deadlocks and doesn't execute any further because of locks are being held by threads that are attempting to access synchronized code.

Immutable objects are a huge advantage in that an individual immutable object requires no synchronization. This is because an immutable object can't be modified, and therefore you don't have to fear that another thread will update the state of an object. However, immutable objects still require some locks since, after all, the reference to an immutable object must be established, and therefore a lock is required. Hence, immutable objects reduce dramatically the number of locks required, but don't eradicate them.

Don't Instantiating and Copying Make an Application Slower?

Assuming that you accept immutable objects are faster from a synchronization point of view, there is still a concern regarding resources. Where immutable objects can be slower is the constant thrashing of memory due to allocation and freeing of objects. That thinking, while correct in theory, is incorrect in practice, or at least mostly incorrect.

In the past, memory allocations were considered very expensive. When using C and C++, the buffer is allocated from a subdivided heap. When allocating a buffer in C and C++, the memory allocation routines search a list of pointers and check whether a heap subdivision is large enough. If the piece of memory is too large, it's subdivided into two pieces. When the piece of memory is freed, the pointer is added to the list of available subdivisions. When two freed subdivisions exist beside each other, they are merged into one piece of free memory. The cost of finding, splitting, and merging memory blocks is expensive and inefficient.

.NET does the same thing as C and C++ in that it searches, allocates, and releases memory. Where .NET and other runtimes are different is that they make assumptions on how to search, allocate, and free memory. These assumptions, which are available to C and C++ in the form of runtimes, dramatically increase the performance of an application.

The result is that allocating and freeing objects using a runtime costs less time from a CPU perspective than using synchronization. Granted, more resources are required, but these days, with 1GB RAM–equipped machines, it's feasible to make those assumptions. As smart as the new generation of memory managers are, there are limits on what should be repeatedly allocated and freed. For example, if an object is 40MB in size, then it shouldn't be allocated and freed as often as an object that is only 1MB. It's still possible to use large immutable objects via the Object Pool pattern.

Following are three different types that illustrate the differences in performance:

```
class Regular {
    private int _value;

    public Regular( int initial) {
        _value = initial;
    }
    public Regular Increment() {
        _value ++;
        return this;
    }
}
```

```
class Immutable {
    private readonly int _value;

    public Immutable( int initial) {
        _value = initial;
    }
    public Immutable Increment() {
        return new Immutable( _value + 1);
    }
}

struct structImmutable {
    private readonly int _value;
    public structImmutable( int initial) {
        _value = initial;
    }
    public structImmutable Increment() {
        return new structImmutable( _value + 1);
    }
}
```

Regular is a typical read-write–capable class that allows editing of its data members. Immutable is a typical immutable class that defines its data members as readonly. In the implementation of Immutable.Increment, a new Immutable instance is instantiated. The structure structImmutable is like the class Immutable, except a structure is used. When a structure is defined, the data members are value types, meaning manipulation occurs on the stack.

The objective is to know the performance characteristics between the three different types when incrementing the internal data member _value. An example of the code used to test Immutable is as follows:

```
public static void IncImmutable() {
    int counter;

    Immutable obj2 = new Immutable( 0);
    for( counter = 0; counter < total; counter ++) {
        obj2 = obj2.Increment();
    }
}
```

The other test script routines are identical, except they use the appropriate type. Before presenting the results, common sense would say that Regular is quickest, followed by structImmutable, and Immutable would be the slowest. When the routines are executed, the overall percentage execution times are as follows:

```
Regular             0.05%
Immutable           0.25%
structImmutable     0.20%
```

The theory was correct, in that allocating objects causes the program to require five times as much computing time. What is interesting, though, is that using a structure is slightly quicker than using a class. Let's modify Increment of Regular to include a lock block as illustrated by the following code:

```
class Regular {
    private int _value;

    public Regular( int initial) {
        _value = initial;
    }
    public Regular Increment() {
        lock( this) {
            _value ++;
        }
        return this;
    }
}
```

Rerunning the performance tests, the following results are generated:

```
Regular           0.46%
Immutable         0.52%
structImmutable   0.45%
```

This time the numbers indicate that it doesn't matter which type is used, as they are all executing at the same performance levels. You may be tempted to believe that it's still best to avoid immutable objects because they are slow. But remember, you haven't yet seen any synchronization scenarios, just an acquiring and releasing of a lock. Adding synchronization will dramatically change the behavior of your application. It's possible with a well-written application to keep the performance advantage of a read-write object. However, this is very difficult and it's simpler to use an immutable object.

Some Rules of Thumb for Immutable Classes

When creating immutable classes, you should be aware of certain rules of thumb regarding their use:

- Immutable classes often consist of data classes. A data class holds data only and doesn't provide many operations that relate to application logic. The class might have a large number of methods that relate to manipulating the data such as the String class.

- An immutable class doesn't reference a read-write class. Essentially what this means is that an immutable class doesn't publicly expose a type that is read-write capable.

- Immutable classes typically don't implement interfaces. But a very useful technique is the implementation of an immutable interface by a read-write class. An immutable interface is an interface that has read-only operations. The immutable interface allows a class implementation to optimize when synchronization is necessary.

- Immutable classes can be serialized and are typically transported across networks or AppDomains. Rarely will a type hold a remote reference to an immutable type.

Now that you understand the basics behind immutable classes, let's take a look at how to use them with the Flyweight pattern.

Using Immutable Classes in the Flyweight Pattern

An immutable class is a single class, but when used as a collection, it makes up the basis of the Flyweight pattern.[2] The problem that the Flyweight pattern solves is a common scenario. Let's say that you're writing an application, and some pieces of the application are objects that have a constant value or are immutable throughout their entire life. Having the client instantiate an object with the same value repeatedly is wasteful of CPU time and resources.

In the following source code, a new object is repeatedly instantiated with the same values:

```
interface IBase {
}

class ImmutableImplementation : IBase{
    public ImmutableImplementation( int initialValue) {}
}

class Factory {
    static public IBase CreateImplementation( string parameter) {
        if( String.Compare( "somevalue", parameter) == 0) {
            return new ImmutableImplementation( 10);
        }
        throw new NotImplementedException();
    }
}
```

The interface IBase is implemented by the class ImmutableImplementation. The method Factory.CreateImplementation instantiates the class ImmutableImplementation with a certain initial state. The initial state is dependent on the value of the variable parameter. Imagine if the method CreateImplementation were called one hundred times where the parameter variable is equal to somevalue. Then the same state-defined immutable object would be instantiated one hundred times. This is wasteful of resources.

The flyweight optimizes this not by instantiating a new object, but by reusing an old instance. Also imperative is the use of the factory, which knows when to reuse an object instance and when to allocate a new object instance. (Chapter 3 introduced the Factory pattern.)

Let's take a look at an example of the Flyweight pattern before delving into its architecture.

---

2. Erich Gamma et al., *Design Patterns: Elements of Reusable Object-Oriented Software* (Boston: Addison-Wesley, 1995), p. 195.

An Example of the Flyweight Pattern

You probably have been using the Flyweight pattern without even knowing it. In the .NET runtime, strings are both immutable and use the Flyweight pattern. For example, if you reference two strings with the exact same contents, there is only one string value. Even if the two buffers have been assigned with the same contents, there will be a single value of the buffer in memory. The two buffers will reference the same piece of memory.

How the string routines implement the Flyweight pattern is as follows:

```
[TestFixture]
public class TestString {
    [Test]
    public void Test() {
        String flyweight = "flyweight", pattern = "pattern";
        String flyweight2 = "flyweight", pattern2 = "pattern";

        // Test 1
        Assert.IsTrue( Object.ReferenceEquals( flyweight, flyweight2));
        // Test 2
        Assert.IsTrue(Object.ReferenceEquals( pattern, pattern2));

        String distinctString = flyweight + pattern;
        // Test 3
        Assert.IsFalse( Object.ReferenceEquals( distinctString,
"flyweightpattern"));

        String flyweightpattern = String.Intern(flyweight + pattern);
        // Test 4
        Assert.IsTrue( Object.ReferenceEquals( flyweightpattern,"flyweight"));
    }
    [Test]
    public void TestFlyweightReadOnly() {
        ImmutableClass cls1 = new ImmutableClass( "hello", 10);
        ImmutableClass cls2 = new ImmutableClass( "hello", 10);

        Assert.IsFalse( Object.ReferenceEquals( cls1, cls2));
    }
}
```

The method TestString contains multiple Assert statements with a comment and test identifier above each of the lines. Following is an analysis of each of the tests:

- Test 1: The variables flyweight and flyweight2 are two different buffers assigned the same value separately. At runtime, .NET will assign flyweight and flyweight2 to reference the same value. The test ReferenceEquals verifies the optimization.

- Test 2: This test does the same thing as Test 1.

- Test 3: This test illustrates how comparing two identical value strings during the course of execution results in creation of two different values.

- Test 4: This test is identical to Test 3, except the flyweightpattern variable is the result of calling the Intern method. The Intern method adds a string value to the "flyweight" table of strings, which is useful when reusing certain buffer values in an application.

What the tests demonstrate is how the Flyweight pattern optimizes string usage in the .NET runtime. The method TestFlyweightReadOnly shows that the Flyweight pattern only applies to the .NET string type. ImmutableClass is a type defined by the user, and when two immutable classes are instantiated, two unique distinct values result. What is important to realize is that all of the data members within ImmutableClass are defined as readonly, and therefore the runtime could optimize and implement the Flyweight pattern like the string type.

A Generic Flyweight Architecture

A generic Flyweight pattern implementation is a cross between a collection and a factory. It's a collection in that a Flyweight pattern implementation manages the cross-reference between identifier and implementation. A Flyweight pattern implementation is also a factory, because if an identifier doesn't cross-reference with an implementation, then an object must be instantiated.

In formal UML terms, the Flyweight pattern is defined as shown in Figure 7-1.

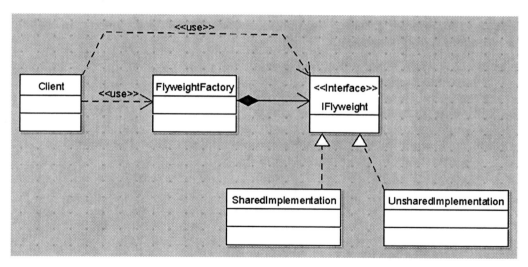

Figure 7-1. *UML diagram that illustrates the architecture of the Flyweight pattern*

The Client interacts with the FlyweightFactory class and IFlyweight interface. The FlyweightFactory class is a factory, but also contains the logic to cross-reference a specific IFlyweight instance based on an identifier. The identifier is supplied by the Client passed to FlyweightFactory for cross-referencing purposes, and its meaning is understood by an IFlyweight implementation. Based on the identifier, FlyweightFactory can give the client a new instance or an already existing instance. FlyweightFactory knows about the types SharedImplementation and UnsharedImplementation.

The implementation of the Flyweight pattern uses two previously defined topics: the method GetHashCode and a transformer functor. In contrast to the UML diagram in Figure 7-1, FlyweightFactory is also an implementation of an interface that can be shared to instantiate a flyweight object. The interface isn't necessary, but is added so that it's possible to use the Flyweight factory in remote and dynamic loading contexts.

Following is the source code for the Flyweight factory interface:

```
public interface IFlyweightCollection< type> {
    type GetItem( object descriptor);
}
```

The name IFlyweightCollection<> is used instead of a factory because a generic architecture is being defined. The purpose of IFlyweightCollection<> is to retrieve an instantiated instance compatible with the generic parameter type. The client using IFlyweightCollection<> doesn't know or care where the instantiated type comes from. The client uses the method GetItem, where the parameter descriptor is an object that describes the type to instantiate. descriptor is of type object so that it allows a maximum amount of flexibility. Ideally, descriptor will implement the Dynamic Extension pattern or the Static Extension pattern and be used by the IFlyweight interface as constructor information. One of the problems of a constructor is knowing how to pass the appropriate constructor information. Using the Dynamic Extension pattern, it's possible to combine various interfaces into one object instance.

In the implementation of FlyweightFactory, shown in the following code, the various flyweight instances are managed as a collection that cross-references the descriptor with the instance. The full FlyweightFactory implementation uses the transformer functor to transform the descriptor into an instance.

```
public sealed class FlyweightFactory< type> :
    IFlyweightCollection< type> {
    DelegateTransformer< object, type> _transformer;
    Hashtable _collection = new Hashtable();

    public FlyweightFactory( DelegateTransformer< object, type> transformer) {
        _transformer = transformer;
    }

    public type GetItem( object descriptor) {
        type retval = (type)_collection[ descriptor];
        if( retval == null) {
            retval = _transformer( descriptor);
            _collection[ descriptor] = retval;
        }
        return retval;
    }

}
```

FlyweightFactory<> implements the interface IFlyweightCollection<>, and both are Generic types. The data member _collection references a Hashtable that cross-references the descriptor with an instance. The data member _transformer is of the type DelegateTransformer, which represents a transformer functor. The purpose of DelegateTransformer is to act like a factory and instantiate a data type. This may seem odd using a transformer functor, but consider that the idea behind the flyweight is to cross-reference an identifier descriptor with an instance. Hence, using a transformer functor is logical.

The method GetItem retrieves the instance using a two-step strategy. The first step is to retrieve an instance from the Hashtable data member _collection. This will only work if descriptor has implemented the GetHashcode method. As a side note, if the default .NET-provided GetHashcode method is used, a reference equality test is performed, and most likely the Flyweight pattern implementation won't work properly. The exception is if the descriptor is the string data type.

For the second step, if the retval variable is a null value, then the instance must be created using the _transformer functor. The returned instance is then added to the _collection hash table. It's important to realize that if the transformer functor can't instantiate an instance from the descriptor, an exception is thrown. As mentioned in earlier chapters, a null value shouldn't be returned. Under the circumstances defined by the Null Object pattern (which was discussed in the preceding chapter), it's acceptable to return a null object.

Now that you're familiar with the architecture of the Flyweight pattern, I'll show you how to use it in the next section.

Using the Generic Flyweight Architecture

Using the generic Flyweight pattern implementation isn't complicated and is well suited in a component situation. What is important about using the generic Flyweight pattern implementation is that it should be hidden in the context of a builder.

Let's say that the following interface and implementations are instance types that a client is interested in:

```
public interface ITestFlyweight {
    string Identifier {
        get;
    }
}

class TestFlyweightA : ITestFlyweight {
    public String Identifier {
        get {
            return "TestFlyweightA";
        }
    }
}

class TestFlyweightB : ITestFlyweight {
    public String Identifier {
        get {
            return "TestFlyweightB";
        }
    }
}
```

The interface ITestFlyweight has a single property, Identifier, that retrieves a property value. In your own solutions, the interface could have as many methods or properties as needed, but the interface needs to be immutable. Additionally, an interface doesn't need to be used; instead you could employ a base class. Or if desired, in the declaration of FlyweightFactory you can include the type object, which allows the referencing of any object instance. In the example, TestFlyweightA and TestFlyweightB both implement the ITestFlyweight interface and a rudimentary implementation of the property Identifier.

The following Builder class illustrates a complete Flyweight pattern implementation:

```
class FlyweightBuilder {
    public static ITestFlyweight Transformation( object desc) {
        if( String.Compare( (string)desc, "TestFlyweightA") == 0) {
            return new TestFlyweightA();
        }
        else if( String.Compare( (string)desc, "TestFlyweightB") == 0) {
            return new TestFlyweightB();
        }
        throw new NotSupportedException();
    }
    public static IFlyweightCollection< ITestFlyweight, string> Instantiate() {
        return new FlyweightCollection< ITestFlyweight, string>(
            new DelegateTransformer< string, ITestFlyweight>(
                FlyweightBuilder.Transformation));
    }
}
```

FlyweightBuilder has two static methods: Instantiate and Transformation. The method Instantiate instantiates the FlyweightCollection class, where the Generic parameter is defined to be ITestFlyweight. This means that this Flyweight pattern implementation creates objects of type ITestFlyweight. The method Transformation instantiates either TestFlyweightA or TestFlyweightB depending on the value of parameter desc. If desc doesn't resolve to one of the two values, an exception is thrown.

Using the Flyweight Implementation

The last step in this demonstration of the Flyweight pattern is to have FlyweightBuilder instantiate some types based on a descriptor. Following is the related NUnit test code:

```
[TestFixture]
public class TestFlyweight {
    [Test]
    public void TestSimple() {
        IFlyweightCollection< ITestFlyweight, string> var =
FlyweightBuilder.Instantiate();

        ITestFlyweight var1 = var.GetItem( "TestFlyweightA");
        ITestFlyweight var2 = var.GetItem( "TestFlyweightB");
```

```
        Assert.AreEqual( "TestFlyweightA", var1.Identifier);
        Assert.AreEqual( "TestFlyweightB", var2.Identifier);

        ITestFlyweight var1a = var.GetItem( "TestFlyweightA");
        Assert.IsTrue( Object.ReferenceEquals( var1, var1a));

        ITestFlyweight var2a = var.GetItem( "TestFlyweightB");
        Assert.IsTrue( Object.ReferenceEquals( var2, var2a));
    }
}
```

An instance of the `IFlyweightCollection<>` interface is instantiated using the method `FlyweightBuilder.Instantiate`. Then the method `GetItem` is called twice and assigned to the variables var1 and var2. The variable var1 references an instance of `TestFlyweightA`, and the variable var2 references an instance of `TestFlyweightB`. The subsequent `Assert` statements verify that the correct instances are instantiated.

The variable var1a uses the same descriptor as was used to assign the variable var1. The Flyweight pattern dictates that both var1 and var1a reference the same object instance. The proof is the validation using the method `Object.ReferenceEquals` of var1 and var1a; `Assert.IsTrue` then checks to see whether the method returns a `true` value. The same test is performed for the variables var2 and var2a.

Let's consider the ramifications of this implementation:

- There is no way to test whether the returned instantiated type is immutable. The Flyweight pattern dictates that it's immutable, but there is no way to verify it. A way to ensure that only immutable objects are used is to periodically check the hashcode of such an object and ensure that it isn't modified.

- It's possible to use class instances that can be altered. However, that means multiple clients will be manipulating the same object instance. This violates the Flyweight pattern and introduces state corruption, as multiple threads might be manipulating the same data. But if the objects do change, use the hashcode to check for changes and perform some additional action not defined by the illustrated implementation.

- There has to be a way to describe the objects you're interested in. In the example, the description consisted of a text buffer, but you could also use an enumeration or a configuration file entry. I previously mentioned that the descriptor should implement either the Dynamic or Static Extension pattern because that makes the descriptor definition flexible.

- A flyweight descriptor can only refer to one unique state. It isn't possible, nor should it be attempted, to switch the meaning of a descriptor while a Flyweight implementation is being used. In other words, combining the Flyweight pattern with the State pattern isn't a good idea.

- A very good way of implementing the transformation functor is to use the Chain of Responsibility pattern. This gets away from the hard-coded `if` statement block given by the example.

This wraps up the discussion on the Flyweight pattern. Next, I'll introduce you to another pattern that helps you create efficient code: the Object Pool pattern.

The Theory of Object Pools

The Object Pool pattern[3] could be considered controversial because .NET in conjunction with COM+ provides an object pooling facility. The Object Pool pattern uses an approach whereby a container represents a factory and manages class instances. If COM+ object pooling isn't used, there is another approach that can be used specific to .NET.

You use object pooling when you don't want to constantly instantiate an object because the resulting cost in terms of time and resources is very large. The instantiation cost is high because, for example, a file needs to be parsed or a network server needs to be queried for information. Both of these examples require that the application retrieve data from a medium that is slower than the computer's RAM. Using an object pool, the object is instantiated with the slower-to-read information once, and thereafter the object operates on that information. An object pool isn't a flyweight because a flyweight has a single state for a single descriptor, whereas an object pool has a single state that is loaded by multiple objects.

Object Pools and COM+

Before the Object Pool pattern is discussed, I'd like to share a quick note about how object pooling relates to COM+. COM+ has implemented object pooling, as this example illustrates:

```
[ObjectPooling(MinPoolSize = 10,MaxPoolSize = 20)]
public class Example :ServicedComponent
{ }
```

The attribute `ObjectPooling` marks the class `Example` as being poolable. This means when the type `Example` is instantiated, COM+ intercepts the call and manages the object instances. The parameters `MinPoolSize` and `MaxPoolSize` indicate the minimum and maximum of objects in the pool. Other parameters control the object instantiation timeout, and so on. Overall, though, many other rules apply such as state, and this requires some additional thought before using COM+ object pooling. Also included are details like object referencing, etc.

I've just covered COM+ object pooling in two paragraphs and did so deliberately. When I was writing this material, I learned that to give COM+ object pooling justice, I could either cover it quickly or cover it thoroughly. I chose the former because to cover COM+ object pooling in detail, I would need an entire book, since a discussion of COM+ object pooling requires a discussion of COM+ and everything that it entails. However, the focus of this book isn't COM+, but object-oriented design and .NET patterns.

The result is that I will illustrate the Object Pool pattern in terms of .NET. This means that you either choose COM+ or choose my Object Pool pattern implementation. The implementation outlined in this book doesn't even come close to being as deep as a COM+ implementation. It's meant for those situations when COM+ is too much extra work or not necessary, because after all, using COM+ requires additional design and deployment considerations.

---

3. Alan Shalloway and James Trott, *Design Patterns Explained: A New Perspective on Object-Oriented Design, Second Edition* (Boston: Addison-Wesley, 2004), p. 371.

So, without further ado, let's first look at the architecture of the Object Pool pattern, followed by an exploration of how to use this pattern.

The Theory of Object Pools

The UML diagram in Figure 7-2 presents a way to implement the Object Pool pattern.

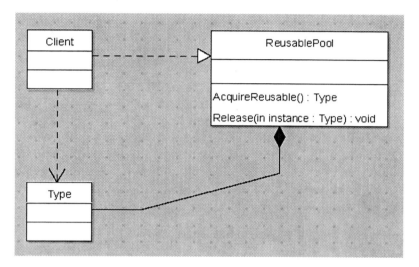

Figure 7-2. *UML diagram that illustrates the architecture of the Object Pool pattern*

In Figure 7-2, the Client interacts with a class called ReusablePool. ReusablePool has two methods: AcquireReusable, and Release. The method AcquireReusable retrieves an instance from the pool, and the method Release puts the object back in the pool.

An object pool is responsible for instantiating and managing the object instances. The object pool maintains an internal collection of objects representing objects that will be "instantiated." The object pool can be as simple or complicated as needed. In the simplest case, the object pool wouldn't reference any instantiated objects, only instantiating them when necessary. Then as processes complete their work, the objects are returned to the object pool and reused by another caller.

Where an object pool becomes more complicated is if there are requirements such as minimum or maximum number of objects, and maximum idle time. Other complications include threading and AppDomain management.

Implementing an Object Pool Pattern in .NET

A complete Object Pool pattern implementation in .NET is a bit more complicated than the UML diagram in Figure 7-2. For example, in general, object pools should have an external factory that instantiates the individual object.

Figure 7-3 shows another UML diagram of the Object Pool pattern.

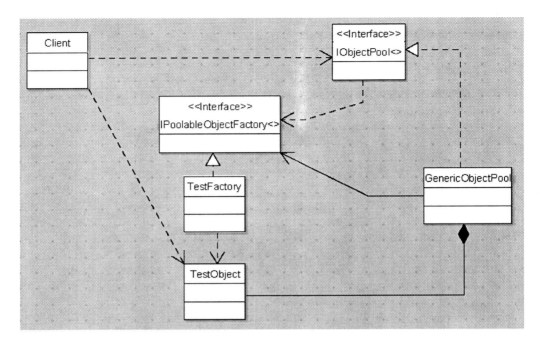

Figure 7-3. *UML diagram for .NET Object Pool pattern implementation*

When compared to Figure 7-2, the UML diagram in Figure 7-3 appears more complicated, due mainly to the refactoring of the object pool collection functionality that is separate from the factory and the use of interfaces. The interface IObjectPool<> defines the core object pool collection functionality. IPoolableObjectFactory<> is an interface that a developer implements and uses to instantiate an object when requested by an IObjectPool<> implementation.

The class TestFactory implements the IPoolableObjectFactory<> and is responsible for instantiating TestObject, which is used by Client and managed by GenericObjectPool. GenericObjectPool references an IPoolableObjectFactory<> instance. In the example, GenericObjectPool references the type TestObject directly, but it's possible to reference an interface instance.

Hooking into .NET Finalization

What is radically different from the original Object Pool pattern is the use of .NET finalizers. A .NET finalizer is like a destructor that is called before the .NET runtime disposes of an object. It's used because it makes the Object Pool pattern implementation self-managing.

Let's say that you're instantiating an object that will be pooled. You ask the pool for the object, and an object is removed from the inactive pool and moved into the active pool. Then when you're done, you need to give the object back to the pool. This additional step of returning the object to the pool is the dilemma. Coders might forget to do this additional step, and an object pool will hand out objects without the caller pooling any of them.

A possible alternative would be to add a finalizer to a pooled object that, when called, would resurrect the object again. Following is an example pooled object with a finalizer declaration:

```
class TestPoolAllocation {
    IObjectPool< TestPoolAllocation> _parent;

    public TestPoolAllocation( IObjectPool< TestPoolAllocation> parent) {
        _parent = parent;
    }
    ~TestPoolAllocation() {
        _parent.ReturnObject( this);
    }
}
```

The class TestPoolAllocation has a constructor parameter parent, which represents the object pool collection manager. The parent parameter is assigned to the data member _parent. A pooled object has a reference to the object pool collection that instantiated it. When a client finishes using a pooled object, the .NET garbage collector will collect the pooled object and call the finalizer (~TestPoolAllocation). This in turn causes the pooled object to call the method _parent.ReturnObject, which creates a strong reference to the pooled object by the pool, thus resurrecting the pooled object.

There is a catch in this pooled object scenario, namely that the object pool collection can't reference the pooled object when a client is using the pooled object. The garbage collector will only call the TestPoolAllocation finalizer if no references exist to the instance. Were the pool collection to have a reference, there would be no need to garbage collect the object, thus the garbage collector never calls the finalizer. The only time when the object pool collection can reference the pooled object is if the pooled object is available for reuse.

Making an object poolable requires the additional steps of adding a constructor with a parameter and adding a finalizer (*destructor*). This might deter usage because it requires modifications of already existing types. However, to convert an existing object into a pooled object does require some changes. Consider the scenario of adding a pooled object back into the pool. Before the pooled object can be used, it has to be reset to some initialized state. Not doing that would cause objects to use an object that has the state from previous client interactions.

Implementing the Object Pool Collection

Regardless of which object pool strategy is implemented, the interface IObjectPool<> has to be implemented, and is defined as follows:

```
public interface IObjectPool< type> {
    type GetObject();
    void SetFactory( IPoolableObjectFactory< type> factory);
    bool ReturnObject( type obj);
}
```

The interface IObjectPool<> has three methods: GetObject, SetFactory, and ReturnObject. The method GetObject retrieves an object from the pool. The method SetFactory assigns a factory to the object pool collection. And the method ReturnObject is called by the pooled object to indicate that the object is available for reuse.

The factory assigned by the method IObjectPool<>.SetFactory is defined as follows:

```
public interface IPoolableObjectFactory< type> {
    type MakeObject( IObjectPool<type> parent);
    void ActivateObject(type obj);
    void PassivateObject(type obj);
}
```

IPoolableObjectFactory<> also has three methods: MakeObject, ActiveObject, and PassivateObject. The method MakeObject instantiates a new object instance, when the object pool collection implementation needs a pooled object instance. The methods ActiveObject and PassivateObject initialize and reset the state of the pooled object, respectively. For example, when an object is given back to the object pool, the method PassivateObject is called. An implementation of PassivateObject would release and reset any resources before the object is added to the available object list. The method ActiveObject is called whenever an object is about to be consumed and initializes the object, so that the consumer gets a "fresh" object without any previous state.

For the scope of this book, a simple object pool is implemented as follows:

```
public class GenericObjectPool<type> : IObjectPool< type> {
    IPoolableObjectFactory< type> _factory;
    Stack< type> _availableObjects;
    bool _allowRegistrations;

    public GenericObjectPool() {
        _availableObjects = new Stack< type>();
        _allowRegistrations = true;
    }
    ~GenericObjectPool() {
        lock( this) {
            _allowRegistrations = false;
        }
    }
    public virtual type GetObject() {
        lock( this) {
            type retval;
            if( _availableObjects.Count == 0) {
                retval = _factory.MakeObject( this);
            }
            else {
                retval = _availableObjects.Pop();
            }
            _factory.ActivateObject( retval);
            return retval;
        }
    }
```

```
        public virtual bool ReturnObject(type obj) {
            lock( this) {
                if( _allowRegistrations) {
                    _availableObjects.Push( obj);
                    _factory.PassivateObject( obj);
                    GC.ReRegisterForFinalize( obj);
                    return true;
                }
                else {
                    return false;
                }
            }
        }
        public virtual void SetFactory(IPoolableObjectFactory<type> factory) {
            _factory = factory;
        }
    }
```

GenericObjectPool<> implements the IObjectPool<> interface. The data member
_availableObjects is a stack data type, chosen for a specific reason that will be outlined in a
moment. The data member _factory is a factory that is responsible for instantiating new
objects, initialization, and resetting of existing objects.

Let's look closer at GetObject in this example. The first step is to check whether the stack is
empty by checking whether the property _availableObjects.Count equals zero. If the stack
is empty, then the _factory is called to instantiate an object. If an object does exist on the stack,
then that object is activated by calling the method _availableObjects.Pop. Before the object is
returned to the client, the method _factory.Activate is called, which prepares the state of the
object before it's returned to the client.

Before getting to the explanation of ReturnObject, you need to understand a couple of
points. Instead of a Stack, a list or array could have been used to reference available pooled
objects. Doing this might be wrong, because of the referencing issue. Remember that the.NET
implementation of the Object Pool pattern makes use of finalization, which means no references to
the object can exist. So, for example, if a list is used, and the element isn't removed from the list,
then a dangling reference will occur. The dangling reference will cause the finalizer to not be called.
If, however, the GenericObjectPool<> type needed to keep a reference to the instantiated object,
then you should use the class System.WeakReference. Using System.WeakReference allows you
to reference an object without stopping finalization. Many will call this dangling reference a
resource leak, even though the garbage collector is tracking the resource. The problem is that
the program has a dangling reference, and the garbage collector can't track the resource due to
an application logic error.

The method ReturnObject is a bit more complicated because of the way finalization
happens. Finalization isn't guaranteed to execute in any particular order, nor is it known when
it will happen. You don't know if the pooled object will be finalized before the object pool or
vice versa. Therefore, you can't make assumptions on the pooled object reregistration process.

Going through the process when the finalizer for the pooled object executes, the pooled object will reference the IObjectPool<> instance and reregister itself. In ReturnObject, the method GC.ReRegisterForFinalize is called. When an object is resurrected, the finalizer won't be called again. Calling the method ReRegisterForFinalize will cause the garbage collector to call the finalizer again, even though the object has been resurrected. The trouble with this strategy is that sometimes it isn't desirable to resurrect an object. This occurs when the finalizer of object pool has been called. Then the object reregistration won't happen because the variable _allowRegistrations will be a false value, and the finalizer won't be reregistered. Doing otherwise will result in a never-ending loop of finalizations method calls.

A Small Discussion on the Garbage Collector

Another strategy that could be used that wouldn't require a reregistration flag is the class WeakReference. WeakReference allows one class to reference another class without creating a strong reference to the other class. Without a strong reference, the class can be garbage collected.[4] In theory, the pooled object could reference the IObjectPool<> instance using a weak reference, and then in the pooled object's finalizer the weak reference is tested before reregistration. The problem with this strategy is that finalizers are called in any order by the garbage collector. And that could mean that the weak reference finalizer for the pooled object will be called before the finalizer of the pooled object, which would result in an object been returned to memory even though the IObjectPool<> instance still existed.

Another solution to the Object Pool pattern is to not implement a finalizer, but use the IDisposable interface as illustrated by the following:

```
class TestPoolAllocation : IDisposable {
    WeakReference _reference;

    public TestPoolAllocation( IObjectPoolBase<TestPoolAllocation> parent) {
        _reference = new WeakReference( parent);;
    }

    public void Dispose() {
        if( _reference.Target != null) {
            ((IObjectPoolBase<TestPoolAllocation2>)_reference.Target).
                ReturnObject( this);
        }
    }
}
```

In the modified example, the class TestPoolAllocation implements the IDisposable method, which uses the WeakReference class. The WeakReference class contains a reference to an IObjectPoolBase<> class instance. In the implementation of the Dispose method, the weak reference is tested for a null value, indicating that the object has been garbage collected. If the Target value isn't null, then the IObjectPoolBase<> instance still exists, and the object can be reregistered for reuse.

---

4. http://blogs.msdn.com/brada/archive/2004/4/28.aspx: "Why does my WeakReference throw an InvalidOperationException when I use it from my finalizer?"

The safe bet is to use the IDisposable interface technique, because it will work in all instances. The safe bet is also an extra step because it explicitly requires the client to call the Dispose method. Another potential decision-making factor is that from a performance point of view, not implementing a finalizer is faster as the garbage collector doesn't need to explicitly call a method.

Using the finalizer is acceptable so long as you understand that there might not be an order in which the objects are finalized. This means sometimes you could have strange side effects. The strange side effects only happen when you use things like COM+ or other containers that make extensive use of AppDomains and threading. If you're writing an application where you control the threads or a simple ASP.NET application, then using the finalizer will solve the problem.

Letting a Client Use the Object Pool Implementation

When using an IObjectPool<> implementation, you need to provide an IObjectPoolableFactory<> implementation. The object pool implementation expects you to instantiate, activate, and passivate the individual objects. An example factory is defined as follows:

```
class TestPoolAllocationFactory : IPoolableObjectFactory< TestPoolAllocation> {
    public TestPoolAllocation MakeObject(
        IObjectPoolBase<TestPoolAllocation> parent) {
        return new TestPoolAllocation( parent);
    }
    public void ActivateObject(TestPoolAllocation obj) {
        obj.Identifier = 0;
    }
    public void PassivateObject(TestPoolAllocation obj) {
    }
}
```

The method MakeObject acts like a factory method and should be treated as such. Where things become complicated is if the instantiation of TestPoolAllocation requires additional constructor information. One possible solution, not shown here, is to use the Dynamic Extension pattern and typecast the IObjectPoolBase<> to the required interface.

The method ActivateObject activates the object before it's manipulated by the client, and the method PassivateObject prepares an object for storage in idle mode. ActivateObject and PassivateObject seem similar, but serve very distinct purposes. Imagine an object that loads a file and internally keeps a list of a subset of the file elements. The method PassivateObject would release the list of subset file elements to conserve memory because the list is transitory and only relevant in the context. The method ActivateObject would instantiate a fresh list that contains no elements.

Having ActivateObject and PassivateObject attached to the factory might not make sense. A better solution might be to attach those methods to the object itself, since the pooled object needs to be passivated and activated. The reason for adding those methods to the IPoolableObjectFactory<> is to allow references external to the pooled object to be passivated and activated.

Then to use the pooled objects and factory, employ the following test code:

```
[TestFixture]
public class TestObjectPool {
    void Method1(GenericObjectPool< TestPoolAllocation> pool) {
        TestPoolAllocation obj = pool.GetObject();
        obj.Identifier = 100;
        NUnit.Framework.Assert.AreEqual( 1, pool.NumActive);
    }
    void Method2(GenericObjectPool< TestPoolAllocation> pool) {
        NUnit.Framework.Assert.AreEqual( 0, pool.NumActive);
        TestPoolAllocation obj = pool.GetObject();
        NUnit.Framework.Assert.AreEqual( 100, obj.Identifier);
        NUnit.Framework.Assert.AreEqual( 1, pool.NumActive);
    }
    [Test]
    public void TestAllocateFreeAndReallocate() {
        GenericObjectPool< TestPoolAllocation> pool =
            new GenericObjectPool< TestPoolAllocation>();
        pool.SetFactory( new TestPoolAllocationFactory());

        Method1( pool);
        GC.Collect();
        Thread.Sleep( 500);
        NUnit.Framework.Assert.AreEqual( 0, pool.NumActive);
        NUnit.Framework.Assert.AreEqual( 1, pool.NumIdle);
        Method2( pool);
    }
}
```

In the NUnit test code method TestAllocateFreeAndAllocated, the variable pool represents the GenericObjectPool< TestPoolAllocation>. From the pool, the individual TestPoolAllocation objects are instantiated. This test code has one small change in the method TestPoolAllocationFactory in that ActivateObject and PassivateObject aren't implemented. This is done on purpose to illustrate that an object is reused. In this NUnit test code, Method1 allocates an object instance and assigns the Identifier property a value of 100. Then in Method2, when an object is retrieved from the pool, the Identifier property value of 100 is tested to indicate that an object has been recycled. Notice in the implementation of TestAllocateFreeAndReallocate the methods GC.Collect and Thread.Sleep are called to give the garbage collector a chance to execute the finalizer.

Now that you've seen how object pooling works, let's move on to creating applications with multiple threads.

Multithreaded Applications

Writing applications that make use of multiple threads is a complicated undertaking because when you use multiple threads, multiple things are happening at the same time. The best way to understand this complexity is to think of pairs figure skating.

When two people figure skate, they skate together in synchronization. It's expected of each to do the right thing at the right time. For example, let's say the pair does a double axel. One picks up the other and spins the person like a top, who then amazingly lands on one skate to continue skating. Writing threaded applications is like pairs skating, except that there might be more than a pair of skaters trying to skate together at the same time. The more threads, the more skaters, the more likely something is going to go wrong.

Debugging and visualizing threads is futile. It's like asking one of the skaters to stop midway in the routine for inspection. The other skater will probably fall flat on his or her face because the skater who is being inspected isn't at the place that the other skater expects him or her to be at. Therefore, as a word of warning, don't believe those tools that promise to solve your threading problems in one quick-and-easy step. The only way to manage multiple threads is to use a correct architecture with targeted debugging.

Applications developed today require a developer to understand threading, as computers will include central processing units (CPUs) that will have multiple cores. *Multiple cores* means multiple processors, which means for an application to achieve scalability, the application needs to be threaded.

A Simple Thread Example

Running multiple threads in .NET is simple, and involves the instantiation of a delegate that is passed to a class that calls the delegate. The following source code provides an example:

```
class StaticMethodThreads {
    public static void Thread1() {
        for(int i = 0; i < 10; i++) {
            Console.WriteLine("Thread1 {0}", i);
        }
    }
}
[TestFixture]
public class TestSimpleThreading {
    [Test]
    public void RunStaticMethodTests() {
        Thread tid1 = new Thread(new ThreadStart(StaticMethodThreads.Thread1));
        tid1.Start();
    }
}
```

The class StaticMethodThreads has a single static method, Thread1, which has no parameters and no return value. The method RunStaticMethod instantiates the type Thread, and the constructor is a delegate of type ThreadStart. When the method tid1.Start is called, the delegate ThreadStart that is part of the method StaticMethodThreads.Thread1 is executed. When the method tid1.Start returns, the calling thread that is executing is doing so at the same time as the thread executing the method StaticMethodsThreads.Thread1.

When a thread executes concurrently with another thread, they can both manipulate the same data. You could consider it as two applications executing at the same time, though this is a very simplistic way of looking at threading. It's also possible to execute multiple threads running in different AppDomains. In that case, the rules of calling across AppDomains still apply as illustrated in the Client-Dispatcher-Server pattern discussion in Chapter 4.

Implementing the Singleton

The Singleton pattern[5] solves the problem of instantiating a class that is reused by multiple clients that don't know about each other. The classical singleton implementation doesn't consider how the class is instantiated or from where it's instantiated. It also doesn't consider how the data of the singleton is exposed. Those issues are delegated, but the implementation of the classical singleton has to be dramatically modified. The reason why you do need to consider threading and a reader-writer is because singletons are nasty from a resource and performance point of view and need more functionality to be useful.

Singletons are also nasty because they are so simple to implement. The problem with the Singleton pattern is that the implementation doesn't make a reader aware of the ramifications. In the simplest terms, a singleton is a like a global variable—there can only be a single instance. Yet let's think about this: does it mean a single instance per application? That isn't entirely correct, because when an application is composed of multiple AppDomains, then it includes multiple singletons. So what does a singleton really mean? The answer is that there is no answer because a singleton depends on the scope. For example, it's possible to create a singleton per AppDomain, or a singleton per application, or a singleton per user, or a singleton per computer, or a singleton per group configuration. And yet all of these singletons aren't implemented as many Singleton patterns are implemented today.

The Classical Simple Singleton

The following represents the classical Singleton pattern:

```
class Singleton {
    public static Singleton Instance() {
        if(_instance == null) {
            lock(typeof(Singleton)) {
                if(_instance == null) {
                    _instance = new Singleton();
                }
            }
        }
        return _instance;
    }

    protected Singleton() { }
    public int Value;
    private static volatile Singleton _instance = null;
}
```

When implementing the Singleton pattern, the class itself becomes the singleton. The data member _instance is declared as static and volatile. This means that for the class Singleton,

---

5. *Design Patterns: Elements of Reusable Object-Oriented Software*, p. 127.

only one instance of the data member _instance can exist. The keyword volatile ensures that a multithreaded application will retrieve the most current value and not one from a cache.

To retrieve an instance of the Singleton class, the client uses the method Instance. In the implementation of Instance, a double-checked lock is used. Imagine an application that is executing and references the method Instance for the very first time. The data member _instance will equal null, and that is an indicator to instantiate a Singleton class. However, an application might have multiple threads, and therefore multiple threads will realize that they need to instantiate a Singleton instance. This is the purpose of the lock statement; it ensures only one thread will instantiate a singleton. If a thread has control, a check is made to ensure that the _instance data member is still null, because another thread might have created an instance. If the data member _instance is null, then the class Singleton is instantiated.

A client would use Singleton as follows:

```
Singleton.Instance().Value;
```

The example singleton implementation illustrates how to instantiate a singleton using a method reference. The advantage of using this approach is it enables the singleton class to be constructed using a configuration file or some other global information.

If a simple instantiation is desired, and the application isn't required to have loaded all information, then the following Singleton class implementation is adequate:

```
sealed class Singleton {
    private Singleton() { }
    public static readonly Singleton Instance = new Singleton();
}
```

In this example, the Singleton type is instantiated when the Singleton class is referenced for the first time. This technique has no synchronization and is possible because the .NET Framework ensures that only a single thread initializes static data members.

Outlining What Is Wrong with the Classic Singleton Implementation

A few things are wrong with the classical Singleton pattern implementation shown in the previous section:

- A singleton is only a singleton in its own AppDomain. Other AppDomains would need to instantiate their own singleton, causing potential data consistency issues. For example, imagine having to share configuration information in multiple AppDomains.

- It isn't easily possible to shut down a singleton, and therefore data might be lost.

- Every class that wants to be a singleton needs to implement a singleton type class structure, requiring changes.

- To make the class thread-safe, additional code is needed.

In general, implementing a singleton using the classical approach isn't that versatile, even though for a confined context it works extremely well. The point to remember is that its scope its limited.

Let's see how to implement a versatile singleton.

Implementing a Versatile Reader-Writer Singleton

The problem with the classical singleton isn't the Singleton pattern, but the way that it's implemented. The original pattern mixed together multiple techniques that should have been separated. Specifically, what shouldn't have been made part of the singleton implementation is the instantiation and data type reference.

A versatile singleton should include the following attributes:

- A singleton should act as a container and delegate as much functionality as possible to other interfaces.

- Instantiation is delegated to a factory that allows the instantiation of a class that may exist in the local AppDomain, or, using .NET remoting, on another computer. The singleton only manipulates a local class that may be a proxy.

- The singleton data should be immutable to increase performance.

- The singleton implementation should be responsible for calling functionality that verifies the correctness of the immutable singleton data. If the singleton data needs updating, the singleton implementation manages the calling of the external factory.

Figure 7-4 is the UML diagram of the versatile singleton implementation.

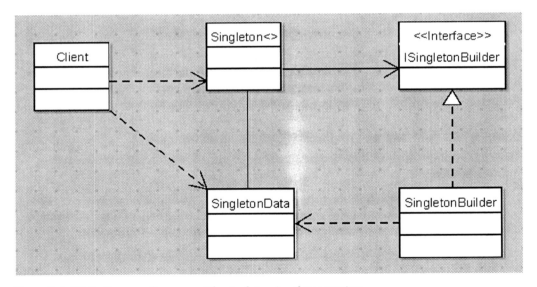

Figure 7-4. *UML diagram for a versatile singleton implementation*

As you see in Figure 7-4, the client interacts with two classes, Singleton<> and SingletonData. Singleton<> is a general class that defines all singletons. SingletonData is a user-defined class that will be used in a single instance.

ISingletonBuilder<> and SingletonBuilder represent the classes used to instantiate SingletonData. The idea is that delegating the instantiation to SingletonBuilder, a local AppDomain singleton could in fact be a proxy to another singleton executing in another AppDomain or on a remote machine. The SingletonBuilder is in complete control.

From an execution point of view, the way the versatile singleton considers SingletonData is as immutable. The SingletonData class is updated using external means that the consumer of SingletonData doesn't know about. Internally, Singleton<> implements a verification and update of the SingletonData mechanism.

Immutability and Threading

The user is responsible for defining a builder that instantiates, verifies, and indicates how the internal Singleton<> update process executes. Following is the definition for the ISingletonBuilder<> interface that the user is responsible for:

```
public interface ISingletonBuilder< type> where type: class {
    DelegatePredicate< type> IsValid {
        get;
    }
    DelegateTransformer< object, type> NewObject {
        get ;
    }
    int SleepTime {
        get;
    }
    bool KeepPolling {
        get;
    }
}
```

The interface definition provides no method to directly instantiate the type SingletonData. The approach chosen is to use functors to instantiate and verify the object. Functors were chosen because they make it possible to combine operations and use the Chain of Responsibility pattern. Then whenever a request is made for instantiation of a singleton data object, one transformer in the chain can perform the action. The other properties relate to the execution of the Singleton<> update mechanism.

The other methods of the ISingletonBuilder<> interface relate to the topic of updating the data of the singleton. A singleton is a performance bottleneck. You'll have multiple clients accessing the same data, and if the data is updated, then you'll need synchronization.

The best strategy when developing singletons is to consider the data mostly read-only. This means the data from the singleton will be read-only for the most part and occasionally modified. If a singleton ends up being read-write, then most likely you don't need a singleton, but a producer-consumer. A type of producer-consumer is implemented in the next section.

A Multithreaded Singleton Implementation

The singleton implementation is multithreaded and manages the updates as necessary, and the full implementation is as follows:

```
public class Singleton< singletonupdate, type>
where singletonupdate: ISingletonBuilder< type>, new()
where type : class {
    private static Singleton< singletonupdate, type> _instance;

    private ISingletonBuilder< type> _builder;
    private type _data;
    private ReaderWriterLock _lock;

    Thread _thread;

    private Singleton() {
        _builder = new singletonupdate();
        _lock = new ReaderWriterLock();
        _thread = new Thread( new ThreadStart( SingletonThread));
        _thread.Start();
    }

    private void SingletonThread() {
        while( _builder.KeepPolling) {
            try {
                _lock.AcquireReaderLock( -1);
                if( _data != null && !_builder.IsValid( _data)) {
                    _lock.UpgradeToWriterLock( -1);
                    _data = null;
                }
            }
            finally {
                _lock.ReleaseLock();
            }
            Thread.Sleep( _builder.SleepTime);
        }
    }
    public static type Instance( object obj) {
        if( _instance == null) {
            lock( typeof( Singleton< singletonupdate,type>)) {
                if( _instance == null) {
                    _instance = new Singleton< singletonupdate, type>();
                }
            }
        }
        type retval = null;
        try {
```

```
            _instance._lock.AcquireReaderLock( -1);
            if( _instance._data == null) {
                _instance._lock.UpgradeToWriterLock(-1);
                if( _instance._data == null) {
                    _instance._data = _instance._builder.NewObject( obj);
                }
            }
            retval = _instance._data;
        }
        finally {
            _instance._lock.ReleaseLock();
        }
        return retval;
    }
}
```

The Singleton<> class is a Generic class that has two generic parameters: singletonupdate and type. The type is an implementation of the ISingletonBuilder<> interface. It's specified as a template parameter because of the nature of the singleton. Unfortunately, the singleton is a static type that is instantiated without knowing any reference information. Using a singleton within the singleton is a futile endeavor, as that would create a recursion, and attempting to reference a configuration file creates an unwanted dependency. The only solution is to define the type as a generic parameter. The generic parameter type defines the singleton data, which in the example of Figure 7-4 was SingletonData.

Singleton<> has two methods: SingletonThread and Instance. The method Instance functions identically to the classical singleton implementation of the method Instance. The method SingletonThread is a threaded method that scans and queries whether the singleton data needs to be updated.

The best way to understand Singleton<> is to explain the order of events when a client executes the following source code (it's assumed that the Singleton<> class with the specified types has never been referenced in the application):

```
Singleton< MySingletonBuilder, SingletonData>.Instance( null).Buffer = "hello";
```

The .NET compiler will convert the Generic type Singleton<> into a unique type based on the generic parameters MySingletonBuilder and SingletonData. The method Singleton<>.Instance is called with a null parameter indicating that there is no constructor information. Shifting focus to the implementation of the Instance method, the first check is to see whether the data member _instance has been instantiated. If _instance equals a null, which means no instantiation, then _instance is assigned an instance of Singleton<>.

When Singleton<> is instantiated, the constructor instantiates an ISingletonBuilder<> instance and assigns it to the data member _builder. After the _builder variable has been assigned, a ReaderWriterLock is instantiated and assigned to the data member _lock. The variable _lock will be discussed in more detail in a moment. The last thing the constructor does is create a thread and execute the method SingletonThread. The method SingletonThread is a polling thread that periodically checks for the validity of the singleton data. What is different about the polling is the while loop that doesn't lock the data, but uses something called a *reader-writer lock*.

The idea behind the reader-writer lock is that when a piece of data is being read, it's being considered immutable. And immutability means allowing multiple readers at the same time poses no problem. Where the problem begins is if a thread wants to write data. Then only one thread can write, while all of the others have to wait. Relating this back to the method SingletonThread, this means that it's possible to read the data member _data, but not manipulate it. To acquire a read-only lock, the method AcquireReaderLock is called. The if block that calls _builder.IsValid DelegatePredicate<> tests whether the singleton data needs to be updated. If the predicate returns true, then _lock is upgraded to a writer lock using the method UpgradeWriterLock. Then the _data variable is assigned a value of null, indicating that the client needs to instantiate a new instance before using the singleton data. The reason why _data is assigned a null and not instantiated is because that is the task of the method Instance. The lock is released using the method ReleaseLock.

Once the constructor and thread have finished, the Instance method will continue and also acquire a read-only lock to the data member _data. If _data is null, then the read lock will be upgraded to a write lock and the method _instance._builder.NewObject is called. The NewObject method is responsible for instantiating a new instance of the singleton data.

In both SingletonThread and Instance, the try-finally construct is used. This is done on purpose so that if within the try block an exception is generated, the lock will be released and not cause a deadlock scenario. Doing otherwise could result in threads waiting for a lock to be released that never will be released.

Building a Full Implementation

Putting all of this together, what results is a singleton implementation that periodically checks for any updates to the singleton data. If there are updates, then the object is newly instantiated. It's important to understand that singleton data isn't updated on the singleton, but through some other technique. The singleton data is considered a snapshot of the data that should be considered "global" data.

Following is a class definition that represents the singleton data:

```
[Serializable]
class SingletonData {
    public readonly string FileData;

    public SingletonData( string filedata) {
        FileData = filedata;
    }
}
```

Notice how SingletonData is both serializable ([Serializable]) and immutable (uses only readonly properties). Doing both of these things makes it very easy to serialize SingletonData across a network or AppDomain.

Singleton<> requires an ISingletonBuilder<> instance, and it's defined as follows:

```
class SingletonBuilder : BaseSingletonDelegation< SingletonData> {
    private string _path;
    public SingletonBuilder() {
        //_path = some configuration file entry
    }
```

```
protected override bool IsObjectValid( SingletonData obj) {
    FileInfo file = new FileInfo( _path);
    if( file.Exists) {
        return false;
    }
    else {
        return true;
    }
}
protected override SingletonData InstantiateNewObject( object descriptor) {
    FileStream filestream = new FileStream( _path, FileMode.Open,
        FileAccess.Read, FileShare.None);
    StreamReader stream = new StreamReader( filestream);
    SingletonData retval = new SingletonData( stream.ReadLine());
    stream.Close();
    FileInfo info = new FileInfo( _path);
    info.Delete();
    return retval;
}
}
```

SingletonBuilder is responsible for validating and instantiating SingletonData. The data for SingletonData is based on a file that is defined by a configuration file entry. The details of the configuration file entry have been removed for simplicity. However, illustrated is the need for a configuration file or database, or registry entry. The implementation of IsObjectValid doesn't include the parameter obj. The validation is based on the existence of a file. If the file exists, then a false is returned, indicating that the singleton data should be updated.

In the implementation of the method InstantiateNewObject, again the parameter descriptor is ignored. Then a number of file operations are performed to read the contents of the file and create a new instance of SingletonData. The new instance is returned to the caller and will serve as the new singleton data.

In the example implementation, the parameters to the methods were ignored. This isn't always the case, for it depends on the scenario. For example, the input parameters could themselves contain references for validation or instantiation. In the case of InstantiateNewObject, the parameter descriptor could be an object that uses the Extension pattern for constructor information.

Putting It All Together and Thinking About What All This Means

It's necessary to step back and consider what the versatile Singleton pattern implementation means. The implementation of the singleton includes three main pieces: singleton container, singleton data, and singleton data builder. Separating all three makes it possible to have the singleton builder located on another machine, and yet have the singleton data in the local AppDomain.

As an example, consider the following singleton data builder, which is designed to be called using .NET remoting:

```
class SingletonMultiAppDomainBuilder : BaseSingletonDelegation< SingletonData> {
    private string _path;
    private static SingletonData _data;
    private static bool _needUpdate;
    private static ReaderWriterLock _lock = new ReaderWriterLock();

    public SingletonMultiAppDomainBuilder( string path) {
        _path = path;
    }
    protected override bool IsObjectValid( SingletonData obj) {
        try {
            _lock.AcquireReaderLock( -1);
            FileInfo file = new FileInfo( _path);
            if( file.Exists) {
                _lock.UpgradeToWriterLock( -1);
                _needUpdate = true;
                return false;
            }
            else {
                return true;
            }
        }
        finally {
            _lock.ReleaseLock();
        }
    }
    protected override SingletonData InstantiateNewObject( object descriptor) {
        try {
            _lock.AcquireWriterLock( -1);
            if( _needUpdate) {
                FileStream filestream = new FileStream( _path, FileMode.
                    Open, FileAccess.Read, FileShare.None);
                StreamReader stream = new StreamReader( filestream);
                _data = new SingletonData( stream.ReadLine());
                stream.Close();
                FileInfo info = new FileInfo( _path);
                info.Delete();
                return retval;
            }
            return _data;
        }
        finally {
            _lock.ReleaseLock();
        }
    }
}
```

I don't want to explain the entire class `SingletonMultiAppDomainBuilder` because to a large degree it's a reimplementation of `SingletonBuilder`. What you should consider is that in the implementation, static data members and reader-writer locks are used. This is because when using .NET remoting, it's desirable to have only a single builder managing the configuration data.

Think about the problem as follows. You start out with an application that reads the global data from a file on the local computer. Without using the `Singleton<>` implementation, you create some local AppDomain classical singleton. As the demands of the application grow, a network of computers results. You still need the same file to be updated. The application remains the same, and a classical singleton is used. This means each computer on the network needs to get a copy of the updated file. The task of updating your application has been delegated to the administrator. You're happy because your program doesn't need to change. But your administrator isn't happy, as he or she has yet another task to add to his or her list of tasks.

Using the `Singleton<>` class, it's possible to call a singleton builder on a remote machine (for example, via the Client-Dispatcher-Server pattern) that passes to the local machine the singleton data. From the coder perspective, not much has changed, other than the singleton data to a central server. I will admit the `Singleton<>` class needs some tweaks to make .NET remoting calls, but needs no tweaking to make .NET web service calls.

Creating a more sophisticated singleton by combining the Singleton pattern with a Flyweight pattern provides some food for thought. The two would be an ideal combination because a flyweight creates references to commonly used objects. A flyweight is instantiated multiple times, and therefore there would still be multiple instances. Combining the Singleton pattern with a Flyweight pattern would result in a multiple-instance-typed singleton.

How Not to Solve an Unknown Implementation Problem

In C# 2.0, it's possible to use partial classes. One of the problems with a singleton is how to define an implementation that specifies the factory for the singleton without using an external configuration file. One possible solution would be to use partial classes as illustrated by the following example:

```
namespace HowNotToSolve {
    interface ISingletonBuilder { }
    partial class Singleton {
        private static ISingletonBuilder _builder;
        static Singleton() {
            _builder = Singleton.GetMyBuilder();
        }
    }

    partial class Singleton {
        class MySingletonBuilder : ISingletonBuilder { }
        static ISingletonBuilder GetMyBuilder() {
            return new MySingletonBuilder();
        }
    }
}
```

This example of using partial classes works, but should, never, never—I say NEVER—be used. The problem is that partial classes solve a different problem, which relates to code generation. Using partial classes in this context results in a class that is included in multiple assemblies with a different signature. This could be considered dynamically changing polymorphism, which isn't object oriented, and just plain wrong. So don't do it!

This admonition may seem out of place in this book, as I'm usually not so harsh. However, what bothers me is that once I saw a presenter illustrate a technique similar to what I explained, and that person thought it was a cool way to use partial classes. Wrong, it isn't a cool way!

Managing Multithreaded Problems Using the Producer-Consumer Technique

The producer-consumer technique has never been defined as a pattern, but is used very often. It has some similarities to the Observer pattern, but doesn't include the asynchronous callback. The producer-consumer technique is more generalized than the Pipes and Filters pattern outlined in Chapter 4. The difference is that the producer-consumer technique is simpler in scope and context.

This raises the question as to whether or not to cover the producer-consumer, and the answer is yes, the reason being the producer-consumer is the counterpart to the reader-writer. The reader-writer technique is very useful, but is geared towards synchronization scenarios where the data is mostly read. It's possible to use the reader-writer in a scenario of less read and more write, but that would cause a slowdown of the overall implementation, as there would be more writer lock wait times.

A Producer-Consumer Example Without the Name

An obvious producer-consumer example is probably one you know about, but never realized was a producer-consumer implementation. In Windows Forms, multithreaded applications aren't allowed to access user interface components if they aren't the thread that created the UI element. To get around this problem, the Windows Forms library created the Invoke method, which is illustrated as follows (note the GUI application uses another thread to periodically increment a counter that is displayed in a textbox):

```
public partial class Form1: Form {
    public Form1() {
        InitializeComponent();
    }

    private int _counter;
    private void IncrementCounter() {
        txtMessage.Text = "Counter (" + _counter + ")";
        _counter++;
    }

    delegate void DelegateIncrementCounter();
```

```
    private void PeriodicIncrement() {
        while(1 == 1) {
            Invoke(new DelegateIncrementCounter(IncrementCounter));
            Thread.Sleep(1000);
        }
    }
    Thread _thread;

    private void Form1_Load(object sender, EventArgs e) {
        _thread = new Thread(new ThreadStart(PeriodicIncrement));
        _thread.Start();
    }
}
```

When Form1 is loaded, the method Form1_Load is executed, which instantiates a new thread that then executes the method PeriodicIncrement. Within the implementation of PeriodicIncrement is a never-ending loop that calls the Form.Invoke method. Passed to the Form.Invoke method is a delegate. The delegate is the method IncrementCounter, which increments a counter and outputs the result to the textbox txtMessage.

From a user perspective, it would seem obvious to call the method IncrementCounter directly from the other thread (_thread). However, hidden in the implementation of Invoke is a producer-consumer implementation. The producer is the Invoke method that adds to a queue a delegate that needs to be called. The consumer is the Windows.Forms.Form class, which periodically checks its Invoke queue and executes the delegates contained within.

In a nutshell, a producer-consumer is nothing more than a handoff of information from one thread to another thread. The reason why this is effective is that the producer and consumer are separate and manage their own concerns. The only common information between the producer and consumer is a queue or list that is synchronized and contains information both are interested in.

Implementing a Generic Producer-Consumer

The architecture implemented by Windows Forms is a very good way of implementing a producer-consumer architecture. The reason why it's good is because it's elegant and self-containing.

Following is the source code that implements a generic producer-consumer architecture:

```
interface IProducerConsumer {
    void Invoke( Delegate @delegate);
    void Invoke( Delegate @delegate, Object[] arguments);
}

class ThreadPoolProducerConsumer : IProducerConsumer {
    class Executor {
        public readonly Delegate _delegate;
        public readonly Object[] _arguments;
```

```
        public Executor( Delegate @delegate, Object[] arguments) {
            _delegate = @delegate;
            _arguments = arguments;
        }
    }

    private Queue< Executor> _queue = new Queue<Executor>();

    private void QueueProcessor( Object obj) {
        Monitor.Enter( _queue);
        while( _queue.Count == 0) {
            Monitor.Wait( _queue, -1);
        }
        Executor exec = _queue.Dequeue();
        Monitor.Exit( _queue);
        ThreadPool.QueueUserWorkItem( new WaitCallback( QueueProcessor));
        exec._delegate.DynamicInvoke( exec._arguments);
    }

    public SingleThreaderProducerConsumer() {
        ThreadPool.QueueUserWorkItem( new WaitCallback( QueueProcessor));
    }
    public void Invoke( Delegate @delegate, Object[] arguments) {
        Monitor.Enter( _queue);
        _queue.Enqueue( new Executor( @delegate, arguments));
        Monitor.Pulse( _queue);
        Monitor.Exit( _queue);
    }
}
```

ThreadPoolProducerConsumer has a single public method, Invoke, which is used in the same fashion as the Windows Forms Invoke method. What makes the generic producer-consumer work is its use of the Monitor synchronization class. Monitor is a special type of synchronization class that has the ability to indicate something has changed.

To understand how Monitor works, let's consider the overall workings of a producer-consumer implementation. The consumer thread (QueueProcessor) executes, constantly waiting for items in the queue (_queue). To check the queue, the method Monitor.Enter is called, which says, "I want exclusive control for a code block that ends with the method call Monitor.Exit." To check the queue, a while loop is started, which waits until something appears in the queue. The thread could execute, constantly waiting for something to be added, but while the thread is looping, it has control of the lock. This means a producer thread can't add anything to the queue.

The consumer needs to give up the lock, but also be able to check whether anything is available in the queue. The solution is to call Monitor.Wait, which causes the consumer thread to give up the lock and say, "Hey, I'm giving up the lock temporarily until somebody gives me a signal to continue processing." When the consumer thread gives up its lock temporarily, it goes to sleep, waiting for a pulse.

The producer thread (Invoke) also enters a protected block using the method Monitor.Enter. Within the protected block, an item is added to the queue using the method Enqueue. Because an item has been added to the queue, the producer thread sends a signal using the method Monitor.Pulse to indicate an item is available. This will cause those threads that gave up the lock temporarily to wake up, for example, the consumer thread. However, the consumer thread executes when the producer thread calls Monitor.Exit; until then the consumer thread is ready in execute mode.

There is one additional optimization with the producer-consumer implementation. In the simplest case, a single thread would constantly execute QueueProcessor. There is an optimization that can be implemented: a thread pool can be used. In the ThreadPoolProducerConsumer constructor, the method ThreadPool.QueueUserWorkItem uses thread pooling to execute the method QueueProcessor. In the implementation of QueueProcessor, the method ThreadPool.QueueUserWorkItem is called again before calling the delegate. This has the effect that there is always one thread waiting for an item in the queue, but multiple threads may be executing concurrently, processing items from the queue.

Using the Generic Producer-Consumer

Using the Generic Producer-Consumer is nearly identical to using the Windows Forms Invoke method, as shown in the following example:

```
[TestFixture]
public class TestProducerConsumer {
    delegate void TestMethod();

    void Method() {
        Console.WriteLine( "Processed in thread id (" +
            Thread.CurrentThread.ManagedThreadId + ")");
    }
    [Test]
    public void TestSimple() {
        IProducerConsumer producer = new ThreadPoolProducerConsumer();
        Console.WriteLine( "Sent in thread id (" +
            Thread.CurrentThread.ManagedThreadId + ")");
        producer.Invoke( new TestMethod( Method));
    }
}
```

The TestSimple method instantiates ThreadPoolProducerConsumer type. Then the method Invoke is called using the delegate TestMethod, which executes the method Method. With respect to Windows Forms, a different type is instantiated, but the same Invoke method is used. The implementation is also a bit different in that the consumer isn't a single thread, but as many threads as necessary.

Some Final Thoughts

When I first started writing this chapter, I wondered what I was going to write. Sure, the material on immutable classes, reader-writer processes, flyweights, and so on was plentiful. My doubts were how to present this material to make it obvious that you need to implement these things in your daily development. What I was especially concerned with was the topic of immutability.

It's one of those topics that sounds good (for example, eat healthy, exercise daily, don't smoke, etc.), but due to real-life circumstances and contexts is hard to realize.

Yet after using the techniques discussed in this chapter, I'm convinced of the advantages of immutability, flyweights, and so on. What especially surprised me are the advantages of immutable objects in a multithreaded context. While investigating the implementation of the string class, I was awed at how sophisticated .NET strings are, and yet very fast. Also interesting was the implementation of the producer-consumer in Windows Forms.

Overall, the message is that to be able to write effective multithreaded applications, immutability, flyweights, reader-writer, producer-consumer, and object pools are patterns and techniques that you need. And with CPU producers such as Intel and AMD producing multicore CPUs, that need to write effective multithreaded applications will become ever more vital.

CHAPTER 8

■■■

Data Persistence

Of all the chapters in this book, this is probably the most controversial, because persisting data is fraught with debate. Mention a persistence framework, and you'll probably get hundreds of answers. Want to start an argument about something greater than where to place the curly brackets, talk about persistence. What is peculiar is that many pattern books don't address persistence. It isn't discussed, almost as if it wasn't important. The fact of the matter is that persistence *is* important.

Think of it as follows. You own a car, and people like to tinker with their cars. They add 400-horsepower engines, 1,000-watt stereo systems, and racing leather seats. Yet in all of this discussion, nobody talks about the slick black tires. And without these tires, a car goes nowhere, and closely reassembles a 1-ton paperweight. Persistence is important because an application must operate on data that it retrieved from somewhere. Without data, an application is like a car without wheels.

This book doesn't attempt to answer all questions regarding persistence. In fact, this chapter only scratches the surface of persistence, since persistence patterns are a book unto themselves.

The purpose of this chapter is to provide a new direction for how an application can persist data. The ideal persistence technique is one in which you don't have to think as much about the technology, and are able to focus on the data. The reason why so much discussion arises over persistence is because persistence is what makes or breaks an application. Once a leading Microsoft Transaction developer said, "VB or C++—it doesn't matter, because the slowest part of your application is going to be the database."

This chapter covers two main persistence techniques. The first is serialization, and how to integrate it into your application. It's important to understand serialization properly and its ramifications. Not doing so will result in overengineered objects that don't solve the problem efficiently. The second persistence technique I cover is object-to-relational (O/R) mapping. O/R mapping is very useful because there exists an object-to-relational impedance mismatch.[1] An additional book that complements the materials presented here is Scott Ambler's *Agile Database Techniques* (Indianapolis: Wiley Publishing, 2003).

---

1. http://www.agiledata.org/essays/impedanceMismatch.html

Serialization in .NET

Serialization is the process of converting the state of an object in memory into a state of another medium that is a complete representation of the object. Other media include hard disks and networks. Serialization is implemented using the Serializer pattern.[2]

In a general sense, the Serializer pattern is implemented using two pieces: a serializable class and a serialization reader or writer class. The serializable class dictates what data to serialize. The serialization reader or writer class deals with transferring the contents of the serializable class to and from the other medium. The idea is that by separating what's transferred and how it's transferred, the possibility exists of dynamically changing the medium without changing the implementation of the serializable class.

In UML terms, the Serializable pattern is similar to what you see in Figure 8-1.

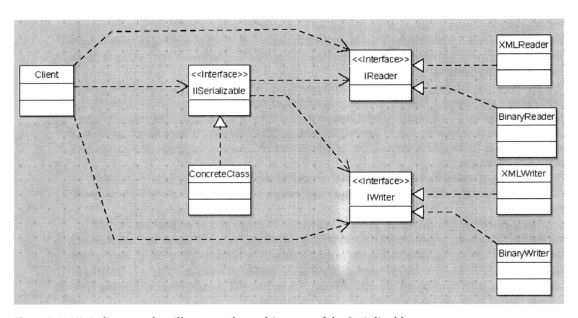

Figure 8-1. *UML diagram that illustrates the architecture of the Serializable pattern*

Figure 8-1 shows three main interfaces: ISerializable, IReader, and IWriter. A class will implement the ISerializable interface, which usually has two methods: ReadFrom and WriteTo. The method ReadFrom transfers the contents of the object from the medium to memory. The method WriteTo transfers the contents of the object from memory to the medium. As an example, to save the class ConcreteClass to XML, you'd use the XMLReader and XMLWriter classes. If instead it's desirable to read and write binary files, then you'd use the classes BinaryWriter and BinaryReader.

You have multiple ways to serialize a class in .NET, two of which I'll discuss here: binary serialization and XML serialization.

---

2. Robert C. Martin et al., *Patterns Languages of Program Design 3* (Boston: Addison-Wesley, 1997), p. 293.

Binary Object Serialization in .NET

Probably the most common means of serializing a class in .NET is through binary serialization, as it's used for files and remoting. Binary serialization is unique in that the footprint of the object's data in memory is almost identical to the footprint of the data in the other medium.

To illustrate how the Serialization pattern is implemented for binary serialization, consider the following class declaration:

```
[Serializable]
class SampleClass {
    private int _value;
    private string _buffer;

    public SampleClass(int value, string buffer) {
        _value = value;
        _buffer = buffer;
    }

    public int Value {
        get {
            return _value;
        }
    }
    public string Buffer {
        get {
            return _buffer;
        }
    }
}
```

SampleClass has been marked serializable because of the [Serializable] attribute. This means when doing binary serialization, all data members of SampleClass will be serialized regardless of the scope of the data member. Binary serialization iterates each data member and writes the contents of it to the data stream. For SampleClass, this means that _value and _buffer will be serialized.

The Serialization pattern indicates the serializable type implements the methods ReadFrom and Writeto. Because .NET binary serialization uses the metadata of the type to perform serialization, those methods aren't necessary. This modification of the Serialization pattern is acceptable, because part of the reason for the methods is that the pattern assumes a type doesn't have any metadata. For example, the C++ Microsoft Foundation Classes (MFCs) fully implement the Serialization pattern. This is because C++ MFCs don't have metadata information.

Getting back to serialization, binary serialization is a bit of challenge because everything is serialized. Maybe some data members shouldn't be serialized because the state can't be carried across media. An example could be delegates or database connections. These data members are transient and only applicable when the object is executing in memory. Applying the attribute [NonSerialized] to a data member causes the data member to be ignored when serialization is executed.

Following is some code that illustrates how to serialize the class SampleClass to a file:

```
SampleClass obj = new SampleClass(10, "hello");
Stream stream = File.OpenWrite( @"C:\sampleclass.bin");
BinaryFormatter bf = new BinaryFormatter();
bf.Serialize(stream, obj);
stream.Close();
```

The class `SampleClass` is instantiated and assigned to the variable `obj`. Then a file stream is opened using the method `File.OpenWrite`. It's important to realize that a plain vanilla file is being opened. Then `BinaryFormatter` is instantiated, which represents a serializer assigned to the variable `bf`. The sample class instance `obj` is written to the file stream using the `bf.Serialize` method. After the object has been serialized, the file stream contains a representation of the object instance `obj`. What is interesting is that the binary serializer isn't part of the file. This makes it possible to perform a binary serialization to a file or to a network connection. The way that the binary serializer does this is by manipulating the stream interface.

The resulting binary file would appear similar to the following text:

```
^@^A^@^@^@????^A^@^@^@^@^@^@^@^L^B^@^@^@
&test, Version=0.0.0.0,Culture=neutral^E^A^@^@^@^
KSampleClass^B^@^@^@^F_value^G_buffer^@^A^H^B^@^@^@
^@^@^@^F^C^@^@^@^Ehello^K
```

The funny characters (@? etc.) represent binary data used by the formatter. Ignore these characters and look at the data that is text based. Notice the identifier `SampleClass`, which represents the class that has been serialized. Then `_value` and `_buffer`, which represent the data members of `SampleClass` that have been serialized. The remaining textual value, hello, represents the value of the data member `_buffer`. The value of the data member `_value` exists, but is encoded using a numeric value, and hence hidden in the funny characters. What you should remember is that the stream of characters can only be written and read by the class `BinaryFormatter`.

To re-create the class, the source code used to deserialize `SampleClass` is as follows:

```
FileStream stream=new FileStream(
    @"C:\\sampleclass.bin", FileMode.Open);
BinaryFormatter bf = new BinaryFormatter();
SampleClass obj = bf.Deserialize(file) as SampleClass;
Console.WriteLine( "Object Value (" + obj.Value + ") Buffer (" + obj.Buffer + ")");
file.Close();
```

To deserialize the class `SampleClass`, a file stream (`FileStream`) is opened, and again a binary formatter (`BinaryFormatter`) is instantiated. This time the binary formatter reads an object from the stream using the method `bf.Deserialize`. The read object is typecast to the type `SampleClass` and assigned to the variable `obj`.

XML Object Serialization in .NET

As mentioned previously, another form of serialization in .NET is XML serialization. Unlike binary serialization, the serializer for XML generates XML code, and the representation of the object in XML isn't similar to the object in memory. Using the same class as in the binary serialization, the following class declaration is used for XML serialization:

```
[XmlRoot("SampleClass")]
public class SampleClass {
    private int _value;
    private string _buffer;

    public SampleClass() { }
    public SampleClass(int value, string buffer) {
        _value = value;
        _buffer = buffer;
    }
    [XmlElement( "Value")]
    public int Value {
        get {
            return _value;
        }
        set {
            _value = value;
        }
    }
    [XmlElement( "Buffer")]
    public string Buffer {
        get {
            return _buffer;
        }
        set {
            _buffer = value;
        }
    }
}
```

In contrast to the binary serialization implementation of SampleClass, this has more attributes, and the set parts of the properties have been implemented. The added attributes fine-tune how the data is serialized to XML. The biggest difference between XML serialization and binary serialization is that XML serialization doesn't read the private data members, rather it reads the public properties. And unlike the binary serialization example, a parameterless constructor is required.

Following is the source code used to serialize and deserialize SampleClass to and from XML:

```
public void TestSampleClassSerialization() {
    SampleClass cls = new SampleClass( 10, "hello");
    XmlSerializer s = new XmlSerializer( typeof(SampleClass ) );
    TextWriter w = new StreamWriter( @"c:\sampleclass.xml" );
    s.Serialize( w, cls );
    w.Close();
}
```

```
public void TestSampleClassDeserialization() {
    SampleClass cls;
    XmlSerializer s = new XmlSerializer( typeof(SampleClass ) );
    TextReader r = new StreamReader( @"c:\sampleclass.xml" );
    cls = (SampleClass)s.Deserialize( r );
    r.Close();
}
```

The XML serialization process is identical to the binary serialization in that the serializer is separate from the stream. For XML serialization, XmlSerializer performs the serialization to and from the stream. Because XML is a text format, the stream that is being serialized to and from must be text based, which when writing to a stream involves the classes TextWriter or TextReader.

The generated file that represents the serialized SampleClass is as follows:

```
<?xml version="1.0" encoding="utf-8"?>
<SampleClass
    xmlns:xsd="http://www.w3.org/2001/XMLSchema"
    xmlns:xsi="http://www.w3.org/2001/XMLSchema-instance">
    <Value>10</Value>
    <Buffer>hello</Buffer>
</SampleClass>
```

What should be noticed is that the XML tag identifiers (SampleClass, Value, and Buffer) are identical to the .NET attributes used to describe the properties for SampleClass. The identifiers used by the .NET attributes don't need to be identical to the actual .NET type descriptors. The identifiers can be any text values that you'd like them to be.

Serialization Has Issues!

Two things are obvious when implementing the Serialization pattern using a runtime environment like .NET. The first is that you don't need the WriteTo and ReadFrom methods, because a runtime environment like .NET has the ability to use metadata.

Using metadata is a better solution, because this makes the serializer more flexible to do what is necessary, and it's in control of the serialization. Going back to the C++ MFC example, one of the problems was the inability to convert the serialization routines to XML. Using metadata, that problem is solved. When using a metadata approach, fine-tuning is required, and this is made possible using .NET attributes. In general, this is a good approach. What is tedious is that each serialization (binary or XML) requires its own attributes. Now imagine wanting to serialize to five different mediums—does that mean you use five different sets of serialization attributes?

The second thing to consider is based on the first—specifically, the need to use custom attributes for each medium. Those attributes are necessary, but the real question that must be asked is whether it's even possible to implement a universal Serializer pattern. Ideally, you'd like to be medium independent for now and in the future. The trouble is that it's a holy grail, and not attainable. Binary serialization isn't XML serialization, and each serialization technique requires its own set of fine-tuning. And when I cover O/R mapping, there is yet another set of attributes to learn.

Additionally, the following problems make implementing a Serializer pattern very complicated:

- You have to specifically attach tags and do things that are specific to a serialization technique (for example, XML serialization attributes aren't usable in binary serialization).

- If you change the internal structure of your data class, then binary serialization can become problematic due to data members that are new or have been removed.[3]

- XML serialization breaks the Immutable pattern, because all properties must have a get and set method, and there must be a parameterless constructor. Serialization can conflict with existing architectures and can make them less secure and maintainable.

- You may experience odd behavior in that what works with one serialization technique might not work with another serialization technique.

In a nutshell, serialization is problematic in that you need to decide what medium you want to serialize to. Once you decide, you're locked into that medium. Of course, you can use different attributes, recompile the source code, and run the application to use another medium. But there is no magic solution with respect to serialization and universal .NET attributes. Going back to the introduction of the chapter, this is why persistence is a topic for never-ending debate.

Tweaking and Fixing the Serializer Pattern

The problem of the Serializer pattern isn't the pattern itself, but that it expects utopia when it comes to how data can be stored. So for the purpose of this discussion, let's say that it isn't possible to implement a universal Serializer pattern. What we can be certain about is that a Serializer pattern implementation can be used to generically write a specific format to any medium. For example, if an object supports XML serialization, then the XML can be serialized to any medium (file, network, etc.).

Therefore, the solution to the Serializer pattern is to consider the serialization something that isn't part of the object. If you compare this idea to the Bridge pattern, it means that the type declaration and its serializable declaration are separate from each other. The separation of the type object and its serializable form can be realized through either the Visitor pattern[4] or the Memento pattern,[5] which we'll explore in this section. You may question the reason for illustrating the Visitor pattern in a serialization context. I chose to employ this technique because it's a very convenient and instructive scenario for when a Visitor pattern is applicable.

You may also question the necessity of separating the serialization from the executing objects, considering that too much work. But, and this is a big but, imagine writing an application that supports both binary and XML persistence. And this application has had three or four releases. How will you write the application so that application version 4 can read and write data from application version 1? The problem of application versions and/or different mediums isn't insignificant and shouldn't be underestimated. Just idly adding more attributes and data members is acceptable only for quick-and-dirty applications.

---

3. The article "Format Your Way to Success" (http://msdn.microsoft.com/msdnmag/issues/04/10/AdvancedSerialization/default.aspx?print=true) illustrates some of the finer details on how to minimize the problems of version changes.
4. Erich Gamma et al., *Design Patterns: Elements of Reusable Object-Oriented Software* (Boston: Addison-Wesley, 1995), p. 331.
5. *Design Patterns: Elements of Reusable Object-Oriented Software*, p. 283.

Accessing an External State: The Visitor Pattern

The purpose of the Visitor pattern is to enable external object access to the internal workings of a class. This doesn't mean internal access to the data, rather a detailed understanding of how the class works. The Bridge pattern separates the intention from the implementation. A consumer will use the intention, which is represented by a base class or interface. The Visitor pattern says, "Throw the Bridge pattern out the window, and the consumer will have a direct reference to the implementation."

In this section, I give you a look at the theory behind the Visitor pattern, followed by advice for using this pattern in your code.

Visitor Pattern Theory

The Visitor pattern flies in the face of everything this book has said shouldn't be done. In particular, the Visitor pattern advises a Generic type to reference specific types. What this means is that an application that employs the Visitor pattern has a direct reference to the types that are part of the calling chain. This is useful in scenarios like persistence where it's necessary to know what the type is.

Figure 8-2 illustrates the UML diagram of the Visitor pattern.

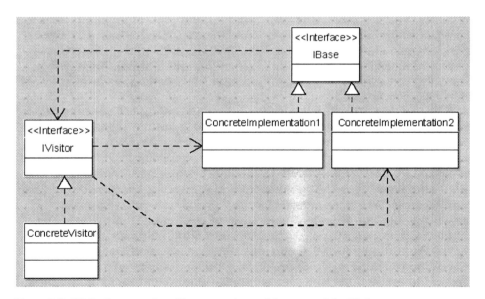

Figure 8-2. *UML diagram that illustrates the architecture of the Visitor pattern*

Figure 8-2 shows two IBase implementations: ConcreteImplemtation1 and ConcreteImplementation2. IBase is an implementation that is to be inspected by an external type. IBase uses IVisitor, which is the inspector. The IVisitor implementation ConcreteVisitor has direct knowledge and reference of ConcreteImplementation1 and

ConcreteImplementation2. This can be a problem, because it isn't possible to define IVisitor in a separate assembly. Doing so will create a recursive reference that can't be compiled.

To understand this recursive nature, consider the following source code, which holds the definitions of the interfaces IBase and IVisitor:

```
public interface IBase {
    void Accept( IVisitor visitor);
}
public interface IVisitor {
    void Process( ConcreteImplementation1 obj);
    void Process( ConcreteImplementation2 obj);
}
```

The interface IBase is the interface that is implemented by all classes that would like to expose themselves for inspection by the Visitor pattern. The interface IVisitor contains methods for all of the types that will be visited.

An implementation of the interfaces would be as follows:

```
public class ConcreteImplementation1 : IBase {
    public void Accept(IVisitor visitor) {
        visitor.Process( this);
    }
}
public class ConcreteImplementation2 : IBase {
    public void Accept(IVisitor visitor) {
        visitor.Process( this);
    }
}
```

In ConcreteImplementation1 and ConcreteImplemetation2, the method Accept is implemented by calling the visitor.Process method. The visitor.Process method can then do whatever it needs to with the type ConcreteImplementation1 or ConcreteImplementation2. The inspector knows about the different objects, but the objects being inspected don't know about the visitor.

Any class that implements IVisitor will be able to manipulate the types Concrete➥Implementation1 and ConcreteImplementation2 directly. For example, XML serialization in which the object is written to the stream could have been implemented using the Visitor pattern. Like XML serialization, the IVisitor implementation only knows about the type, and the methods and properties that are exposed, not the internal workings of the type.

Implementing the Visitor Pattern

The Visitor pattern in theory has a major problem in that IVisitor can't be defined in a general fashion in a separate assembly. As per my original Bridge pattern implementation, an interface is implemented. The interface could be defined in one assembly and the implementations in another assembly. The Visitor pattern as Figure 8-2 defines it doesn't allow this. The problem is that IVisitor references types that would be defined in a separate assembly. This causes the "interface" assembly to reference the "implementation" assembly, and the "implementation" assembly to reference the "interface" assembly. This is recursive, and thus can't be compiled. Hence both interface and implementation have to be defined in the same assembly.

What is possible is the definition of IVisitor interface could be in one assembly, and the implementation of IVisitor could be in another. However, the types referenced in IVisitor then need to be defined with public scope, which defeats the purpose of the Bridge and Factory patterns.

There is a way to have your cake and eat it too. The better solution is to use Generics and modify the IVisitor interface to the following:

```
public interface IVisitor {
    void Process< type>( type parameter) where type : class ;
}
```

In the new definition of IVisitor, the method Process has been altered to use a Generic type. The Generic type is the parameter of the type being inspected. Using Generics in this way delegates the responsibility of identifying the type to the implementation of IVisitor. The advantage of this approach is that it's possible to move both IBase and IVisitor to an interfaces-only assembly for reference by an implementations assembly.

To demonstrate these principles, I'll show you XML serialization to a stream via a Visitor pattern. The modified SampleClass from the XML serialization example is defined as follows:

```
[XmlRoot("SampleClass")]
public class SampleClass : IBase {
    private int _value;
    private string _buffer;

    public SampleClass() {

    }
    public SampleClass(int value, string buffer) {
        _value = value;
        _buffer = buffer;
    }
    [XmlElement( "Value")]
    public int Value {
        get {
            return _value;
        }
        set {
            _value = value;
        }
    }
    [XmlElement( "Buffer")]
    public string Buffer {
        get {
            return _buffer;
        }
```

```
        set {
            _buffer = value;
        }
    }
    public void Accept( IVisitor visitor) {
        visitor.Process( this);
    }
}
```

The modification to SampleClass is minimal and only requires the implementation of the IBase interface. Like the examples before, the method Accept calls the visitor.Process method. When using the Visitor pattern, the inspectee will usually only go so far, and leave the heavy lifting to the inspector (IVisitor implementation).

Following is an IVisitor implementation:

```
public class VisitorImplementation : IVisitor {
    private string _path;

    public VisitorImplementation( string path) {
        _path = path;
    }
    public void Process< type>(type parameter) where type: class{
        if( parameter is SampleClass) {
            XmlSerializer s = new XmlSerializer( typeof( SampleClass ) );
            TextWriter w = new StreamWriter( _path);
            s.Serialize( w, parameter as SampleClass );
            w.Close();
        }
    }
}
```

The class VisitorImplementation implements the IVisitor interface. The method Process<> checks the passed-in type using an if statement that tests whether the parameter is a specific type. If the type is SampleClass, then the XML serialization proceeds; otherwise nothing happens.

Putting everything together, the following source code executes the Visitor pattern:

```
VisitorImplementation visitor = new VisitorImplementation( @"c:\sampleclass.xml");
IBase @base = new SampleClass( 20, "SampleClass");
@base.Accept( visitor);
```

VisitorImplementation and SampleClass are both instantiated, and then the method Accept is called, resulting in the creation of the XML file.

The Visitor pattern implementation has the following advantages:

- Like the Bridge pattern, the Visitor pattern makes it possible to separate definition from implementation. In the example, this means separating the serializable class from the serialization class.

- Making an existing class usable as an inspectee requires a minimum of additional code.

- The Visitor pattern is a good way to modify, update, or tweak a collection of objects with a universal operation, without having to manually iterate each type.

- The heavy lifting is always managed by the IVisitor implementation, and not by the inspectee. The inspectee is oblivious to the entire process.

Refactoring the XML Serialization

The Visitor pattern implementation is complete, but what isn't to our liking is the problem of having to associate XML attributes with the inspectees. Frankly, the current Visitor pattern implementation is both trivial and overkill. What would be of interest is to use the Visitor pattern to serialize an already existing type, without having to use XML attributes. It's possible to do this and relatively trivial to realize.

For this example, the SampleClass used is from the earlier binary serialization example (the immutable SampleClass) minus the serializable attribute. The modified IVisitor implementation is defined as follows:

```
public class VisitorImplementation : IVisitor {
    private string _path;

    public VisitorImplementation( string path) {
        _path = path;
    }
    public void Process< type>(type parameter) where type: class{
        if( parameter is SampleClass) {
            XmlTextWriter writer = new XmlTextWriter( _path, null);
            SampleClass cls = parameter as SampleClass;
            writer.WriteStartDocument();
            writer.WriteStartElement( "SampleClass");
            writer.WriteStartElement( "Value");
            writer.WriteString( XmlConvert.ToString( cls.Value));
            writer.WriteEndElement();
            writer.WriteStartElement( "Buffer");
            writer.WriteString( cls.Buffer);
            writer.WriteEndElement();
            writer.WriteEndElement();
            writer.WriteEndDocument();
            writer.Flush();
            writer.Close();
        }
    }
}
```

In the modified implementation of the method Process, instead of instantiating XmlSerializer, XmlTextWriter is instantiated. XmlTextWriter is a useful utility class that you can use to write an XML stream. An IVisitor implementation knows the details of the type being manipulated, and hence knows which data members exist. Therefore, it isn't difficult for IVisitor to manually convert the properties into a series of XML elements. The individual XML elements are serialized using the methods WriteStartDocument, WriteStartElement, and so on.

The advantage of this approach is that the serializable object needs to do nothing, and the IVisitor implementation does all of the heavy lifting.

Thinking about this approach, it's easy to conclude that the Serializable pattern has been indirectly implemented. That thinking is correct, because in this instance the Visitor pattern directly resembles the serialization to the medium part (WriteTo) of the Serializable pattern. What needs to be understood is that the Visitor pattern only implements the browsing of an object hierarchy, and not the deserialization aspect of the Serializable pattern.

Browsing a Hierarchy of Types

The example Visitor pattern implementation was for a single object, and not a hierarchy of objects. The question is, when you are confronted with a hierarchy of objects, who calls whom? Let's say that you have a parent and child types. Does the IVisitor implementation, when confronted with the parent type, automatically process the child? Or does the parent type, when being inspected, call thereafter the child type to be inspected? You have two options, in that the IBase implementation iterates through the hierarchy or the IVisitor implementation iterates through the hierarchy. To illustrate the difference, I'll demonstrate both means of iteration.

Here an IBase implementation iterates through the hierarchy of child objects:

```
class SingleClass : IBase {
    private string _buffer;
    public SingleClass( string buffer) {
        _buffer = buffer;
    }
    public string Buffer {
        get {
            return _buffer;
        }
    }
    public void Accept( IVisitor visitor) {
        visitor.Process( this);
    }
}


class CollectionClass : IBase {
    private IList< SingleClass> _elements = new List< SingleClass>();
    public CollectionClass() { }
    public void AddElement( SingleClass cls) {
        _elements.Add( cls);
    }
    public void Accept( IVisitor visitor) {
        visitor.Process( this);
        foreach( SingleClass element in _elements) {
            element.Accept( visitor);
        }
    }
}
```

```
public class VisitorImplementation : IVisitor {
    public void Process< type>(type parameter) where type: class{
        if( parameter is CollectionClass) {
            Console.WriteLine( "CollectionClass");
        }
        else if( parameter is SingleClass) {
            SingleClass cls = parameter as SingleClass;
            Console.WriteLine( "SingleClass (" + cls.Buffer + ")");
        }
    }
}
```

The class CollectionClass has a data member, _elements, that is a collection of SingleClass instances. Both CollectionClass and SingleClass implement the IBase interface and the associated Accept method. The implemented method SingleClass.Accept is similar to the examples that have been illustrated thus far. What is different is the implementation of the method CollectionClass.Process. The first call to Process is for the instance of CollectionClass. Then a foreach loop iterates the instances in the collection _elements. For each iterated instance, the method element.Accept is called, which calls the method SingleClass.Accept.

In this scenario, the VisitorImplementation.Process only reacts to the immediate object instance being passed to it. The IVisitor implementation doesn't know about child objects and doesn't attempt to know about them.

Before an analysis of this technique is done, let's contrast that to an example IVisitor implementation that iterates through the child elements:

```
class SingleClass : IBase {
    private string _buffer;
    public SingleClass( string buffer) {
        _buffer = buffer;
    }
    public string Buffer {
        get {
            return _buffer;
        }
    }
    public void Accept( IVisitor visitor) {
        visitor.Process( this);
    }
}

class CollectionClass : IEnumerable, IBase {
    private IList< SingleClass> _elements = new List< SingleClass>();
    public CollectionClass() { }
    public void AddElement( SingleClass cls) {
        _elements.Add( cls);
    }
```

```
    public IEnumerator GetEnumerator() {
        return _elements.GetEnumerator();
    }
    public void Accept( IVisitor visitor) {
        visitor.Process( this);
    }
}

public class VisitorImplementation : IVisitor {
    public void Process< type>(type parameter) where type: class{
        if( parameter is CollectionClass) {
            Console.WriteLine( "CollectionClass");
            CollectionClass cls = parameter as CollectionClass;
            foreach( SingleClass item in cls) {
                item.Accept( this);
            }
        }
        else if( parameter is SingleClass) {
            SingleClass cls = parameter as SingleClass;
            Console.WriteLine( "SingleClass (" + cls.Buffer + ")");
        }
    }
}
```

In this implementation variation, the methods CollectionClass.Accept and SingleClass.Accept have been kept minimal. The iteration of CollectionClass has been delegated to VisitorImplementation.Process.

So which to use, IBase or IVisitor? The answer is that there is no best approach. It really depends on the context, and what is desired.

- If IVisitor iterates the children, that is reinforcing the principle whereby the IVisitor implementation is responsible for all of the heavy lifting. The inspectees are kept simple.

- If IVisitor iterates the children, then when iterating the children, before and after events can be generated. This is because the IVisitor implementation is responsible for calling the children.

- If the inspectee iterates the children, then an IVisitor implementation only needs to react to the types that are of interest to it. This is useful when processing a hierarchy of objects and, for example, executing a running total on certain types. In this scenario, the IVisitor implementation doesn't know or need to know about the object hierarchy.

- Regardless of which IVisitor implementation is used, the Process method has to reference the types directly, and no attempt should be made to abstract the reference types of the IVisitor implementation.

Some Conclusions on the Visitor Pattern

The Visitor pattern is a good way to postprocess specific data types to extract specific pieces of information. The Visitor pattern could be combined with a closure functor to process certain types in certain contexts. Serialization is one way to use the Visitor pattern, but more often it's used to perform tasks that can only be done by accessing the implementation directly.

Even though the Visitor pattern requires that an IVisitor implementation have a direct reference to the types it manipulates, the IVisitor implementation can be used generically. This makes it possible to use a factory and wire together an IBase implementation and IVisitor implementation without having the consumer of each know about the specific implementations.

Accessing an Internal State: The Memento Pattern

As mentioned earlier, another way to perform a serialization is to use the Memento pattern. The Memento pattern differs dramatically from the Visitor pattern and Serializer pattern in that it abstracts the state of an object from the object. The state transferred is the minimal amount of information needed to uniquely describe a type instance. The Memento pattern is similar to the Visitor pattern in that specific knowledge about the implementation is shared with another class. Where the Memento pattern differs from the Visitor pattern is that it's specifically geared towards transfer of state.

Following is an overview of the theory behind the Memento pattern, followed by an example of how to use it in your code.

Theory of the Memento Pattern

In a nutshell, the Memento pattern has a type definition that the public is exposed to. The type definition has a method that extracts and assigns the state of the type. The Memento pattern is in essence the Serializer pattern, except the other medium is another type. The main objective of the Memento pattern isn't serialization, but transferring of state. Figure 8-3 presents a UML diagram of the Memento pattern.

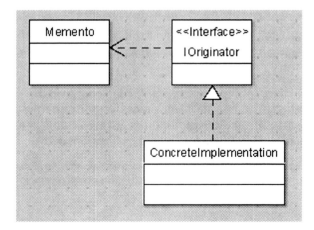

Figure 8-3. *UML diagram that illustrates the architecture of the Memento pattern*

The UML diagram of the Memento pattern is extremely simple in that Concrete➥ Implementation implements the interface IOriginator. The interface IOriginator has two methods, CreateMemento and SetState, that create the state of the object and assign the state of the object to the type Memento. In code terms, the Memento pattern is implemented by the following source code:

```
class Memento {
    private string _buffer;
    public Memento( string buffer) {
        _buffer = buffer;
    }
    public string Buffer {
        get {
            return _buffer;
        }
        set {
            _buffer = value;
        }
    }
}
interface IOriginator {
    Memento CreateMemento();
    void SetState( Memento state);
}
class Simple : IOriginator {
    private string _buffer;
    public Simple( string buffer) {
        _buffer = buffer;
    }
    public Memento CreateMemento() {
        return new Memento( _buffer);
    }
    public void SetState( Memento state) {
        _buffer = state.Buffer;
    }
}
```

The class Simple implements the method IOriginator, which has two methods, CreateMemento and SetState. The method CreateMemento instantiates the type Memento and assigns to Memento the state of a Simple instance. The method SetState assigns to Simple a state, which is stored in the Memento type. In the preceding example, Simple and Memento are nearly identical. The main difference is that Memento will always be a data object with read and write properties, and it represents the internal state of Simple, whereas Simple is an application logic object that is immutable, and may or may not expose its internal state. Realize that Simple is a pure object-oriented object that doesn't expose its internal state. On the other hand, Memento isn't a pure object-oriented object, and its internal state is its external state. The state in Memento is a copy of the state in Simple. This is very important to remember when an object hierarchy needs to be created. The Memento instance never contains references that both Memento and Simple share. When Memento is assigned the state of a reference object, a clone is made.

Realizing a Memento Pattern Implementation

Implementing the Memento pattern using the classical pattern definition isn't useful, and will prove complicated. The main problem has to do with the method CreateMemento. The idea behind this method is to instantiate the type that will transfer the state. The trouble with this approach is that the class that transfers the state might not always know what the state object is.

Think of it as follows. Let's say you have an immutable object. The immutable object can be serialized using binary serialization. The immutable object can't be serialized using XML serialization because of the differences in serialization implementation. To be able to serialize using both binary and XML, the immutable object has to be converted into a mutable object. Through the Memento pattern, the possibility exists whereby the immutable object transfers its state to an XML serializable state class. But let's get back to the original problem of serializing both to binary and XML. To do that, two different state classes are needed, as was shown in previous examples. The question is which state class CreateMemento instantiates. The answer is that the IOriginator implementation has no idea.

A better approach to state transfer isn't to use static types, but to use .NET Generics, and replace the CreateMemento method with a GetState method. Using GetState, it's simpler to substitute implementations that can be used in different serialization contexts. This moves the responsibility of instantiation from the IOriginator implementation to the caller of IOriginator, and it allows the IOriginator to focus on the transfer of state and not care what happens to that state. The modified IOriginator<> interface is defined as follows:

```
interface IOriginator< type> {
    void GetState( type state);
    void SetState( type state);
}
```

Continuing this serialization line of thinking, the Memento pattern is going to be used to serialize the object using binary or XML serialization. The focus this time will be to make the state transfer for serialization as flexible as possible. The first modification is to convert Memento into an interface, which is defined as follows:

```
interface IMemento {
    string Buffer { get; set; }
    int Value { get; set; }
}
```

The interface IMemento has two properties that represent the state of SampleClass. The modified SampleClass that uses IMemento and IOriginator<> is defined as follows:

```
class SampleClass : IOriginator< IMemento> {
    private int _value;
    private string _buffer;
```

```
public SampleClass() { }
public SampleClass(int value, string buffer) {
    _value = value;
    _buffer = buffer;
}

public int Value {
    get {
        return _value;
    }
}
public string Buffer {
    get {
        return _buffer;
    }
}
public void GetState( IMemento state) {
    state.Buffer = _buffer;
    state.Value = _value;
}
public void SetState( IMemento state) {
    _buffer = state.Buffer;
    _value = state.Value;
}
}
```

SampleClass implements the IOriginator<> interface, and the interface that represents the state is IMemento. Then in the implementation of the method GetState, the state from SampleClass is transferred to the IMemento instance. And in the implementation of SetState, the state is transferred from IMemento to SampleClass. SampleClass has no idea what the final destination is of the state. From the viewpoint of SampleClass, there is no such thing as serialization, only transfer of state. Serialization is possible because the IMemento implementation could implement it. That extra step is the responsibility of IMemento.

What is interesting about this transfer of state is that only the state that pertains to the unique definition of the object is transferred. For example, a database connection wouldn't be transferred, as a database connection is specific to the instance of the object. The Memento pattern could be combined with the Object Pool pattern to transfer the state of objects to already existing objects that are immutable. Or the Memento pattern could transfer the state between multiple versions of object instances (for example, version 1 and version 2 of a type). And finally, the Memento pattern could be used for integration purposes of two dissimilar applications.

Getting back to the serialization example, following is an implementation of IMemento that contains the state of SampleClass. (The declaration of the class will remarkably resemble the XML serialization example, other than the implementation of IMemento. This is a coincidence, because back in the XML serialization example, the class contained only data members.)

```
[XmlRoot("XMLSampleClass")]
public class XMLSampleClass : IMemento {
    private int _value;
    private string _buffer;

    public XMLSampleClass() {

    }
    public XMLSampleClass(int value, string buffer) {
        _value = value;
        _buffer = buffer;
    }
    [XmlElement( "Value")]
    public int Value {
        get {
            return _value;
        }
        set {
            _value = value;
        }
    }
    [XmlElement( "Buffer")]
    public string Buffer {
        get {
            return _buffer;
        }
        set {
            _buffer = value;
        }
    }
}
```

To serialize SampleClass, use the following code:

```
SampleClass cls = new SampleClass( 40, "Memento");

XMLSampleClass state = new XMLSampleClass();
cls.GetState( state);

XmlSerializer s = new XmlSerializer( typeof( XMLSampleClass));
TextWriter w = new StreamWriter( @"c:\sampleclass.xml" );
s.Serialize( w, state);
w.Close();
```

The variable cls represents the SampleClass used in the application. The variable state represents the state of XMLSampleClass, which initially contains nothing. To transfer the state contents of SampleClass to XMLSampleClass, the method cls.GetState is called. Once the state has been transferred to the variable state, serialization to XML can be carried out. The deserialization occurs in the same fashion, except the method SampleClass.SetState is called.

When using the Memento pattern, the class that implements the IOriginator interface and follows the Immutable pattern will need a parameterless constructor, because the state that is transferred to it isn't known when the immutable object is instantiated. A possibility does exist where a constructor is created that is the same type as the IOriginator<> interface. Then when the immutable object is instantiated, the constructor can call the IOriginator<>.SetState method to assign the initial state. Being able to assign state during the lifetime of an immutable object creates another problem with respect to the immutable object in that synchronization is required. A solution to this problem is to change the implementation of SampleClass to the following:

```
class SampleClass : IOriginator< IMemento> {
    private int _value;
    private string _buffer;

    public SampleClass( IMemento state) {
        _buffer = state.Buffer;
        _value = state.Value;
    }
    public SampleClass(int value, string buffer) {
        _value = value;
        _buffer = buffer;
    }

    public int Value {
        get {
            return _value;
        }
    }
    public string Buffer {
        get {
            return _buffer;
        }
    }
    public void GetState( IMemento state) {
        state.Buffer = _buffer;
        state.Value = _value;
    }
    public void SetState( IMemento state) {
        throw new NotSupportedException();
    }
}
```

In this modified example, the SetState method will throw an exception. It's only possible to assign the state using the IMemento constructor when the object is instantiated. Another solution is to implement SampleClass with a reader-writer synchronization. Using a reader-writer synchronization adds additional overhead, but most likely won't slow down the manipulations of the object. This is because in such a scenario, assigning the state is rare, and most locks will be reader locks.

Some Concluding Remarks About Memento

The Memento pattern is a very useful and powerful way to transfer state from one object to another. The other object is shared among multiple other implementations. The Memento pattern is especially useful when different versions of applications need to exchange data. This is because the application type and internal state have been separated, and each application type can pick and choose among states.

Where I found the Memento object to be of great use is in my NUnit tests. Very often I would manipulate objects, and then want to know the state of my object. Specifically, I wanted to know if certain internal state variables were properly assigned. These internal state pieces could have been exposed externally, which is bad object-oriented programming. More appropriately, the objects implemented the Memento pattern, and when needed, the state was extracted and tested. This made it possible to cleanly separate the unit tests from the assemblies. Otherwise, I had to declare the internal data as internal, and run the unit tests within the assembly.

This finishes our exploration of data persistence through serialization. Next, let's take a look at the second method of data persistence I mentioned at the beginning of this chapter, O/R mapping.

Object-to-Relational Data Mapping Using NHibernate

For the rest of the chapter, I'm going to cover the Open Source O/R mapping toolkit named NHibernate,[6] a port of the very successful Java toolkit Hibernate.[7] The NHibernate toolkit isn't an implementation of a single pattern, but more generally an implementation of the Serializer pattern. And it isn't a general toolkit for all sorts of persistence problems, rather it focuses on the persistence of .NET objects to relational databases.

To have a program persist its data to a relational database, you would use ADO.NET. Using ADO.NET, a connection is created, some commands are executed, a transaction is executed, and voilà, the data exists in a relational database. ADO.NET isn't difficult. What is difficult is mapping the data in memory to data in a relational database. This gets more complicated when data sets are involved, and larger amounts of data need to be transferred. The Memento pattern separates the object from the state, but the state still needs to be converted into data for a relational database. The Memento pattern in this context doesn't help. NHibernate changes this in that the programmer doesn't even touch an ADO.NET command. In essence, everything seems to happen magically. Sounds too good to be true, but Hibernate in the Java world has shown that it's possible.

An object-to-relational mapper operates from class to relational database. At a conceptual level, you start with the class, and then define the relation to a database. The reality is that the database is designed first, and the O/R mapping is fitted on top. This means most likely two

---

6. http://wiki.nhibernate.org/display/NH/Home
7. http://www.hibernate.org/

individuals will be involved when creating a relational database application. One individual is responsible for the design of the relational database, and the other individual is responsible for the mapping and programming. Databases are a skill unto themselves.

In the upcoming text, I'll present a simple NHibernate example, explore one-to-many relationships, and briefly survey other relationships and using HQL in this continued discussion on data persistence.

A Simple NHibernate Example

Creating an NHibernate application requires three pieces: configuration files, objects that are persisted, and a calling application. The three pieces have to be synchronized with each other to make a persistence function properly. It may seem complicated to have three pieces, but there is an advantage in that each piece can vary independently. For example, an object could be associated with multiple configuration files, which can be associated with multiple databases. The advantage of this approach is that it's possible to keep objects and tables somewhat consistent across multiple databases and applications.

Defining a Type to Be Persisted

The first step is to define the type that will be persisted. In this example, a book description will be persisted, and this description is defined as follows:

```
public class Book {
    private string _isbn;
    private string _title;
    private string _author;

    public Book() { }
    public Book( string isbn, string title, string author) {
        _isbn = isbn;
        _title = title;
        _author = author;
    }
    public string ISBN {
        get {
            return _isbn;
        }
        private set {
            _isbn = value;
        }
    }
    public string Title {
        get {
            return _title;
        }
```

```
        private set {
            _title = value;
        }
    }
    public string Author {
        get {
            return _author;
        }
        private set {
            _author = value;
        }
    }
}
```

The class declaration Book has a minimal declaration, but can include application logic methods. NHibernate can persist already existing types, and for the most part requires only minimal extra declarations. NHibernate doesn't fight developers when they realize their implementations for the following reasons:

- NHibernate for the most part requires property getters and setters to be declared. To avoid violating the Immutability pattern, the setters can be scoped private, even though the getters are public.

- For this version, there are no NHibernate-specific attributes, and everything is based on configuration files. This makes it possible to persist plain vanilla objects. In the future, though, attributes will be an option, but not a required option.

What is very clever about NHibernate is that, like binary serialization, private data fields can be serialized. But unlike binary serialization, what are serialized are the properties, and not the individual data members. This makes the NHibernate persistence very flexible, as is binary serialization, in that only specific pieces of the state are persisted.

Defining a Relational Database Table

The Book class declaration has to have an associated relational database table. The associated table could be a view, but that is a choice for the developer. In the Book example, the table is called BOOKS, and is defined as follows:

```
CREATE TABLE "BOOKS"
{
    "ISBN" VARCHAR(20) NOT NULL,
    "TITLE" VARCHAR(120) NOT NULL,
    "AUTHOR" VARCHAR(50) NOT NULL,
    PRIMARY KEY( "ISBN")
};
```

The table BOOKS has three columns, which are all varchar, or variable length strings, that can't contain null values. The primary key index is ISBN, and it's expected to be unique. When using NHibernate, it isn't necessary for a table to declare a primary key.

Defining the Class Type Mapping Configuration File

NHibernate encompasses the notion of attributes, but they are defined in configuration files. For the Book class, NHibernate, when resolving how to persist Book, will search for the configuration file Book.hbm.xml or the configuration file that is bound as a resource in an assembly. In most cases, the configuration file is added to the assembly as an embedded resource, and there can be multiple embedded configuration files. Book.hbm.xml is defined as follows:

```
<hibernate-mapping xmlns="urn:nhibernate-mapping-2.0">
    <class name="Chap08.ObjectRelational.Book,Chap08.ObjectRelational"
        table="Books">
        <id name="ISBN">
            <generator class="assigned" />
        </id>
        <property name="Title"/>
        <property name="Author"/>
    </class>
</hibernate-mapping>
```

The XML tag hibernate-mapping specifies the root-level NHibernate parsing point that contains a number of subelements defining the mapping between the class and relational database.

The XML tag class represents the .NET class that will be mapped. The attribute name represents the name of the class to load, which follows .NET type naming conventions. From the example, this means specifying at a minimum the class identifier and assembly. Not specifying the assembly will cause NHibernate to generate a "class not found" exception. The attribute table specifies the table that contains the data for the class Book. The table can be a view, but remember, whether or not data can be added or updated depends on the relational database implementation of view. Contained within the XML tag class are various child tags used to cross-reference the data members of class Book and the table Books.

In a relational database, most tables have a primary key, but it isn't a necessity. When defining a class in NHibernate, there has to be a primary key, and the simplest is to use the XML tag id. The id tag has a single attribute, name, which references the name of the property that uniquely identifies an object instance. The case of the value for the name attribute has to match the case of the referenced property. If the case doesn't match, then an error is generated.

When NHibernate transfers the state from the property to the relational table, the default is to search for a column with the same name as the property. If the column is named differently from the property, then, a hidden attribute called column can be used. The attribute column is the name of the column in the table that is used by NHibernate to transfer to and from the property.

Contained within the id XML tag is a generator XML tag. The generator tag defines how the property and column value will be generated. Consider it as follows. You are adding a record to a database. To be able to distinguish one record from another, there usually needs to be a primary key. The problem with the primary key is how to generate a unique value. The simplest is to count from zero and update the counter for each record. In the example, the XML tag generator has assigned the attribute class to assigned, meaning that the primary key value for the property Book.ISBN will be assigned by the program.

The remaining child XML tag's property represents the individual mapping of the class properties to relational database columns. Like the id XML tag, the attribute name represents the class property identifiers. Additionally, since there is no `column` attribute, the default column mapping to the relational database is the `name` property.

Defining the Database Configuration File

The database configuration file is used by NHibernate to connect to a database. It isn't necessary to use a configuration file, as the configuration information can be defined programmatically. The configuration information is usually stored in the application configuration file, but could be stored in a separate XML file that is then loaded manually. Following is a sample configuration file:

```
<configuration>
    <configSections>
        <section
            name="nhibernate"
            type="System.Configuration.NameValueSectionHandler,
                System, Version=1.0.5000.0,Culture=neutral,
                PublicKeyToken=b77a5c561934e089"
        />
    </configSections>
  <nhibernate>
    <add key="hibernate.connection.provider"
      value="NHibernate.Connection.DriverConnectionProvider"
    />
    <add key="hibernate.dialect"
      value="NHibernate.Dialect.FirebirdDialect"
    />
    <add key="hibernate.connection.driver_class"
      value="NHibernate.Driver.FirebirdDriver"
    />
    <add key="hibernate.connection.connection_string"
        value="User=SYSDBA;Password=masterkey;
        Database=c:/db/nhibernate.fdb;DataSource=localhost;Port=3050;"
    />
  </nhibernate>
</configuration>
```

The NHibernate configuration information is specified using key-value pairs, which are represented as child elements of the XML tag `nhiberate`. The minimum number of keys to specify are four, and they are defined as follows:

1. `hibernate.connection.provider`: This setting defines the class that provides a database connection when `hibernate` reads and writes objects. The default value as illustrated in the example indicates that NHibernate should do everything.

2. `hibernate.dialect`: This setting is used by NHibernate when converting to and from the relational database. A dialect is necessary because each database has its specifics that aren't portable across databases. The dialect class provides NHibernate with a lowest-common-denominator functionality. To find out the dialect of your database, inspect the namespace `NHibernate.Dialect`.

3. `hibernate.connection.driver_class`: This setting defines the connection class used by NHibernate when connecting to the database. The driver class doesn't replace the ADO.NET connection driver, as it's still required.

4. `hibernate.connection.connection_string`: This setting defines the connection string used to connect to the database, and is specific to each database.

Instead of a configuration file, the same connection settings could have been defined using the following example source code:

```
_cfg = new Configuration();
_cfg.SetProperty( "hibernate.dialect", "NHibernate.Dialect.FirebirdDialect");
_cfg.SetProperty( "hibernate.connection.provider",
    "NHibernate.Connection.DriverConnectionProvider");
_cfg.SetProperty( "hibernate.connection.driver_class",
    "NHibernate.Driver.FirebirdDriver");

_cfg.SetProperty( "hibernate.connection.connection_string",
        @"User=SYSDBA;Password=masterkey;
        Database=c:\db\BOOKS.FDB;DataSource=192.168.1.103;Port=3050");
```

It's important to call the configuration settings right after the instantiation of `Configuration`, as otherwise some exceptions might be generated.

Putting It All Together

Finally, let's put everything together into an application. The following source code adds a book to a database:

```
Configuration _cfg;
ISessionFactory _factory;
ISession _session;
_cfg = new Configuration();
_cfg.AddAssembly("Chap08.ObjectRelational");
_factory = _cfg.BuildSessionFactory();
_session = _factory.OpenSession();
ITransaction transaction = _session.BeginTransaction();
Book book = new Book( "1-59059-540-8"
    "Foundations of Object Oriented Programming Using .NET 2.0 Patterns",
    "Christian Gross");
_session.Save( book);
transaction.Commit();
_session.Close();
```

A typical usage of NHibernate involves several steps:

1. The NHibernate environment is initialized, which involves instantiating Configuration. Configuration references the information used by NHibernate when types are being persisted to and from a relational database. It's up to the programmer to make sure that the persistable types and database configuration information have been completely defined before attempting any persistence operations.

2. Using the method call AddAssembly causes NHibernate to load the assembly and search for embedded mapping files. When a mapping file is encountered, it's processed and added to the Configuration data mapping.

3. Instantiation of the session occurs using the methods BuildSessionFactory and OpenSession. The resulting session object instance (_session), after having called OpenSession, is the client's connection to the database. It's important to consider what to do with the session object instance because using it involves resources. After having used the session object, the session is closed using the method Close.

4. For most operations, a transaction is started using the method BeginTransaction, which is then committed using the method Commit.

5. Once a transaction has been started, the session object instance saves an object to the database using the method Save.

To read the object back into memory, the following source code is used (note that the configuration and initialization haven't been displayed for brevity, but are identical to persisting an object):

```
Book myBook = (Book)_session.Load(typeof(Book), "1-59059-540-8");
```

To load the object back into memory, the method Load is called, with the primary key used to reference the book. If the object isn't found, an exception is generated, which can be caught. If the object is found, it's loaded, and the data members are assigned. For the method Load, the first parameter is the class description of the object that is to be loaded into memory. NHibernate will use that description to cross-reference a class mapping configuration and instantiate an object.

Updating the Details of the Object

The declaration of Book is an immutable object. Or at least Book is immutable to any class that isn't Book, as the set part of the properties have been declared private. So let's say the contents of Book need to be updated, which means creating a new object because of the immutability. A new object is instantiated and added to the NHibernate session. NHibernate will be confused because there are two object instances with the same primary keys.

To get around this problem, the only real option is to delete the object from the relational database, and then add the object again. Following is the source code to delete the object:

```
ITransaction transaction = _session.BeginTransaction();
Book myBook = (Book)_session.Load(typeof(Book), "1-59059-540-8");
_session.Delete( myBook);
transaction.Commit();
```

The code example carries out two steps: loading of the object and then deleting it from the database. As an optimization, it isn't necessary to load the object, as the method Delete has been overloaded. One variation of Delete is to use a string buffer representing a query string that references the primary key and allows a direct deletion of the object.

Deleting and re-creating the object is a very simple and logical approach when working with immutable objects in memory. However, with respect to a database, this isn't a logical solution, because it requires too many resources. This doesn't mean that immutable objects are wrong for O/R mapping, but it means you don't always use immutable objects. A good example of where you would use an immutable object is if the data being loaded is cross-reference information that rarely changes.

One of the major problems of deleting and re-creating an object is the loss of referencing information. In the case of Book, the primary key was defined by the application, and it's the ISBN. But there are other situations where the primary key is automatically generated. Thus, when deleting and re-creating the key, a new primary key is generated, and all of the old references in the other tables will cease to exist. Performance considerations aside, this single issue alone makes immutable objects impossible to implement.

There is a solution to the immutability problem, one that can make both O/R mapping and the .NET runtime happy. The solution is to not use the private keyword on the set part of a property, but to use internal. Remember that immutability doesn't require synchronization in concurrent situations. The wait times that result from synchronization slow down applications. Therefore, the objective is to implement O/R mapping in such a way that the application isn't slowed down, but still allows for modification.

Consider the following modified O/R mapped immutable Book class (for clarity, the reader-writer locks have been omitted):

```
public class BookUpdater {
    public static void UpdateAuthor( Book book, string author) {
        book.Author = author;
    }
}
public class Book {
    private string _isbn;
    private string _title;
    private string _author;

    public Book() { }
    public Book( string isbn, string title, string author) {
        _isbn = isbn;
        _title = title;
        _author = author;
    }
    public string ISBN {
        get {
            return _isbn;
        }
        internal set {
            _isbn = value;
        }
    }
}
```

```
    public string Title {
        get {
            return _title;
        }
        internal set {
            _title = value;
        }
    }
    public string Author {
        get {
            return _author;
        }
        internal set {
            _author = value;
        }
    }
}
```

The trick in this solution is the use of `internal` for all `set` parts of the properties, and the use of a class `BookUpdater` to update the contents of the book. It's assumed that `Book` and `BookUpdater` are defined in the same assembly. From an external assembly perspective, `Book` is immutable, and if an update to the book is required, then `BookUpdater` is used.

Looking at this solution, you'll probably say, "Huh?" This confusion stems from the fact that a separate class modifies the contents of a class. Even though you have the ability to use object-oriented programming techniques, they seem to be ignored by adding a separate class. The problem here isn't the separate class, but how NHibernate, and many other frameworks for that matter, persist its data using properties. As defined in Chapter 1, object-oriented design requires that you don't expose the internal state of the class. Yet for persistence, you have to.

The reality is that the problem isn't the exposure of the internal data, but the ability to modify the internal data. What you really need to be concerned with is the exposure of the properties. Immutable objects might expose internal data members, but using read-only access. With NHibernate, you have the option of applying the `private` scope to all property getters and setters, which means that no external exposure of the internal data occurs.

The real reason, though, why you want to use a `BookUpdater` type strategy is because changing an individual property, regardless of scope, can corrupt the state of the class. Let's say you make the property setters of `Book` public. This would allow you to update the title without updating the other properties. This is incorrect because an unwritten fact is that a title and its ISBN are connected at the hip. Changing the title most likely means changing the ISBN of the book. Of course, there are exceptions, like the title being mistyped, or the title being updated. But these are exceptions, and they won't happen often. The general case is that the ISBN and title are connected, and changing one means changing the other. This means changing the ISBN or title, deleting an old book instance, and creating a new book instance. Changing the author of a book doesn't change the semantics of the book, and hence it's possible to directly access the `Author` property.

Knowing what you know of the semantics of `Book`, exposing all of the `set` properties as public data members is incorrect. The more appropriate solution is to use a method that assigns the properties like `BookUpdater`. In the example, the method is part of another class, but there is nothing to stop you from adding the method to the Book class. The important part is to use methods that manipulate the internal state of the object. Of course, this creates an object that isn't purely immutable, but mostly immutable. It isn't always possible to create a purely immutable class, even though you might like to.

Here's one last bit of code to finish the example of updating a book without deleting the book instance:

```
Book myBook = (Book)_session.Load(typeof(Book), "1-59059-540-8");
BookUpdater.UpdateAuthor( myBook, "Different Author");
_session.Flush();
```

The Book instance is loaded using the Load method. Then calling the method UpdateAuthor will change the author. This changes the value of the author, which means when the method _session.Flush is called, the new value will be saved in the database. Calling Flush has the effect of committing the transaction.

Not Saving the Content

When an object is loaded, it's associated with a session. The session was created using the method call _factory.OpenSession in the earlier section, "Putting It All Together." A session has resources that could be equated to a workspace. Objects are loaded and saved from the workspace. Closing a session means saving and discarding the contents of the session. It's possible to separate a session from the transaction by opening and committing a transaction manually, as illustrated when the Book object was initially saved. Sometimes you'll want to leave a session open, which is made possible by using the methods _session.Disconnect and _session.Reconnect.

NHibernate is clever in being able to detect changes of an object, which are then automatically persisted when the NHibernate transaction is completed. The problem is that such a solution might be too clever, because you might want to update the class, but not save the contents. Following is the source code that removes an object from a session, which means that the contents of the object aren't saved if it's modified:

```
Book myBook = (Book)_session.Load(typeof(Book), "1-59059-540-8");
_session.Evict( myBook);
```

The method Evict removes the object reference from the session. The object instance myBook can still be manipulated and referenced, but it's disconnected from the database.

Mapping One-to-Many Relationships

For most scenarios, you won't be adding, deleting, and removing data from a single table or view. More likely what you'll be doing is creating two tables, and have one table reference another. Unlike object-oriented programming, the referencing of data in a relational database is through keys. A *key* is a value in one table that is identical to a key of another table. The key of the other table is almost always unique, meaning that there is a one-to-one reference between a record of one table and a record of another table. Often in a relational database, multiple records of one table reference one record of another table, creating a one-to-many relationship.

Defining Comments Using a SQL Table

Let's extend the simple book application and add the ability to associate comments with a book. From an architectural point of view, there would be multiple comments associated with a particular book. A comment will only be associated with a single book. The SQL used to create the tables is as follows:

```
CREATE TABLE "BOOKS"
(
  "ISBN"     VARCHAR(20) NOT NULL,
  "TITLE"    VARCHAR(120),
  "AUTHOR"    VARCHAR(50),
  PRIMARY KEY ("ISBN")
);

CREATE TABLE "COMMENTS"
(
  "ID"     VARCHAR(40) NOT NULL,
  "PARENT_ISBN"    VARCHAR(40),
  "COMMENT"    VARCHAR(1024),
  "AUTHOR"    VARCHAR(40)
);
```

The BOOKS table hasn't changed, but what will change in the declaration of the class Book is the inclusion of a list of available comments. New is the COMMENTS table, where PARENT_ISBN is the column that associates a particular comment with a particular book.

Modifying Book to Reference Comments

The modified Book declaration is as follows (there are missing property declarations, which have been removed for clarity):

```
public class Book {
    private string _isbn;
    private string _title;
    private string _author;
    private IList _comments;

    public Book() { }
    public Book( string isbn, string title, string author) {
        _isbn = isbn;
        _title = title;
        _author = author;
    }
    public IList Comments {
        get {
            return _comments;
        }
```

```
        internal set {
            _comments = value;
        }
    }
}
```

The new property declaration Comments is of the type IList. When an instance of Book is loaded, NHibernate will select from COMMENTS the associated comments. These are then loaded into a list that is assigned to the property Comments. If you happen to know Hibernate or NHibernate, please don't question my previous statement. I'll get to the nitty-gritty details in a moment. For now, just consider that, when loading Book, the associated Comments are selected and loaded. From a SQL perspective, the following statements are executed when loading an instance of Book (note that actual NHibernate SQL statements reference the fields individually, but I use a * to keep things simple):

```
SELECT * FROM BOOKS WHERE ISBN=?
SELECT * FROM COMMENTS WHERE PARENT_ISBN=?
```

For reference, this means in the default case of loading Book, there will be two SQL statements executed for every book that is loaded.

The association of IList to Comments isn't something that NHibernate can figure out on its own. The mapping configuration file for Book has to be modified to include a reference to the Comments as follows:

```
<hibernate-mapping xmlns="urn:nhibernate-mapping-2.0">
    <class name="Chap08.ObjectRelational.Book, Chap08.ObjectRelational"
        table="BOOKS">
        <id name="ISBN" column="ISBN">
            <generator class="assigned" />
        </id>
        <property name="Title" />
        <property name="Author" />
        <bag name="Comments">
            <key column="PARENT_ISBN" />
            <one-to-many
    class="Chap08.ObjectRelational.Comment, Chap08.ObjectRelational" />
        </bag>
    </class>
</hibernate-mapping>
```

What is new in the Book mapping configuration file is the XML tag bag. NHibernate associates a bag as a collection. Like the XML tag property, the name attribute defines the name of the property, which must be of the type IList. The bag tag is straightforward; it associates a collection of comments with a book. Within the XML tag bag are two child tags. The child tag key represents the column of the other table that will be associated with the XML tag id. Simply put, whatever ISBN equals for the BOOKS table, it must match PARENT_ISBN in the other table. What is yet unknown is the other table. That is resolved by using the XML tag one-to-many. One-to-many defines the class identifier (Chap08.ObjectRelational.Comment) that will be stored in the IList collections.

Implementing Comments

To make this relationship work, the class Comment and its associated mapping configuration file need to be created. Following is the definition of the class Comment:

```
public class Comment {
    private string _comment;
    private string _whoMadeComment;
    private string _ID;

    public Comment() { }
    public Comment( string comment, string whoMadeComment) {
        _comment = comment;
        _whoMadeComment = whoMadeComment;
    }
    public string ID {
        get {
            return _ID;
        }
        set {
            _ID = value;
        }
    }
    public string Text {
        get {
            return _comment;
        }
        internal set {
            _comment = value;
        }
    }
    public string WhoMadeComment {
        get {
            return _whoMadeComment;
        }
        internal set {
            _whoMadeComment = value;
        }
    }
}
```

Included are three different fields: ID, Text, and WhoMadeComment, but in the declaration of the COMMENTS table, there are four columns. Missing as a property is the column PARENT_ISBN, because it isn't necessary in this example of a one-to-many relationship. The individual comments are managed as part of a collection managed by Book, and therefore adding the PARENT_ISBN record isn't necessary.

The mapping configuration file for Comment is defined as follows:

```
<hibernate-mapping xmlns="urn:nhibernate-mapping-2.0">
    <class name="Chap08.ObjectRelational.Comment, Chap08.ObjectRelational"
        table="COMMENTS">
        <id name="ID">
            <generator class="uuid.hex">
                <param name="format">N</param>
                <param name="separator">-</param>
            </generator>
        </id>
        <property name="Text" column="COMMENT" />
        <property name="WhoMadeComment" column="AUTHOR" />
    </class>
</hibernate-mapping>
```

What is unique about this example mapping configuration file is that the generator XML tag doesn't use assigned, but uses uuid.hex. The generator uuid.hex is a built-in primary index generator that uses the Guid.NewGuid method call to generate a unique key. The XML param tags refer to how the generated GUID will be formatted. More details about this generator and others appear in the NHibernate documentation.

It should be apparent that the Comment declaration is like the original Book declaration in that the it lives and acts on its own and doesn't know it's part of a collection managed by Book.

Putting It All Together Again

Now let's put everything together and create an example where a Book is loaded and a comment is associated with the book:

```
Book myBook = (Book)_session.Load(typeof(Book), "1-59059-540-8");
foreach( Comment comment in myBook.Comments) {
    Console.WriteLine( "Comment (" + comment.Text + ")");
}
Comment newcomment = new Comment( "some comment", "my author");
myBook.Comments.Add( newcomment);
_session.Save( newcomment);
_session.Flush();
```

In this example, the Book is loaded like it is previously without any reference to a Comment. The two SELECT SQL commands would be executed, and if they find any comments, then the comments are loaded. The comments can be iterated using a foreach loop, and the text of the comment is output.

The next line after the loop instantiates a Comment object, which is assigned to the variable newcomment. At this moment, the object instance is referenced only in the memory of the .NET runtime. When the method myBook.Comments.Add is called to add the Comment instance to the book, a reference is created. But the reference only exists in the sense of an abstract reference. The state of the O/R mapping is inconsistent because an object from the database is referencing an object that doesn't exist in the database. This is why it's imperative to call the method _session.Save so that the Comment instance is added to the COMMENTS table. Then calling the Flush method writes the Comment object instance and its associated reference to the database.

Auto-Saving of the Child Objects

Adding an object to a list and then having to explicitly save the object using the Save method is tedious. In some cases, you want this behavior. For example, imagine a scenario where the table references a set of constants. It would be very silly to add a new constant to the table whenever an association between two classes is made.

In this example, where a comment is only associated with a single book, it isn't efficient. Using the attribute cascade, it's possible to have an object saved automatically, if it needs to be saved. Following is the slightly modified mapping configuration file for Book:

```
<hibernate-mapping xmlns="urn:nhibernate-mapping-2.0">
    <class name="Chap08.ObjectRelational.Book, Chap08.ObjectRelational"
        table="BOOKS">
        <id name="ISBN" column="ISBN">
            <generator class="assigned" />
        </id>
        <property name="Title" />
        <property name="Author" />
        <bag name="Comments" cascade="all">
            <key column="PARENT_ISBN" />
            <one-to-many
    class="Chap08.ObjectRelational.Comment, Chap08.ObjectRelational" />
        </bag>
    </class>
</hibernate-mapping>
```

The cascade attribute is associated with the XML tag bag. The attribute value of all indicates that all children of the object will be saved or updated. Another variation, all-delete-orphan, deletes all children when the parent is deleted. It would seem that all-delete-orphan isn't necessary because, by default, all children should be deleted. However, there are some situations in which you would want parent objects to be loaded and deleted without having deleted all of the children.

The cascade attribute would seem like a life saver, but it's a double-edged sword. If a specific Book object instance is deleted, then all of the children will also be deleted. This can be useful when you want to maintain the consistency of the database, but could be problematic if by accident an object is deleted or if the children reference constants stored in another table.

Understanding the Parent-Child Relationships

Thus far it would seem all is OK in the example book application, when in fact under the covers, so to speak, multiple things are happening. First, the addition of a comment into the relational database isn't a single SQL statement, but two. The first is an INSERT statement that adds a comment to the COMMENTS table. The second is an UPDATE statement that associates the comment with the book.

The two SQL statements are problematic because when the INSERT statement is executed, the PARENT_ISBN value is null. A few sections ago when the COMMENTS table was defined, there was no NOT NULL constraint, which allowed the addition of the comment. In most database designs, though, the PARENT_ISBN will have a constraint in that the value can't be null. Trying to execute an INSERT without a value for PARENT_ISBN will result in a database constraint error.

The reason two SQL statements are being executed is because of ownership rules. As the relationship stands, the parent, which is Book, is responsible for maintaining the parent-to-child relationship. In the case of Book and Comment, this sort of arrangement is acceptable, because only one Comment is ever associated with one Book. There will never be the situation where a comment will be referenced with another book.

There are some instances where this type responsibility isn't acceptable, and the child should be responsible for the referencing. The configuration mapping file needs to be updated. The updated one for Book is as follows:

```
<hibernate-mapping xmlns="urn:nhibernate-mapping-2.0">
    <class name="Chap08.ObjectRelational.Book, Chap08.ObjectRelational"
        table="BOOKS">
        <id name="ISBN" column="ISBN">
            <generator class="assigned" />
        </id>
        <property name="Title" />
        <property name="Author" />
        <bag name="Comments" inverse="true" cascade="all">
            <key column="PARENT_ISBN" />
            <one-to-many
    class="Chap08.ObjectRelational.Comment, Chap08.ObjectRelational" />
        </bag>
    </class>
</hibernate-mapping>
```

Again, the XML tag bag is modified to include an attribute, inverse, with a value of true. This tells NHibernate that the responsibility of the parent-child relationship is managed by the child instance. If the C# code in the "Putting It All Together Again" section were executed again, the child would be created, and there would be only one SQL statement, INSERT. The single statement is good, but if there is a NOT NULL constraint, an error would still be generated. The problem is that the child is fulfilling its responsibility and creating an association to the BOOKS table. What is needed is a reference to the PARENT_ISBN column because the child Comment hasn't been modified to manage the PARENT_ISBN data. Remember from the "Implementing Comments" section that there is no property for the PARENT_ISBN column.

Comment is updated to include a reference to the parent as follows:

```
public class Comment {
    private string _comment;
    private string _whoMadeComment;
    private Book _parent;
    private string _ID;

    public Comment() { }
    public Comment( string comment, string whoMadeComment, Book parent) {
        _comment = comment;
        _whoMadeComment = whoMadeComment;
        _parent = parent;
    }
```

```
public string ID {
    get {
        return _ID;
    }
    private set {
        _ID = value;
    }
}
public string Text {
    get {
        return _comment;
    }
    internal set {
        _comment = value;
    }
}
public string WhoMadeComment {
    get {
        return _whoMadeComment;
    }
    internal set {
        _whoMadeComment = value;
    }
}
public Book Parent {
    get {
        return _parent;
    }
    internal set {
        _parent = value;
    }
}
}
```

The property Parent is of type Book, which references the parent book. To indicate that an association exists, the Comment mapping configuration file needs to be updated to the following:

```
<hibernate-mapping xmlns="urn:nhibernate-mapping-2.0">
    <class name="Chap08.ObjectRelational.Comment, Chap08.ObjectRelational"
        table="COMMENTS">
        <id name="ID">
            <generator class="uuid.hex">
                <param name="format">N</param>
                <param name="separator">-</param>
            </generator>
        </id>
```

```
        <property name="Text" column="COMMENT" />
        <property name="WhoMadeComment" column="AUTHOR" />
        <many-to-one name="Parent"
    class="Chap08.ObjectRelational.Book, Chap08.ObjectRelational"
            column="PARENT_ISBN"
            not-null="true" />
    </class>
</hibernate-mapping>
```

In the mapping configuration file, the XML tag many-to-one is added, indicating that the property Parent is associated with the class attribute. The many-to-one tag indicates that many Comment instances are associated with a single Book instance. NHibernate needs to know this information when data is deleted or updated. The attribute not-null with a value of true indicates that the property should never be a null value.

The Book class could and should be modified to the following (note the properties discussed previously have been omitted for clarity):

```
public class Book {
    private string _isbn;
    private string _title;
    private string _author;
    private IList _comments;

    public Book() { }
    public Book( string isbn, string title, string author) {
        _isbn = isbn;
        _title = title;
        _author = author;
    }
    public void AddComment( Comment comment) {
        _comments.Add( comment);
        comment.Parent = this;
    }
}
```

The additional method AddComment performs a cross-referencing of the parent to child, and child to parent. It isn't necessary to use a method like AddComment, but it's necessary to perform a child-to-parent and parent-to-child association. Then when the Comment object instance is written to the database, only one SQL INSERT statement is used, and the key column PARENT_ISBN can have a NOT NULL constraint. Now, if the Book object instance were deleted, the child Comment instances would also be deleted. To test this code, you would use the same C# source code as in the section "Putting It All Together Again," except the method call to children.Add would be replaced with AddComment.

What is powerful about this is that if you load a child, and then reference a parent, it will be loaded automatically. This makes it possible for you to search for a specific child, load the parent, and then navigate a relational database like you would an object hierarchy.

Lazy Loading

Imagine iterating through your book collection, and displaying the results in a dialog box for further selection. The example code as it's written would load all of the data. This means loading all books and their associated comments—a data retrieval explosion that could lead to very slow reaction times. What you want in this instance isn't to load everything, but only to load the immediate information.

NHibernate has a technique called *lazy loading*, where the data is loaded when it's needed. To implement lazy loading, it's only necessary to change the Book mapping configuration file to the following:

```
<hibernate-mapping xmlns="urn:nhibernate-mapping-2.0">
    <class name="Chap08.ObjectRelational.Book, Chap08.ObjectRelational"
        table="BOOKS">
        <id name="ISBN" column="ISBN">
            <generator class="assigned" />
        </id>
        <property name="Title" />
        <property name="Author" />
        <bag name="Comments" inverse="true" cascade="all" lazy="true">
            <key column="PARENT_ISBN" />
            <one-to-many
  class="Chap08.ObjectRelational.Comment, Chap08.ObjectRelational" />
        </bag>
    </class>
</hibernate-mapping>
```

Again, the bag XML tag is modified to include an additional attribute, lazy, with a value of true. This tells NHibernate to not load everything at once. Instead, the data will only be loaded when it's referenced.

Other Types of Relationships

There are other types of relationships, like many-to-many, and other types of collections, like maps and sets. For example, if the XML tag map were used, then NHibernate would associate an IDictionary instead of an IList with a child collection. The techniques for dealing with these relationships are based on the same techniques illustrated in the simple example of the parent-to-child relationship.

The difference for these other relationships isn't complexity, but getting the mapping configuration file correct. So for a many-to-many mapping, instead of only having a bag XML tag in the parent, there would also be a bag tag in the child referencing back to the parent. These topics are beyond the scope of this book.

Using HQL

The examples thus far illustrate how to find a single book and its associated comments. Let's say, though, that you want to find a series of books, and then display those books in a list box.

For that, you would need to use Hibernate Query Language (HQL).[8] Hibernate Query Language is similar to SQL, except it's specific to an object-oriented persistence layer like NHibernate. The web address referenced in the footnote is for the Hibernate HQL language, which is identical to NHibernate HQL. This section only illustrates two examples; you can get more details in the Hibernate documentation.

As a simple example, let's say you want to open the COMMENTS table, and then iterate all of the comments while displaying the parent book. Here's the source code to do that:

```
IList list;
list = _session.CreateCriteria( typeof( Comment)).List();
foreach( Comment comment in list) {
    Console.WriteLine( "Comment (" + comment.Text + ")");
    Console.WriteLine( "Parent (" + comment.Parent.Title + ")");
}
```

In the example, the variable list represents a list of elements that will be searched for from the COMMENTS table. The COMMENTS table is queried using the method CreateCriteria, which defines a filter of all elements that should be found. The "filter" is relatively simple in that all Comment instances should be searched because the criteria is specified as typeof(Comment). Then the .List() method is called to return the list of all Comments.

The variable list is then iterated using a foreach loop, and the comment.Text property is referenced. Notice the property comment.Parent.Title is also referenced. This is a very clever ability of NHibernate in that it lets you navigate a database hierarchy like an object hierarchy without having to explicitly load the parent. This ability alone makes an O/R mapper an extremely useful and time-saving tool.

To search for a set of comments that match a specific criterion, use the following source code:

```
IList list;
list = _session.CreateQuery( "from Chap08.ObjectRelational.Comment
        as comment where author = 'me'").List();
foreach( Comment comment in list) {
    Console.WriteLine( "Comment (" + comment.Text + ")");
    Console.WriteLine( "-- Parent (" + comment.Parent.Title + ")");
}
```

In this example, the method CreateQuery is used instead of CreateCriteria. The buffer that is passed to CreateQuery is HQL and can be considered an object-oriented SQL. Missing is the SELECT part, because it's assumed. Because we are dealing with objects, it would be rather silly to specify the properties, as they would all be loaded. Having said that, it's possible to specify properties, but rarely is this done. The object that is being referenced is Chap08. ObjectRelational.Comment, or comment as the alias.

The selection of the author is accomplished after the where keyword and uses the same notation as SQL, and the author references the column from the table comments. It's possible to write the query entirely using object references, as illustrated by the following example:

```
list = _session.CreateQuery( "from Chap08.ObjectRelational.Comment
        as comment where comment.WhoMadeComment = 'me'").List();
```

---

8. http://www.hibernate.org/hib_docs/reference/en/html/queryhql.html

Notice in this example the query is based on the property WhoMadeComment, which is cross-referenced by the Comment mapping configuration file as the column AUTHOR from the table COMMENTS.

Some Final Thoughts

Like many pattern authors, I cringe at persistence. There are plenty of pattern books, but so few on data access. The problem with data access and persistence is that it's a never-changing debate—hence why I was apprehensive of covering it in the first place. Frankly, I thought, "What can of worms are you getting yourself into, Christian?"

Something interesting happened when I wrote this chapter. It turned out that persistence in .NET is frighteningly easy. I always thought one of the biggest benefits of a managed environment was its ability to garbage collect your objects. But it turns out that there is another huge benefit, and that is persistence. When I used to code in C and C++, persistence was an absolute pain in the butt, and any change in my application caused my program to come to a grinding halt. With a managed runtime, saving information is easy.

When I needed to write the materials that make it simpler to persist data into a relational database, I kept getting visions of complex frameworks that nobody understands or wants. So while looking on the Internet, I visited the web site for Hibernate, which I heard of through my experience with Java. I was skeptical of O/R mapping because, well, my encounters with object relational mapping and object databases were extremely discouraging. And again, I was pleasantly surprised. Hibernate is extremely popular in the Java world, and I came to understand why while using NHibernate.

So the moral and focus of this chapter is that you should never ever need to write a low-level routine to persist an object. There is no need to read an individual line of text, nor is there a need to manually parse XML, nor is there a need to use ADO.NET directly. The functionality offered by the .NET base classes and NHibernate take care of the lower-level details, making it possible for you to only think in terms of objects. This chapter did not go into a large amount of detail because doing so would have required writing another book entitled *Persistence in .NET*. Persistence is an entire subject unto its own. Here I attempted to explain the basics of what you should be doing and how you should be doing it when it comes to persistence.

Finally, if you're skeptical, don't be. I was wowed and am convinced. I find it odd how sometimes previous convictions can become wrong after being forced to confront one's fears.

CHAPTER 9

■■■

Refactoring to Patterns

I didn't come up with the idea of refactoring to patterns—that honor goes to Erich Gamma.[1] Erich, who wrote one of the first design pattern books, was giving an interview and explaining how he applied patterns. From reading the interview, my impression was that the ideal way to develop software is to write some code, write some tests, and then refactor the code.

The idea that Erich Gamma proposed was to get a feeling for the application by writing some code, understanding how the application works by testing it, and then finally fixing up the code to use patterns. The result is code that both fulfills the requirements and is architected for future bug fixes and extensions. The focus of this chapter is to illustrate some common code scenarios that can be refactored to known patterns.

Sometimes a refactoring is performed to an antipattern.[2] An *antipattern* is like a pattern, except it references a pattern of code that is incorrect. The antipattern then proposes a way to correct, or refactor, the code. Missing in the antipattern discussion is the refactoring to patterns, an oversight I hope to rectify here.

A very important reminder to all readers: I will be refactoring mostly from the .NET base class library. The reason is simple: I want to illustrate something that everybody understands. This doesn't mean that the base class libraries are bad, but it does illustrate that .NET developers are human, just like everybody else. And remember that hindsight is 20-20, so when refactoring and critiquing, be kind and gentle.

Test-Driven Development and Refactoring

Coding isn't a simple task. Often designers and architects will attempt to find the best architecture ahead of time for their purposes. But the problem is finding the best architecture. It isn't that it's impossible or difficult, rather that it's tedious. Reports have to be generated, studies have to be carried out, and findings have to be analyzed. Imagine doing these tasks when all you wanted to know is how to write an assembly. The software industry does research to uncover findings for how the software needs to operate. Typically this is called *requirements*. When coding, executing large amounts of research is simply too tedious and in fact unnecessary. Software is malleable, and therefore can be made to be whatever the coder wants it to be. We should never ignore this.

---

1. http://www.artima.com/lejava/articles/gammadp.html
2. William J. Brown et al., *Anti Patterns: Refactoring Software, Architectures, and Projects in Crisis* (Indianapolis: Wiley Publishing, 1998).

What the software industry does need to realize is that being malleable is both a good and a bad thing. We're constantly looking for the holy grail—the perfect algorithm. The answer is that there is no holy grail, because there are multiple "good enough" algorithms. Test-driven development was discussed in Chapter 2, but not discussed was the automatic refactoring. As you implement your application, you need to look at the resulting code and see if it resembles a design pattern. And if you find such a design pattern, then the code needs to be modified to resemble the design pattern.

It may seem counterproductive to create some code and then fix it up. It isn't because you're learning about your code and what works best. Over a decade of coding has taught me that as much as developers would like to find the ideal design ahead of time, it's nearly impossible. There are simply too many permutations and combinations.

What is important in this cycle is the implementation of small pieces of functionality. The trouble with refactoring is that the larger the time deltas between refactorings, the more costly the process becomes. Normally, you would think that refactoring is dependent on the size of the code, but in fact that isn't true.

Consider it as follows: say you're building a house. You build the foundation, build the frame, and add the siding. Only after adding the siding do you inspect your work to see if everything is done correctly. If you realize that you built a house that is partially on another property, there will be quite a bit to tear down. Yet if you built the foundation and then checked if everything was OK, only the foundation needs to be ripped down. This is because the foundation has been checked and verified and assumed correct. Granted, it can happen that after building the house, the house still needs to be ripped down. The likelihood of that happening, though, is fairly remote.

Writing That First Line of Code

So let's say that you need to write that first line of code, and have no idea where to start. Well, as the famous Nike commercial says, "Just do it." Write your code without regard to anything. Because if you're free in your mind, you'll make it happen. Of course, that doesn't mean you write your application with any old code.

When implementing test-driven development, many believe it's best to write the tests first, and then implement the code. I differ in this opinion because it will confuse more than assist. Most modern integrated development environments (IDEs) are based on the idea of having a base functionality that they know about, and you want to manipulate. IntelliSense, compilation, and so on are all based on this idea. Hence, by going the other way, you're forced to remember method signatures, assembly names, and the like. This is baggage that you don't need to carry around. By implementing first, and then testing, you can focus on the higher-level semantic issue of making your application function.

Implementing first doesn't mean writing lines and lines of code, and then testing. What it means is implementing an idea and then testing. The idea could be implemented in five minutes, ten minutes, three hours, maybe even two days. Of course, the idea should be simple and singular, not complex like "Creating an invoice for a client." Creating an invoice for a client encompasses multiple ideas, namely creating the invoice, creating the client, associating the invoice with the client. Right there you have three ideas that can each be implemented and tested individually.

This process of defining an idea, implementing the idea, and then testing the idea is an iterative test-driven development process. What you should realize is that the concept idea can be replaced with a requirement. I didn't mention requirements because often requirements are like the complex idea "Creating an invoice with a client" and contain multiple requirements that are implied. Developers need to break those requirements into microrequirements.

After That First Line of Code

Once that first line of code has been written and tested, what follows next is a refactoring. You'll want to inspect your code and see that it contains no shortcuts, and that it will work and be robust. Of course, having written the tests, it's trivial to see if your refactoring works. If the tests fail, then the refactoring must be fixed.

Overall, though, test-driven development that includes refactoring follows these steps:

1. Implement a piece of functionality by writing some code.

2. Write test scripts to test the functionality.

3. Run the test scripts.

4. Refactor the written code.

5. Rerun, verify, and fix the refactored code.

6. Go back to the first step.

Even though you'll try to apply patterns in step 1, it's difficult, because it's hard to see how a system will behave ahead of time. Of course, you'll have general directions and general ideas. Compare this to growing a garden. Sure, you know the dimensions of the garden, and you know what you want to grow. What you don't know is whether you'll get any fruits and vegetables. You might get a snail or bug invasion. Weeds might grow rampantly, and there might be too much sun or too much rain. To make a garden successful, you need to adapt it. The same applies to code. This doesn't mean to implement code without thinking about design patterns ahead of time, rather you still need to think about things and plan—hence why it's important to be flexible.

Kinds of Refactorings

When writing the first line of source code, it's important to understand what the context of the first line of code is. There are four unique contexts, defined as follows:

- *Cleanup*: You're not adding any code, but modifying existing code.

- *Extension*: You're adding new code, but not modifying existing code.

- *Maintenance*: You're modifying existing code, but only insofar as to fix certain problems.

- *New*: You're creating entirely new code. The new code might be part of an already existing code base.

The following sections explain these different contexts, and the text thereafter explains various refactorings that can be used in the different contexts. It's important when writing code that one of these contexts be applied. With each context, certain boundaries are defined.

These boundaries are artificial and can easily be overstepped. However, the point of the boundaries is to make the software process manageable and, more importantly, controllable from a developer and manager perspective.

Cleanup

The purpose of the cleanup context is to reengineer code. You're given a code base and told to make it faster or make it work on another platform. Ideally, a manager would ask for code to be cleaned up as part of an overall development cycle. However, simply performing a cleanup with no goal has no tangible benefits. Please note that cleanup does mean refactoring. Having developed the code, refactorings will have been performed. Often, though, at the end when everybody sees the big picture, some refactorings are postponed and hence not implemented. This results in code that may have problems. Often a cleanup is a tweaking of the code, focusing on a single goal such as faster performance or consumption of fewer resources, or things that have been postponed and need attention.

What is unique when performing cleanup is that the test scripts don't change, even with the possible addition of new test scripts. If the original test scripts were to change, that would defeat the purpose of the cleanup. A cleanup is the improvement of the existing code for a specific purpose. A cleanup won't extend or change any functionality. When performing a cleanup, it's absolutely vital that the test scripts are well written and cover the most important situations, as you want to be assured that your changes will be tested.

Extension

When writing an extension, the objective is to enhance an already existing functionality. Typically, an extension requires you to implement a set of predefined interfaces. The test scripts will already be written, and it's only necessary for your extension to fulfill the needs of the test. Additional test scripts may be added, but existing test scripts won't be modified.

An extension typically involves writing new code. The new code will require testing and refactoring. But importantly, the tests written for the new code from a test or pass perspective are irrelevant. What is relevant is the success or failure of the interfaces that are being implemented. Lazy developers would even use those test scripts as the only tests for their extensions. Using only the extension tests isn't advisable, because the extension tests may be badly written, resulting in a badly written extension.

Maintenance

Maintenance is the simplest of all contexts in that there is no cleanup, no additional test scripts, and no new code. The only requirement when coding in a maintenance context is that the application work. A maintenance context happens when the application doesn't work.

There is one exception to no additional test scripts: if a user uses the application and causes a bug to appear for which no test script exists. Logically, if a bug appears, it's because there is no test script. Hence, a developer has to write a test script to fix the code.

New

The new code context is one of the most complex and demanding contexts. This should be the context where the least amount of time is spent, because when writing new code, there are no boundaries, no test scripts—just brand new code and brand new tests.

A good development strategy is to write new code that is then extended using the extension context. The idea is to define an infrastructure and overall architecture using the new code context. And then to finish the application, the team only needs to implement a series of extensions. Extensions are simpler to implement and test and lead to an overall development process that is controllable.

Classes, Methods—Everything Is Too Big

When writing code, it often happens that there is a class, interface, or structure that is modified and enhanced. Multiple enhancements result in a type definition that seems large. It seems that there are too many methods and properties, and that makes developers unhappy.

As much as we hate large declarations, sometimes they are necessary, because the type is complicated. When designing types, the need for a refactoring isn't the size of the type, but the abstraction.[3] A base type should embody only one feature, abstraction, or responsibility. Let's consider this for a moment in the context of a help desk application. Whenever a help request comes in, a ticket is issued. The ticket is used in multiple steps of the help desk workflow. For the workflow, there will be only one type of ticket that will contain all of the actions. But the only actions contained relate to the ticket. This means the workflow will reference the ticket, and not the other way around. The moment multiple responsibilities are combined in a single base type, you're asking for problems.

Where multiple responsibilities are confusing is in the Extension pattern. The Extension pattern explicitly implements multiple responsibilities in a single type. The difference with multiple responsibilities is the definition and implementation. The Extension pattern implements multiple responsibilities, but considers them as individually exposed personalities. In a nutshell, the strategy is to define base types as simply as possible that are pulled together using an implementation of the Extension pattern.

There are two major reasons to split a type:

- Helps simplify the type, making it more flexible for the implementations to pick and choose the base types to implement or extend

- Makes it possible to implement functionality that is consistent and doesn't violate constraints

The key thing to remember with this refactoring is that you want to divide and conquer. Split apart each individual item into its single responsibility, and then reassemble using patterns. Keep in mind that typically this refactoring is applied to interfaces or base classes, and not to classes that implement the Extension pattern.

---

3. Arthur J. Riel, *Object-Oriented Design Heuristics* (Boston: Addison-Wesley, 1996), p.19.

Let's say you're confronted with some problem code that contains multiple ideas. This code is called a Blob antipattern.[4] What essentially happens is that one type requires all of the attention, and the rest of the type declarations revolve around the functionality of the blob class. The main problem with the blob type is that if the blob is modified, the ramifications are immense in that many other types need to be changed. This makes the application brittle and hard to change.

The following class declaration for System.IO.Stream is an example of code with too many responsibilities:

```
public abstract class Stream : System.MarshalByRefObject, System.IDisposable {
    public static readonly System.IO.Stream Null;
    protected LocalStream() {}
    void System.IDisposable.Dispose() {}
    public virtual void Close() {}
    protected virtual System.Threading.WaitHandle CreateWaitHandle() {}
    public abstract override void Flush();
    public abstract override int Read(byte [] buffer, int offset, int count);
    public virtual int ReadByte() {}
    public abstract override long Seek(long offset, System.IO.SeekOrigin origin);
    public abstract override void SetLength(long value);
    public abstract override void Write(byte [] buffer, int offset, int count);
    public virtual void WriteByte(byte value) {}
    public virtual System.IAsyncResult BeginRead(byte [] buffer, int offset,
        int count, System.AsyncCallback cback, object state) {}
    public virtual System.IAsyncResult BeginWrite(byte [] buffer, int offset,
        int count, System.AsyncCallback cback, object state) {}
    public virtual int EndRead(System.IAsyncResult async_result) {}
    public virtual void EndWrite(System.IAsyncResult async_result) {}
    public abstract bool CanSeek {
        get {}
    }
    public abstract long Position {
        get {}
        set {}
    }
    public abstract bool CanWrite {
        get {}
    }
    public abstract long Length {
        get {}
    }
    public abstract bool CanRead {
        get {}
    }
}
```

---

4. *Anti Patterns: Refactoring Software, Architectures, and Projects in Crisis*, p. 73; and Michael Feathers, *Working Effectively with Legacy Code* (Upper Saddle River, NJ: Prentice Hall, 2004), p. 245.

The class declaration of the Stream is relatively large. The size shouldn't matter, but what should is if there are multiple responsibilities. Stream doesn't have just a single responsibility, even though it would seem it does. The apparent single responsibility is to be able to read and write data either synchronously or asynchronously from a medium. Yet try to decipher the single responsibility, and it's apparent that Stream has multiple responsibilities.

A good test of whether a base type has multiple responsibilities is to try and generically implement the base class and consider how many times a NotImplementedException is necessary as illustrated in the following example:

```
public class MyImplementation : Stream {
    public abstract long Position {
        get { throw NotImplementedException(); }
        set { throw NotImplementedException(); }
    }
}
```

NotImplementedException indicates a functionality that a class doesn't need or can't implement for one reason or another. If the exception is used, then it's the first sign of an interface or base type defining multiple responsibilities.

The Stream class contains three responsibilities: read from a medium, write to a medium, and read/write asynchronously to a medium. It would seem that reading and writing asynchronously are two responsibilities, but in fact they constitute a single responsibility because they extend the read and write responsibilities. It's important to create three responsibilities because it enhances the flexibility of the implementations.

When the Pipes and Filters pattern was discussed in Chapter 4, the Stream base type wasn't used because of the responsibilities defined. In the Pipes and Filters pattern, there were input streams and output streams. It isn't allowed to write data to the input stream and read data from the output stream. Imagine using the Stream base type. An element in the Pipes and Filter chain may write data that would never be processed, or attempt to read data that doesn't exist. The implementation of the input and output streams may bind together input and output streams, but the personalities are exposed individually. Single responsibility base types ensure a minimum amount of coding errors.

Refactoring the Stream Class

When refactoring a big type into a smaller type, the following rules apply:

- Define the responsibilities of the type.

- Subdivide the type into types that implement each responsibility, adding, removing, or manipulating new methods or properties as appropriate.

- If a method or property is applicable to multiple responsibilities, then copy the method or property to multiple responsibilities. It must be noted that some methods or properties fit into no responsibility because they aren't applicable. For the Stream example, the method CanRead is a method that isn't needed in the refactoring.

From the new set of types, perform a refactoring of an already existing implementation that implemented the old base type. A subset of the test scripts should be rewritten to use the new types. When the test scripts are completed, execute the scripts and see what happens.

The idea is to understand the ramifications of the refactoring. To make sure the test scripts don't fail, fix the source code, but not the test scripts. If the modifications seem too large and complex, maybe some responsibilities have been defined incorrectly.

Following is the refactored Stream class:

```
public interface ReadStream {
    void Close();
    int Read(byte [] buffer, int offset, int count);
    int ReadByte();
    long Position {
        get;  set;
    }
    long Seek(long offset, System.IO.SeekOrigin origin);
    long Length {
        get;
    }
}

public interface WriteStream {
    void Close();
    void SetLength(long value);
    void Write(byte [] buffer, int offset, int count);
    void WriteByte(byte value);
    void Flush();
}

public interface ASynchronousReadStream : ReadStream {
    System.Threading.WaitHandle CreateWaitHandle();
    System.IAsyncResult BeginRead(byte [] buffer, int offset,
        int count, System.AsyncCallback cback, object state);
    int EndRead(System.IAsyncResult async_result);
}

public interface ASynchronousWriteStream : WriteStream {
    System.Threading.WaitHandle CreateWaitHandle();
    System.IAsyncResult BeginWrite(byte [] buffer, int offset,
        int count, System.AsyncCallback cback, object state);
    void EndWrite(System.IAsyncResult async_result);
}
```

There are four abstract base interfaces: ReadStream, WriteStream, ASynchronousWriteStream, and ASynchronousReadStream. The responsibilities have been divided into two categories: reader and writer responsibility. The asynchronous responsibility is an extension of the reader and writer base classes. Notice that the Stream abstract class has been converted into a number of interfaces. Interfaces are preferable to abstract base classes because they offer more flexibility.

You might have been tempted to make the abstract base classes use .NET Generics. The idea would be to write a stream using one set of types. The problem is that no stream encompasses a single type. More often, streams represent multiple types, hence .NET Generics doesn't make the interfaces more flexible.

Problems of Refactoring the Stream Class

Refactoring the Stream class into four other interfaces is very simple since Stream was crying out for refactoring. An implementation such as file would use the base interfaces as follows:

```
public class FileImp : ReadStream, WriteStream {
}
```

The declaration of FileImpl seems logical, and it would employ the Extension pattern.

For this discussion, let's say that it wasn't possible to convert the Stream class into four interfaces. For reasons beyond the scope of this discussion, the new types would have to be defined using abstract base classes. In this case, FileImpl as a declaration wouldn't work as it isn't possible to subclass two classes. Besides using interfaces, there is another solution, and it's illustrated here:

```
class FileWriteImpl : WriteStream { }
class FileReadImpl : ReadStream { }
```

To write a file, the type FileWriteImpl is instantiated, and the base type WriteStream is used. Then the stream instantiated is FileRealImpl, and the base type ReadStream is used. This solution is logical, but the types are separate and not related to each other. Consider the case where data isn't written to a file, but to memory. Implemented would be the types MemoryWriteImpl and MemoryReadImpl. The question is, If the memory data is a private memory variable, and the consumer uses WriteStream or ReadStream, how can the data be extracted or assigned? To fully understand the problem, consider the following source code:

```
public class MemoryWriteImpl : WriteStream {
    private Byte[] _data;
}
```

The class MemorWriteImpl implements WriteStream, and the data is written to the data member _data. The problem is that the consumer of InMemoryImp or WriteStream can't access the data that is written. In the old implementation of Stream, that wouldn't have been a problem, because it would have only been necessary to rewind the reference and read the data.

If interfaces were used, then both the WriteStream and ReadStream interfaces would be implemented. Because WriteStream and ReadStream are abstract classes, it isn't possible. The solution is to consider other patterns, specifically the Memento pattern. The purpose of the Memento pattern is to assign or extract state, in this case, extract or assign the memory data. The MemoryWriteImpl class would implement the Memento pattern as illustrated by the following example:

```
public class InMemoryImp : WriteStream, IOriginator {
    private Byte[] _data;

    public void GetState<type>( type data) { }
    public void SetState<type>( type data) { }
}
```

In the modified implementation of MemoryWriteImpl, the interface IOriginator is implemented, but the methods are left empty for illustration purposes. The client that uses WriteStream can use the Static Extension pattern to cast to IOriginator and extract the state of the written data. Using the Memento pattern is the best solution because the Memento pattern keeps the state consistent and doesn't involve "hacking" in a method to assign or retrieve data. In the implementation of MemoryWriteImpl, there would be additional data members that relate to the current cursor position and size of the written data, and the data member _data most likely will contain empty values for reserve. Using the Memento pattern, a single state exists for the buffer, where there are no extra pieces of data.

Refactoring a Class and Not a Base Type

Refactoring Stream was relatively simple, because it was an abstract class that had no implementations. But refactoring a class to a simpler class is more complicated because there are implementation details. Often a large class is created because it was simpler to keep adding functionality to the already existing class than to cleanly separate the functionality. In effect, the hardest type of large class to refactor has been created in that within the implementation the data members reference each other even though they are part of different responsibilities.

When separating the class into its individual subclasses, the idea is to separate the subclasses and then use patterns to make them fit each other. There is no magic rule, just that you separate and divide and then re-create the classes using patterns. In an Open Source project, I found the following example of class that needed refactoring because it fell into the category of being too big. The class declaration itself isn't too large, but the problem is that the class declaration combines multiple responsibilities.

```
public class Channel {
        [XmlAttribute] public string Name = "";
        [XmlAttribute] public string Url = "";

        // Used when updating the feed
        [XmlAttribute] public string LastModified = "";
        [XmlAttribute] public string ETag = "";
        [XmlAttribute] public string Type = "";

        public int NrOfItems {  }
        public int NrOfUnreadItems {  }

        ArrayList mItems;
        [XmlElement ("Item", typeof (Item))]
        public ArrayList Items {   }

        public Channel() { }
        public Channel(string name, string url) { }

        public void Setup() {   }
        public Item GetItem(string id) {  }
        public bool MarkAsRead() {     }
```

```
    private ArrayList mUnupdatedItems;
    public void StartRefresh() {  }
    public void FinishRefresh() {}

    public bool UpdateItem(string id, RssItem rssItem) { }
    public bool UpdateItem(string id, AtomEntry entry) { }
    public void MarkItemIdAsRead(string id) { }
}
```

The class Channel looks to be fine, but most likely this is version 1.0 of a class that should be updated. Remember that all classes will need to be reengineered at one time or another. That is the nature of software. Getting back to Channel, it would seem that everything is OK. A parent-child relationship exists between Channel and Item. The parent-child relationship is acceptable, but the question that must be asked is who has the responsibility for what.

The following things could be considered design problems:

- There are two lists: a list of items and list of nonupdated items (whatever that might mean). This could cause a redundancy of the data whereby an item might be deleted from one list, but not another.

- On the one hand, there is the method MarkItemIdAsRead, yet there is also a method on Item, which is called Setunread. This means to mark something read you have to reference one class, but to mark it unread you have to reference another class.

- Most of the methods are implemented using foreach, which is repeated in a number of places. Replication requires more changes when a single tweak of foreach is required.

- The classes Channel and Item have overloaded methods RssItem and AtomEntry, which are used to fill the channel and items. The problem is that each type is similar and is only needed when parsing an RSS or Atom feed. If another feed format were created, it would require yet another overloaded method.

- When finding items in a collection, the GetHashcode and Equals methods aren't implemented, meaning finding the item from the collection is based on instance references, not content value. This could result in two object instances having the exact same data.

- Some of the data members are declared as public items, and others are declared as public properties. This is an inconsistency that would confuse a programmer or consumer.

Many of the things that appear wrong might be wrong because no other viable solution was available, and hence the problems can't be fixed. However, those situations are fewer than we think. The overall problem is that Channel and Item have a split responsibility, yet the partitioning of that responsibility remains unclear.

The refactoring of Channel changes the dynamics of the parent-child relationship, where Channel is only responsible for the organization and Item is responsible for its own actions and data. Specifically, what is applicable is the Composite pattern. The overall purpose of the Composite pattern is to enable traversing a hierarchy of objects that can be treated as one. The parent shouldn't be responsible for managing the individual items. Also problematic is the fact that Channel and Item are responsible for two different feed types. Imagine the scenario when a third feed type needs to be added. Will the Channel and Item classes be updated again?

To avoid updating these classes again, the first step in our refactoring is to separate the serialization from the overall architecture. The new serialization structure is defined as follows:

```
interface ISerialization {
        Channel ReadChannel();
        void WriteChannel( Channel channel);
}

class RssSerialization : ISerialization { }
class AtomSerialization : ISerialization { }
```

A generic interface is defined, called ISerialization, which has two methods to read a channel and write a channel. Then two classes implement the interface ISerialization: RssSerialization, which handles RSS serialization, and AtomSerialization, which handles Atom serialization. It wouldn't seem useful to have a WriteChannel method because a blog reader is always reading content from other web sites. However, what if the developer of the newsreader wanted to extend the functionality and create a news aggregator that generates a feed based on other feeds? Having both reading and writing functionality makes it very simple to create an aggregator. Or imagine the situation where a reader literally reads thousands of blog entries a day. Instead of saving the contents to a file, maybe a database using NHibernate would be appropriate. In that situation the NHibernate persistence layer would only need to implement the ISerialization interface.

The serialization has been removed from the Channel and Item classes, which means that the individual methods that reference the data types RssItem and AtomItem are unnecessary. Also unnecessary are the XML attributes, as the implementations of ISerialization will manage those details.

The next step is to implement the Composite pattern. To illustrate the solution, but keep the implementation simple, I'll show you the method MarkAsRead. The idea is to mark a series of Item instances as read.

```
public class Item {
    private Item _next = null;

    public Item() { }
    public Item( Item next) {
        _next = next;
    }
    public bool Unread = true;
    public void MarkAsRead() {
        if( _next != null) {
            _next.MarkAsRead();
        }
        Unread = false;
    }
}
public class Channel {
    public Item _items;
}
```

The class `Channel` doesn't reference an `ArrayList` for `Item`, but references a single instance of `Item`. The type `Item` contains a `_next` data member that references a chain of `Item` instances. Removing the `ArrayList` from `Channel` and replacing the list with a single reference could be considered problematic because a `foreach` loop can't be used.

Using a `foreach` loop means to use the Iterator pattern. In .NET 2.0, the Iterator pattern can be implemented using classes that don't support lists. A solution to iterate the individual elements would be to use the `yield` keyword. The solution that is used doesn't iterate the elements, but lets each element take care of the next element. Consider the implementation of `Item.MarkAsRead`. Calling that method causes the referenced `Item` instance to be flagged as read, and if `_next` isn't null, then the `_next` element will be marked as read. The end result is a cascading effect that can be used in place of an iteration.

I Can't Understand the Code

One of the incredible things about Open Source is that it works considering the context. Thousands of developers around the world who probably rarely talk to each other in person are solving problems in conjunction with other developers without a single game plan. Yet Open Source applications still work. Still, in some corporations, there'll be a group of developers who see each other every day who can't agree what to name a variable. It begs the question of how Open Source developers do something that others can't. The answer is rigorous coding practices that don't always involve writing easy-to-understand comments.

Not all Open Source projects are successful or exhibit good programming practices. And not all corporations have developers who can't understand each other. My point is that it's expected that corporations develop good software and that Open Source not develop good software.

Approaching Unknown Code

The "I Can't Understand the Code" syndrome isn't solved with refactoring, but through a way of understanding the code when you're responsible for performing some maintenance or cleanup work. To be able to understand code that already works, and most likely you didn't write, is a major undertaking. Such a task should never be underestimated. It's possible to understand the code if you take your time and follow some steps. The purpose of the following steps is to provide a reproducible way of understanding code in different circumstances:

1. Install the sources on a computer and rebuild the sources yourself using a build process you created yourself. If this step is too complicated, then you can skip it, but the objective is to understand the build process, so you understand the dependencies, and thus you know the overall layout of the application.

2. Add your own scripts that test the functionality you want to modify. Writing your own test scripts gets you to understand how the types at the different levels interoperate with each other.

3. Run the tests scripts with the addition of tracer code. Tracer code helps you figure out what your code is doing and why.

Each of these steps isn't used to improve the code, but to improve your understanding of the code. The first step defines the dependencies of the application with respect to assemblies, files, database connections, and other external pieces of information. The second step defines the dependencies of the components within the application. From the tests that are executed at the different levels, the dependencies of the various components become understandable. And the last step, tracer code, makes it possible to understand what the individual code pieces are doing.

Tracer Code

Tracer code is a topic that isn't discussed using that particular term. But change the code from tracer code to logging code, and then it's apparent what tracer code is. I don't like the term *logging code* because it implies code used for logging problems. Tracer code implies the development of code that traces what it's doing. Tracer code was discussed in Chapter 2, and the class Tracer demonstrated.

When implementing tracer code, it should be distributed during runtime, but not active during normal operation. As illustrated with log4net, tracer code is activated by using either the info or debug levels. When writing tracer code, the debug level is most appropriate. The tracer code should perform tests and output messages indicating what the code is doing. Then if something goes wrong, a developer can inspect the logs to see what happened.

Breaking Some Code

Once the logs have been investigated, tests executed, and application built, the best way to know what is going on is to break some code. It's absolutely imperative to break code.[5] Of course, before you break the code, it isn't executing from the main branch, but a local branch. The theory behind breaking code is that if you break code, you can see what your application does when things go wrong.

Injecting executing errors into an application doesn't test the stability of an application. This is because you're causing the application to run in a disabled state. For example, imagine testing a car and removing one of the wheels. There is no real situation that can test if that car will behave properly, as cars aren't meant to be driven with three wheels. However, what can be tested in such a scenario is to see whether the car reacts in a way it should have. Injecting errors are bizarre situations that most developers have never encountered, and as such maybe bizarre things will happen in your application.

There are two ways to break code. The first is to break the test scripts and make them do things that they shouldn't be doing. Maybe a configuration isn't properly instantiated, maybe a method call is made when it shouldn't be. The generated output of the tracer code should highlight where things went wrong. If it doesn't, then you know something isn't correct in the code. The second way to break code is to use the tests that work and modify the internal source code. Then what should have worked doesn't work, and the test scripts and tracer code should react appropriately. If there is improper behavior, then it can be inspected.

Breaking code is useful for seeing what an application does because it's very similar to figuring out how a machine works by pushing some buttons. The only difference is that the

---

5. Jeffrey M. Voas and Gary McGraw, *Software Fault Injection: Inoculating Programs Against Errors* (Indianapolis: Wiley Publishing, 1998).

worst that can happen is a crashed machine. When buttons are pushed, reactions can be inspected, and then cross-references can be made. For example, not specifying a database connection might cause other objects to not instantiate. This creates the cross-reference where a database connection is directly related to some object instantiations.

It would seem that breaking code is a good way to ensure quality in an application. While I agree with this statement, the problem with breaking code is that it's a shot in the dark. You can't come up with all the bizarre ways that somebody will use the code. It simply takes too much time to implement without tangible results. Imagine trying to tell your manager, "Oh yeah, we had hackers test the code to see the bizarre ways our application will crash." Unless you're delivering a consumer product, most managers will ask, "Is there a quantifiable reason?" That's why when you need to understand code, it's simpler to convince a manager to "break code."

The Code Feels Similar, Yet Is Different

Unfortunately, Windows developers are plagued with the infamous code "Copy and Paste" sticker. There is some truth to this sticker, because many books reference this behavior as something to avoid.[6] What is odd is that if so many references exist to copying and pasting code, why do it in the first place? The answer is because it can provide advantages, and it's easy.

Why Copying and Pasting Code Works

Many people will probably reference this section as something that I shouldn't have written about because it's controversial. Copying code into another application creates duplication. Duplication isn't something people do inadvertently. Your editor doesn't force you to copy and paste some code. You do it knowingly. Duplication means that you take something from somewhere else and paste it into your code to solve your problem.

Let's get back to the duplication behavior and focus on why duplication happens. I stated that duplication happens knowingly. However, in some situations, duplication occurs unknowingly, and not because of a copy-and-paste operation. In those situations, duplication happens because two developers happen to be developing the same type of code without knowing it. A classic example involves the universal string class used when developing C++ code. Everybody and their grandmother had a pet project on developing the best string implementation. With the introduction of STL, this behavior is stopping, but it does happen with other pieces of functionality.

Another reason for duplication is that it's imposed. This happens when source code is too complicated for somebody to understand. So instead of refactoring the code to make it understandable, that programmer rewrites the same piece of code, but using his or her improved coding style.

So if you do duplicate code knowing the problems that it will generate, there must be a perceived benefit. The perceived benefit can easily be illustrated. Consider the following declaration:

---

6. *Anti Patterns: Refactoring Software, Architectures, and Projects in Crisis,* p. 133; and Andrew Hunt and David Thomas, *The Pragmatic Programmer* (Boston: Addison-Wesley, 1999), p. 26; *Working Effectively with Legacy Code,* p. 269.

```
class Working {
    public void CoolMethod() { }
}
```

The class Working has a method, CoolMethod, which has no parameters. The implementation works well. From a quality perspective, Working and CoolMethod are tested, working, and considered finished. Along comes a developer who sees that CoolMethod does everything he or she needs it for, except for one thing. And that one thing is absolutely necessary. Sadly, that one thing can't be added as a post- or precall step of CoolMethod, so CoolMethod has to be modified.

The developer has a dilemma. He or she could modify CoolMethod and extend its functionality. That would mean rerunning the tests and ensuring the viability of the changes that won't impact already working code. If the developer went to his or her manager, the manager would say, "OK, but it's your responsibility." And those are the magic words that cause the programmer to copy and paste code. The developer doesn't mind responsibility, but doesn't want responsibility for something that he or she didn't create or even understand fully. And asking the original developer of CoolMethod to include those changes is probably futile, as the original developer probably has enough work.

The developer copies the code into his or her own program and changes the pasted code so that the one thing works. The developer is happy when the test results are positive and the application works without a hitch. But the program has a hidden time bomb that isn't known at the time of distribution. If CoolMethod needs to be updated, then most likely the pasted-and-modified code needs to be modified as well. If the modified code isn't updated, then the bomb explodes: bugs show up that appear identical to the fixed bug, causing developers to scratch their heads. The worst part is that this time bomb may explode at the most terrible moments.

Refactoring Duplicated Code Using the Template Method

Duplication behavior needs to be stopped whenever possible. It's destructive and causes problems in the long term. Oddly enough, duplication may help as a short-term fix, at the expense of a long-term solution. I suppose one could classify duplication in the same category as taking out a large loan at a very high interest rate. You have the money, but it has to be paid back, and that is usually where the problems start.

The Template pattern is a pattern that supplies some base functionality, supplemented by a custom class or implementation. It's possible to use the Template pattern in its own context. The problem is that often you don't know what represents common functionality. You can guess common functionality, and probably use base classes for most of it. The problem is that the Template pattern can be applied everywhere, because, after all, isn't object-oriented programming about getting some base class to do some work, and another class to do the rest? Yet the Template pattern exists, and must have a purpose. The purpose is to refactor duplicate code that looks similar, but isn't.

A Duplicate Code Example

The following example contains duplicated code. That example will be refactored using the Template pattern. (Note that the data members have been declared as public and not properties to simplify the declaration. Normally properties would be used.)

```
class Item {
    public int Id;
    public bool MarkedFlag = false;

    public Item( int id) {
        Id = id;
    }
}

class DuplicatedInternal {
    private IList _items = new ArrayList();

    public Item GetItem(int id) {
        foreach(Item item in _items) {
            if(item.Id == id) {
                return item;
            }
        }
        return null;
    }
    public bool MarkItems() {
        bool updated = false;

        foreach(Item item in _items) {
            if(!item.MarkedFlag) {
                item.MarkedFlag = true;
                updated = true;
            }
        }
        return updated;
    }
}
```

This example demonstrates a classical parent-child relationship, where DuplicatedInternal is the parent for Item. The parent contains an array of child elements. This forms the basis of most object hierarchies. When a child element needs to be manipulated, it's necessary to iterate through the individual elements. The methods GetItem and MarkItems perform two different functionalities, but each contains a foreach loop. In the Blob refactoring, the Composite pattern was used to navigate the individual elements. However, even with the Composite pattern, some code has to be repeated in multiple places.

The problem with iteration is that it's the same operation of looping through the data. What is different is the code that manipulates the iterated element in the loop. In the methods GetItem and MarkItems, the loops are repeated, but the iterated Item is manipulated in different scenarios. The foreach loop is a very simple example of duplicated code, but it illustrates the architecture of duplicated code.

Refactoring the Duplicated Code Example

Refactoring duplicated code is easy from a theoretical point of view, but requires some thought from a practical perspective. The Template pattern says that a large percentage of the code is delegated to a common type, and the rest is custom implementation.

Implementing a Template Pattern Using Inheritance

Without regard to whether the Template pattern is properly implemented for the context, the following source code is an initial refactoring of the class DuplicatedInternal:

```
class RefactoredIterator< type> {
    private IList< type> _list;

    public RefactoredIterator( IList< type> list) {
        _list = list;
    }
    public void Iterate() {
        foreach( type item in _list) {
            ProcessItem( item);
        }
    }
    public virtual void ProcessItem( type item) { }
}
```

RefactoredIterator<> is a Generic class that contains the common code of the class DuplicatedInternal. The duplicated code is the iteration of a list of elements. So that RefactoredIterator<> remains flexible, the Generic parameter is the type being iterated, and for DuplicatedInternal, that would be the type Item. For each iteration, the method ProcessItem is called, which is defined as a virtual method. The idea is that DuplicatedInternal should subclass RefactoredIterator<> and implement the method ProcessItem. In the implementation of ProcessItem, the code would be the loop contents of GetItem or MarkItems.

Stepping back, you might notice a disjoint: refactoring out the common code is easy, but making it do the custom work won't work. This is the crux of the problem of why duplicated code isn't recommended. The original developer either knowingly or unknowingly couldn't abstract the duplicated code to use a common code piece. Don't underestimate the complexity of such an undertaking, because it isn't simple to do elegantly.

The refactored class RefactoredIterator<> is one solution, but there are some extra details that may or may not be optimal. To understand what I am trying to point out, consider the following refactored DuplicatedInternal class declaration:

```
class DuplicatedInternal {
    IList< Item> _list = new List< Item>();

    public DuplicatedInternal() {  }
    private class InternalGetItem : RefactoredIterator< Item> {
        public int Id;
        public Item FoundItem;
```

```
        public InternalGetItem( IList< Item> list, int id) : base( list) {
            FoundItem = null;
            Id = id;
            Iterate();
        }

        public override void ProcessItem( Item item) {
            if( item.Id == Id) {
                FoundItem = item;
            }
        }
    }
    public Item GetItem(int id) {
        return new InternalGetItem( _list, id).FoundItem;
    }
}
```

In the modified DuplicatedInternal class, a private internal class InternalGetItem is declared. This is necessary because DuplicatedInternal can't be derived from RefactoredIterator<>. Doing so would only allow the solving of either GetItem or MarkItems. The private class implements the method ProcessItem, which executes the same logic as the original GetItem method. The iteration is executed in the context of the constructor. This makes it possible for GetItem to instantiate the type InternalGetItem, and then directly reference the data member FoundItem, which represents the found element.

The approach used by the private class InternalGetItem makes the implementation of GetItem very compact and simple. There is no separate instantiation, variable assignment, method call, and retrieval of the return data. The main problem of this approach is how to pass the data of GetItem to InternalGetItem, and then return the data.

The strategy used is to pass all of the data to the constructor of InternalGetItem. Once the data has been assigned to the constructor, the process method within the constructor is executed. Normally, a developer would call the method explicitly, but that would mean having to write additional lines of code. The return value is stored in a property accessed from the instantiated object. In effect, what will happen is that an instance of InternalGetItem is created, isn't assigned, but is accessed for a return value. If there is no single return value, then out parameters could be used on the constructor. It's acceptable to use this strategy because the class being instantiated is private.

Implementing a Template Pattern Using Delegates

Using inheritance to implement the Template pattern works, but that could mean if you have ten methods that use looping, you'll also have ten private classes. Another way to implement the Template pattern is to use .NET 2.0 anonymous delegates. When using delegates, an iterator class doesn't call a virtual method, rather it calls a delegate, as illustrated by the following example:

```
delegate bool Processor<type>( type element);

class RefactoredIterator < type> {
    IList _list;
    Processor< type> _processor;

    public RefactoredIterator ( IList list, Processor< type> processor) {
        _list = list;
        _processor = processor;
    }
    public bool Iterate() {
        foreach( type element in _list) {
            if( !_processor( element)) {
                return false;
            }
        }
        return true;
    }
}
```

In this new definition, the RefactoredIterator<> constructor requires both a list to iterate and a delegate that will be called by the foreach loop. The implementation of the loop is identical to the previous example that called a virtual method.

Now consider the following example that refactors the GetItem method using the new class and anonymous delegates:

```
class DuplicatedInternal {
    public IList _items = new ArrayList();

    public Item GetItem( int id) {
        Item found = null;
        new RefactoredIterator< Item>( _items, new Processor< Item>(
            delegate( Item item) {
                if( item.Id == id) {
                    found = item;
                    return false;
                }
                return true;
            })).Iterate();
        return found ;
    }
}
```

In the implementation of the method GetItem, the class RefactoredIterator<> is instantiated, and then the method Iterate is called. Like the previous example, the RefactoredIterator<> instance isn't assigned to any variable. The delegate that is passed to Processor is an anonymous delegate, where the implementation of the delegate is defined in the method GetItem. In the example of using a virtual method, that challenge was to pass the parameter information to a `RefactoredIterator` instance and return a value.

The trick is the anonymous delegate and how it allows the use of variables defined in the scope of the `GetItem` method. Notice how the comparison `if( item.Id == id)` uses the parameter ID, and the return value is assigned to the local variable found. This is a very powerful feature of anonymous delegates. The overall structure of the code is identical to that of the `foreach` loop, except that the `foreach` loop is replaced with the instantiation of `RefactoredIterator`.

The advantage of this approach to the virtual method is that it's possible to use common code declared in another class, and have the specific code stored in the local method. When using inheritance, the developer must maintain a custom class and the local method.

Duplication That Is Acceptable

Even though duplicate code should be avoided, as mentioned previously, sometimes duplicate code is desirable. Consider the example of implementing a proxy. The proxy hides a method that is very time consuming. Because of this required time, the proxy creates a cache that stores the results for specific queries. So whenever a client makes a query that the cache stores, the answer is returned from the cache. This duplication in information about the query is stored in two places. The information duplicated could be even simpler than a query; for example, it could represent an item count or username.

When duplication results from a cache or a second variable, then it's due to a particular reason such as performance. The cache increases performance, but also increases maintenance, as the code to maintain the cache accurately has to be written. Sometimes that is desired because the performance outweighs the increased maintenance.

Time Is Short, Make It Quick

Time is something software engineers don't have enough of, something I hear time and time again. One of the shortcuts to save time for the short term is to use duplication. But duplication is bad in the long term, and I demonstrated a refactoring as a solution. The refactoring solves the problem of duplication, but it doesn't address one of the reasons of why duplication was done in the first place, namely lack of time.

There is a partial solution to the lack of time that also solves the duplication problem. The solution involves using the Adapter pattern to integrate two dissimilar systems. Let's look back at the refactoring of the Blob antipattern, where a class was refactored into something simpler. The refactoring was successful, but it requires a new implementation. Supposing time doesn't allow a new implementation, a possible time saver for the short term is to use the Adapter pattern.

Following is an abbreviated implementation of the refactored `ReadStream` interface:

```
public class StringReadStream : ReadStream {
        private MemoryStream _memoryStream = new MemoryStream();

        public StringReadStream( string buffer) {
            _memoryStream = new MemoryStream( Encoding.Unicode.GetBytes( buffer));
        }
```

```
public override int Read(byte[] buffer, int offset, int count) {
    return _memoryStream.Read( buffer, offset, count);
}
}
```

The abstract base class ReadStream is the new base type definition. The class StringReadStream is the new type that needs to be implemented. In the implementation, the type MemoryStream, which is used because it already exists, implements the full Stream abstract base class. To implement the Read method, a delegation to the MemoryStream.Read is executed.

This implementation of ReadStream is very quick and works correctly. This begs the question of if you're going to use a legacy class, why define a new interface and use old implementations. The answer is as follows:

- Legacy is usually tested and it works, so why not use something that already works? Combining old with new minimizes development time and risk.

- A new type can, when properly implemented, make code flexible and adaptable in a way that an old type can't.

The Adapter pattern provides a very useful refactoring when time is short and old code already exists. This means instead of duplicating code by copying and pasting, use an adapter in combination with the Template pattern to solve your problem. The code won't be pretty, but it will work. Having written all of this, I should say this approach doesn't give any developer carte blanche to use the Adapter and Template patterns for all code. But when you want to implement some things quicker, and you have already existing code, use this approach.

If the code doesn't already exist, can the Adapter pattern be used? It depends on whether or not the code can be bought in terms of a library, or another Open Source library accomplishes most of the task. Very often other libraries solve the problem at hand, but don't integrate with the overall application. The Adapter pattern saves the day in that it allows a smooth integration using an already existing piece of software.

I Wish This Code Was Removed

One of the last things that this book will cover isn't refactoring, but deleting of code. As a code base expands, it's necessary to clean up the code and remove old types that are replaced with new types. While it would be nice to delete a type and expect everyone to use the new type, that simply isn't possible. What is needed is an upgrade path. Developers need time to adapt and fix their code.

Upgrading code should happen in four phases:

- *Phase 1*: Old code and new code execute concurrently.

- *Phase 2*: Old code is marked as obsolete, causing any code that is recompiled to generate a set of warnings.

- *Phase 3*: Old code is implemented using a series of exceptions that are thrown if the method is used.

- *Phase 4*: Old code is removed from the code base.

Developers can mark their code as being obsolete so that anybody who uses the code will get a warning indicating that the method or type is going to be phased out. Following is a declaration that marks a method as obsolete:

```
public class Type1 {
    [Obsolete( "Don't use it")]
    public void Method() {
        Console.WriteLine( "method");
    }
}
```

Whenever any type uses the method Type1.Method, the compiler will generate a warning similar to the following:

```
/Users/cgross/Chap09.Refactorings/toolittletime.cs(16)
warning CS0618: 'Chap09.Refactorings.Type1.Method()' is obsolete: 'Don't use it'
```

It's also possible to mark a type as being obsolete as illustrated by the following example:

```
[Obsolete( "Don't use it")]
public class Type1 {
    public void Method() {
        Console.WriteLine( "method");
    }
}
```

When a type such as class or interface is marked as obsolete, then when some code uses the type, and the code is compiled, a warning similar to the previous one is generated. Having a series of warnings being generated makes it possible for any developer to understand that the programming construct being used is to be refactored. Usually, it's helpful in the warning to provide a message like, "Don't use it, do the following." The message could hint at another method, property, or type, or some help text. Only saying to not use the code is extremely unhelpful.

Some Final Thoughts

And there you have it: a book on object-oriented programming illustrated through a number of patterns. I suppose this book should really be entitled *Foundations of Object-Oriented Programming Using .NET 2.0 Patterns, Test-Driven Development, and Refactoring.* If there is anything positive in this title, it's the fact that it would win at buzzword bingo. However, it isn't my intention to win at buzzword bingo. My intention is to illustrate that object-oriented programming isn't about inheritance or encapsulation, but about tests, patterns, and refactorings. Modern object-oriented programming is about software engineering, which sometimes I missed with traditional object-oriented programming techniques.

It wouldn't have been inappropriate for me to introduce you to refactoring earlier in this book, because it would have broken the tension on writing that first line of source code. After all, the biggest problem of coding isn't the tests or getting it done on time—it's our pride in writing good code that others will look at and say, "Cool, this code is really slick!" I know of no software engineer who writes bad code on purpose! However, I chose to present this chapter last, because refactoring assumes you understand the patterns presented earlier. In doing so, this last chapter closes the circle: after you've written the source code and executed your tests, you need to refactor your code to patterns.

Index